Teaching
the
Gifted
Child

Teaching the Gifted Child

Second Edition

JAMES J. GALLAGHER
University of North Carolina

Allyn and Bacon, Inc.
BOSTON · LONDON · SYDNEY · TORONTO

Library of Congress Cataloging in Publication Data

Gallagher, James John, 1926–
    Teaching the gifted child.

    Bibliography: p.
    Includes index.
    1. Gifted children—Education. I. Title.
LC3993.G3 1975   371.9′5   74–28093

ISBN 0–205–04689–4

Eighth printing . . . August, 1978

Contents

Contents

Contents

Contents

Teaching
the
Gifted
Child

"The Creator has withheld from Man the shark's teeth, the bird's wings, the elephant's trunk and the hound's or horse's racing feet. The creative power planted in a minority of mankind has to do duty for all the marvelous physical assets that are built into every specimen of Man's non-human fellow creatures. If society fails to make the most of this one human asset, or if, worse still, it perversely sets itself to stifle it, Man is throwing away his birthright of being the lord of creation and is condemning himself to be, instead, the least effective species on the face of this planet."

ARNOLD TOYNBEE
Is America Neglecting Her Creative Minority?
Ac'cent on Talent, 2 (2), 1968

Organization

Ordinarily, I would give my reasons for writing a book, and for its particular organization, in a preface. However, I am well aware that prefaces are spectacularly unread documents, rivaled only by appendices and epic poems in being aggressively ignored by readers.

On the other hand, the reader will probably find it very helpful to have in mind, as he proceeds, the topic areas into which the individual chapters fall; I shall therefore start the book with a brief statement of that organization.

SECTION I: THE GIFTED CHILD AND HIS SCHOOL

In Chapter 1, "Definition and Identification of the Gifted Child," I attempt to define the term "gifted" and present the standard means used to identify a gifted child. You will meet four gifted children, *Cranshaw, Zelda, Sam,* and *Joe,* who appear throughout the book to illustrate specific points. The second chapter, "Characteristics of Gifted Children," delineates the unique properties of various subgroups of gifted children, with special reference to those characteristics which pose specific educational problems or challenges for the educator.

Chapter 3, "The Changing School Program for the Gifted," presents the general issues that schools face generally in trying to adapt the standard or usual curricular program to the specific needs of the gifted student.

SECTION II: CONTENT MODIFICATIONS FOR THE GIFTED

In this part separate chapters are devoted to some of the suggested curricular adaptations in the fields of mathematics (Chapter 4), science (Chapter 5), social studies (Chapter 6), and language arts (Chapter 7).

1

Common to all these chapters are two themes: (1) teaching the gifted student the most abstract and important ideas possible, and (2) providing the opportunity for gifted children to be active learners, seeking out answers rather than waiting passively for knowledge to be poured into them.

SECTION III: STIMULATION OF PRODUCTIVE THINKING

In this section, two chapters provide ideas as to how gifted students can become more skilled in two important intellectual areas, problem solving and creativity. Chapter 8, "Problem-Solving Strategies for the Gifted," analyzes various methods by which the learner can use the information provided to reach the logical and direct solution. Computer-based learning is included as an example of organizing problem-solving sequences. Chapter 9, "Creativity in the Gifted," explores both the creative person and the creative process and some means by which teachers can enhance these skills.

SECTION IV: ADMINISTRATION AND TRAINING FOR THE GIFTED

Section II covers special *content* and Section III the *skills* that can be taught to the gifted child. This section examines the organization of resources that can facilitate the implementation of the ideas of Sections II and III.

Chapter 10, "Administrative Changes for the Gifted," deals with program design of special classes, resource rooms, and acceleration programs. Chapter 11, "Training Educational Personnel for the Gifted," focuses on the kind of training programs that can prepare teachers and administrators to provide a more stimulating educational experience for gifted students.

SECTION V: SPECIAL PROBLEM AREAS

This section deals with two very special issues that require some distinctive approaches in gifted education, the underachiever and the culturally different child. Chapter 12, "Gifted Underachievers," focuses on the unique characteristics of a group of children whose performance is consistently poorer than their ability and discusses the variety of educational strategies that have been devised to improve performance. Chapter 13, "The Culturally Different Gifted," focuses on a special group of youngsters who come from vastly different family and cultural backgrounds—minority-group children whose talents may be hidden and who need special types of educational attention and stimulation.

After each chapter some of the major unresolved issues are noted, together with a list of readings that are particularly pertinent to the material of the chapter.

SECTION I

The Gifted Child and His School

Section I, which contains the first three chapters of the book, is designed to set the stage for the sections that follow. In order to discuss intelligently what should be done for gifted children in the educational setting, we must (1) describe whom we are talking about; (2) discuss the special nature and characteristics of these youngsters; and (3) discuss the nature of the intersection of these characteristics with the school system as it traditionally exists.

In the area of definition and identification, recent findings have made the situation more complex than it was in past decades. Twenty years ago, an IQ score would have been considered all that was necessary to identify gifted children. By implication if not actual statement, genetics was considered to control the presence or absence of giftedness in the individual.

At the present time there is a strong tendency to view giftedness on a much broader conceptual level, so that although the IQ is still a valuable tool, other indicators of other dimensions of giftedness are also called for. In addition, the role of environment, in interaction with heredity, has been more clearly seen, particularly with regard to such topics as the nature of gifted women, where social factors have clearly shaped some of their characteristic response patterns and performance.

The more we know about any topic, the more we tend to subdivide and see differences within that class of things. This generalization is reflected in our increasing knowledge of the gifted child. In the past we were satisfied to describe the gifted child by a general overall list of characteristics.   Now we are able to distinguish several subgroups of the gifted.   [Those gifted youngsters who come from culturally different families are so important and so distinctive that we need a separate chapter (Chapter 13) to deal with that special issue.   The same applies to the subgroup of youngsters who seem to have great talent and do not use it, the gifted underachievers (see Chapter 12).]   Currently, there is great interest in the nature of creativity and the special characteristics of children who have a special talent in this direction; we deal with this subject at some length in Chapters 2 and 9.

Finally, in Chapter 3, we discuss the diversity of ability among school-aged children in light of the American principle of universal education.   In other cultures and countries this diversity is often handled by allowing children to leave school early, or by focusing on only a very small percentage of elite leadership types who are encouraged to go forward to higher education.   Without regard to the morality of such a decision to reserve leadership opportunities to a particular social class, it would be impossible for a technological society, needing the talents of all of its citizens, to survive for long with such a strategy.   Therefore, the design of programs for the gifted has to be organized within the framework of the total needs of a modern technological society.

When we discuss the needed changes in the school program for the gifted, we will focus on three elements introduced in this part: the nature of change in the content, in the teaching of special skills, and in the modification of the learning environment.

1

Definition and Identification
of the Gifted Child

Who are the gifted children in our society? Those individuals who will
be the creators, the leaders of the next generation? As we shall see,
many of the children discussed in this book will be key members of the
next generation of leaders and producers of our society. How they fare
in the American educational system and in American society in general
will influence strongly the character and future of that society.

We Americans are justly proud of our egalitarianism, of our demand
for equal education for all, but we are equally proud of our goal of
individualization to fit the program to the child's needs. We have
moved far toward providing access to education for all, but we are less
effective in meeting the differing needs and abilities of individual children. For those children at the extremes—the handicapped and the
gifted—the commitment to individualization has been halting and incomplete. Failure to help the handicapped child reach his potential
is a personal tragedy for him and his family; failure to help the gifted
child reach his potential is a societal tragedy, the extent of which is
difficult to measure but which is surely great. How can we measure the
sonata unwritten, the curative drug undiscovered, the absence of political
insight? They are the difference between what we are and what we
could be as a society.

In 1859, Charles Darwin wrote the *Origin of the Species,* in which
he propounded his notion of the survival of the fittest; but who are the
fittest in our modern culture—the heavyweight champion of the world,
the President of the United States, a nuclear scientist, an artist, a physician? I suspect that each of us harbors the idea that the essence of
fitness is made up of traits somewhat like his own. The athlete thinks
of physical prowess and skill; the teacher of the ability to pass on im-

portant ideas from one generation to another; and the minister of the moral leadership that distinguishes humanity from the animal. Each of us defines "fittest" to suit his own needs.

The teacher, faced with overwhelming daily pressures, is hard-pressed to gain perspective on the problems of gifted children and is eagerly seeking specific guidance. Often justifiably impatient with esoteric discussions about definition, the teacher and others in our society fail to recognize that the definition of "giftedness" is culture-bound. It is as much a part of the mid-twentieth century as television, nuclear reactors, and moon walks. Flanagan, Dailey, Shaycoft, Gorham, Orr, and Goldberg (1962, p. 19) have some pertinent things to say about talent and its definition in past eras:

> The definition of talent in a primitive tribe is likely to be quite simple. Where the tribe depends primarily on hunting wild game for survival, the definition of talent will focus on the ability to become an outstanding hunter. To the warring tribe, the ability to carry battle to the enemy is most prized.
>
> Even nations which produced men whose brilliant insights and ideas are still recognized today had a limited view of man's talents. The Greeks honored the orator and the artist—but failed to appreciate the inventor. Rome cherished the soldier and the administrator—but failed to recognize the many other potential talents of either its citizens or its slaves.
>
> What is our present concept of talent and how has it developed? It is not surprising that a complex society such as ours has a complex view of talents.

There are many different versions of a definition of gifted children for our society and the one that follows (*Education of the Gifted*, 1972, p. 10) is as acceptable as any. It reflects the current concern with a variety of dimensions of giftedness.

> Gifted and talented children are those identified by professionally qualified persons who by virtue of outstanding abilities are capable of high performance. These are children who require differentiated educational programs and services beyond those normally provided by the regular school program in order to realize their contribution to self and society.
>
> Children capable of high performance include those with demonstrated achievement and/or potential ability in any of the following areas.
> 1. General intellectual ability
> 2. Specific academic aptitude
> 3. Creative or productive thinking
> 4. Leadership ability
> 5. Visual and performing arts
> 6. Psychomotor ability

The ability to manipulate internally learned symbol systems is perhaps

the *sine qua non* of giftedness. It allows the gifted student to learn on his own, to imagine and create new forms and products, without waiting for a teacher or his environment. Such symbol systems thus give the learner autonomy. Although the prime symbol system for our culture is language and the linguistic facility of the student is predominantly what is tested when one tests for IQ, there are many other symbol systems around us and students can be gifted or talented in any of them. For example, mathematics, music, chemistry, and the more private symbolism of art—all constitute symbol systems. Children who come from culturally different homes often express themselves in the idiom or style—that is, symbol system—of that culture. But how does one take such broad philosophic statements and translate them into such practical matters as finding gifted children in a particular classroom?

THE OMNIPRESENT IQ

It is difficult to go very far into the discussion of giftedness without raising the topic of the IQ. In an era where our lives seem to be controlled and regulated by numbers, social security or phone or credit card, a special place is reserved for the IQ score. It has been said that once a person has received information about his or her IQ score, that number becomes indelibly etched in his cortex as if it had been burned there with hydrogen flouride. He may forget his address, his phone number, his spouse's name, but he will never forget that number, his IQ. If it appears to be high enough, it can suddenly appear uninvited in casual conversation at parties or in chats with neighbors. Notwithstanding, there is very little real appreciation of what it really means. Few lay persons realize that their IQ score is a function of a particular test, so that interpretation is impossible without reference to the tool used to obtain it. The same person can quite legitimately get IQ scores ranging as much as 25 or 30 points, depending on the test used.

Since the IQ score remains one of the strongest measures of intellectual giftedness, it is worth a brief review of just what we are talking about when we refer to the IQ. Actually, there are two quite different ways of obtaining an IQ score. The older of these is obtained by asking a child to respond to a series of questions that previous experience has shown will be responded to at different rates by different age levels of children. By allowing the child to respond to a range of questions we can obtain a mental age score that allows us to compare his or her performance with that of other children. Thus a mental age score of 9 years means that this would be the score expected from an average child who was 9 years old. One can then form a ratio of *mental age* to *life*

11

age and obtain an index that is referred to as an intelligence quotient. For example,

$$IQ = \frac{\text{mental age}}{\text{life age}} = \frac{12 \text{ years}}{8 \text{ years}} \times 100 = 150$$

We can see intuitively that an IQ score of 150, such as that obtained here, is "good." It is clearly better to be advanced in development than it is to be retarded or slow in development. But how much better is it, and how does the child rate with other children of the same age? Extensive experience with the distribution of IQ scores has yielded consistent curves such as that shown in Figure 1-1. The Wechsler scales (Wechsler Intelligence Scale for Children—WISC—and the Wechsler Adult Intelligence Scale—WAIS), both have a mean of 100 and a standard deviation of 15. The 1960 revision of the Stanford–Binet (described later) uses standard scores that have a mean of 100 and a standard deviation of 16. For all practical purposes this one-point difference is of no significance; hence you can also interpret Stanford–Binet IQs by referring to the WISC and WAIS scale in the figure.

Here we can see that a score of 150 falls above the 99th percentile,

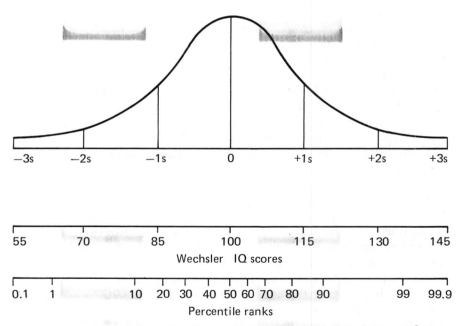

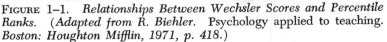

FIGURE 1-1. *Relationships Between Wechsler Scores and Percentile Ranks.* (*Adapted from R. Biehler.* Psychology applied to teaching. *Boston: Houghton Mifflin, 1971, p. 418.*)

meaning that the person obtaining such a score would be performing better than 99 persons of his age level and less well than only one person out of a theoretical 100. The typical IQ curve also shows that as one approaches the upper and lower limits, there are fewer and fewer persons, so that an IQ score of 130 or above on this type of measure would identify the top 3 percent of a particular group.

Another slightly different way of obtaining an IQ is to give a series of items to a child that has previously been given to a representative sample of children of the same age. The score of that child compared with that of all children of that age (and not of various ages as with the Stanford-Binet can give a comparative measure called a deviation IQ (how far the child deviates from the average performance of his or her age group). These deviation scores can then be translated into IQ scores and interpreted in the same way as those in Figure 1-1.

The IQ score actually yields two different kinds of measures, both of importance to educators. First, it gives some indication of the current mental level of the child in comparison with his own age group; second, it makes a prediction as to the rate of the child's mental growth in the future. Although IQ tests clearly do not measure all of what we consider to be important in our discussions of intelligence, they do measure much of what is necessary to current academic success. Thus the predictive power of an IQ score for future academic attainment remains impressive and has been the reason for its enormous influence in educational circles.

"GIFTED" DEFINED

Table 1-1 gives four types of mental functions and some sample test items used to measure the individual's performance. A large number of preliminary tryouts of the prospective test item will establish an age level at which you would expect the average child to succeed and by which you can discover if the children's performance follows expected practice (i.e., older children should find the item easier than younger children). Although there are disagreements among psychologists about just how many important intellectual functions there are, the ones listed in the table are usually included in any comprehensive list.

The list itself is interesting because not all these mental functions are sampled equally on "intelligence tests." Which ones are not? And why? The memory items are familiar to all students, particularly the vocabulary or long-term memory items. As noted, this type of item stresses the importance of rich language and conceptual understanding. The youngster from a culture that does not stress language, even a talented one, is likely to do *relatively* more poorly on such items than

13

TABLE 1-1. *Samples of Intelligence Test Items.*

MENTAL FUNCTION	SAMPLE ITEM	SUPPOSED CULTURAL INFLUENCE
Short-term memory	Repeat exactly as I say it: cow–zebra–giraffe–mongoose.	Very little influence of experience except for the set of attending to an adult.
Long-term memory	What is an ocelot ? What do we do with a wrench?	Substantial influence of culture. Experience, particularly reading experience, can build substantial vocabulary.
Association linkage	*Ball* is to *bat* as *puck* is to _____ . Name the one that doesn't belong: blue sweet red orange	The richness of language depends partly on experience and partly on ability to store and retrieve associations and concepts; in part, environment and in part, constitutional influences.
Reasoning convergent	If Jerry is taller than Peter and Pete is taller than Moe, then _____ is taller than _____ .	Relatively small influence of culture. Basically an internal intellectual process.
divergent	What would happen if all the water were shut off from your city?	Depends on self-confidence and freedom from criticism and knowledge of subject area.
Evaluation	Compare and judge Capote and Mailer for their portrayal of the male figure in the novel. Which would you rather have–$5 to spend now or $25 at the end of the week?	The criterion used to choose a proper answer has to be culturally learned.

14

on reasoning items or on short-term memory, which are less dependent on past experience.

The two items *least* frequently observed on intelligence tests, although they are undoubtedly important in charting the talents of gifted children, would be *divergent reasoning* and *evaluation*. Since both these characteristics are deemed important for imaginative and creative work, why are such items so infrequently seen on standard tests compared to the prevalence of memory, linkage, and convergent reasoning items? There would seem to be both a logical and a practical reason. First, the primary purpose of the intelligence test is to predict school achievement. If school achievement consists primarily of memorizing facts and doing simple kinds of problem solving, test items that measure memory and convergent reasoning will be sufficient to predict which students will do well. Even in classes for gifted students it is often rare to find much emphasis in class discussions on divergent or evaluative thinking (Gallagher, Aschner, & Jenné, 1967).

The second reason is less kind to the test constructors. It is simply that such items are painfully difficult to handle. If we include such divergent items as

"Tell me all the words you can think of when I say 'round',"

or

"Tell me what would happen if everybody in the world went deaf,"

how will you score the answers? You can't simply count all the responses; some of them may be silly or redundant. The placement of such an item on a group intelligence test would cause havoc and could not be keyed properly for scoring.

Similarly, evaluation test items are difficult to score. If you ask a question such as "What is best. . ." or "What is most appropriate. . .," you can get legitimate differences of opinion on what the right answer ought to be.

One of the standard evaluative questions we ask ourselves as a society is "Which candidate is better for a particular political office?" and it is easy to see what violent differences of opinion can be obtained from such a simple item. The ability to use good judgment is a crucial element in our intelligence, but it is abominably hard to measure. So, as long as the easily scored items seem to do the predicting job (school performance), there is a tendency to go along with the existing measures.

The true nature of the cultural relativity of our definitions of "gifted" can be realized when we discuss other types of gifted persons, not typically considered. For example, how about the "gifted" student in the ethical and moral dimension? Wouldn't it be just as important to

15

identify and cultivate these talents as to cultivate reasoning ability? Or more so?

Getzels and Jackson (1962, p. 135) have given us a list of characteristics that might help us in such a search, as follows:

A moral person characteristically
1. Chooses the ethical rather than the expedient alternative when faced with an interpersonal dilemma;
2. Stands against public sentiment when such sentiment threatens to compromise his values;
3. Feels allegiance and responsibility for principles and causes;
4. Identifies with humanity beyond the immediate confines of his own group;
5. Feels compassion for wrongdoers without condoning their specific acts;
6. Perceives and admits to his own shortcomings;
7. Holds to personal ideals transcending such qualities as appearance and social acceptability.

We have few such identifications or programs for gifted moralists. Is it because we believe that giftedness is inherent and morality is learned? Or is it merely that we, as a culture, have not come to grips with morality and feel more comfortable with technology and engineering?

IDENTIFICATION OF GIFTED CHILDREN

The identification of gifted children has long been a favorite topic of discussion in educational circles in this country. This has often puzzled laymen, who do not seem to understand the reason for all the fuss. "After all," the layman asks, "can't you spot these children easily?" The answer is, of course, that you can spot *some* of them very easily. They identify themselves with their advanced thinking and achievement. Any reasonably alert person can see that children such as these are special. However, many children with a high ability to conceptualize are not easy to find through observation; these should be the special concern of the teacher, the administrator, and the psychologist.

It is only natural to assume that identification procedures evolve from the definition of "gifted children." So they do, in part. By classifying a child as "intellectually superior," we rule out tests of physical fitness as appropriate identification measures. What is just as true, but much harder to recognize, is that the identification procedures also *determine* the operational definition of gifted children. Let us take one of the more popular general definitions of giftedness: "consistent excellence in any field of human endeavor." This definition has the advantage of sounding erudite and is general enough so that anyone could agree with it. Its disadvantage is that it has little relationship to educational practice.

A few rather well-established devices have been used to locate gifted students when a school system has decided to take notice of them. Table 1–2 shows the procedures used in the Illinois program. The second column

Table 1–2. *Major Procedures Used and Recommended in the Identification of Gifted Students.*

MAJOR IDENTIFICATION PROCEDURES	PERCENT USING	PERCENT RECOMMENDING
Teacher observation and nomination	93	75
Group school achievement test scores	87	74
Group intelligence test scores	87	65
Previously demonstrated accomplishments (including school grades)	56	78
Individual intelligence test scores	23	90
Scores on tests of creativity	14	74

Source: S. P. Marland, *Education of the gifted and talented.* Washington, D.C.: U.S. Office of Education, 1972, p. 261.

represents the percentage of programs using a particular procedure, and the third column describes what experts suggested regarding the procedures. Although teacher observation and nomination have been the most frequently used devices, the "experts" preferred the use of individual intelligence tests and previously demonstrated accomplishments, for obviously economic reasons. Most of the studies that have examined the question carefully (for example, Pegnato and Birch, 1959) find that teachers will overlook many gifted children that a well-designed test will find, and, conversely, many may be overly impressed by the dutiful and hard-working child and overrate him. The experts show their concern about the limited usefulness of a group IQ test by ranking it lowest in efficiency.

The current pattern is not to rely exclusively on any one of these approaches but to use combinations of them (i.e., school grades and IQ tests). Although the experts ranked the use of the new creativity measures highly, such measures have obviously not caught on with school personnel.

The means of identification of gifted children in the first two decades of this century was by teacher nomination. In many rural areas of the country it remains the only one. In this situation, the actual definition of gifted children becomes "those children who are doing very well in school, much better than their companions." What is wrong with this particular definition? Many children who have a high aptitude for reasoning and conceptualization are *not* performing well in school. Such a definition would then rule them out. Albert Einstein, Thomas

17

Edison, and Winston Churchill would constitute three classic cases that would not be labeled "gifted" by teacher nomination.

Table 1–3 gives one example of the type of rating scales that have been utilized to aid teachers in finding high-ability children. Note the wide range of characteristics used.

Teacher judgment has been gradually replaced as the prime identifying technique by standard tests of mental ability. The operational definition of gifted children then becomes: "those children who score high on IQ tests." This definition is only as good as the tests being used, no better. If the tests do not happen to measure all that we think is important in intellectual giftedness, we will again miss some youngsters by using this type of definition.

TABLE 1–3. *Sample Scale Items: Behavioral Characteristics of Superior Students.*

	LOW 1	2	3	HIGH 4
Part I: Learning Characteristics				
Has unusually advanced vocabulary for age or grade level: uses terms in a meaningful way; has verbal behavior characterized by "richness" of expression, elaboration, and fluency.	___	___	___	___
Is a keen and alert observer; usually "sees more" or "gets more" out of a story, film, etc. than others.	___	___	___	___
Reads a great deal on his own; usually prefers adult level books; does not avoid difficult material; may show a preference for biography, autobiography, encyclopedias, and atlases.	___	___	___	___
Column Total	___	___	___	___
Weight	1	2	3	4
Weighted Column Total	___	___	___	___
Total	___			
Part II: Motivational Characteristics				
Is easily bored with routine tasks.	___	___	___	___
Strives toward perfection; is self-critical; is not easily satisfied with his own speed or products.	___	___	___	___
Is quite concerned with right and wrong, good and bad; often evaluates and passes judgment on events, people, and things.	___	___	___	___
Column Total	___	___	___	___
Weight	1	2	3	4
Weighted Column Total	___	___	___	___
Total	___			

Table 1-3 *(Cont'd)*

	LOW 1	2	3	HIGH 4
Part III: Creativity Characteristics				
Displays a great deal of curiosity about many things; is constantly asking questions about anything and everything.	___	___	___	___
Displays a keen sense of humor and sees humor in situations that may not appear to be humorous to others.	___	___	___	___
Displays a good deal of intellectual playfulness; fantasizes; imagines ("I wonder what would happen if . . ."); manipulates ideas (i.e., changes, elaborates upon them); is often concerned with adapting, improving, and motivating institutions, objects, and systems.	___	___	___	___
Column Total	___	___	___	___
Weight	1	2	3	4
Weighted Column Total	___	___	___	___
Total		___		
Part IV: Leadership Characteristics				
Is self-confident with children his own age as well as adults; seems comfortable when asked to show his work to the class.	___	___	___	___
Adapts readily to new situations; is flexible in thought and action and does not seem disturbed when the normal routine is changed.	___	___	___	___
Tends to dominate others when they are around; generally directs the activity in which he is involved.	___	___	___	___
Column Total	___	___	___	___
Weight	1	2	3	4
Weighted Column Total	___	___	___	___
Total		___		

Source: J. Renzulli and R. Hartman. Scale for rating behavioral characteristics of superior students. *Exceptional children*, vol. 38, no. 3, 1971, pp. 243–248. Reprinted by permission of the authors and The Council for Exceptional Children.
Note: 1, seldom or never; 2, occasionally; 3, considerably; and 4, almost always.

FOUR GIFTED CHILDREN

The one factor that youngsters labeled "gifted" have in common is the ability to absorb abstract concepts, to organize them more effectively, and to apply them more appropriately than does the average youngster. Apart from that, however, the range of other variables, such as social abilities and personality, is almost as great as one would find in a random selection of youngsters of a given age.   Therefore, it is not meaningful from the standpoint of the teacher to talk about the social abilities of gifted children or the emotional adjustment of gifted children, since gifted children vary so widely in these characteristics.

To aid in the discussions of past research and programming, the author would like to introduce four children, aged 10, all of whom would fit the label of "intellectually gifted" but who differ quite markedly in their other characteristics.   The reader would be well advised to study carefully these personal descriptions and refer back to them from time to time as they are looked at in light of different research findings and educational programming.

Cranshaw is a big, athletic, happy-go-lucky youngster who impresses the casual observer as the "all-American boy" type of youngster.   He seems to be a natural leader and to be enthusiastic over a wide range of interests.   These interests have not yet solidified.   One week he can be fascinated with astronomy, the next week with football formations, and the following week with the study of Africa.

His past history in school has suggested that teachers have two very distinct reactions to Cranshaw.   One is that he is a joy to have in the classroom.   He is a cooperative and responsible boy who can not only perform his own tasks well but be a good influence in helping the other youngsters to perform effectively.   On the other hand, Cranshaw's mere presence in the class also stimulates in teachers some hints of personal inferiority and frustration, since he always seems to be exceeding the bounds of the teachers' knowledge and abilities.   The teachers secretly wonder how much they really are teaching Cranshaw and how much he is learning on his own.

Cranshaw's family is a well-knit, reasonably happy one.   His father is a businessman, his mother has had some college education, and the family is reasonably active in the community.   Their attitude towards Cranshaw is that he is a fine boy and they hope that he does well.   They anticipate his going on to higher education but, in effect, say that it is pretty much up to him what he is going to do when the time comes.   They do not seem to be future-oriented and are perfectly happy to have him as the enthusiastic and well-adjusted youngster that he appears to be today.

Zelda shares similar high scores on intelligence tests to those manifested by Cranshaw.   Zelda is a rather unattractive girl who is chubby, and wears rather thick glasses that give her a "bookish" appearance.   Her clothes, while reasonably neat and clean, are not stylish and give the impression that neither her mother nor Zelda have given a great deal of thought to how they look on this particular child.   Socially, she has one or two reasonably close girl friends but is not a member of the wider social circle in the classroom and, indeed, seems to reject it.

Teachers respond to Zelda with two generally different feelings. They are pleased with the enthusiasm with which Zelda attacks her school work and the good grades that she gets. At the same time, they are vaguely annoyed or irritated with Zelda's undisguised feeling of superiority toward youngsters who are not as bright as she is; they tend to repel Zelda when she tries to act like an assistant teacher or to gain favors that are more reserved to the teacher.

Zelda and her family seem to get along very well with each other. The main source of conflict is that the family, itself, has values that Zelda has accepted wholeheartedly but that are getting her into difficulty with her classmates. Her father is a college professor and her mother has an advanced degree in English literature. They seem to value achievement and intellectual performance almost to the exclusion of all other things.

Their social evenings are made up of intellectual discussions of politics, religion, or the current burning issue on the campus. These discussions are definitely adult-oriented and Zelda is intelligent enough to be able to enter into such conversations occasionally. This type of behavior is rewarded much more by the parents than is the behavior that would seem more appropriate to her age level.

Figure 1–2 shows the range of abilities in different developmental areas for Zelda and Cranshaw. If all the points on the scale were at the same height as their mental ability, there would be little trouble in placing them educationally. Cranshaw shows a wide variation from the physical development of an average 11-year-old to the mental abilities of an average 15-year-old. This means that any standard placement at any level will displace Cranshaw physically, academically, or socially.

Zelda has an intellectual and academic profile similar to Cranshaw's. Both are doing as well as might be expected on the basis of these measurements. Zelda is slightly inferior to Cranshaw in arithmetic. However, it is in the personal–social area where real differences are apparent. While Cranshaw's adjustment here has the same superior rating as his academic record, Zelda has social difficulties. She is not accepted by her peers and worries about it. Table 1–4 shows some sentence completion results from Zelda. In this task, Zelda was supposed to finish some incomplete sentences. The italicized words are the sentence stems and the rest of the sentences shown in Table 1–4 indicates how Zelda finished each one. Intellectual striving and social yearning are both quite apparent. Her inability to understand how her own behavior causes antagonism is also apparent—*and quite important.*

Whereas the two preceding children have in common a high academic performance, the following cases are low-producing children.

Joe is a tall, lanky youngster of age 10 who seems to have, in common with Cranshaw, only his score on an intelligence test. Joe has a certain amount of charm and has a good many friends in his peer group, but he is

21

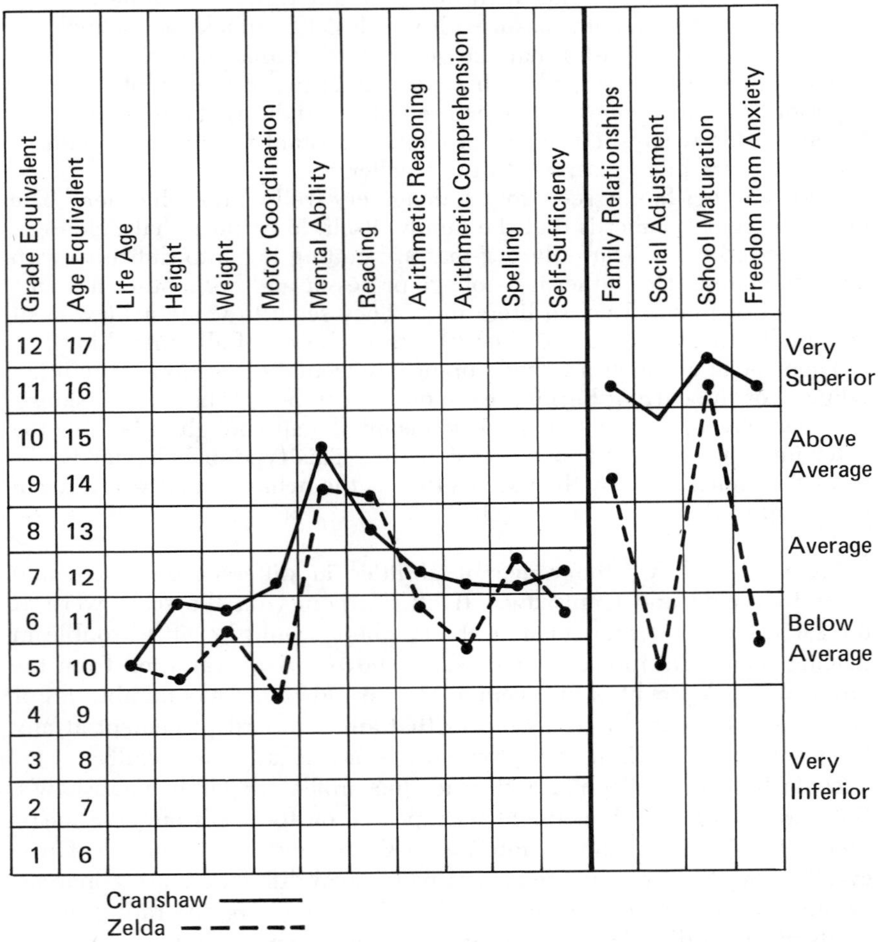

The figure is a profile chart. The vertical scale has two leftmost columns (Grade Equivalent and Age Equivalent) paired with qualitative descriptors on the right. The column headers across the top and the scale rows are transcribed below.

Grade Equivalent	Age Equivalent	Life Age	Height	Weight	Motor Coordination	Mental Ability	Reading	Arithmetic Reasoning	Arithmetic Comprehension	Spelling	Self-Sufficiency	Family Relationships	Social Adjustment	School Maturation	Freedom from Anxiety	Descriptor
12	17															Very
11	16															Superior
10	15															Above
9	14															Average
8	13															
7	12															Average
6	11															Below
5	10															Average
4	9															
3	8															Very
2	7															Inferior
1	6															

Cranshaw ———
Zelda — — — —

FIGURE 1–2. *Profiles of Gifted High Producers.*

anything but a leader. Whenever any responsible task comes up, he is likely to default. Moreover, in a group, he tends to be a complainer, one who operates against the effective operation of the group itself. Joe is described by his teachers as a "foot dragger," a "work dodger," and a monument of passive resistance. As such, he has been a source of pain and frustration to teachers throughout his five years in school. Teachers report considerable difficulty in getting Joe to do any more than the bare minimum that is requested of him. This is doubly frustrating since they all know, through his scores on intelligence tests, that these assignments should be easy tasks for him. They have all tried, in their

TABLE 1–4. *Sentence Completion Items from Zelda.*

There are times when I am mad at the world.
My mind is underdeveloped as yet.
My greatest trouble is friends.
Many of my dreams are nightmares.
Secretly I wish to be like Marie Curie.
I cannot understand what makes me tick. Why I am so unlikable to
    certain people.
My worst trait is that I argue.
My chief worry is getting along with people.
My teachers don't like me.
It is fun to solve what has been unsolved.
If I could have three wishes, I would wish for:
    1. Universal peace.
    2. Goodness to all.
    3. As many other wishes as I wanted.

various ways, to get him to do something extra: to read another book, to do a report, to become interested in something more than the direct assignments given the average youngsters.

Joe has a complete battery of excuses and reasons why he should not do these things. He seems to feel that he is being unjustly pushed and that the demands upon him are entirely unreasonable. He tends to reject the notion that he is smart, saying, "Who says so?" and generally does not seem to be happy in school except when in the company of his friends.

His family wants Joe to do well and is more than a little irritated with him about his attitude. His father is an attorney; he has almost despaired of this youngster and of his future, if the boy maintains his present attitude. There doesn't seem to be a great deal of understanding between the father and Joe. The father reacts to his son's resistance by increasing the pressure on him. This, in turn, increases Joe's resistance.

Of the four children discussed in this book, *Sam* probably is the least likely, from the standpoint of background and family situation, to be found in a program for gifted students. But unlikely things happen all the time in school, and this is one of them.

Sam is a physically mature 10-year-old black boy whose family immigrated to a northern urban community some three years ago. The family consists of the mother and grandmother and two younger siblings. Sam remembers his father as a big, burly, laughing man, with terrifying bursts of temper, who hasn't been around for almost two years. His mother and grandmother know very little more about Sam's father's absence than he does.   They have heard that he may be in jail in another state but aren't sure.   Sam himself is puzzled, and his mother will not share with him any of her own thoughts on this matter.   As the oldest boy, he somehow feels both the responsibility of trying to be the "man in the family" and his own lack of competence for that task.

His mother now works part-time and the grandmother is caring for the household.   Sam spent his first two years in school in the rural South and does not remember much about his school except that it was easy and pleasant.   When he moved, his third-grade teacher perceived through the ragged clothes his alertness and responsiveness.   A year later he was given tests to determine his ability; he scored very high for his cultural subgroup, but not so high as Cranshaw and Zelda.   Most psychologists would suggest that, given different circumstances—perhaps the same environmental background that Cranshaw and Zelda had— Sam would score ten to fifteen IQ points higher than he scores today.

Despite these abilities, Sam is not doing particularly well in school, and there are hints that he will be troublesome from a behavioral standpoint, since he has formed friends with a peer group who seek excitement and adventure.   Sam is already aware of drug traffic and crime firsthand, even though the neighborhood that his mother and grandmother live in is not one of the worst in the city.   The challenge for the school, and for society as well, is to provide a future goal of importance and practicality for Sam so that his intellectual talents will be used to constructive purposes.

For Sam, who was raised in a culture much more interested in the wail of the blues than in the clever turn-of-phrase honored in Cranshaw's and Zelda's homes, it was natural that some of the expression of talent came through this different medium.   One of Sam's recreational joys is to play drums for the local drum-and-bugle corps, and to accompany TV rock and roll stars when his mother can stand it.   He has a sense of rhythm that comes not from any presumed black superiority at music but rather as a combination of interest and of a lack of inhibition that slows and clouds the motor reactions of his more middle-class colleagues. When he is "beating the skins," Sam has a kind of sense of order and rightness of things that seems akin to the joy of the mathematician in solving a formula or the poet who has found just the right alliteration for his stanza.

Should we support the development and encouragement of diverse talents or the single dimension of verbal excellence?   The gifted and talented have a rare flair for confronting us with questions about our basic educational values.

Figure 1–3 shows the profiles of Joe and Sam.   It is easy to see that Joe's high performance on a mental-ability test represents his only really high point on the scale.   His achievement test scores are only a little advanced for his grade level and the teacher claims that his classwork is below average for his grade level.   In the personal–social area he shows

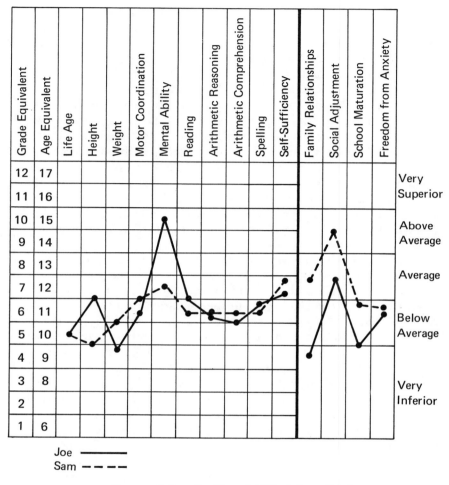

Joe ———
Sam — — — —

FIGURE 1–3.   *Profiles of Gifted Low Producers.*

poor family relationships and school motivation that probably relates to
his ineffective performance.

Sam's profile shows less academic performance, only average for his
age group. This is somewhat understandable, in view of his language
difficulties. His mental-ability score seems to be quite an achievement,
considering the handicaps he has surmounted in his environment. His
problems do not seem to be in the personal–social area but in cultural
problems related to his background. In school programs it is somewhat
natural to assume that problems lie within the child rather than in his
surroundings. With Sam, that is a clearly wrong assumption.

SUMMARY

The definition and identification of a special subgroup of children, such as gifted children, is not a simple matter. Such a definition is linked to the culture that creates this subgroup. Thus, "giftedness" reflects those dimensions that the culture values. As the values of the society change, the views toward the nature of excellence also undergo subtle change.

In the past decade these changes in values have been reflected in changes in the definition of giftedness and in the nature of the identification techniques used to find talented and gifted children. Until the middle 1960s, the operational definition of giftedness was a rather straightforward one. It included those children who performed in an advanced fashion on measures of verbal development and logical thinking as measured by standard IQ tests. Excellence in these dimensions allowed children to achieve well in further academic work and in traditional areas of professional and technical skills that have been highly valued by the society.

In the late 1960s a genuine societal change began, marked by our increasing concern about the nature of artistic excellence, moral behavior, and that unpredictable, but highly prized, dimension of creativity. We wished to add these dimensions to the definition of giftedness, and the result of those additions is contained in the broader statement of a gifted child, as reflected in the most recent definition, reported in this chapter.

No matter how elaborate and all-encompassing the definition of giftedness, the specific identification tools that are actually used are often the real determiner and the real definer of giftedness in a school setting. The standard intelligence test, despite recent criticism, still remains predominant in such identification, although it is now usually supplemented by a range of other instruments purporting to measure such dimensions as creative and imaginative abilities. There is a renewed interest in accepting teacher judgment on such hard-to-measure dimensions as "initiative" and "originality." This attempt to broaden the range of identification tools in nominating children for special educational programs is sound, particularly in those educational settings that focus on culturally different talented children.

There is strong suspicion that the different values and different experiences of talented youngsters coming from less advantaged or traditional homes would show them at a disadvantage. However, they may well show talent and excellence in other intellectual domains, and the prevailing thought is to encourage talent in those areas as well.

It is the ability to manipulate symbolic systems, whether that of language, or of less traditional areas, such as music or even social sensitivity, that has encouraged us to include a slightly different group of children under the rubric of giftedness than would have been assembled in the 1940s or 1950s. Consequently, the nature and direction of programs for gifted children also have changed to adjust to differences in definition, as will be apparent in later chapters.

UNRESOLVED ISSUES

No book that addresses a major educational issue should imply at any point that all the issues are settled. In the field of the gifted, as in other major topics in education, there is much to be learned that we don't know, much that needs to be discarded from what we think we know today. The author wishes to give his estimate of the most important questions remaining in each of the major topics covered by this book. Two or three of these will be included at the end of each chapter.

1. If the environment is partially responsible for the development or the suppression of giftedness, is it possible to create special environments to increase the total number of children that we could call gifted?

2. If the IQ test is not totally satisfactory as an identification tool, where are other tests or scales that measure such characteristics as aesthetic sensitivity, creativity, and imagination which we can use to support the broadened definition that we want?

3. If our definition of gifted changes as the values of our society change, what will the definition look like in 1985? What values will be downgraded and what values more highly regarded?

READINGS OF SPECIAL INTEREST

BAYLEY, N. Development of mental abilities. In P. Mussen (Ed.), *Carmichael's manual of child psychology.* Chicago: Rand McNally, 1970.
A fine scholarly review of what is known about the development of mental abilities in young children. Focuses particularly on changes in mental growth and performance in young children.

GUILFORD, J. P. *The nature of human intelligence.* New York: McGraw-Hill, 1967.
A comprehensive statement about the structure of intellectual processes in human beings by one of the foremost theoreticians of the past two decades. More than any other single person, Guilford's ideas have transformed and broadened the definition of giftedness.

MARTINSON, R. *The identification of the gifted and talented.* Los Angeles: National/State Leadership Training Institute of the Gifted and Talented, 1973.
A summary of the latest views and procedures on identification of the gifted. Presents a series of scales and checklists with assessments of their usefulness.

Newell, A., Shaw, J. C., & Simon, H. H.   The process of creative thinking.   In H. Gruber, G. Terrill, & M. Wertheimer (Eds.), *Contemporary approaches to creative thinking*.   New York: Atherton, 1962.

A highly innovative attempt to explain mental processes by means of computer analogies. Particularly useful in the understanding of basic operational aspects of information-processing in human beings; suggests mechanisms for creative thought.

Torrance, E. P.   Broadening concepts of giftedness in the 70's.   In S. Kirk & F. Lord (Eds.), *Exceptional children: Educational resources and perspectives*.   Boston: Houghton Mifflin, 1974.

This author stresses the importance of multitalent concepts of giftedness, with particular emphasis on the creative child. Discusses ways to stifle and stimulate individuality.

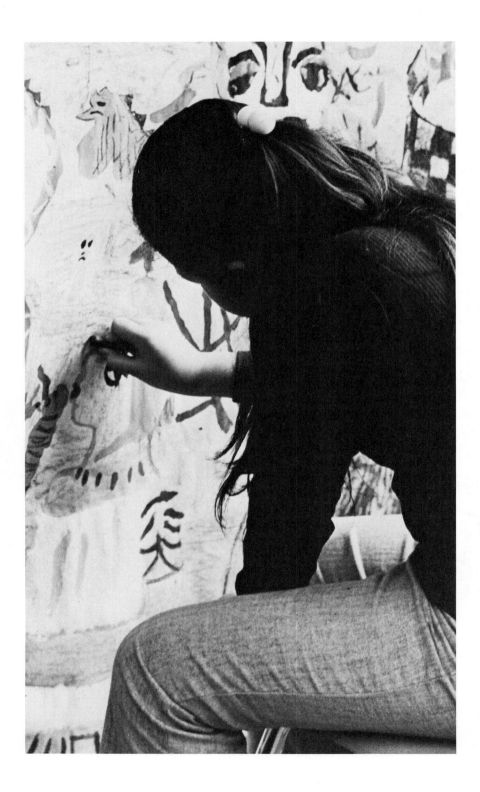

2

Characteristics of Gifted Students

What are gifted children really like? If you are identified as a professional who works with such children, you will be certain to be approached formally or informally by people wishing an answer to what seems to be a simple and straightforward question. But it is not. And before we pursue the various interesting facts related to the issue, it would be well to see what the qualifications are that should be considered.

As we have seen through the brief descriptions of Cranshaw, Zelda, Sam, and Joe, a superior performance in measures of intelligence does not guarantee homogeneity in family, social, or academic characteristics. So whatever general statements are made, there will always be plenty of exceptions.

A common experience in the schools can illustrate this problem. A psychologist may be invited to give a talk on the characteristics of gifted children. He states that research indicates that gifted children are more emotionally stable than average children. This stimulates a teacher who has had a good deal of experience to ask a question. "If what you say is true, how is it that I had a very emotionally unstable gifted child in my class last year?" The teacher then proceeds to document her statement with examples of the behavior and problems of this particular child. The psychologist responds by saying that he was talking about the "typical gifted child." The teacher then remembers another child who contradicts the generalization the psychologist has made. In all too many instances, adequate communication is never reached. The teacher goes away mumbling that if only psychologists would get down to the teachers' level and experience the classroom situation, what he says could be of more use to the teacher. The psychologist goes away muttering to himself that teachers can't seem to go beyond their own experiences in such discussions.

The major difficulty in using an individual case to try to establish a general rule is this very problem of "typicalness." If the approximately 3 million children of 12 years of age were lined up on the turnpike from New York, they could form a line extending all the way to Chicago. If a teacher then drove from New York to Chicago, he could get a reasonably good picture of the physical characteristics of the children. Suppose that the youngsters whom we have called gifted children tied red bandanas around their necks; we could then get some general impression of whether, on the average, they tended to be larger or heavier or more pleasing to look at than average children.

If someone came to the teacher after this interesting drive and asked him what he thought about the physical characteristics of gifted children, he might very well say, "Well, I thought they were a little bit heavier than the other children." At the same time, however, he would carry in his memory the very thin, scrawny boy he saw east of Toledo who, although he had a red bandana around his neck, didn't fit the general statement that he had just made.

To make this discussion of characteristics more meaningful we will review those features that seem representative of various subgroups; the high-performing gifted, talented girls and women, highly creative children, and the like.

Another issue that needs to be recalled is that this information reveals facts related to giftedness without implying some causation. For example, a discovery that gifted students are more popular should not cause one to jump to the conclusion that a high IQ will cause you to have greater social popularity; it may very well be that a factor such as "high family status" in the community is related and responsible for both.

HIGH-PERFORMANCE GIFTED

The group of children who have high mental aptitude as measured by IQ test scores have probably been studied more thoroughly than any other group—probably because they are the easiest to discover. Cranshaw is a fine example of this type of child. He has been thought of as special by his teachers since he entered school. His manifest ability and leadership qualities have endeared him to teachers. Despite his favorable status, however, some interesting and important questions have been raised concerning Cranshaw and other children like him. Some of these are:

Is their intellectual aptitude equally distributed across various subject fields?
Do their high-ability scores suggest high adult adjustment and achievement?

Does high mental ability hinder, or facilitate, social and emotional adjustment? Does the very high IQ child have special adjustment problems?

Prior to careful scientific studies devoted to describing the general characteristics of gifted children, we had only the observations of physicians or other professional observers on various children. One set of observations that was most influential in guiding our earlier beliefs about the nature of genius and giftedness was provided by Cesare Lombroso (1893, p. 361), an extraordinarily influential professor of legal medicine at the end of the last century. This view, now considered highly inaccurate, was as follows:

> The frequency of genius among lunatics and of madmen among men of genius explains the fact that the destiny of nations has often been in the hands of the insane; and shows how the latter have been able to contribute so much to the progress of mankind. . . . It seems as though nature had intended to teach us respect for the supreme misfortunes of insanity; and also to preserve us from being dazzled by the brilliancy of those men of genius who might well be compared, not to the planets which keep their appointed orbits, but to falling stars, lost and dispersed over the crust of the earth.

How can such a brilliant observer as Lombroso apparently be so wrong? One reason is that as a psychiatrist he may have seen a very atypical sample of gifted individuals. His mistake was not in his individual observations but in trying to generalize from them to the larger group. It is a classic example as to why observations have to be supplemented by careful research.

The Terman Research

Many of the facts in the research available on high-IQ children are the results of the remarkable contributions of Lewis Terman and his associates, who organized a longitudinal study on approximately 1500 children which now been in progress for over forty years. This sample of children was drawn from California schools but that fact is unlikely to distort the general portrait. Terman did depend on teacher ratings to locate children for study and that probably resulted in overlooking such children as Sam and Joe who might not be found impressive by some teachers. Terman's description (1954, pp. 222–223) of the development of his thinking on this project is worth recording:

> I was a senior in psychology at Indiana University and was asked to prepare two reports for a seminar, one on mental deficiency and one on genius. . . . The reading of those two reports opened up a new world to me, the world of Galton, Binet and their contemporaries. . . . Then

I entered Clark University, where I spent considerable time during the first year in reading on mental tests and precocious children. . . . By the time I reached my last graduate year, I decided to find out for myself how precocious children differ from the mentally backward, and accordingly chose as my doctoral dissertation an experimental study of the intellectual processes of fourteen boys, seven of them picked as the brightest and seven as the dullest in a large city school. . . . The experiment contributed little or nothing to science, but it contributed a lot to my future thinking. . . . My dream was realized in the spring of 1921 when I obtained a generous grant from the Commonwealth Fund of New York City for the purpose of locating a thousand subjects of IQ 140 or higher.

Field studies were conducted again on this sample in 1927–1928, 1939–1940, and 1951–1952, with mail follow-ups periodically interspersed, the last of which was conducted in the late 1950s.

It is no coincidence that Terman is noted for his development of the Stanford–Binet Intelligence Test, as well as for his work with the gifted, since the test itself was the instrument by which he identified his superior children. His findings of their overall superior school adjustment were influential in exploding the then popular notion that gifted children were weak, puny, unpopular, and disturbed. A summary of the findings on the general characteristics of this group follows (Terman & Oden, 1951, pp. 23–24):

1. The average member of our group is a slightly better physical specimen than the average child. . . .
2. For the fields of subject matter covered in our tests, the superiority of gifted over unselected children was greater in reading, language usage, arithmetical reasoning, science, literature and the arts. In arithmetical computation, spelling and factual information about history and civics, the superiority of the gifted was somewhat less marked. . . .
3. The interests of gifted children are many-sided and spontaneous, they learn to read easily and read more and better books than the average child. At the same time, they make numerous collections, cultivate many kinds of hobbies, and acquire far more knowledge of plays and games than the average child. . . .
4. As compared with unselected children, they are less inclined to boast or to overstate their knowledge; they are more trustworthy when under temptation to cheat; their character preferences and social attitudes are more wholesome, and they score higher in a test of emotional stability. . . .
5. The deviation of the gifted subjects from the generality is in the upward direction for nearly all traits. There is no law of compensation whereby the intellectual superiority of the gifted tends to be offset by inferiorities along nonintellectual lines.

Even if we can show that there is one group of children in the school system superior to the rest in ability to learn and who are above average in other characteristics, can we demonstrate that such superiority will last? The great contribution of longitudinal studies is that children can be followed into adulthood to see how they adjust in later life. Terman and his associates used two measures of later success: performance on ability tests and career performance.

In this connection, an interesting investigation was carried out by Bayley and Oden (1955). From 1939 to 1952, 768 of the gifted subjects making up Terman's gifted sample were given the Concept Mastery Test, a group measure of intellectual ability. Bayley and Oden (p. 96) report:

> The scores at the later testing, when the subjects are approximately 12 years older, are consistently higher than for the first testing. The increases in scores . . . are highly significant . . . for both the men and the women.

In short, far from slipping back, as the "early ripe, early rot" notion would have it, these individuals actually *improved* their relative status on mental ability test scores in adulthood.

Terman and Oden (1951) provided some interesting personal notes on the achievement of various members of this group. A few of the outstanding accomplishments noted as of 1945 are summarized in Table 2–1.

TABLE 2–1. *Sample Accomplishments of Terman Gifted Group (by middle or late thirties in age).*

Men:
   physicist—director of major atomic energy laboratory
   physiologist—codirector of the most important investigation made on physiological, biochemical, and psychological effects of prolonged semistarvation
   head of major department of public health in leading medical school
   psychiatrist—made official examination of Nazi war criminals in Nuremburg trials
   oceanographer—chief of a technical staff at Bikini atomic tests
   brigadier general—Army Air Force
Women:
   Far fewer women than men have made records of outstanding achievement. This is hardly surprising—only a small minority have gone out wholeheartedly for a career. Among these are:
      a gifted woman poet
      successful novelists and journalists
      talented actress and author of successful Broadway play

Source: Adapted from L. M. Terman & M. Oden. The Stanford studies of the gifted. In P. Whitty (Ed.), *The gifted child.* Boston: D. C. Heath, 1951, pp. 33–34.

Terman (Terman & Oden, 1951, pp. 33–34) summarized the follow-up career performance of 800 men in his sample as follows:

> The achievement of the group at midlife is best illustrated by the case histories of the 800 men, since only a minority of the women have gone out for professional careers. By 1950, when the men had an average age of 40 years, they had published 67 books (46 in the field of science, arts, and the humanities, and 21 books of fiction). They had published more than 1400 scientific, technical, and professional articles; over 200 short stories, novelettes, and plays and 236 miscellaneous articles on a great variety of subjects. They had also authored more than 150 patents. The figures on publications do not include the hundreds of publications by journalists that classify as news stories, editorials, or newspaper columns, nor do they include the hundreds if not thousands of radio and television scripts. . . . The level of education attained by this group was over ten times that expected of the general population.

On the evidence of both the life history follow-up and the test–retest information, it is fair to say that this group gave little evidence of declining from its lofty position attained on the tests in middle childhood. On the contrary, they have shown a tendency to *increase* their advantage over the average individual. In this fashion it seems that the intellectually rich get richer. However, all was not milk and honey for all the members of this gifted group. A later chapter will focus on the information available on the "underachievers" in this sample.

Oden (1968, pp. 50–51) in the last available report on this remarkable group reported:

> All the evidence indicates that with few exceptions the superior child becomes the superior adult. . . . Two thirds of the men and almost as large a proportion of the women consider that they have lived up to their intellectual abilities fully or reasonably well.

It must also be noted that no one of the singular brilliance of an Einstein or Edison or Lincoln has yet emerged from this group. It is likely that great fame relies upon so many imponderables, and is so statistically unlikely, that even a sample as large as Terman's with its distinguished membership would not be expected to yield the genius that appears once or twice in a generation.

The Functioning of High-IQ Students

What are the capabilities of the gifted children who are performing as might reasonably be expected, without individual debilitating social or personal problems? We can review the evidence available on the gifted from middle-class backgrounds. Do the results of other studies match the results of the Terman studies? (The late 1960s and the early 1970s have shown a marked reduction of studies on characteristics of the gifted; much of the research reported here, therefore—with the exception of that on creativity—is a decade or more old.)

ACADEMIC PERFORMANCE. We commented in the previous chapter on how closely our definition of intelligence is dependent upon the way in which we try to measure it. It is important for teachers to reflect that what we call "achievement" in our school children is determined mainly by the construction of what we call "achievement tests." If the intelligence tests do not measure all of what we would like to measure in intelligence, we will be missing important segments of giftedness. It is also true that if our achievement tests fall short in various dimensions, we may be deceiving ourselves in terms of the amount of achievement attained by gifted children.

The following example is one of many that could be chosen. Terman commented that his group appeared less effective in arithmetic computation than in reading, social studies, or science. Gallagher and Crowder (1957) investigated the adjustment of thirty-five highly gifted elementary children (Binet IQ 150+) and found the same result. That is, in their sample, 68 percent of the children were more than three grades above their own grade level in paragraph meaning, and 58 percent were three grades above their grade level in science; *but* only 27 percent were three grades or more above their grade level in arithmetic reasoning, and only 3 percent were three grades or more above their grade level in arithmetic computation. What does this mean? Is this a condemnation of the current practices in teaching arithmetic? Does it mean that gifted children have inherent deficiencies in numerical abilities?

The more reasonable explanation would seem to lie in the construction of the achievement tests. Once the basic skills of readings have been learned, there are almost no additional barriers that need to be surmounted before the youngster can go ahead, often on his own, in rapidly improving his breadth of knowledge and skill. His performance on achievement tests, linked to reading, requires no further learning of skills.

However, in the area of arithmetic, achievement is measured by the student's ability to progress through a series of well-defined skills. Thus, the third-grade child, in order to attain a score in arithmetic computation at the sixth-grade level, would not necessarily have to have great depth of mathematical knowledge but merely knowledge of such arithmetic operations as subtraction of fractions or long division.

If it is true that the results of arithmetic competence are dependent upon the way the tests were constructed, then, perhaps, results in other areas are dependent upon the tests also. A gifted child may score four grades above his own grade level in social studies, but that may merely mean that he has absorbed an extensive collection of isolated facts and does not necessarily have a comprehensive knowledge of the basic concepts or ideas of social studies or how to apply these ideas in other situations. Until we can become more effective constructors of achievement tests that measure depth of understanding as well as breadth, these skyrocketing achievement scores obtained by gifted students may mean much less than we would like them to mean.

Martinson (1972, p. 81), commenting on a study of over 1000 gifted children, reported the kind of academic advance that is both a source of pleasure and a headache to educators who are used to planning for children on the basis of their chronological age or their grade level.

> In the kindergarten group, the average performance of gifted students was comparable to that of second grade students. . . .
>
> The average for fourth and fifth grade gifted children was beyond that of seventh grade students.
>
> The average for gifted eighth grade students was equal or beyond the typical performance of 12th grade students.

In short, the individual profiles of Cranshaw and Zelda that show them three or four years in advance of their agemates are by no means uncommon, and *unless* some special programming is provided for them they will be condemned to review material in their school that they had mastered two or three years ago.

It is always interesting to compare results in such studies with children from different cultures. Lovell and Shields (1967) reported on the first fifty youngsters who scored an IQ of 140 or more in two large cities in the north of England. They used similar rating scales to that used by Terman and found that the mean rating given by British teachers for this sample was very close to that given by American teachers to Terman's sample forty years ago. The children who scored in this high IQ range were rated outstandingly high in desire to know, originality, truthfulness, will power, perseverance, and sense of humor, among other characteristics. The poorest rating, which was still rated about average, was freedom from vanity and egotism, which seemed to be particularly a problem with boys. This type of confirmatory evidence gives confidence that the basic pattern revealed by Terman seems to be confirmed by youngsters who score high on IQ tests from a distance of 6000 miles and forty years.

Social Status.   Several questions have been raised concerning the social adjustment of gifted or high-IQ children. Are they popular? Whom are they interested in having as their friends? Are there other factors besides mental ability influencing the results of these sociometric studies? There is little or no question about the general social status of high-IQ elementary school children. It is high. Figure 2–1 shows the social popularity of the groups related to IQ levels in an investigation by Gallagher (1958) in the elementary schools in a midwest university town.

Similar results showing the positive relationship between IQ scores and popularity have been shown by a large group of investigators (Grace and Booth, 1958; Grupe, 1961; Johnson and Kirk, 1950; and Miller, 1956).

Other miscellaneous facts concerning social status of high IQ children can be presented briefly:

1. The social status of gifted children seems to show a relative decrease at the secondary level.
2. Gifted children are able to identify correctly the social status of others and themselves better than the average.
3. Gifted children tend to choose each other for friends when they are removed from the classroom for a period of time each day.
4. Gifted children lose some general social acceptance when removed from the classroom for a special workshop.
5. Acceleration at the elementary level does not seriously affect their social adjustment.

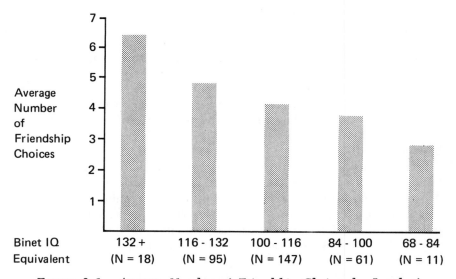

FIGURE 2–1. *Average Number of Friendship Choices by Level of Intellectual Ability.* (*Adapted from J. J. Gallagher. Social status of children related to intelligence, propinquity, and social perception. Elementary School Journal, 1958, 58, p. 228.*)

6. Gifted children seem to serve as an ego-ideal to the average child, who chooses him even though he sees differences between himself and the gifted youngster.

But why are high-IQ children popular? Is it their intellect or is it other characteristics? Tannenbaum (1959) made an attempt to identify important factors for social choice in an urban secondary school. He found that academic brilliance was neither socially acceptable nor unacceptable *per se* but depended on other pertinent factors (i.e., athletics, studiousness). The most unfortunate combination of factors, from a social status standpoint, was a brilliant and studious student who was a nonathlete, whereas the student who ranked high in athletics *and* who was involved in social activities was most highly regarded.

If good social and personal adjustment can be the result of high intelligence *or* the strong family background often found in conjunction with high-ability children, perhaps a study could be conceived that would hold social background factors constant; one could then see whether IQ still made a difference.

Such a study was executed by Smith (1962). He compared forty-two intellectually gifted adolescents with forty-two adolescents of average intelligence on six different criteria of personal and social adjustment. Most important, the two groups were equated on variables of sex, social class, religion, nationality, and age.

Tests of personality and attitude, as well as teacher and peer evaluations, were used in the comparison. Smith discovered that the gifted students were different from the average in one major area—a tendency to display more dominant, forceful, independent, and competitive types of behavior.

In all other dimensions, such as accuracy of self-perception, personality integration, self-acceptance, and the like, no differences between the groups were found, leading Smith to conclude that factors other than intellectual ones were largely responsible for the high adjustment shown by most gifted samples.

Such information can provide some insight as to the individual differences obtained on the four children under discussion in this book. Although Cranshaw was popular, the results were quite different with Zelda, who irritated other youngsters with her superior, know-it-all attitude and who did not seek out a large number of other friends. She would not obtain more than one or two friendship choices from her class. So the generalization that high-IQ children are popular does not serve the teacher very well in Zelda's case. What it *does* tell the teacher is that intellectually gifted children are usually popular or unpopular for the same kinds of reasons that other children are popular or unpopular. To the degree to which these children have desirable characteristics they are popular. To the degree to which they do not, social popularity will desert them regardless of their ability level.

Joe is quite a different matter from either Zelda or Cranshaw in this regard. Joe would probably get a number of social choices, but this is not likely to bring much of a feeling of comfort to the teacher. A close examination of the children who are choosing Joe would probably reveal that they are difficult children to handle in the school situation, with a history of troublemaking. The grouping together of these students could well mean more trouble for the teacher. In order to use sociometric examinations effectively, it would therefore be desirable to investigate further to discover *why* particular people are being chosen, in order to evaluate whether the teacher should be happy or disappointed with the results of the sociometric technique.

PERSONALITY CHARACTERISTICS. Whenever one finds a group of children who receive high social acceptance, it is very likely that he will also find good personal adjustment. By and large, this seems to be the case in the investigations so far. Not only did Terman's group seem well adjusted in childhood, but they showed a slightly below-average incidence of suicide and institutionalization for mental illness in later life. The results of studies of the personality problems of high-IQ children consistently show them to have more freedom from problems than average groups (Gair, 1944; Gallagher and Crowder, 1957; Hildreth, 1938; Lightfoot, 1951; Mensh, 1950; Ramaseshan, 1957). The emphasis on personality problems of the gifted stems, no doubt, from an attempt to examine the popular belief that there is a relationship between emotional instability and genius. These studies, despite their consistent results, have not settled this issue, since the instability that is noted may be found in subgroups other than high-IQ children (i.e., the high creative).

Some studies have abandoned the global approach to personality and have investigated more specific characteristics. One personality factor that seems related to high ability is the characteristic of *independence*. A study by Lucito (1959) illustrates this point. He compared fifty-five bright and fifty-one dull sixth-grade children on a task that measured conformity to group judgment. The task that the children were given (in groups of six) was to identify which of three lines was the longest. There was no problem in perceptually identifying which line was the longest (the children had previously demonstrated the ability to tell the difference), but the problem was complicated by the experimenter, who provided each of the children with false information on the performance of the other five youngsters in the group. In some instances, a youngster was given the information, before he made his decision, that the other five members of his group had chosen the wrong line. His choice was either to follow the group members in a decision that was

41

manifestly wrong or to reject the group and trust his own perceptions. Results indicated that the bright children, as a group, were significantly less conforming to their supposed peer opinions than were the dull children.   None of the dull children qualified for the most independent category of behavior as defined by Lucito, whereas 29 percent of the bright children fell into such a category.

One method in psychological clinics that has been used to elicit information about inner wishes, desires, and fears has been the Sentence Completion Test.   Table 2–2 shows some selected excerpts from the

TABLE 2–2.   *Excerpts from Sentence Completion Test.*

MARY	MONA
Our family is very big.	*Our family* is close.
My mother is sweet and understanding.	*My mother* is pretty.
Secretly I wish everybody was well fed and taken care of.	*Secretly I wish* I was pretty.
I cannot understand what makes me so awfull (*sic*).	*I cannot understand what makes me* so ugly
My father is very mean at times but very nice at other times.	*My father* is strong.
My worst subject in school is Social Studies.	*My worst* trouble is beuty (*sic*).
I envy people who play golf.	*I envy* pretty girls.
My looks are fair.	*My looks* are bad.
My chief worry is how we can help poor people.	*My chief worry is* looks.
I am sorry for the death of people.	*I am sorry* I was born ugly.
At home I have a wonderful time.	*At home* I am nothing.
I am ashamed of my manners.	*I am ashamed* of my looks.

If I could have any 3 wishes, I would wish for:

1. All the people in the world to be well fed, cared for, and happy.	1. I would wish for beuty (*sic*).
2. Not to let anyone die. It just brings sorrow to others.	2. For a billion dollars to give to charity.
3. I'd wish to stay just the way I am happy and content not rich not real poor just happy and content.	3. Everyone in the world would be happy.

Sentence Completion Tests taken by two girls, Mary and Mona.   As in Chapter 1, the italicized parts represent the stems of the sentences that the children responded to, and the rest constitutes the answers that the children wrote.   Read both, and see if you can perceive the different view of life that each of them has.

Mona seems quite disturbed about her own looks and physical appearance, whereas Mary does not. What makes these two girls of particular interest to us is that both of them are in the intellectually superior range and are *identical twins!* Despite the fact that Mary and Mona can be distinguished from each other only by very close acquaintances, there are considerable differences in their perceptions of themselves. Also, since both of them have about the same level of intellectual ability, one couldn't say that Mona's feeling about her physical appearance stems from her being bright.

Many of the personal problems of gifted children stem from the same general sources as those of average-ability children. Since there is a tendency for the high-IQ children to be a little better off in family stability and physical health, they are less likely to have problems than is the average child. This does not mean, however, that one cannot find gifted youngsters who are in a great deal of emotional trouble and in need of a good deal of special help and assistance.

VERY HIGH ABILITY CHILDREN

If a child attains a remarkably high IQ score—say a Binet IQ of 170 or 180 (achieved by 1 child in about 100,000)—does this set him too far apart from his fellow students, socially and intellectually? Many people feel that it does. Tim is an example of a child who scored an IQ of over 200 on the Stanford-Binet. This meant that his mental-age score was double that of his chronological age. As an 8-year-old, he had a mental-age score of 16 years. At the age of 8, in the middle of the second grade, Tim was capable of giving definitions like this:

> Diamond: *a hard rock mined in Africa that sparkles and is of high value.*
>
> Gamble: *to risk something, to take chances.*
>
> Shilling: *a dollar in some other country.*
>
> Microscope: *like a short-range telescope to see something very small.*
>
> Belfry: *a bell tower.*

His fund of information was truly remarkable. Even when he was missing some quite advanced questions, he was revealing his superiority, as in the following examples:

> *What does the stomach do? Takes your food and throws it all over your body.*
>
> *What is the capital of Greece? Rome.*

43

Where does turpentine come from?   Maple Trees.
What does C.O.D. mean?   Careful on Delivery.

Can this boy, and other children like him, ever communicate effectively with their age mates?   In this instance, Tim was having trouble socially, but it had to do only indirectly with his ability.   In reality, his trouble was a sense of inferiority—not intellectual inferiority, of course, but physical inferiority.   In order to hide his feelings about his poor ability in sports, he tried to impress other children with his mental ability; this was not a striking success.   However, his father found some time to help him with his physical coordination and sports skills.   His obnoxious mannerisms were reduced coincident with his better performance in the physical area.

One of the earlier investigators deeply concerned about the problems of extremely high ability children was Leta Hollingworth (1942).   One of her projects was an intensive analysis of twelve children who scored above 180 Binet IQ.   According to test standardization data, such children should appear about once in 1 million cases.   Hollingworth felt that these youngsters were so far beyond the abilities of their age group that they would have difficulties in making both educational and social adjustments.   She suggested that there were five general conduct problems with which they must learn to deal (p. 299):

1. To find enough hard and interesting work at school.
2. To suffer fools gladly.
3. To keep from becoming negativistic toward authority.
4. To keep from becoming hermits.
5. To avoid the formation of habits of extreme chicanery.

Naturally, a child who appears only once in a million times is of such an unusual nature and character that the school program cannot possibly be drastically revised or changed in order to fit his particular needs.   What is needed may be special tutoring sessions on an individual basis, with a skilled person who realizes the particular pitfalls awaiting this type of youngster.

These observations on highly gifted children have been supported by Terman and Oden (1947), who suggested that for such a youngster social adjustment is one of his most difficult tasks.   From a total of twenty-five youngsters of this intellectual level, Terman found that few received top ratings on a social-adjustment scale, whereas over 35 percent of them fall in the bottom two categories.   They seemed to be poor mixers and solitary children.   Both Terman and Hollingworth concluded that the IQ level most compatible with the school society, as it is now constituted, probably ranges between 125 and 155.   At this level there are enough peers of similar ability to avoid intellectual isolation.   They are not so different from the group that they could not operate as adequate leaders in various activities.

Cox (1926) utilized a unique method of examination of the biographies and papers of 301 eminent men and women in order to estimate their intellectual ability at an early age. The average estimated IQ score of this group was from 135 to 145, and the range from 100 to 190. The high intellectual eminence of this group seemed apparent from an early age. The very high scores were most often found among writers and scientists, with lesser aptitude necessary for military and political leaders.

Kirk (1972), drawing on the work of Cox, makes the interesting point that many of the extraordinarily intelligent men of the past did not receive benefits from the formal education of that era and instead were privately tutored. To support his case, Kirk chose John Stuart Mill, Norbert Wiener, Albert Einstein, Werner Von Braun, and Thomas Edison, all undeniably in the top echelon of ability and performance. What happened in their education?

John Stuart Mill wrote at length about his early experiences. "My father's scheme of education could not have been accomplished if he had not carefully kept me from having any great amount of intercourse with other boys." His father kept him out of school and away from other children to avoid the "contagion of vulgar modes of thought and feeling." Mill concluded, "I consequently remained long . . . inexpert in anything requiring manual dexterity. . . . The education which my father gave me was in itself more fitted for training me to *know* than to *do*" (1972, p. 115).

Norbert Wiener is a remarkable example of an accelerated student. At the age of 7 he entered school and was placed in the third grade. By 9 years of age he was admitted to high school, by 11 he entered Harvard College, and by 18 he had a Ph.D. in mathematics. He had to spend several years in relatively low-level occupations since people were wary of hiring an 18-year-old Ph.D. But was formal schooling the major contributor to Wiener's performance? Wiener himself reports that his father tutored him at home and that other specialists tutored him as well. His father was a perfectionist and severe taskmaster who accepted only high level performance and accuracy.

Wiener's early expertise in mathematics finally became translated into his origination of a new field, that of cybernetics. In many ways, our computer-based society owes much of its origins to the genius of Norbert Wiener. Wiener himself paid a high personal price for this, in terms of periodic mental illness and general personal unhappiness. Was all of that early family pressure and drive to achieve for Norbert worth it? Of whom shall we ask that question? Of Wiener himself or of the generation of people who live better lives for his excellent, if personally tormented, work? We might get different answers.

Albert Einstein is another person who did not have particularly happy school experiences. His lack of verbal ability—he was quite slow in developing language skills—did not encourage his teachers to believe that he was something special. Einstein's interest in mathematics was stimulated by his uncle. After some initial adventures in mathematics he studied on his own, apart from the school program, and continued to compile a mediocre record in school in areas dependent on language. Could he get into a first-rate college today? Of course, you say? If a college placed great emphasis on scholastic aptitude tests based on language, Einstein would not have looked very good. His great accomplishments were built on a base of knowledge that was largely self-learned, not school-learned.

Thomas Edison's talents surely cannot be attributed to his formal education. His indignant mother, outraged that a teacher called Thomas "addled," removed him from school and taught him at home. He flourished in this tutorial program, mastering many difficult masterpieces in literature at a young age and cultivating a creative engineering mind that was later to produce important inventions, if not great ideas.

Of the five men noted by Kirk, only Werner Von Braun had an apparently normal schooling. He attended regular schools in Germany but was accelerated markedly through the school program, as was evidenced by his obtaining a Ph.D. in mathematics at the age of 22. His interest in rocketry, which eventually made him famous, apparently stemmed from some self-initiated reading about interplanetary rockets. His accomplishments were attained without the help of a single course or formal study in this special area.

Kirk raises three serious questions arising from these case studies (p. 116):

1. Is it necessary to segregate *very* superior children from their childhood peers in order to educate them for a scholarly career?
2. Can such an education be accomplished in a school situation?
3. Is such achievement, described here, the result of a tutorial system which can begin at an early age, uncontaminated by a school curriculum and grade placement?

ORIGINS OF GIFTEDNESS

The search for the origins of giftedness is a fascinating one. Is heredity foremost? Environment? Or are they equally important? If the environment is influential, which environment? At what age level?

There is no question, certainly, that talent is inherited to at least some extent. Educators are so involved in environmental changes that they often overlook or underestimate the influence of heredity. Our general observation that most gifted families resemble those of Zelda and Cranshaw, whereas many fewer are like Sam's, does not help us answer the question. If a child has both highly intelligent parents and a rich environment, we still don't know to which characteristic, or in which combination, we can assign the favorable results.

One approach that has received some attention as a way to sort out the various factors is to compare results obtained on identical twins (children from the same fertilized egg, hence with the same heredity) with the performance of fraternal twins (who come from two different eggs fertilized at the same time). If heredity is important, we would expect greater similarity in the performance of identical as compared with fraternal twins.

Recently, Nichols (1965) identified 700 identical twins and 500 fraternal twins who had participated in the National Merit Scholarship program and were highly talented students. The correlation on total test scores for identical twins was .87; for fraternal twins, .63. These results correspond closely to values obtained in eight previous twin studies published during the last forty years and conducted in several different countries and in several different languages. Using these data, Nichols concluded that approximately 70 percent of the total performance of the student can be attributed to heredity. That still leaves a lot of room for the educator to work in, but he should not assume that each child is starting from a blank slate and that his performance is determined solely by environmental influences.

Another not entirely explained phenomenon is the tendency for first-born children to be more talented than their subsequent siblings. Again among National Merit finalists from two-child families, there are about twice as many first-born as second-born. In three-child families there are as many first-born finalists as second- and third-born combined. The same result was obtained on a group of 600 talented black students (Altus, 1966).

It is one thing to observe a clear phenomenon and another to explain it. Both physiological and psychological reasons can be used to explain the data. You might try your hand at explaining it yourself.

GIFTED GIRLS AND GIFTED BOYS

Zelda is a member of a minority group—a group that has nothing to do with her religion or skin color or ethnic characteristics. She is a girl—a gifted girl. Even at her early age, Zelda has had a taste of what awaits her in her struggle to become accepted as a person with a superior intellect without having people refer to her sex. She has heard an aunt say, "She is so bright, it is too bad she wasn't born a boy." She has been told by teachers and her peers that girls "don't like science and mathematics."

Like other minority groups, gifted girls are in dire danger of behaving according to the stereotype constructed for them by the culture. After all, if people are told often enough that they are lazy, or greedy, or drug prone, or any of the other stereotypes circulated for minority groups, many of the members of that group will start to act that way. If a girl has learned that girls don't argue with the opinions of others and are somewhat unimaginative, she may begin to believe it and act accordingly.

Walberg (1969), in reviewing the performance of gifted girl students in physics programs in the secondary school, concluded that they tended to be conforming, dependent, docile, uninterested in risk-taking, and he suggested that they "hold back intellectually for conformity to the feminine role and social approval" (p. 52).

Gallagher, Aschner, and Jenné (1967) reported a similar finding in analyses of tape recordings of classroom interaction in twelve classrooms of gifted junior high school classes. The boys in these classrooms were eight times as likely to quarrel with the opinions of their peers or teacher than the girls. Also, the girls did not express themselves in class discussion as much as the boys, even though their written expressiveness compared favorably with that of the boys.

In six biology classes, Gallagher (1967) identified the most orally expressive and nonexpressive students, both boys and girls, in terms of their total verbal output during three days of classroom discussion. The expressive students were superior in aptitude, in knowledge of biological concepts as revealed by formal tests, and they obtained better test grades and overall course grades. These results are consistent across instructors, and for both boys and girls. A comparison of expressiveness in the six classes, however, showed that in four of the six classes, boys were more expressive than girls, with the other two classes showing no significant relationship.

Are there meaningful differences between the sexes in the development of superior ability? The folklore of many cultures carries the expectation that there are differences in sex in certain kinds of abilities, such as the boy's being more skilled in science and mathematics and the girl's being more talented in the arts and social sensitivity.

A second question is, if differences are found, are they due to innate sex-linked characteristics or to differential cultural stimulation? Here is a classic "chicken and egg" problem. Does the greater aptitude of boys in mathematics preshape the cultural acceptance of math as part of the male role, or does the traditional social acceptance of math as a non-female role discourage girls who might otherwise show substantial aptitudes in mathematics?

Astin (1972) took samples of junior-high-aged boys and girls participating in math and science contests, thus presumably drawing the most highly motivated boys and girls in a metropolitan area, and found that boys scored significantly higher than girls on tests of mathematical and scientific aptitude. There was some suggestion that girls lose interest in math and science as they get older, that parents tended to encourage boys in these interest areas more than they did girls, and that such encouragement seems reflected in girls' choosing more artistic and social types of occupations.

If it is true that family and cultural expectations can play an important role in the development of different styles or approaches to life, one rather special application of this notion could be a closer look at the effect of sex differences on these characteristics. Sears, Maccoby, and Levin (1957) and Bayley and Schaefer (1960) report longitudinal studies that stress the marked differences in the developing patterns of boys and girls.

It is slight exaggeration to say that boys and girls grow up in markedly different worlds, where different social roles and different life patterns are imposed from without, by both family and culture. If one key philosophy related to creative production is the "take a chance" position versus the "play it safe" notion, there would be sound theoretical grounds for suggesting that girls are less creative than boys, since they tend to be encouraged more to adopt the "play it safe" or dependent philosophy.

This idea is seemingly borne out in some results now becoming available. Generally, girls have been found to do as well as or better than boys in the area of school achievement. Yet, in adulthood, they seem to become relatively few high-level creative scientists, writers, or musicians. This limited production does not seem to be explained entirely by the traditional dual role that women play as wife–mother and career person. A moment's reflection will suggest that these different sex roles begin at an early age. Common parental admonitions such as "Big boys don't cry" and "Nice girls don't get dirty" begin to set patterns before the child is in school.

Torrance (1959) discovered that certain toys had achieved sex role status as early as in the primary grades. When asked to think of ways of improving certain kinds of toys, girls produced significantly fewer ideas about toys which have a masculine identification—such as a fire engine. On the other hand, boys produced more ideas for a fire engine than they did for a nurse's kit. Some boys first felt compelled to change it to a doctor's kit before giving answers. Some of the children felt so strongly about the sex preference and identification of these toys that they would even refuse to answer the question about a toy that they felt really belonged to the opposite sex.

The girl who does show tendencies toward creative ability apparently runs risks in peer acceptance not shared by boys. Torrance selected the top-scoring boy and girl in each of twenty-three classes on a test battery of "creative" thinking, and compared them with a group of control children with whom they were equal in sex, grade, class, race, and IQ. The creative children were identified on a sociometric device according to whether they had more ideas "off the beaten track." Perhaps as a consequence of this, there was a tendency for them to gain a reputation for having wild or silly ideas, and for being characterized by a sense of humor and a playfulness superior to that of the control group. Although being divergent did not seem to influence the popularity of the boys in the sample, it did significantly influence the popularity of the girls—the more divergent girls being less frequently chosen. Here, again, we see another of the forces that discourages girls from expressing more of the characteristics relating to creativity.

Gowan and Groth (1972) explored the vocational choices of young girls in a summer school program for gifted students. The girls ranged in age from 7 to 14 and there were over 200 in the total sample. When asked their vocational choices, their responses reflected more their perceived expectation of the society rather than personal choices at this early age. However, of the girls, 37 percent chose an occupation in the general area of nurturance, such as a nurse or a teacher or a stewardess, as against only 7 percent of the males in these dimensions. On the other hand, only 10 percent of the girls chose science, although that figure increased as the girls became older; 33 percent of the males chose the science area.

The girls chose the area of the performing arts three times as often as the boys, and neither group chose the area of trade or business in any significant amount. These choices tended to reflect the still-powerful sex expectations in terms of occupation, regardless of ability.

Flanagan (1970) reported on the educational outcomes for nationwide Project Talent students who fell in the highest academic aptitude quarter of the children tested *but* in the lowest socioeconomic quarter—the brightest but poorest 25 percent. Although 80 percent of the men in that group did go to college, only half of them completed college, suggesting a delayed inhibiting role.

With the women in the study, the problems appeared to be much more severe. Less than half the women in the highest quarter in academic aptitude went to college, and only 30 percent completed college. Although it is an oversimplification to attribute the failure to complete college solely to economics (there might be different values in the students' coming from different socioeconomic levels), it is at least a point worthy of more careful study.   Many students, boys and girls who come from low economic backgrounds, with high talent, are not finishing their educational program.   When one reflects on the needs for leadership in the poorer segments of society, the inability of these talented students to complete their education is a serious societal problem.

What are the characteristics of those women who overcome the discouragement of teachers, job discrimination, and slow advancement to become professional women who use their superior intellect?   Bachtold and Werner (1970) studied the personality profiles of 124 women psychologists.   There were major differences between the women psychologists and average women.   They were more socially aloof, serious, and dominant.   It was a general portrait of an individual of purpose, not easily swayed by social pressures.   That pattern is confirmed by superior scores by the women psychologists in security, self-sufficiency, and unconventionality.

Sanford (1956, p. 37), in a set of four case studies of gifted Vassar women, gave some tentative notions of factors related to that high achievement.

> In all four cases, one or the other of the parents was highly educated or placed high values upon scholarly attainments, and held high hopes and expectations for their daughter.   In all four cases there was early, close involvement with the parents and early and persistent awkwardness in social relations with peers.

The stress on the unfairness of not opening many professional careers to gifted women, and the perception of women being unfairly forced to stay at home, have threatened to rob the role of *mother* of intellectual respectability.   Torrance (1972, p. 1602) reports on one gifted woman reflecting on her education in a university high school as follows:

> University High failed us in a sense by directing their female students solely toward careers in all fields other than domestic.   No one ever told us how creative and rewarding the role of mother and wife can be, combined of course with other interests if so desired.

Bertrand Russell, the English philosopher, once reported on a primitive tribe that preached celibacy as the holy way of life, depending, according to Russell, on man's natural sinfulness to provide the tribe with the next generation of disciples.   Similarly, those who urge women to abandon the role of mother and wife must secretly expect that not every woman will agree, else we will all be members of the final generation of mankind.

COMPARATIVE GROUP RESEARCH.   The educational implications of comparing boys and girls seem quite limited.   The fact that there is an *average* difference between boys and girls with regard to performance on this test or that variable does not have implications for individual children.

Some girls will obviously show stronger interests and greater aptitude for mathematics and science than some boys, despite an average difference in favor of the boys, and such girls should be encouraged in these interests.

Probably what it means is that the only way we can really find out whether such differences as described here are due to social and environmental characteristics is to eliminate the social bias or pressures that would tend to embarrass or discourage girls and boys from going into fields that have been traditionally denied them. If under conditions of complete freedom of choice and acceptability, there remained a difference between the sexes, we would know then that such a difference does relate to genetic sex-linked characteristics.

RACIAL AND ETHNIC DIFFERENCES

One often-asked question is: How much of a rarity is Sam? Does the fact that he is black and gifted make him an extraordinarily unusual person? Is the discovery of Sam and his talents a rare discovery? According to the research available in this area, the answer is that it is *not* unusual, but it *is* less likely. Although gifted and talented students can be found in all walks of life and in all racial and ethnic groups, they are more likely to be found in some groups than in others. The groups with high incidence of the gifted place a great emphasis on intellectual values and have more extensive opportunities to develop talents and skills already present in the child.

Another finding, reproduced a number of times, is that although more boys and girls are found generally in searches for gifted and talented youngsters, in black populations high-ability girls outnumber the boys more than two to one. While it is unwise to jump to conclusions, the lack of opportunities for black boys compared to those available to black girls in the culture leads one to speculate that part of the full realization of intellectual potential lies in perceived opportunities in the adult society by the youngsters involved. The same reasoning is a possible explanation as to why more gifted boys than gifted girls are found in the general population. It is one more piece of evidence that the schools cannot be viewed apart from the society and the culture in which they exist. The "failure" of schools to develop black potential can be partially ascribed to the culture, which does not provide sufficient models or opportunity.

There are two general statements that can be made regarding ethnic differences in ability at the highest levels of performance. First, ability at the highest level can be found in every ethnic and racial group. Second, there are clear differences in the proportion of youngsters being identified as gifted in various ethnic and racial groups. Adler (1967) did a brief review of studies relating intelligence to ethnic groups and found consistently the highest-ranking groups in proportion of talent discovered were Jewish, German, English, and Scottish, while the lowest proportions of talent were Negro, Italian, Mexican, and American Indian.

There is a rather suspicious correlation here between these rankings and the groups that have the most favorable social status in the society and which have been members of the dominant culture for the longest period of time. Perhaps only the Jewish subgroup of the favored populations has had substantial handicaps or barriers placed in its way in relation to other groups in the society. The long-accepted emphasis in Jewish and Chinese families on family life and on learning is also a pertinent observation.

Terman and Oden (1947) noted the high incidence of Jewish children found in their longitudinal study (over 10 percent of the sample—far larger than their population incidence would anticipate). A comparison of Jewish and non-Jewish samples along dimensions of school achievement, marital happiness, personality ratings, and so on yielded few differences, as Terman and Oden state (p. 310):

> The conclusion suggested by these detailed comparisons is that the Jewish subjects in the study differ little from the non-Jewish except in their greater drive for vocational success, their tendency toward liberalism in political attitudes and somewhat lower divorce rate.

However, it is precisely in the motivational area that the key difference may lie.

THE "CREATIVE" CHILD

For many years psychologists were satisfied with an operational definition of intelligence; namely "intelligence is what an IQ test measures." This is a useful definition only if what is being measured fits reasonably with our larger view of intelligence. It took a theoretical psychologist, J. P. Guilford, to firmly demonstrate that there are a number of dimensions of intellectual performance that are *not* measured by standard IQ tests— prominent among these, divergent thinking and evaluative thinking.

In his attempt to determine the extent and limits of the intellectual processes, Guilford (1968) drew a clear distinction between the operations of divergent thinking (which included characteristics of fluency, flexibility, and foresight) and convergent thinking (which represented the kind of abilities often measured on standard intelligence tests).

Some examples of the distinction between the two types of test items are given in Table 2–3. Sample items are shown from typical IQ tests

Table 2–3.   *Contrast Between IQ and Creativity Test Items.*

TYPICAL IQ TEST ITEMS	TYPICAL CREATIVITY TEST ITEMS
1. What is a brick?	1. How many uses can you think of for a brick?
2. If a boy goes to the store and buys 3¢ worth of candy and gives the man 10¢, how much change will he get back?	2. How many different ways can you think of that will get an answer of 4?
3. Find the absurdity in this picture. (A wheel off a car or a man hammering with the wrong end of the hammer.)	3. Take this toy dog and think of ways that it could be changed to bring more fun to boys and girls.
4. Glove is to Hand as Shoe is to ————.	4. Write all the words you can think of to the word "bolt."

and from the divergent-thinking tests.   The reader will notice that the characteristics which the IQ test items have in common are that they all have one correct answer and that they result in a narrowing of the subject under consideration to one appropriate response.

In contrast to this, the "creativity" test items stress the importance of many answers.   Indeed, one of the criteria for successful performance on these tests is the number of answers given.   Such factors as originality and flexibility are also scored by evaluating the quality and direction of responses to such a question as, "How could we improve a toy dog?"

As the new tests of fluency, flexibility, and foresight have been put into greater use, it has been discovered that children who score very high on these tests are not always the same youngsters who score high on IQ tests.

Some of the differences in originality in two children of similar high IQ can be illustrated in the contrasting stories of Zelda and Cranshaw to the same assignment, "My Interesting Trip."   First, Zelda's story:

> One day last spring our family went to Uncle Ned's house.   He lives in the city and we have to drive a long time to get there.   He has many interesting things in his house, cellos, violins, bass fiddles and other musical instruments.   Sometimes he will play his violin for us.
>
> He always finds a quarter hidden in my ear even when I know it isn't there.   It is a lot of fun to visit Uncle Ned's.   I would like to go there again.

Here is Cranshaw's story:

> One day when I was coming down our rickety stairs I tripped over my sister's pull toy.   I sprained my ankle and had to stay in bed for a week.
>
> I read seven books.   While reading them I traveled to Africa, the North Pole, to prehistoric days, and down the Santa Fe Trail.   I shared the adventures of brave men.   I was hot and cold, happy and sad, scared and excited with them.   That is why my trip down the stairs was my most interesting trip this year.

Is Zelda's fear of unstructured situations a manifestation of a deeper personality characteristic? Is it a legacy from family attitudes and values, or has the school program discouraged her so much in the past that she fears to strike out in unexpected territory? Where is the Solomon to weigh these possible factors? Yet some progress has been made in the search for factors associated with tendencies to high and low creativity.

High-Convergent Versus High-Divergent Children

Getzels and Jackson (1962) conducted what appeared to be a deceptively easy study that set a pattern for a decade of research on this topic. They decided to draw a comparison across many different academic and social dimensions of those children who were very good at tests of convergent thinking but not very good at divergent thinking with those children who were very good at tests of divergent thinking but not very good at convergent thinking. The following figure illustrates the basic idea.

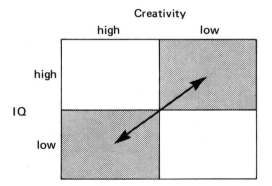

What appeared uncomplicated, however, turned out to be complex, and we are still trying to interpret the information obtained by this and subsequent studies. For one thing, Getzels and Jackson refer to one of their groups as "high creative." But these students are so labeled on the basis of high scores on divergent-thinking tests. We are faced with a new version of the old operational definition. "Creativity is what 'creativity tests' measure." But that certainly is not true; for this reason the reader must bear in mind that the term "high creative" in our discussion of these children has a very specific meaning, one that will become clear as our discussion progresses.

Another problem is how low is "low IQ," or "low-creativity" for that matter. The "low-IQ" children in Getzels and Jackson's study had an *average* IQ score of over 120, which is in the top 15 percent of ability nationally and would be called super high in many schools. Since the study was done at a university laboratory school, all the children turned out to be fairly bright, so "low IQ" is a very relative term here. Getzels and Jackson did not separate out the sexes either, and, as we saw in the previous section, that was a major contaminating factor.

Despite all these reservations, however, there is no doubt that these investigations stumbled onto something quite distinctive; it is therefore worthwhile to detail some of their findings. The reader is warned to keep the above reservations in mind, however.

The distinctions between the two groups seemed to demonstrate a general personality style that showed itself in the children's attitudes toward school, family background, choice of friends, thoughts about future occupation, and so forth. As the authors state (p. 135), "Whatever terms are used, it is clear that one process represents intellectual acquisitiveness and conformity (high IQ), the other, intellectual inventiveness and innovation (high creativity)."

School Achievement

One of the many interesting findings of the Getzels and Jackson study had to do with the scholastic achievement of the high-creative group. Despite the fact that they scored, on the average, twenty-three IQ points below the high IQ children, they were their equals in performance on achievement test scores. Both groups far outdistanced the average pupil achievement for the school.

Torrance (1959) replicated the study on another laboratory school sample at the elementary level and found that high-creative scorers were high in achievement as well. Further studies by Torrance (1960), however, indicated that the high-creative students do not always fare so well. In a rural and a parochial school, where more traditional controls over behavior were applied, they were not a match for the high-IQ children in achievement. Such studies urge us to be cautious about generalizing too fast from what happens in *one* school, particularly in a laboratory school, where the atmosphere, skill of instruction, and other factors could differ considerably from those in other schools.

Family Factors

According to Getzels and Jackson (1962), one of the central concepts that differentiates the high-creative child from the high-IQ child, is his ability or predisposition to take risks. This willingness to take risks shows itself in the child's not being afraid to make unusual contributions to the group, to depart from the group's ideas, and to produce unique

56

and individualistic results. Getzels and Jackson have identified several family variables that seem to discriminate the creative from the non-creative family environment. The creative family does not mention finance or financial hardship as much as the high-IQ family. Mothers in the creative family are more often employed; they see less unfavorable qualities in their children and are more dissatisfied with their own child-training practices.

The implication (still unproven) to be drawn from these findings is that financial hardship may tend to place a single-minded emphasis on success as a way of alleviating the trouble. The mother who is less critical of the child and who is less often physically present may encourage greater independence in the child. Finally, a tendency was discovered in the creative family to stress internal characteristics such as "a sense of values, interest in something, and openness, rather than external characteristics such as good family, good manners, and being studious." Thus, the patterns of the creative family seem to favor risk taking and independence, whereas the high-IQ family seems to place a stress on adapting to proper methods of behavior.

Attitudes and Values

This central philosophy of "take a chance versus play it safe" can be seen in the kinds of values and choices the student makes in a wide variety of situations. Getzels and Jackson (1962, pp. 52–53) show a vivid contrast between the high-IQ and the creative child's performances in storytelling ability. The students were shown a picture that was most often interpreted as a man sitting in an airplane, returning from a conference or a business trip, and were then asked to make up a story about it.

> *The high-IQ subject.* Mr. Smith is on his way home from a successful business trip. He is very happy and he is thinking about his wonderful family and how glad he will be to see them again. He can picture it, about an hour from now his plane landing at the airport and Mrs. Smith and their three children all there welcoming him home again.
> *The high-creative subject.* This man is flying back from Reno where he has just won a divorce from his wife. He couldn't stand to live with her anymore, he told the judge, because she wore so much cold cream on her face at night that her head would skid across the pillow and hit him in the head. He is now contemplating a new skid-proof face cream.

The different reactions of the two groups again are shown in the reaction to a picture most often perceived as a man working late (or very early) in an office.

> *The high-IQ subject.* There's ambitious Bob, down at the office at 6:30 in the morning. Every morning it's the same. He's trying to show his

boss how energetic he is.   Now, thinks Bob, maybe the boss will give me a raise for all my extra work.   The trouble is that Bob has been doing this for the last three years, and the boss still hasn't given him a raise. He'll come in at 9:00, not even noticing that Bob had been there so long, and poor Bob won't get his raise.

The high-creative subject.   This man has just broken into this office of a new cereal company.   He is a private-eye employed by a competitor firm to find out the formula that makes the cereal bend, sag, and sway.   After a thorough search of the office he comes upon what he thinks is the current formula.   He is now copying it.   It turns out that it is the wrong formula and the competitor's factory blows up.   Poetic justice!

Note the cautious approach of the high-IQ storyteller.   He gives a standard story on a standard respectable theme.   No one can say that the stories are wrong or inappropriate.   He is minimizing any possible losses or criticism by this approach.   In contrast, the high-creative subject breaks free from the stimulus, and gives unusual tales that may deal with such socially unacceptable themes as divorce and robbery; and he throws in some ironic humor for good measure.   In other words, he is willing to run the risk of teacher or peer disapproval in order to give free rein to his own imagination—and a clear risk it is too.   Torrance and his associates (1959, p. 81) have pointed out that:

> In most classrooms, the child who expresses an unusual idea or offers an unusual production takes a calculated risk!   In such a setting, it takes a great deal of courage for a child to press for presentation of his unusual ideas.   Such ideas are frequently hooted at and depreciated as 'silly' or 'screwy'.

Does the high-creative child realize this fact?   The two groups in the Getzels and Jackson study were asked to rank thirteen descriptions of children in terms of whether they wanted to be like them, whether these characteristics will lead to success in adult life, or whether teachers would like each of the children.   These characteristics included such variables as creativity, moral character, goal directedness, and sense of humor. The high-IQ child revealed a very close relationship between the values he wanted for himself, the values that he thought would lead to adult success, and those that teachers would like.   In contrast, the high-creative child saw little relationship between his own values and the values that he thinks the teacher and society prefer.   He *saw* the difference, but apparently did not *care*.   The one value that appeared to be weighed quite differently by the two groups was "sense of humor."   It was given a high ranking by the high-creative group but not by the high-IQ sample.

The reader who wonders why the high-creative youngster, with his sense of humor and his independence, should be less preferred by teachers to the high-IQ student should grasp the point through the following class excerpt.

The teacher, by judicious planning and organization, has tried to get across the concept of *revolution* to his social studies class. For two weeks various types of revolutions have been studied and reports made—now, fifteen minutes away from the weekend, the teacher is ready to try to bring forth the larger generalization of *revolution* as a concept.

T: Now we have learned a little bit about the French, Russian, and American revolutions, and we have seen that, although they each had their own local characteristics, perhaps they had some things in common too—what do you see as some of the common elements?

Sharon: Well, they each had a rebel and a loyalist faction.

T: All right; that is one thing in common.

Bob: Yeh—If the English had won, Benedict Arnold would have been a hero—

Mike: Nuts—he was a traitor to his country.

Mary: No one who deserts his own side is a hero.

Pete: Aw, he [Bob] is just trying to start an argument again.

John: Wait a minute, maybe he has a point there.

Jean: (incredulously) You mean you think that Benedict Arnold was a hero, too?

The teacher stands frozen as the last five rapid-fire comments occur in the space of about ten seconds. What to do? Bob had done it again—derailed the class discussion and started the class off in a different direction. As he surveys the rapidly deteriorating scene, the teacher sees five or six students with hands waving frantically, wanting to get their opinions heard on Benedict Arnold. As the precious sands of time drain away, the teacher realizes that there is no time to get the class back on the track again; he will have to start all over again on Monday. How can he help but feel some resentment toward Bob, whose fertile—but undisciplined—mind had thrown a monkey wrench into many such discussions during the year, sometimes with relevant diversions and sometimes just to hear himself talk?

If there is a *single* purpose or goal to the activities of a class, the divergent thinker is bound to be an abrasive, an irritant guaranteed to win few bouquets from the teacher. It should be clear that the high-creative youngster can be an irritation in the classroom, in that he would not be as docile or as pliable as other students. Since he does not seem to be particularly dependent upon teacher approval, it is no particular surprise to find that teachers, in the Getzels and Jackson study, generally preferred the high-IQ to the high-creative child when questioned as to the desirability of having him or her in the classroom. These results were confirmed in further investigation by Torrance (1959) at the elementary school level. He concluded that "Two of the most consistent findings are for the high IQ pupils to be better known by their teachers and to be considered more desirable as pupils than the highly creative subjects."

What kinds of situations are handled more effectively by the high-IQ student, and which more effectively by the high-creative? There is little assurance that the youngsters identified as high-creative by Getzels and Jackson will really be more creative in adult life than will the high-IQ children. What has been discovered, however, are two groups of youngsters who approach life from drastically different orientations. We also seem to have considerable evidence that the teachers are more likely to overlook one group than the other, and more likely to favor one group than the other.

The study by Getzels and Jackson stirred great interest, and many similar studies soon followed. One of the more important was carried out by Wallach and Kogan (1965), who compared the performance of 151 fifth-graders, the entire school population of a suburban middle-class school on measures of creativity and intelligence. Wallach and Kogan divided the youngsters into the same general categories as Getzels and Jackson but looked at all four boxes in the model on p. 55 and took all the children rather than just the extremes. The description they give of the four separate groups (p. 303) is worth reviewing, particularly that of the children who were high in both creativity and IQ scores, a group not studied by Getzels and Jackson.

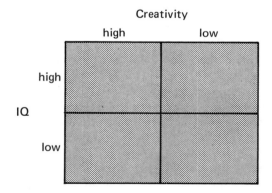

High creativity–high intelligence.   These children can exercise within themselves both control and freedom, both adultlike and childlike kinds of behavior.

High creativity–low intelligence.   These children are in angry conflict with themselves and their school environment and are beset by feelings of unworthiness and inadequacy.   In a stress-free context, however, they can blossom forth cognitively.

Low creativity–high intelligence.   These children can be described as "addicted" to school achievement.   Academic failure would be perceived by them as catastrophic, so that they must continually strive to make excellent grades in order to avoid the possibility of pain.

Low creativity–low intelligence.   Basically bewildered, these children engage in various defensive measures, ranging from useful adaptations such as intensive social activity to regression such as passivity or the development of pychosomatic symptoms.

The ability of the creative person to show both mature and childlike behavior is remarked upon in studies of creative adults.   Barron (1969) calls the creative person both more primitive and more cultured, more destructive and more constructive, crazier and more sane than the average person.

Another way of looking at this situation is that the creative syndrome is really a set of personality characteristics distinguished by a strong self-concept that pays little attention to the academic and social sanctions that force most of us to not use all our skills for fear of social disapproval. The high creative of Getzels and Jackson, like the creative artists and scientists of Barron, just do not care that much about the opinions of teachers and peers and are free to explore unusual and sometimes non-sanctioned intellectual paths.

The unproven assumption that high-divergent test scores will predict adult creativity has bothered many educators. A very different approach to the problem was taken by Martinson and Seagoe (1967). They started from the point of manifest creative production with the purpose of exploring the characteristics of children judged as creative. Five ungraded classes at a university elementary school with life ages usually found in grades three to six were subjects in the study.   The products were obtained across a number of areas:

Science: *Construct new investigations and think of communications on the moon.*

Creative writing: *a poem and written story.*

Social studies: *"My Idea of Utopia" and "How To Survive on a Desert Island."*

Art: *paintings and clay models.*

Music: *filmed interpretive rhythms.*

Some of the product samples rated high and low are presented to give the reader a feel for the kinds of differences obtained (pp. 22, 24).   Here are several examples of both high-creative and low-creative poems, followed by examples of "creative writing" on the topic of utopia:

HIGH CREATIVITY	LOW CREATIVITY
Is a blackboard alive?	My friend is a very special person
I do not think it is.	Who is almost always at my side.
But whenever somebody pulls a chalk	She doesn't argue with me.
across it too hard, it squeaks.	Whenever I am right.
The wind is a very funny thing	My friend is good at sports,
As it whistles through the trees	And cares a little about boys,
Do you know what it really is?	She really is the nicest person
Its when everybody sneezed.	And that is why she is my friend.
Deep down, dark and cool.	
Where witches sleep and ghosts grow	
cold.	
There lies a chest full of gold.	
Deep down, dark and cold.	
The chairs are stacked on one another	
In hopes of reaching the sky	
I know that they will not make it	
But then neither will I.	
The bulletin board is full of holes	
From this I say it must be cold.	

HIGH CREATIVITY	LOW CREATIVITY
My idea of Utopia is that all of the people would be born with advanced minds so that they would know almost everything they need to know.	My idea of Utopia is when I have a billion dollars and I have a Rolls Royce, servants and servants, and I can just lay around in my own mansion.
There would be no bad people and you could live forever and stay at any age you wanted.	Give a hundred dollars to every poor person in my country.
All people would have equal rights.	And I'd like to own a whole chain of department stores. Have all of
Everybody would have all the money they wanted.	my money in a bank I'll buy out. Then I'll buy all the stock I can
You could get anything you wanted by pressing a button.	buy and let other people buy stock and then draw out all my stock out
I would not make the whole world perfect because then everybody would be lazy and there would be no excitement.	and let the other people gain a little then just take out all my stock and I will have gained a thousand.

A number of judges rated the production, and composite ratings were used to give final scores to children. Although there was the usual difficulty in getting judges to agree on just what originality was, differences were clearly found between high-creative and low-creative children on IQ, with high-IQ children turning up more often in the high group, except in art and music.

The same was not true, however, when a battery of divergent-thinking tests were used. No differences were found between high- and low-creative groups on their performance on these measures. In short, IQ scores were more important than divergent-thinking scores in identifying children who produced creative work, especially in the verbal or semantic domain.

After all the dust has cleared, it is likely that we will find that divergent thinking is an important mental process and is related to a more open life style but that it is less important to traditional school attainment than the skills of memory and logical thinking that are found on IQ tests. The section on productive-thinking stimulation will pursue these ideas further.

SUMMARY

It is important for educators to understand the nature of the characteristics discussed in this chapter, because these characteristics should provide the base for special educational programs for the gifted. The broadened definition of giftedness, noted in Chapter 1, has modified earlier characterizations of "gifted," in that one must now consider not only the nature of the entire group fitting the definition but also the distinctive nature of several subgroups.

The traditional description of high-performance children relies in large measure on the data obtained from the monumental half-century longitudinal study of gifted children by Terman and his associates. The results of that study have finally put to rest the myths that gifted children are generally emotionally unstable and that they perform poorly as adults. Instead, Terman's subjects appeared to be superior academically, socially, and emotionally to the average student and to have made many extraordinary contributions to society in adulthood.

Special attention has been paid recently to the changing role of women in the society, thereby highlighting the distinctive nature of gifted girls. Such information as is available suggests that there are major sex differences, with gifted girls being more diffident and less intellectually aggressive in educational settings than gifted boys.

Girls have traditionally been expected to be more concerned about peer attitudes and pressures, and the available research suggests that they do seem to be more affected and inhibited by such pressures. Whether the changing attitude of the society toward a greater acceptance of intellectual performance of gifted women will change the performance of gifted girls in educational settings will be interesting to note.

Another subgroup of highly creative children has also been identified, although questions remain as to how "creative" they really are. In other words, we do not yet have the evidence that high performance on tests of creativity results in highly creative and imaginative adults. We do know that such youngsters seem less inhibited, more able to produce unique and unusual answers, are less influenced by peers, and are more able to follow their own intellectual directions and stimulation. The characteristics of two other subgroups—the culturally different gifted and the gifted underachiever—will be dealt with in more detail later.

UNRESOLVED ISSUES

1. Most of our knowledge of the characteristics of gifted children comes from careful longitudinal study of children who have scored high on intelligence tests and who have come from very advantageous social and economic backgrounds. We need to discover to what extent the favorable outcome observed was due to the family background and to what extent a superior intelligence. For example, do gifted children from broken or unhappy homes still turn out to be more emotionally stable than the average child? If the answer is "yes," then high mental ability has a greater influence than previously considered. If the answer is "no," the favorable results may be attributed more to the good family than to high IQ.

2. Are there identifiable developmental threads that lead to consistent creative performance in adulthood? Perhaps hyperactivity in early childhood, when combined with parental rewards for intellectual activity, is predictive of purposeful autonomous intellectual action in later childhood. The stages through which the creative adult passes as he moves through the various levels of infancy, early childhood, primary school, elementary school, junior high, senior high, and college, are currently shrouded in mystery, and attempts to stimulate "creativity" in young children may well be making unwarranted assumptions about the nature of that developmental process.

3. Does the rapidly changing attitude toward women in American society render out-of-date all existing data on sex differences between gifted boys and gifted girls? A replication of those studies of the 1940s and 1950s that showed girls to be more hesitant, less intellectually aggressive, and less numerous than gifted boys would be most interesting in this respect.

READINGS OF SPECIAL INTEREST

BACHTOLD, L., & WERNER, E. Personality profiles of gifted women: Psychologists. *American Psychologist,* 1970, **25,** 234–243.

This is one of a number of studies on the special problems and unique characteristics of talented women growing up in American society. Interesting details are provided on the distinction between women psychologists and women taken at random.

GOERTZEL, V., & GOERTZEL, M. *Cradles of eminence.* Boston: Little, Brown, 1962.

This is a biographical approach to the study of giftedness. The authors try to extract from the early lives of noted people some of their relevant or important experiences. Like all such efforts, it is subject to the criticism that the authors selected experiences to fit their own biases, but it remains a thought-provoking effort.

TERMAN, L., & ODEN, M. *Genetic studies of genius,* Vol. 4. *The gifted child grows up.* Stanford, Calif.: Stanford University Press, 1947.

The most comprehensive of the five-volume series spanning a forty-year period of studying 1500 gifted children in California. It remains the most authoritative source on the characteristics of the gifted, if you accept the Terman definition.

WALLACH, M., & WING, C. *The talented student. A validation of the creativity-intelligence distinction.* New York: Holt, 1969.

A detailed and scholarly discussion of the proposed distinction between high-IQ students and high-creativity students. Brings a balanced perspective to an issue too often characterized by the substitution of rhetoric for data and sound research methods.

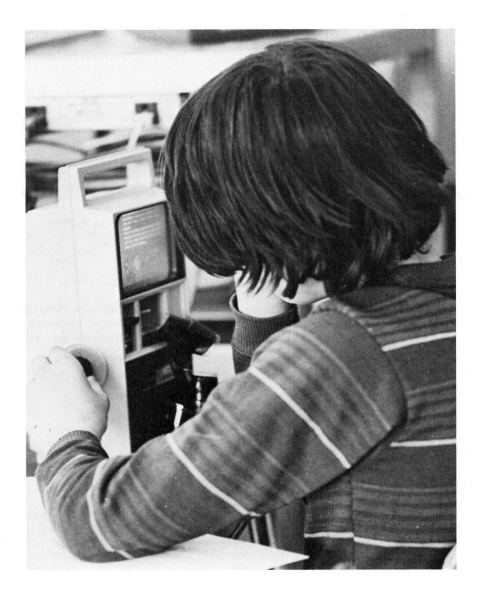

3

The Changing School
Program for the Gifted

We have now seen a variety of portraits of different gifted and talented students. As we get to know some of these youngsters reasonably well, we need to view them from the perspective of the teacher and the school. What meaningful adjustments can be made by the school and by the teacher to better meet the needs of these youngsters? Although we have observed how they differ from the average child with regard to various characteristics, and how they differ from each other in their developmental patterns, we need to demonstrate what those differences mean in terms of the school program.

THE PROBLEM

The average citizen is likely to think that the variety of positive characteristics revealed by many gifted students would be an unambiguous boon to the teacher. Unfortunately, this optimistic approach ignores the problems that this "embarrassment of riches" causes in a school setting. Rice (1970) lists a few of the educational problems created by gifted characteristics (see Table 3–1).

Every experienced teacher has faced the problem of the gifted child with a large vocabulary and special interests. Mrs. Watkins may casually mention hairstyles of Marie Antoinette, only to get buried in a verbal avalanche of interesting, but disruptingly detailed, facts on hairstyles through the ages provided from Zelda's seemingly inexhaustible storehouse of facts.

Scholarliness may be a desirable characteristic in some quarters, but it

TABLE 3–1. *Characteristics of the Gifted and Concomitant Problems.*

CHARACTERISTIC OF GIFTED	POSSIBLE CONCOMITANT PROBLEMS
Critically observes, analyzes; skepticism	Teachers feel threatened; peers censure, try to silence discussion; argumentative
Emphatic response to people; leadership capabilities	Rejection causes intense reaction (e.g., depression or hostility); may seek to dominate rather than understand others
Intellectual interests; intellectuality	Snobbishness; limited recreational outlets; boring to others; intolerance for lesser capabilities
Large vocabulary; verbal facility; high retention	Inappropriate level of communication; dominates class discussion; unnecessary elaboration
Originality	Perceived as "off the subject" by others; impracticality; frequent breaks with tradition; radicalism
Scholarliness	Anti-intellectual reaction by peers; stuffiness; pedantry
Thinks with logical systems; objective, rational problem-solving	Disregard for intuitive, retrospective, or subjective solutions; rejection of belief, revelation as methods.

Source: Adapted from J. P. Rice. *The gifted: Developing total talent.* Springfield Ill.: Charles C Thomas, 1970, p. 237.

would be hard to convince Sam of that. His peer group is predominantly antischool and antilearning, and they look with suspicion on any student who would admit to liking school. Sam uses some of his high intelligence to disguise his intellectual interests. If he wants to read about something, he takes care not to do it where others see him. He avoids the school library, though he sometimes gazes wistfully through the door at this gold mine. Being found in there for anything except a direct assignment is hard to explain to peers, and although Sam has learned how to defend himself physically, he doesn't go out of his way to provoke his neighborhood friends. The danger in Sam's case is that the device of avoiding the appearance of learning can become a genuine habit that prevents him from achieving well in later school years. Each virtue has its concomitant vice or problem, and part of the school's responsibility is to minimize these negative features as much as possible.

Most casual observers tend to drastically underestimate the *range* of performance that is found in the schools at any particular grade level. Martinson (1961) carefully studied 1000 children on a statewide basis in California, at all grade levels, with the following results. The kindergarten group of *gifted* youngsters performed, on the average, at a level comparable to that of the average second-grade children in reading and mathematics. The average for fourth- and fifth-grade *gifted* children in all curriculum areas was beyond that of the normal seventh-grade pupils. Further, nearly three-fourths of the gifted eighth-grade pupils made scores equal to, or beyond, the average of twelfth-grade students on a test battery in six curriculum areas.

As would be expected from our general knowledge of development, as the gifted youngsters get older, the academic gap between them and the average student becomes greater and more noticeable.

Further, in the same set of studies, a group of gifted high school seniors was given the Graduate Record Examination in the fields of social sciences, humanities, and natural sciences. In all these fields, the gifted high school seniors made an average score that surpassed, as a group, the average for college seniors! In other words, even while still in high school, they were performing better than the average college senior.

These findings are reproduced in a variety of other studies and leave no doubt that the gifted youngster, left at his own age level, and presented with material that is three to four or five years below, in complexity and content, what he is capable of, is in the same situation as an athlete trained to high jump and then having someone place the bar at only 2 or 3 feet high. He can soon get tired of such easy work and will certainly develop sloppy and poor habits that will ill serve him when he, in fact, is finally challenged.

A Heterogeneous Classroom

Let us imagine, for the moment, that all four of our friends, Cranshaw, Zelda, Joe, and Sam, have, by some coincidence, been placed in the same fifth-grade elementary classroom. In addition to these four bright youngsters, we have the entire range of ability and achievement that would occur if the class were chosen by such a chance method as assigning the children by alphabetical order. This would mean that the expected range in IQ scores would extend from about 70 to 150 on an individual intelligence test.

Such a range in IQ scores represents a spread in mental-age scores from 7 to 14 years. Sometimes curriculum plans for a fifth grade seem to be developed on the totally unjustified assumption that almost all 10-year-old children should be performing at a fifth-grade level. Instead, in such a heterogeneous class as described here, the range of reading achievement could be anywhere from nonreader to a high school level of proficiency.

In arithmetic, the range of achievement would not be as great because of the greater dependence of the student on the material presented by the teacher; but it still could extend from first- to eighth-grade performance. In such a situation, it would be rather foolish to plan around fifth-grade readers or arithmetic books as if handing them out to all these diverse children represents good educational planning.

Since the subject matter dealt with in the fifth grade depends, to a substantial extent, upon the reading skills that the students possess, it would be worthwhile to look at the problems caused by this range in reading. Mr. Jenkins, the teacher, is faced with the following problem: Eight of his students are not yet ready, from a reading standpoint, for the fifth grade. They have reading skills that range anywhere from first- to fourth-grade ability. They cannot effectively handle material at a fifth-grade level without considerable help. This indicates that some amount of remedial work designed specifically to improve their reading skills (apart from the reading for content that should be done for social studies, science, and language arts) needs to be planned for these youngsters.

While eight of the youngsters are not ready for fifth-grade material, Mr. Jenkins is faced with the problem that eight of the other youngsters are "bored to tears with it." They had obtained a fifth-grade reading level anywhere from two to four years ago, and the program for these youngsters must be predicated upon a much higher level of reading and conceptual difficulty if Mr. Jenkins is going to begin to approach the aptitude and potential of these youngsters. This fast group would include Cranshaw, Zelda, and Joe—but not Sam, whose language problems have slowed his reading progress to an average level. In addition to this, however, Mr. Jenkins has fourteen youngsters who *do* fall within the general age and achievement level that is expected of a 10- or 11-year-old youngster. For these fourteen youngsters, the kind of curriculum and program that is followed in the ordinary fifth grade would seem to be reasonably appropriate.

Thus, Mr. Jenkins actually has three separate reading classes within the physical boundaries of his classroom. One is almost a remedial class, in which the emphasis is still being placed upon the learning of skills that presumably should have been mastered in the primary grades. Another group represents the average, which is developing at a rate to be expected of a normal fifth grader. The third group, the one with which we are particularly concerned, is the group of bright youngsters who have far surpassed the level expected of fifth graders, and who are performing at an eighth- or ninth-grade level.

It is with this group that Mr. Jenkins' own limitations stand out. It is these youngsters who challenge the frontiers of Mr. Jenkins' own knowledge, many times with devastating results. He feels particularly insecure about his poor background in science. He doesn't know very much about such concepts as gravity or the time–space continuum. It is clear to him, and to the other students, that Cranshaw and two or three other youngsters in the class are much more proficient in certain special areas of science than is he himself. As any teacher recognizes, this is an extremely difficult situation because, if it becomes worse, it seriously endangers the concept of the teacher as a reliable informant in areas far beyond the boundaries of science. Every teacher has only so many "I don't knows" to expend before he loses the intellectual respect of his class.

Let us review for a moment Mr. Jenkins' problems. First, his problem lies in the wide range of abilities of the youngsters in his group; this makes planning very difficult and almost forces the conscientious teacher to make many different lesson plans and programs for the different subgroups of youngsters in his class. The second major problem lies in the teacher's own limitation of content knowledge. It is quite obvious to a teacher that his own limitations in certain subject areas, such as arithmetic, social studies, or science, are going to limit severely the depth to which these areas can be investigated by the students. It is all well and good to direct the youngster to other references where he can find out more about things which the teacher does not know; but the teacher is going to need considerable help and assistance before the gifted youngster can profit from such references. The third problem area is the teacher's own lack of knowledge of the appropriate methods of stimulating the high-level conceptualization and productive-thinking ability of the bright group.

Naturally, the teacher wants to stimulate productive thinking at all levels of his class group, but in the advanced group, which includes Cranshaw and his friends, it becomes particularly essential to their future development as scholars, professional men, and independent thinkers.

The range of existing adaptations of school programs for gifted children is quite remarkable and sometimes obscures the fact that they are all attempts to meet these three specific problems: *the wide range of ability, teachers' limitations in content areas,* and *teachers' lack of special methods.* If the reader will keep in mind that practically all the modifications of educational programming and methods attempt to deal with these three fundamental problems, he may be able to avoid becoming too confused by the details of the programs themselves.

What are the elements that educational experts consider to be most important to programs for gifted children? Renzulli (1968) asked twenty-one experts what they felt to be the crucial elements in programs for the gifted. The three selected by these judges most frequently were *the teacher,* with both selection and training seen as major issues; *the curricu-*

71

lum, and how it can be made purposefully distinctive; and *student selection* procedures for the particular program in question.

Such a result could probably be obtained by taking any twenty or twenty-five judgments at random from people who have had experience with programs for gifted students. What is also clear, however, is that despite the general expert consensus that the teacher and the curriculum need special attention, relatively little effort has been expended on either, and the primary allocation of scarce resources remains in the support of excess cost funds to local communities for providing additional educational personnel in this area.

This is not to say that educators are deliberately ignoring such issues as curriculum development or special training; it is just simpler, given the way that education is structured, to hand the local school district some extra funds from the state level to conduct a "gifted program."

PROPOSED CHANGES

No one program that any school could devise could meet the needs of Joe, Cranshaw, Zelda, and Sam. It is obvious that diversity is still a major characteristic of any group of gifted youngsters. In order to evaluate the attempts of the schools to make meaningful changes, we need to think of the three major types of changes a school can make: the content, the method of presentation, and the learning environment.

1. The *content* of the material presented to the students can be changed. Since the gifted child has demonstrated manifest ability to handle a complexity of ideas far beyond his chronological age, it is natural to assume that schools sensitive to this problem will make a genuine effort to modify the content reaching these students to stress the greater complexity and higher levels of abstraction that they can comprehend.
2. The *method of presentation* of material to the students can be changed. Since the process of thinking or the style in which a youngster approaches difficult problems appears important, a significant amount of attention has been given not only to *what* the teacher presents but *how* she tries to present it. The goals of the teacher of gifted students should go beyond the mere absorption of knowledge to help the child develop a learning style that will serve him or her in good stead in later studies and in later life.
3. The third major avenue of change would be to modify the nature of the *learning environment* itself. This means either moving the youngster to a different setting or changing the nature of the setting in which he receives his instruction. Such devices as acceleration to the next-highest grade level, or the use of open classrooms, resource rooms, after-school clubs, or special classes—all represent decisions to change the nature of the learning environment.

72

In some cases programs for the gifted change one of these dimensions but not the others.   Early-admittance-to-college programs, for example, change the learning environment but do little about either content or learning style.   We will be looking at the specifics of change in each of these dimensions in order to make the distinctions clear.

There have been many changes in the school environment and learning environment that have been brought about by decisions far beyond the teacher or even the local school level.   Decisions made at the level of the state department of education or even at the level of the federal government often provide for additional resources that can improve programs for gifted students.   Accordingly, we will pay some attention to the nature of the programs that have developed in recent years in order to present the full range of possibilities.   The teacher interested in gifted children *per se,* and not just in the 30 or 40 children who currently concern him, will probably wish to follow these trends carefully.

It is not easy to change school programs or procedures.   There is a natural inertia that defies movement to all but the most important or critical issues and needs.   Although educational fads occasionally appear on the scene, they rarely endure for long.

If educators and laymen really believed that gifted children could get along just about as well in the regular program as with special care, that nothing could deter their onward rush to glory and achievement, that their gifts would flower whether cultivated or not, then what chance would suggestions for special attention for these youngsters have?   Precious little.   In the 1920s and 1930s these ideas were strongly supported, but there is impressive evidence that if we want gifted children to live up to their potential, we must provide them with special education.

Do the parent and the educator make a difference?   Pressey (1955) was interested in the unusual precocity shown by two quite different groups of children.   In the middle European society of the eighteenth and nineteenth centuries, there were a remarkable number of child prodigies in the area of music.   In twentieth-century America, there have been a number of child prodigies in the area of athletics.   Pressey observed certain similarities between the two cultures (pp. 123–124).

1. Precocious musicians and athletes usually have excellent early opportunities for the ability to develop and encouragement from family and friends.
2. Usually individuals who develop precocious excellence had superior early and continuing individual guidance and instruction.
3. Precocious individuals have had the opportunity frequently and continuingly to practice and extend their special ability and to progress as they were able.
4. The special precocious ability usually brought a close association with

others in the field, which greatly fostered the abilities of all concerned, and led to a still wider stimulating acceptance.

5. As a result of many opportunities for real accomplishment, within his possibilities but of increasing challenge, the precocious musician or athlete has had the stimulation of many and increasingly strong success experiences—and his world acclaimed these successes.

In other words, unusual early accomplishment requires something more positive than merely not interfering with the development of the gifted child. It requires positive encouragement and training along a certain line of development. How many Americans would be willing to preempt their child's decision on the choice of career area, as this approach certainly does, is a moot question. What does seem clear from this example, though, is that it *can* be done if we want it done.

Change in Program Content

In retrospect, it is possible to identify two major trends that have influenced the curriculum for gifted children in the past quarter of a century. There has been the tremendous explosion of knowledge in the area of sciences and a new emphasis on creativity. In many fields of endeavor, more knowledge has been accumulated in five or ten years than had previously been recorded in all of human history. Such terms as "jet propulsion," "atomic energy," "role playing," "nuclear reactor," "fallout," "group dynamics," and "ego strength" have contributed to the production of a new scientific vocabulary. Not only has the vocabulary increased, but ideas and theories have multiplied and changed dramatically. During this time, the scientist has been so eagerly attacking the frontier that has suddenly opened before him that he has had little time to turn around and see how these concepts were being communicated to the next generation.

By the mid-1950s, physical scientists began to become alarmed at what they felt was the inadequacy of the curriculum program, and worried about whether it would challenge or attract first-rate minds into their field of endeavor. The review of existing textbooks showed that their attempts to squeeze new information into the traditional textbooks had only created a weird patchwork quilt, from which the most brilliant student or the most capable teacher was hard put to extract important generalizations. Specialists in liberal arts and social studies have shown similar distress, but could not command either the public hearing or the funds available to the physical scientists.

Actually, this weakness in curriculum is what many critics of the educational scene had been emphasizing all along, saying that the problems of education centered in teachers who were poorly trained in content areas and who did not present the material at as high a conceptual level as possible.

It is hard to quarrel with the fact that a teacher who has had 2 three-hour courses in mathematics at the college level is hardly equipped to present high-level concepts in the world of mathematics to gifted students, or that a teacher whose knowledge of history has been confined to a rather routine examination of military campaigns of the various wars in which America has fought, is hardly equipped to lead the student into more sophisticated knowledge of historical trends through the ages.

Nor does it do much good to suggest that, even though the teacher may not know the subject matter extensively, he can send students to references where they could find out for themselves. When one does not know very much about a content area—and many elementary school teachers, unfortunately, fall into this category—then he cannot send the student to the proper reference source either. The reference he himself used in his college class might be too complex for young minds; hence, important references that could stimulate the child to further endeavor might be missed through ignorance. Unfortunately, much of the criticism of the public schools has been presented in such an emotional tone and the recommendations for the "cure" of the situation have been so patently impractical from the experienced educator's knowledge of the school system that there has been too great a tendency for educators to defend the indefensible (see Silberman, 1970, for example).

Widespread dissatisfaction with the content of existing curricula came to a boil first in the fields of physical science and mathematics. In 1956, the Physical Science Study Committee was formed for the purpose of re-designing the curriculum in physics at the secondary school level. The way in which this subject area was redesigned set the pattern for numerous studies that were to follow. A more detailed account of the committee's activities will be found in Chapter 5, "Science for the Gifted." The goal of these scientists and secondary school educators was to design a curriculum in which the central fabric or *structure* of the content area itself would be illustrated and presented to the student.

A similar movement in mathematics had been initiated by Beberman (1957) at Illinois, through the formation of the University of Illinois Committee on School Mathematics. Many others followed (see Goodlad, 1964). Although different in content, they had very similar goals:

1. To teach the basic structure of the discipline.
2. To have the student approach the subject matter as the specialist approaches it.
3. To introduce important ideas at as early an age as possible.

One example of this emphasis on basic structure is provided by the Biological Sciences Curriculum Study (BSCS) that has produced three

separate curricula with the same nine unifying concepts found in each of
the versions.

1. The change of living things through time (evolution).
2. Diversity of type and unity of pattern of living things.
3. The genetic continuity of life.
4. The biological roots of behavior.
5. The complementarity of organisms and environment.
6. The complementarity of structure and functions.
7. Regulation and homeostasis—the maintenance of life in the face of change.
8. Science as inquiry.
9. The intellectual history of biological concepts.

Although there is great overlap among the three versions, they differ in
emphasis and approach, one being concerned with molecular biology, one
with the biological community, and one with a progression from cellular
biology through ecology. Student investigations play an important part
in all three versions (Schwab, 1964).

Another example of this approach in the social sciences is found in the
economics curriculum developed by Senesh (1965), who presents some
basic ideas or contours that are interwoven in a curriculum from grades
1 through 12, for example (p. 138):

> All people and all nations are confronted with the conflict between their
> unlimited wants and limited resources. The degree of conflict may vary,
> but the conflict is always present.
>
> In all countries, the basic questions to be answered are: What goods
> and services will be produced? How much of these will be produced?
> How will they be produced, and who will receive the goods and services?
>
> In the United States, what and how much will be produced, how it
> will be produced, and for whom are largely determined by the free
> choices of the American people, either as consumers or participants in
> the production process.

This is a long way from playing grocery store or simplistic discussions
of supply and demand, but it is the type of curriculum that will stand
a better chance of saving the next generation of leaders in our nation
from being economic illiterates. As C. P. Snow (1959) has eloquently
pointed out, future leaders must have a grasp of the sciences even if they
are not scientists, since the policy makers must not be ignorant on those
matters upon which they make crucial decisions.

But what if the teacher is not in the school system that has adopted
these new curricula or has not been trained in their use? For many
years, the standard answer for the programming needs of gifted children
has been *enrichment*. Enrichment can be defined as the type of activity
devoted to the further development of the particular intellectual skills
and talents of the gifted child. These might be described as:

1. The ability to associate and interrelate concepts.
2. The ability to evaluate facts and arguments critically.
3. The ability to create new ideas and originate new lines of thought.
4. The ability to reason through complex problems.
5. The ability to understand other situations, other times, and other people, to be less bound by one's own peculiar environmental surroundings.

Kough (1960, p. 147) has listed the requirements that must be met in order for enrichment in the regular classroom to be a reality rather than an illusion:

1. Has each classroom teacher identified and listed the students who are gifted? If teachers are unable to do this, a well-planned classroom enrichment program is not operating. If only some of the teachers have done it, the gifted child program is not reaching all the gifted youngsters in the school.
2. Can each classroom teacher describe the specific curriculum modification being made for each bright youngster? Again, if each teacher cannot do this, there is not a complete enrichment program.
3. Does some person have supervisory responsibility for the entire program? Such a person may help classroom teachers in the identification process and provide motivation, ideas, and materials as the program progresses.

These are difficult criteria for most schools to meet, but no school that does not meet these criteria should be allowed contentedly to claim that it has an adequate enrichment program for gifted children.

It is discouraging to find that many teachers still believe that the primary program adjustment for gifted students is to give them longer and more extensive assignments of the same sort that they would give to the average student. Since gifted students, such as Cranshaw and Zelda, can absorb an almost unlimited supply of facts, they will dutifully attack the new assignments and work hard at them. We may never realize what they are missing—namely, the opportunity to explore larger and more important ideas. Any program designed for an average fourth or fifth grader obviously has limitations for children who are three or more years ahead of that level.

Table 3–2 provides a brief description of how the focus of the same general topic areas can be modified for differing levels of ability among students. In history, we find the slow student profiting best by discussions of his own community and how it works, that is, how he is governed. Similarly, in the area of science the slow student can profit by understanding how to put together a balanced meal from the standpoint of nutrition.

To provide the same intellectual meal to the gifted would be unfortunate. Instead, the gifted student can be thinking in terms of how all types and kinds of cultures can be governed; he can, for example, trace

TABLE 3–2. *Curricular Levels of Abstraction by Ability Levels.*

ABILITY LEVEL	HISTORY	NUTRITION
Bright	Patterns of governing in cultures across time and national boundaries	The biochemistry of food and the translation of food into bodily energy
Average	The beginnings of American government: our historical heritage	Understanding of nutrition: classification of carbohydrates, proteins, fats, etc.
Slow	How local government works and influences me	Kinds of nutritious foods to buy: samples of balanced meals

the changes in governing patterns from primitive to modern times. Similarly, he can be concerned with the biochemistry that lies behind the nutritious meals being selected by the slow student.

The slow student will more than likely live in a world circumscribed by geography, and his own influence will focus on immediate friends and acquaintances. The gifted student's influence can easily be national or international in influence as an adult, and his or her school program ought to reflect that expectation.

Change in Intellectual Skills

But even a fuller understanding of the content fields is not enough. The future is change, and how will our students be prepared for it? When is a gifted child ready for the discovery of new ideas, for independent searching, for inquiry? Sometimes it seems as if the student must wait for graduate school, if then, before he does independent inquiry. When does the idea gatherer become the idea producer? Surely, our educational system has more to offer the gifted student than the prospect of becoming an academic sponge, sopping up facts that pour out when he is squeezed.

Mackworth (1965) has made a useful distinction between two different cognitive styles in his description of *problem solvers* and *problem finders* (see Table 3–3). Although our traditional educational programs have trained a generation of fact gatherers and problem solvers (i.e., the student is presented with a problem and is expected to apply the correct techniques in the proper sequence and come out with the right answer), the needs of the society cry out for talented *problem finders.*

The computer world that lies just over the horizon can easily handle the memory and problem-solving aspects of our problems, but the computers cannot, as yet, choose which problems are important and need

78

attacking. Problems such as population control, nuclear power, and poverty need to be seen far enough down the road so that the reactions to them are planned and not hastily improvised.

This realization lies behind the greatly increased emphasis on the stimulation of creativity and the productive-thinking processes of gifted children. With these goals, it is not the "correct" answer that is sought so much as the unique answer that has quality. We are not as interested in training a gifted student to execute the chemistry experiment correctly as we are that he tell us that the experiment itself is trivial and that he can construct a better one.

Computational accuracy is an undeniable virtue but perhaps not the most important nor the one most eagerly sought after by the instructors of gifted children. Suchman (1965), Torrance (1969), and many others have made useful initial contributions to our initial understanding of these processes and how they are encouraged; Section III, which focuses on this topic, will provide elaboration and examples to this concept.

Change in Learning Environment

There are two major and rather separate goals that concern the educator of the gifted, and for that matter the general educator as well. One of the first tasks is to make the instruction within the existing structure as efficient as possible. This means a primary concentration on the efficacy of instruction of content and methods presented here. A second goal is to imagine and operate on a pilot basis new modes or structures within which instruction could take place that would be impossible under the old system.

For example, for a long time the question posed to educators interested in this area is how to make the teacher more effective if he or she were faced with the problem of dealing with Cranshaw, Zelda, Joe, Sam, and forty-two other randomly selected students from all types of backgrounds and all levels of ability.

Surely there are always some things that can be done to help such a teacher, such as help him to improve his organization of material, help him to recognize talent, or help him to plan for some individualization of instruction.

However, even the most efficient teacher soon comes to the limits of his or her capabilities when faced with that kind of situation. At this point another question can profitably be asked, and that is: why does the elementary school instructional setting have to be one teacher penned up with forty-odd children for an entire day with the exception of recreation or music? Perhaps there is a way of organizing the total learning

TABLE 3–3. *Problem Solving and Problem Finding by Humans.*

	PROBLEM SOLVING	PROBLEM FINDING
Definition	Problem solving is the selection and use of an existing program from an existing set of programs.	Problem finding is the detection of the need for a new program by comparing existing and expected future programs.
Objective	To choose correctly between *existing programs*—in order to select the one program that effectively elicits the required actions from a set of possible responses.	To choose correctly between *existing and expected future programs*—in order to devise new programs and to realize that one or more of these would be more suitable than any of the existing programs in eliciting the required actions.
Method	Experiment more than thought minimizes the mismatch between the desired and apparent actual states.	Thought more than experiment minimizes the mismatch between the desired and apparent actual states.
Outcome	Success is the discovery of one specific acceptable answer to one well-defined problem.	Success is the discovery of many general questions from many ill-defined problems.

Source: Adapted from N. H. Mackworth. Originality. *American Psychologist,* 1965, **20.**

setting to help the individual instructor become more efficient. We shall now consider modifications in the traditional system that apply especially, but not necessarily exclusively, to talented children.

CHOOSING GIFTED STUDENTS FOR A SPECIAL PROGRAM

Although much has been written about the identification of gifted children, such identification does not take place in a vacuum. We have to ask, identification for what? Unless some type of program is going to follow, identification is a relatively useless exercise. The identification of the gifted, then, is tied to the nature of the program since not every intellectually superior child would fit into every special program. Is it an accelerated mathematics program? Then more things have to be taken into account than just a high IQ.

Table 3–4 presents a list of possible candidates for any programs for gifted students from a suburban, average fifth grade and the likely information that the school would have on them. For example, Jane A., 10 years old, has scored an IQ of 132 on a group test, which clearly puts her in the top 5 percent or higher in these measured abilities. Her reading grade-point average (GPA) on achievement tests is two grades above average, her arithmetic GPA one grade or more above average, and her motivation, as rated by teachers, is good. She would be a likely candidate for such an accelerated program.

Contrast this portrait with Bill S., who has almost the same IQ score and reading achievement level but whose arithmetic scores are down and who has a history of not liking arithmetic. One should think twice before tossing Bill into a program that is mainly composed of "gung ho" mathematics students who love the field and exult in the adventure of learning complex mathematical concepts. Although he might accept the challenge, he will more likely become more discouraged and withdrawn from the subject. There would seem to be a need for some preliminary talks or tutorial work at the very least before throwing him in with the mathematical lions.

Another type of program that is gaining in popularity would be special programs in creative writing or language arts. In this instance, a student such as Gert N. would be a genuine candidate even with a mediocre score in arithmetic. In addition to the high-IQ score, she has a record of achievement and enthusiasm in the area that counts. On the other hand, Jim H. has uncertain motivation and not high attainment and would possibly be rejected.

TABLE 3–4. *Candidates for Programs for the Gifted (Normal Fifth Grade).*

	CA	GROUP IQ	READING GPA	ARITHMETIC GPA	MOTIVATION
Jane A.	10.4	132	7.7	6.5	Good
Peter B.	10.5	120	7.2	7.2	Fair
Sam C.	9.8	127	7.5	6.8	Works on his own
Mary D.	10.3	112	5.8	5.9	Excellent
Sally E.	10.2	117	6.4	6.0	Good
Bernice F.	10.3	135	8.3	7.6	Fine student
Paul G.	10.7	109	6.9	7.1	Works very hard
Jim H.	10.3	123	7.2	6.9	Uncertain
John I.	11.1	119	8.3	7.5	Good
Ellen J.	10.6	143	10.5	8.2	Excellent
Ken K.	10.4	119	9.2	7.9	Good: hard worker
Ned L.	10.4	127	7.3	7.1	Fair: erratic
Mame M.	10.1	125	6.7	5.5	Hates math
Gert N.	10.6	137	8.2	5.9	Good in language arts
Zorba O.	10.5	131	8.5	6.8	Poor: foot dragger
Priscilla P.	10.3	115	8.2	6.5	Excellent
Quentin Q.	9.7	125	5.8	5.5	Avoids work
Walt R.	10.4	97	8.4	7.8	Good: first-rate student
Bill S.	10.7	131	7.9	5.8	Doesn't like arithmetic
Jane T.	10.5	126	6.4	7.5	Loves math

Similar judgments can be made on each of the youngsters for whatever program is under consideration. For example, who would or would not be candidates for acceleration, for special class assignment? What additional information would you need to have before coming to that decision? Whom could you rule out right now?

Every school has students such as Mary D., Paul G., and Sally E. With limited ability (compared to the rest of this group), they have achieved well for their grade level. Again, serious second thoughts need to be given about placing them in a special program for talented and gifted since they probably are doing as well as can be expected right now and could easily be overwhelmed by the youngsters of greater ability.

A consideration of "identification for what?" will always bring the realization that there are always multiple characteristics to be considered in student selection for specific programs; a table such as Table 3–4 can be used to give practice both in making choices and in realizing that other information is needed before a selection decision is finally made.

SOCIETAL VALUES AND THEIR IMPACT
ON PROGRAMMING

Whether or not a local school system changes its curriculum, its methods of presentation of concepts, or its learning environment depends to a very large extent on the value systems held by the predominant groups who influence such school policy.   Those who believe that such decisions are made solely, or even predominantly, on the basis of educational research or experience will continue to be confused or puzzled by what actually happens unless they recognize this reality.   A specific example that many have experienced will illustrate the point.

The Palcuzzi Ploy

Mr. Palcuzzi, principal of the Jefferson Elementary School, once got tired of hearing objections to special provisions for gifted children, so he decided to spice an otherwise mild PTA meeting with *his* proposal for gifted children.   The elements of the Palcuzzi program were as follows:

1. Children should be grouped by ability.
2. Part of the school day should be given over to special instruction.
3. Talented students should be allowed time to share their talents with children of other schools in the area or even of other schools throughout the state.   (We will pay the transportation cost.)
4. A child should be advanced according to his talents, rather than according to his age.
5. These children should have special teachers, specially trained and highly salaried.

As might be expected, the "Palcuzzi program" was subjected to a barrage of criticism.   "What about the youngster who isn't able to fit into the special group; won't his ego be damaged?"   "How about the special cost; how could you justify transportation costs that would have to be paid by moving a special group of students from one school to another?"   "Mightn't we be endangering the child by having him interact with children who are much more mature than he is?"   "Wouldn't the other teachers complain if we gave more money to the instructors of this group?"

After listening for ten or fifteen minutes, Mr. Palcuzzi dropped his bomb!   He said that he wasn't describing a *new* program for the intellectually gifted, but a program the school system had been enthusiastically supporting for a number of years—the program for *gifted basketball players!* Palcuzzi took advantage of the silence that followed to review his program again.   Do we have ability grouping on our basketball team? Yes, we do.   No doubt, the player who does not make the first team or the second team feels very bad about it and may even have some inferiority feelings. However, this will not likely cause the program to be changed.

Do we allow part of the school day to be given over to special work? Generally speaking, the last hour of the day can be used, by tradition, for practice of basketball talents.

Do we allow these children to share their talents with other students from other schools and other cities? Yes, we do, and, what is more, we pay the transportation costs involved without very many complaints being heard.

Do we allow gifted basketball players to advance by their talents rather than by their age? Indeed, we do. Any sophomore who can make the team on the basis of his talents gets the privilege of playing with seniors, and no one worries very much about it.

Finally, do we have special teachers who are specially trained and more highly salaried than the ordinary teacher? Yes, we do, and although there is some grumbling about it from the regular teachers, this does not materially affect the program.

What does this tell us? The culture and the community will support the kinds of activities that they find necessary, valuable and/or enjoyable. If they feel that a program is sufficiently necessary or sufficiently enjoyable, all sorts of objections are put aside as being relatively inconsequential. If, on the other hand, the community is not fully interested or involved in supporting such a program, all kinds of objections can be raised as to why these things should not be done, or cannot be done.

The student of human nature knows better than to think that, because Mr. Palcuzzi caught the PTA off balance, he therefore swept on to victory and the PTA unanimously resolved to support the institution of a special program for gifted children.

The opposition to such a program is often deep and emotional. To many people, there is something manifestly unfair about giving Cranshaw, a boy of superior opportunities and abilities, special help to do *more* with his superior abilities, when other children are still struggling to meet minimum requirements. To these people, it is disturbing that there is not a tidy balance sheet for life. The gifted person should somehow be weak, morally or physically. The retarded child should have uncommon strength, so as to compensate for his limited mind. In this way, things would balance out. The fact that this is not so—indeed, it is often just the opposite—is a puzzling thing to them, and attempts to swing the balance even more in favor of the favored (through special educational provisions) is objected to strenuously.

This is not to say that every person who has doubts about the value of special programs is reacting on this basis. It is a plea, however, for an understanding of human emotions which, though often presented in disguised or rationalized argument, determine attitudes and decisions in this area of school policy.   Another inhibitor of school action on the gifted is the frequently heard concern over the consequences we may spawn when we unleash the intellects of the bright students.

The gifted child's ability to use superior logic helps him to penetrate, among other things, current prejudices of the culture and society.   The gifted child is at his most troublesome in the class when he does exactly what we *say* we want him to do—think for himself.   But if he thinks for himself, this means that he is going to want to make up his own mind about the virtues and sins of such controversial subjects as communism, religion, drugs, sex, economics, or politics.   These topics are explosive and controversial, and many school persons try to avoid them.   The movement to make our schools "antiseptic" by systematically ignoring every flesh-and-blood issue in our society has reached alarming proportions.   To a large extent, this is a problem of administrative policy.   If a teacher is sure that he will receive backing from his superiors, he can explore controversial subjects with his students without looking over his shoulder to see which pressure group may descend on him.

Certainly, pressure groups in the community cannot get too aroused over a group of students *memorizing* the Bill of Rights.   This can be done in safety and with a feeling of some patriotism.   However, when the gifted youngsters attempt to *apply* certain parts of the Bill of Rights to their society, and suggest that maybe some of those articles are being actively violated in their own community, there may be some anguished second thoughts about the wisdom of allowing these youngsters to have free rein with their intellects.

In essence, the inquiring gifted child is the true challenge to the educator and his own values, and to the society and its values.   Do the school and the community really believe that the democratic process will triumph in a free exchange of ideas?   Do they really believe that, given the free exchange of ideas, the values that we now cherish would survive and be strengthened by the test?

It is easy enough to say that we believe these things, but it is a little more difficult to practice them.   If we do believe them, then we have the responsibility for allowing these youngsters the opportunity to explore answers other than only those which we think are correct.   If we are honestly committed to helping them think for themselves, then we cannot impress upon them only our own concepts of what is right or what is wrong.   In the first place, they simply will not accept them; they will wonder, "If our values are so good, why are we so frantically trying to stop a fair investigation of them?"   If we actively repress their tendencies to look at all aspects of an issue, all we will have done is delayed a more thorough, and perhaps a more destructive, reaction at a later date.

Finally, if we, as teachers, are to deal effectively with these youngsters, we must understand as thoroughly as possible our own emotional blocks that stand between us and full acceptance of these youngsters. One such block, whether verbalized or not, is that these youngsters are the most thorough threat to the status quo that one could possibly invent. These children are the innovators, the changers, the modifiers, the people who will remold and reshape our culture from the way it is today into the way it will be in the next generation. But this is *our* status quo. With all its faults and sins, we have become adjusted to it, and we may even like it.

The idea that we could actively contribute to its downfall by teaching these youngsters to use their intellectual abilities more effectively is a frightening one to many persons. Although this is an understandable reaction, it is not a very profitable one. The world and culture *are* going to change, whether we like it or not, and despite all that we can do about it. Our only hope is that it will change in a direction favorable for us. The more effectively we help these youngsters to perform, the more we can expect to see, as the fruits of our labor—these youngsters operating at their top capacity to shape their future in ways that will be constructive. This is not to say we shouldn't be concerned about the potential for both benefit and harm that our interest in gifted students can create.

For those readers who are perplexed at the nervousness with which some citizens receive announcements of special programs for gifted children, we wish to include a brief excerpt from John Hersey's outstanding novel *The Child Buyer* (1960). It is the story of a gifted child who has come to the attention of a powerful corporation that wishes to buy him. To explain why, we will let Mr. Wissey Jones, Vice President, United Lymphomilloid of America, Incorporated, speak for himself (pp. 33–34):

My purpose? I buy brains. When a commodity that you need falls in short supply, you have to get out and hustle. I buy brains. About eighteen months ago my company, United Lymphomilloid of America, Incorporated, was faced with an extremely difficult problem, a project, a long-range government contract, fifty years, highly specialized and top secret, and we needed some of the best minds in the country, and we looked around, and we found some minds that had certainly been excellent at one time, but they'd been spoiled by education. By what passes for education. Our schools, particularly at the elementary and secondary levels, speak with great confidence of their "solutions" for what they call the "gifted." . . . There's a great deal of time spent on these so-called solutions, which are for the most part based on psychological and sociological theories and data between twenty and fifty years old, but no one seems to know what really works. . . .

The reason U. Lympho wants to get brains early is connected with a basic difficulty a brilliant youngster has in this country. At an astonishingly early age he goes through a quest for meaning, for values, for the significance of life, and this quest turns, also early, into a struggle to make a place in society and to find values in it that will meet his particular needs. I hardly have to tell you that the culture in which we live is riddled with inconsistencies, from the point of view of a child with a quick mind, who sees that he is punished more than he is rewarded for his brilliance. A bitter inner inharmony results. The individual expends so much emotional energy trying to resolve this inharmony that, having started out in primary and elementary school years the most normal and well adjusted of all his peers, he winds up, before very long, the least so. Our system at United Lymphomilloid is to get the brains early and eliminate this conflict altogether.[1]

If we treat gifted children solely as a natural resource and ignore their individuality, or their rights to seek their own future, we are really acting very much like Mr. Wissey Jones.

SUMMARY

In this chapter we have been concerned with the general strategies by which schools have attempted to adjust to the unique pattern of characteristics of gifted students. Many casual observers assume that the presence of gifted students in school programs is a matter of joy and excitement for the educator. Although this is partially true, it is also true that the presence of gifted students creates serious educational problems and irritations.

If the school has organized its curriculum in a rather rigid and step-wise fashion so that each grade level and developmental level are carefully prescribed, there will inevitably be a problem in dealing with those talented children who are already performing at a level three or four years beyond their chronological age.

In addition, a teacher's limitations, both in knowledge and in the special skills needed to deal with talented children, can cause the teacher severe embarrassment and invoke in him a feeling of resentment against those children who have revealed his weaknesses.

The schools must find some way to counteract or dampen the tendency toward negative reactions on the part of peers to those children who express talent. Otherwise, the gifted child will either hide his talent to obtain greater peer acceptance, or reject his peers as being unworthy of his association; either pattern of adjustment would seem unfortunate.

The schools have three major areas in which they can modify the existing program. They can change the content or material presented, the method of presentation, or the learning environment in which the education takes place. In past decades, strong emphasis was placed on changes in the learning environment, either by acceleration of the gifted

[1] Reprinted from *The Child Buyer* (copyright 1960) by permission of Alfred A. Knopf, Inc.

child through the various stages of the educational system or by the establishment of special classes, in the hope that association with children of similar abilities would more or less automatically encourage superior performance.

In the last decade greater emphasis has been placed on changes in *content*, with particular stress on a higher level of abstract understanding of various content fields. Major curriculum reform and modification efforts in the sciences, history, anthropology, and other content areas have aided this development.

In addition, much attention has been paid to the advancement of new techniques and procedures that encourage independent thinking, problem-solving and problem-seeking behavior. This modification has been based on the notion that a rapidly changing culture makes facts obsolete before they can be used by the growing child, so that the only productive educational strategy is to help the child modify, adapt, and learn how to discover new facts for himself.

Special programs for gifted students, however, must always overcome the strong value of egalitarianism held by society which maintains that essential equality means giving the identical program to all children, regardless of their background or level of development. Although the schools protest that their goal is individualization of instruction, they must face an angry public that does not like to see programs that seem to smack of *special privileges for special people*. The resistance to special programming for the gifted lies not just in increasing expenses, which in fact are very modest, but in a basic ambivalence in the society, which, on the one hand, wishes to reward talent in the Horatio Alger sense, and, on the other hand, deplores the possible existence or emergence of an intellectual or societal elite.

UNRESOLVED ISSUES

1. What type of plan should we develop to continually integrate the new knowledge that keeps pouring out of science's cornucopia and to insert new integrations meaningfully into the school curriculum for young children—particularly gifted children? With the exception of the major curriculum projects, the task of translation and synthesis of new knowledge has been carried out most haphazardly and with little concern for the necessary bridges between elementary, secondary, and college programs. How can important new knowledge be fit into existing programs without lengthening the programs themselves?

2. The education of gifted children is currently caught in a value conflict on the part of society between egalitarianism, where everybody is treated the same, and the Horatio Alger concept that we can achieve any level or status in society that our ambition and talent allows us to.

Which value system will prevail, or what alternative values will take its place?

3. As new educational models, such as open education, *appear on the scene, we need to know their impact on talented students.   Should we organize teams of educational personnel rather than shore up the skills of a particular teacher, or use teams of personnel in the community as well as in the school to bring knowledge to the gifted?   Alternative models should be under continued examination.*

READINGS OF SPECIAL INTEREST

BRUNER, J.   *The process of education.*   Cambridge, Mass.: Harvard University Press, 1960.

This is still the best and clearest rationale for the underlying philosophy of the major curricular reform movement for secondary and, later, elementary schools of the 1960s.   Although this movement was not particularly concerned with gifted students, per se, *the emphasis of these programs on a high level of conceptualization and on training the student in the process of independent inquiry was particularly relevant to the special needs of the gifted.*

MARLAND, S.   *Education of the gifted and talented.*   Report to the Subcommittee on Education, Committee on Labor and Public Welfare, U.S. Senate, Washington, D.C., 1972.

This report to the U.S. Congress on the current status of education for the gifted in the United States points out that general education financing cannot automatically be assumed to benefit gifted students.   Although there are many individual communities conducting special programs for the gifted, the majority of school systems are still paying little identifiable attention to this important issue.

POSTMAN, N., & WEINGARTNER, C.   *Teaching as a subversive activity.*   New York: Delacorte Press, 1969.

This book calls urgently, and sometimes stridently, for reform in education, particularly at the level of the classroom teacher.   Authors describe methods that teachers can use to increase student creativity and individuality with much sympathy for an emphasis on inquiry training and an atmosphere of classroom openness.

SILBERMAN, C.   *Crisis in the schools.*   New York: Random House, 1970.

A highly critical look at the current state of public education.   The author is particularly concerned that the schools, wittingly or unwittingly, cut down the creative student or the imaginative student.   This book is representative of a line of consistent intellectual criticism of the schools and needs to be understood, but not necessarily accepted, by educators.

SECTION II

Content Modifications for the Gifted

One of the three major dimensions of the school program open to possible modification for the gifted is the *content* or curriculum offerings. Should the gifted child be presented the same curricula, additional or supplementary curricula, or different curricula from the average or slow student? The position taken in this book is that a curriculum designed for the gifted student should be different in its greater stress on advanced conceptualizations and important ideas that cannot be easily grasped by students of similar age but of average or below-average ability.

The rapid expansion of knowledge in all content fields in recent years has led to an avalanche of new information. Unless school curricula are carefully constructed, and unless strict self-discipline is practiced by the teachers, the curriculum can be drowned in interesting, but distracting, facts and information.

Various estimates have been made that students in such fields as medicine or psychology could read twenty-four hours a day, seven days a week, and still not be able to cover the new material available in their explosively expanding fields of knowledge. The chase after total mastery of all available knowledge is doomed. What can take its place? One strategy is to emphasize conceptual understanding of the basic principles and processes that lie at the heart of a discipline. One of the major challenges for educators is to interact sufficiently with scholars whose knowledge of content is sophisticated enough to help create valid special curricular materials and experiences to challenge the ready intellect of the gifted student.

The next four chapters explore some possible curricular ideas in mathematics, science, social studies, and language arts that fit this general theme of providing a program of important ideas for gifted students. Most of these ideas can be presented in the regular classroom as well as in special classes.

4

Mathematics for the Gifted

Perhaps no single content area has been so affected by the curriculum research efforts of the 1960s as mathematics. There would seem to be several reasons for this. First, it is an area particularly amenable to organization and structure and thus can be presented in a systematic fashion, more so than economics, for example. Also, it is a subject that was traditionally disliked by many students, gifted and nongifted, so that the desire to change its content and its image was very strong.

The battle cry of the "mathematics revolution" of the 1960s was "Down with rote calculations and up with meaningfulness." In this sense, the revolution has been won with only a few vocal supporters remaining of the old-time rote calculations of multitudes of problems.

But one man's meaningfulness is another man's mystery. The hierarchical nature of mathematical knowledge cries out for some means to individualize the instruction so that the bright student can continue to climb the abstract pyramid as fast as he or she is able, without having to stop for calculations of simple-minded or practical problems, appropriately created for the slow learner but of trivial interest to the quick mind of the gifted student.

Cranshaw is very happy today. He has returned from school beaming proudly, brandishing a report card. He is particularly proud of the "A" he achieved in arithmetic and his parents share his pride. After all, an "A" is a mark of excellence and of considerable accomplishment.

Not that this result was much of a surprise to his parents—Cranshaw had been getting 100s on his homework papers. His teacher had given him extra problems to solve in long division which he completed very easily. When the teacher gave him more complex long-division problems,

Cranshaw, never daunted, swept through them like a hungry grasshopper through a cornfield.

Everyone is happy and all is right with Cranshaw's world of numbers— or is it? There are many people who have serious doubts that the reward for this type of routine work is, in the end, going to help Cranshaw become mathematically proficient in his later academic career. Should he be doing more and more complex long-division problems? Should he be allowed to study the next-higher level of concepts, such as beginning algebra or fractions? Or does he need something much more different and much more complex than this? This is the question that is being asked by educators and mathematicians.

Since mathematics is known as the handmaiden of science, interest in better programming of this area concerns many persons not basically mathematicians. The focus of these new programs has been mainly directed to the academically talented student. One of the first concerns of any serious program of mathematics introduced at the lower grades is to change the image in the minds of students and teachers of what a mathematician is and what he does. Too often the common portrait is of a person who gains great pleasure from manipulating numbers and who delights in the knowledge that all the answers have already been discovered. He has only to present the proper formulas and calculate the answer.

Such a portrait is unfair and almost totally misleading. Mathematics is not merely counting, measuring, or manipulating formulas but, in its essence, is a way of thinking—of deductive and inductive reasoning. It is an area of dynamic changes and exciting new discoveries. Gifted children should be presented this concept if at all possible.

Even gifted students are often unaware of the constantly changing and expanding field of mathematics. In Table 4–1, Wilder (1970) points out that such concepts as lattices, groups, fields, and modules are less than

TABLE 4–1. *Mathematical Levels of Abstraction by Historical Period.*

TOPICS	PERIOD WHEN CREATED
Categories and functions, lattices	Twentieth century
Groups, rings, fields, modules	Nineteenth century
Classical algebra	Middle Ages and Renaissance
Numbers and common arithmetic	5000–2500 B.C.
Primitive types of enumeration, such as tallying	50,000–5000 B.C.

Source: R. Wilder. Historical background of innovations in mathematics curricula. In Edward G. Begle, *Mathematics education.* 69th Yearbook NSSE. Chicago: University of Chicago Press, 1970, p. 19. Used with permission of the National Society for the Study of Education.

a century old. It is true that our number system goes back 7000 years, but that does not mean that creativity and imagination should not be important skills to gifted students interested in mathematics as a career field.

Table 4–2 lists the major elements that lie at the heart of the "new math," the latest curricular effort in mathematics. These principles carry over to major curricular reform efforts in the physical and social sciences as well. The ability of young children, especially gifted children, to understand complex mathematical concepts at an early age is crucial to their comprehension of the world around them. The "discovery" method by which the child is given a set of information on some problems and expected to grasp the larger principle, either intuitively or verbally, is an important element in the way in which the curriculum is supposed to be presented to the students (Bruner, 1966).

The gifted student will sense the excitement of the mathematician as he

TABLE 4–2. *New Curricula Philosophy.*

1. The structure of mathematics should be stressed at all levels. Topics and relationships of endurance should be given concentrated attention.
2. Children are capable of learning more abstract and more complex concepts when the relationship between concepts is stressed.
3. Existing elementary arithmetic programs may be severely condensed because children are capable of learning concepts at much earlier ages than formerly thought.
4. Any concept may be taught a child of any age in some intellectually honest manner, if one is able to find the proper language for expressing the concept.
5. The inductive approach or the discovery method is logically productive and should enhance learning and retention.
6. The major objective of a program is the development of independent and creative thinking processes.
7. Human learning seems to pass through the stages of preoperations, concrete operations, and formal operations.
8. Growth of understanding is dependent upon concept exploration through challenging apparatus and concrete materials and cannot be restricted to mere symbolic manipulations.
9. Teaching mathematical skills is regarded as a tidying-up of concepts developed through discovery rather than as a step-by-step process for memorization.
10. Practical application of isolated concepts or systems of concepts, particularly those applications drawn from the natural sciences, are valuable to reinforcement and retention.

Source: L. Scott. *Trends in elementary school mathematics.* Chicago: Rand McNally, 1966, pp. 15–16. Used with permission of Professor Lloyd F. Scott, University of California, Berkeley.

suddenly sees patterns and relationships that he hadn't understood before. A lesser emphasis is placed in modern mathematics classes on the correct operation of arithmetic skills or operations and much more on adequate comprehension of the major concepts, along with the application of these ideas to science.   The lack of emphasis on calculation skills in modern math has led serious critics and nightclub comics, alike, to portray the "new math" student as understanding the laws of the universe but unable to add a grocery bill.   Such criticisms are open to evaluation.

The program for gifted students at the elementary and junior high school levels probably requires some modification in all three of the major program dimensions noted in Chapter 3—the content, the intellectual skills, and the learning environment.   It seems even more important in this field than in others to individualize instruction.

Shulman (1970, p. 49) has presented an analogy that fits the problems of the gifted and the slow learner in school very well.

> Imagine the mile run if it began with the firing of a gun and ended at the end of four minutes when another gun went off and everyone had to stop wherever they were.   It would be even more startling if about five minutes later another gun went off for the next race and everyone began that race from the same point at which they had ended the previous one.

That is precisely the situation in which students in mathematics find themselves when they are placed in a single curriculum with predetermined competencies to be learned.   Obviously, some substantial modifications need to be introduced that would allow the gifted student to proceed as he is ready and master those concepts that are within his range of comprehension.

MAJOR IDEAS

There appears to be general agreement that the talented child can learn many more important mathematical ideas much earlier in his school career than had been thought possible.   Elementary school students can learn the rudiments of probability, set theory, and a much richer appreciation of the number system, all of which should stand them in good stead when they get to higher mathematics.

Elaboration of the Number System

None of the following examples are presented as a means for teachers to acquire specific skills but rather as illustrations of a variety of approaches that can be used to stimulate the gifted student.   More thorough familiarity and practice than is possible to present here will be necessary for adequate usage.

LATTICES.   One of the more innovative devices for helping young children to see the intricacies of the number system and to begin to appreciate the beauty and fun that is possible in mathematics is to engage in work on number lattices. It can be started as early as the first grade (Page, 1966) and become complicated enough to stir the interest of graduate students. It is therefore a system that can be taught to students with a wide range of ability at the same time. Cranshaw can have just as stimulating a time as the average student in constructing variations on the theme. A simple lattice that all students can understand would be

60	61	62	. . . . .					
50	51	52	53	54	55	56	57	58	59
40	41	42	43	44	45	46	47	48	49
30	31	32	33	34	35	36	37	38	39
20	21	22	23	24	25	26	27	28	29
10	11	12	13	14	15	16	17	18	19
	1	2	3	4	5	6	7	8	9

We are going to have a secret code for writing numbers. It uses that table. Here is a number in code:

   5↑

What number do you guess it stands for?

In the philosophy of teaching followed in this method, student understanding comes not through the parroting of some abstract principle but by inductive reasoning from the correct answers to significant questions.

Teacher: 5 + 13↓.
Student: 8.
Teacher: Right. Who can give the answer in our code?
Another student: 18↓.
Teacher: Good. Who can do it another way?
Third student: 7→.
Teacher: Another way?
Fourth student: 8↓↑→←.
Teacher: OK. Very fancy, very good.

The teacher unfamiliar with this approach to number systems might want to try out his own skills on a variation such as these:[1]

   74↗↓←↗↓←↗↓←
   74↗↗↗↓↓↓←←←

---

[1] The alert teacher should be able to see how the gifted student almost instantaneously arrives at the correct answer (74) in both examples.

While the average student is working his way through standard lattices, such students as Zelda and Cranshaw can be pursuing more sophisticated topics, such as lattices with fractions, nonrectangular lattices—for example:

```
. . . . .
7   8   9   10
4   5   6
2   3
1
```

multiplicative lattices, three-dimensional lattices, and the like.   In this case, these students may wish to pursue for themselves variations that even the teacher had not considered.

Sieve of Eratosthenes.   The reader, at one time or another, has no doubt had a mathematically inclined friend who has stated, "Mathematics is beautiful."   The notion that the painful drudgery of algebra or trigonometry that one wrestled with in high school and college contained beauty is enough to cause a guffaw of laughter and some second notions concerning the sanity of the friend.

The truth is, however, that the mathematician *has* seen a structure and order which, to him, is beautiful in its logic and inevitability.   Often this structure is not clear to one of lesser training.   (Need one say that this is due, in part, to the type of instruction received?)

There are innumerable games and exercises that students can do to aid them in further understanding the unending patterns and complexities represented by the number system.   Just as the novice painter and art critic can stand in front of a great masterpiece for hours seeing different shadings and patterns of the master artist whereas casual viewers see only an interesting portrait, so can the mathematician and budding mathematician see an unending cascade of patterns and relationships in the number system.

Zelda's teacher, in an attempt to break her out of the single-minded pattern of completing the assignment, gave her a special assignment. (She had finished the regular assignment in half the time required by other students anyway.)   She was given the lattice of numbers shown in Figure 4–1 and told that she was to use different colors or shadings to shade out all of the numbers on the Sieve of Eratosthenes from 2 to 9. First Zelda shaded the number 2 and all multiples of 2.   She then followed the same procedure for all numbers up to 9.   When she was done, she had a production such as shown in Figure 4–1.   After Zelda had completed this task, she was asked to tell how many different things she had learned about the number system in the process.

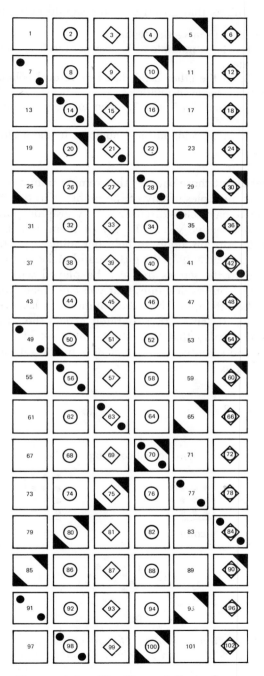

Figure 4–1.   *The Sieve of Eratosthenes.*

A few of the things that gifted students should note are that:

1. The even numbers form vertical columns.
2. The number 4, being a multiple of 2, does not result in any additional numbers being shaded.
3. The number 3, on the other hand, has two vertical columns: one for odd multiples and one for even multiples.
4. Multiples of the numbers 5 and 7, when marked out, appear as diagonal columns.
5. The number 9, as 3^2, adds no new numbers to those already marked for the number 3.

Ah, but what about those squares that remain unmarked? Those numbers must not be multiples of any of the numbers in question, only of the number 1. What has Zelda discovered? A graphic portrayal of *prime numbers* and an effective visual display of them, which is much better than a verbal description alone, to help her understand the concept.

Tasks such as these can help the gifted child make an exciting discovery. There is no end to the games that can be played with numbers—either games made up by others or games that you can create yourself.

Another graphic attempt to show the commutative law is shown in Figure 4–2. Although all students rather routinely accept the notion that $7 \times 9 = 9 \times 7$, a graphic display that the rotation of a set of 3×4 dots really doesn't change the essential number of dots in the set can be an insight for a student. Thus,

$$m \times n = n \times m$$
$$3 \times 4 = 4 \times 3$$

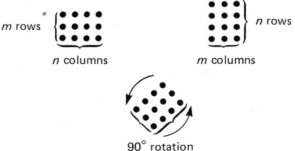

FIGURE 4–2. *Graphic Presentation of Commutative Law in Multiplication. (Adapted from J. Kelley. Number systems of arithmetic. In* Mathematics education. *69th Yearbook NSSE. Chicago: University of Chicago Press, 1970, p. 100.)*

becomes easier to understand because it is presented visually. A reminder at this point of Sam's talents in this area is appropriate. He seems to possess a strong visual sense of balance and proportions and does well when concepts are presented graphically. Sam's early environment has not stimulated his semantic and verbal skills as much as it could have, but his talent in understanding three-dimensional space needs to be recognized and stimulated.

RUSSIAN PEASANT'S MULTIPLICATION. Mr. Jenkins took on a conspiratorial tone one day and announced that he had heard of an astounding discovery—a society on a far Pacific isle that had a number system similar to ours but that had learned to multiply and divide only by two. Is such a thing possible? Could we get along without our multiplication tables? The students were incredulous. Crazy! Impossible!

Cranshaw's hand went up like a rocket. He remembered something he had read. Maybe it was not so impossible after all. When we have two numbers to multiply, if we double one and divide the other in half, the product remains the same—for example, $(4 \times 9) = (2 \times 18) = (1 \times 36) = 36$.

We could solve the problem $4 \times 9 = ?$ without knowing the tables. How about more difficult problems? Mr. Jenkins presented a couple for consideration: (32×122), (64×23).

Cranshaw was insistent. "Yes, it can work; you just have to keep doing it till you reach '1' in the column you are dividing," for example:

DIVIDE BY 2		MULTIPLY BY 2		PRODUCT	DIVIDE BY 2		MULTIPLY BY 2		PRODUCT
32	×	122	=	↑	64	×	23	=	↑
16	×	244	=		32	×	46	=	
8	×	488	=		16	×	92	=	
4	×	976	=		8	×	184	=	
2	×	1952	=		4	×	368	=	
1	×	3904	=	3904	2	×	736	=	
					1	×	1472	=	1472

Let's check it out by regular multiplication. It works! The students are dumbfounded and intrigued, which was one of Mr. Jenkins' purposes from the beginning, of course.

"Wait a minute!" This is Joe entering the conversation! "That crazy system works OK for even numbers, but suppose you are multiplying an odd number?" Mr. Jenkins notes mentally that Joe always seems to enter as an "It doesn't work" specialist. He wishes he could help Joe be a discoverer of new things for once. Oh, well . . .

Let's try one and see what happens:

$$13 \times 65 = ?$$

What do we do? Keep the fraction. "No," Mr. Jenkins suggests, "Let's pretend the odd number is the next-lower even number."

$$13 \times \underline{65}$$
$$6 \times \overline{130}$$
$$3 \times 260$$
$$1 \times \overline{520} = 520$$

Joe is triumphant. "I told you it doesn't work; $13 \times 65 = 845$. I just multiplied it out!" The class is silent. Even Cranshaw looks puzzled and defeated.

Mr. Jenkins can't expect his students to see everything, so he steps in. "Wait a minute. Remember, we pretended something that isn't so. We acted as if we had an even number when we had an odd number. What would happen if we added back the one number we didn't use? We didn't use a 65 when we divided that time; we didn't use a 260 when we divided then. Well, $520 + 260 + 65 = 845$. Voilà!"

The students are encouraged to make up examples of their own. Mr. Jenkins remembers to go over and praise Joe for his perceptiveness in being the first to see the special problem of the odd number, because he noticed that Joe was becoming somewhat unhappy that his negative coup had not worked.

A visitor to the class would have seen energetic and laughing students trying out various examples and having a good time. Some visitors get upset when they see students enjoying themselves in a gamelike situation such as this. "Learning is a serious business," they often remark disapprovingly. So it is. *Much too serious to be solemn.*

The playful exploration of these students will likely teach them more about the number system than any series of already constructed formal problems that they have to plod through. As long as the students are exercising their minds on serious content issues, why not do it with a little fun?

Probability

Another example of adventuresomeness in arithmetic curriculum has been presented by Page (1959), in which he suggests ways of presenting an intuitive understanding of probability theory to children at the elementary school level. The notion here is quite similar to that expressed by Bruner and Piaget that children can understand concepts at an operational level without necessarily being able to state them formally. Thus, these exercises in probability do not demand formal thought or organization on the part of the student but are designed merely to give him some contact with the basic phenomena and to allow him to experience some of the important concepts.

To demonstrate this, Page suggests an experiment in dice casting. If the portrait of a kindergarten youngster eagerly throwing dice is disturbing to adults, spinners could be substituted for the experiment. The student can make a tally of the results of each "experiment." As the student experiences a series of events by throwing the die or by spinning the spinner, Page suggests a number of questions that can be asked to illustrate some of the major probability concepts, such as the understanding of *equally likely events* (pp. 232–233):

> "If we only made six throws, would it have to be that one tally would be placed in each column?"   (No.)
>
> "If we made six throws and then made another six throws and then another six throws and so on, would very many of these six-throws give exactly one mark in each of the six columns?"   (Only a few would. If students don't agree on this conclusion or don't feel strongly about any conclusion, have them carry out the experiment.)
>
> "If you made a hundred throws, would it be possible for one column to be empty?"   (Yes, it would be possible, but it wouldn't happen very often.)

Another fundamental idea that can be learned through experimentation is the concept of *independent events*. Suppose that the children have run a series of throws or events and have placed a tally under the number that has come up in each event, as follows:

die number N	1	2	3	4	5	6	total throws 20
	///	////	//	///	////	///	

The teacher could then ask:

> "Does the location of the first, say, 20 marks in the table affect where the next mark will go? Specifically, suppose that after 20 marks are made, one column is blank. Does that mean that it is pretty certain that a mark will next fall in the blank column?"   (No, but some students may be hard to convince.)

Even an intuitive understanding of the notion of independent events can save much grief in adulthood. Specifically, it might help a person to understand why it is not true that a series of runs of a certain number on an honest roulette wheel means that that particular number is more likely (or less likely) to come up on the next trial, or that a run of bad poker hands means that you are more likely to obtain a good hand on your next turn.

The fundamental concepts of probability underlie all of scientific theory, and a better understanding of these concepts at an early age should provide the proper foundation for easier understanding when they appear in more formal aspects later. Page also describes in further detail how such simple experiments can be expanded to integrate with set theory and to illustrate graphically some of the probability concepts.

Set Theory

One of the current emphases in the teaching of important mathematical concepts to children of a young age has been on set theory. This approach has been central to the work of the School Mathematics Study Group (Begle & Wilson, 1970), a committee concerned with the improvement of mathematics curriculum at secondary and elementary levels.

Suppes (1960) devised a program for teaching the necessary elements of set theory to primary grade children. Naturally, such a program would be of considerable interest to teachers of gifted children, as many of these children will need, and profit by, a more thorough grounding in the area of mathematics. Suppes claims that, by starting with set theory rather than with numerals, it is possible to place arithmetic on a more valid mathematical foundation. As Suppes points out (p. 2):

> The term "set" is a simple concrete term—easy both to explain and understand. A set is simply any collection or family of objects. We may speak of the set or collection of all students now in the first grade, a set or collection of dolls now owned by Mary Jones, a set or collection of all books in this room. . . . Operations upon sets are more meaningful to the student than manipulating of numbers. The putting together of sets of physical objects, for example, is a more concrete operation than the addition of numbers.

Figure 4–3 indicates some of the concepts of set theory as presented to first graders. One of these concepts is that the *order* or presentation of items within a set is of no importance, as shown in the example. It is of no essential mathematical interest which item in the set comes first.

Another concept introduced quite early is the equals sign; this shows that "Set A = Set B" means that "Set A is really the same as, or just, Set B." This is a reasonable and an easily understood concept for gifted children when presented pictorially.

One of the most irritating problems to teachers of primary-aged children has been that of establishing a mathematically sound concept of zero. This problem is simplified considerably by the use of set theory, since zero is referred to as the "empty set." The concept of the empty

Order

Equals sign

Empty set

Counting and numerals

Equals and numerals

Union of sets

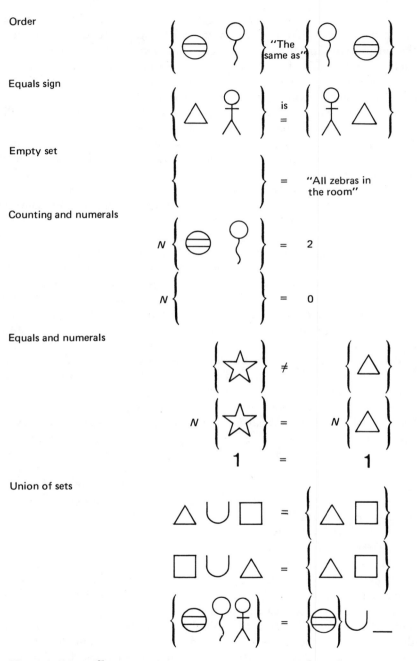

FIGURE 4–3. *Illustrating Properties of a Set. (Adapted from P. Suppes. Sets and numbers. Stanford, Calif.: Stanford University, 1960.)*

set is a relatively easy one for bright children to grasp at a young age, and can be illustrated as representing all the tigers in the classroom, all the people who are 9 feet tall in the classroom, and by numerous other such examples. Children themselves can obtain a great deal of enjoyment from imagining what other empty sets might represent, once the concept has been introduced and established.

Once these notions have been presented through exercise and illustration, the notion that "Numbers are properties of a set, and the operation of the addition of numbers is simply a general way of combining families or sets of things without paying any real attention to the things themselves" can be introduced. As seen in Figure 4–3, the letter N before the set sign requires the students to relate the set to the arabic number symbol by counting, so that the N of the empty set is zero, and the N of the other set is 2.

Once this concept has been reasonably established, it can then be illustrated through the exercises shown in Figure 4–3 under "Equals and numerals." The top example shows that a star is certainly not a triangle and therefore not equal to a triangle. However, the placing of capital N before them means that we are not going to be concerned about the other properties of a set, but will concentrate on the counting operation. In this case, the two statements on the opposite sides of the equal sign are equal to each other, since *one does equal one*.

Part of the operation of addition is introduced through the concept of "Union of sets" and is the final illustration in Figure 4–3. Here the student may notice that the example illustrates the same principle as the commutative law, one of the fundamental principles to be established in the area of arithmetic. What is the advantage of using the union symbol instead of the plus sign? Suppes claims that it rests on a firmer mathematical foundation, and thus is likely to facilitate later learning of more difficult mathematical principles. Furthermore, such an introduction to set theory gives a good grounding for the understanding of the basic principles in arithmetic. Since the student has already learned that order in a set is not important, it is easy for him to understand the commutative law as it illustrated in the figure.

One complaint of critics of the new math is that such programs imply that imagination cannot be used in the presentation of deductive sequences as well. For example, if one does not wish to spend a great amount of time having the students inductively experience the laws of arithmetic, these laws can first be directly presented, as in Figure 4–4. Then students can develop innumerable examples or test the validity of the laws by filling in the blanks. An amusing attention getter for the squares and triangles is to draw them on the blackboard and have the students pretend that they are differently shaped holes that have been sawed in the blackboard, with a little man standing behind the holes

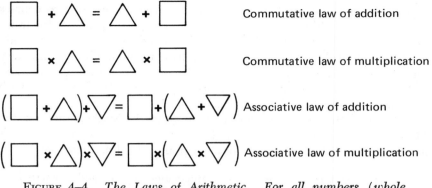

FIGURE 4–4. *The Laws of Arithmetic. For all numbers (whole numbers or fractions, positive numbers, negative numbers, and zero) chosen completely at random, these properties always hold true; they are therefore called the* laws of arithmetic.

holding cards with numbers on them. The students' job is to direct the little man as to what number card he is to hang in each space.

The teacher can stir interest in divergent thinking by telling stories or anecdotes of students, famous or not, who have found novel ways to solve problems. The following story is an example of such (School Mathematics Study Group, 1959, pp. 3–4).

> When Karl Friedrich Gauss was about 10 years old, his teacher wanted to keep the class quiet for a while. He told the children to add all the numbers from 1 to 100. In about two minutes Gauss was up to mischief again. The teacher asked him why he wasn't working on the problem. He replied, "I've done it already!" "Impossible!" exclaimed the teacher. "It's easy," answered Gauss. "I wrote
>
> $1+$ $2+$ $3 + \cdots + 100$ and then I reversed the numbers:
> $100 +$ $99 +$ $98 + \cdots +$ 1 and then I added each pair of numbers:
> $\overline{101 + 101 + 101 + \cdots + 101}$
>
> "When I add, I get a hundred 101's, which gives me $100 \times 101 = 10{,}100$. But I used each number twice, so I divided my answer by 2. The answer is $10{,}100/2 = 5{,}050$."

TEACHER PREPARATION

One of the strongest limiting features in the teaching of mathematics to young gifted students is the inadequate mathematical preparation of the typical elementary school teacher. One can hardly picture Zelda's teacher wandering off into the unknown territory of probability or changing number bases when she herself had barely survived one or two courses in mathematics at the college level. Thus, any special program for training teachers to work with gifted students should include in-depth study of at least one field. Although it is unrealistic to think of one elementary school teacher as an expert in math and science and language arts, and so forth, it is not unreasonable to think of a team of teachers, each with a strong specialty in a different field.

The Committee on Undergraduate Programs in Mathematics for the Mathematical Association of America (1966, p. 5) proposed the following standards for the teacher of elementary school mathematics.

1. Two years of college preparatory mathematics (algebra and geometry).
2. Elementary teachers should be competent in basic techniques of arithmetic.
3. A two-course sequence devoted to the structure of the real-number system and its subsystems.
4. A course devoted to basic concepts of algebra.
5. A course in informal geometry.
6. At least 20% of elementary teachers should have more intensive training in analytic geometry, probability, etc.

Since most elementary school teachers are far from that level of training, some additional approaches need to be found. In summarizing the state of the mathematics field today, Botts (1970, p. 460) concluded:

> For education in the mathematical sciences, however, the truly pressing problem of the day—not just at the secondary level, but at every level from kindergarten to post-Ph.D.—is to produce qualified teachers in sufficient numbers.

One of the clear alternatives to the less-than-knowledgeable teacher in mathematics is computer-assisted instruction (CAI). Through the use of the computer, the gifted student can speak to the highly sophisticated mathematicians and teachers who composed the programs. Suppes and Searle (1971) described a sophisticated program for elementary school mathematics made up of the sixteen strands of problems that comprise all the concepts taught in elementary school mathematics programs. This program is of special interest to gifted educators in that it provides for individualization of problem selection based on the student's performance.

When the student sits down at the console and types out his name, the computer recognizes him from previous lessons and presents a problem from the last strand (i.e., finding multiples of a number or decimals or problem-solving). If he responds correctly, he will be given a problem from another strand. The computer will give the student more problems from the strand in which he is having the most difficulty. This reduces the problem that gifted children often have with programmed learning—that is, having to do a mountain of problems that are easy for them but which add nothing to their learning.

Despite this ingenious approach, CAI has barely moved from an experimental and very limited type of demonstration use. Ways need to be found to make the procedures both more convenient and more economical before many school systems are willing or able to invest in the expensive hardware necessary for the program itself.

Topic Classification: Mathematics

Any teacher who wishes to pursue a planning effort for his gifted students needs some type of model or system by which he can check himself. Table 4–3 shows a two-dimensional matrix which can serve such a purpose. It indicates the level of abstraction of certain concepts and the predominant thinking process required by each topic initiator. Examples are provided. A careful examination of these, going vertically and then horizontally, can give the flavor of the two dimensions involved in the matrix.

At the "data" level, one can focus on individual problems and specific data. Proponents of the new math claim that much of the normal student activity ends up being simple calculations of the descriptive or explanatory type.

At the "concept" level, one begins to see that students are expected to manipulate ideas, instead of numbers or figures. Concepts such as zero or the empty set force the student to think more deeply about the number system and to abandon his focus on strict calculatory accuracy.

For gifted students some degree of mastery at the "generalization" level would seem required. They should not only be efficient in multiplication but understand the distributive law of multiplication. Understanding does not imply the parroting of a verbal definition, but the ability to solve problems based on the law. They should be able to grasp the comparison of number systems of varying bases and produce proofs in support of geometric operations, even as early as elementary school.

A teacher wishing to check his or her own level of presentation can take a blank matrix similar to Table 4–3 and insert his or her own plans of topics that would be covered in the forthcoming week or weeks ahead. If he or she finds no topics at the generalization, or system, level, there is some question regarding the genuineness of challenge of his program for the gifted student, particularly one with special talents in the mathematics area. Teachers who operate in the "discovery" mode could expect to find topics in the expansion area, as a broad range of data and concepts would be needed to aid the student to reach the generalization stage. The type of question used to begin an expansion topic can gen-

TABLE 4–3. *Classification of Mathematics Topics.*

	DESCRIPTION	EXPLANATION	EVALUATION	EXPANSION
Generalization	Distributive law of multiplication, $P = 2(l + w) = 2l + 2w$.	Give a proof to the proposition that in a right angle triangle the square of the hypotenuse equals the sum of the squares of the other two sides.	Compare two number systems, one with base 2 and one with base 10, and state the advantages and disadvantages of each.	Describe our number system if we had three fingers on each hand.
Concept	What is the empty set? All the zebras in this room.	Explain why betting that four straight "tails" will come up in coin tosses is unwise!	Is the "Russian peasant" approach to multiplication a useful technique?	Indicate all the consequences you can think of —if there were no *zero* concept in our mathematics.
Data	Give the 11's in the multiplication table up to 220.	If Joe is taller than Pete and Pete is taller than Sam, what do we know about Joe and Sam?	Which is more, 37 × 22 or 18,370 ÷ 20?	How many different ways can you make 4?

erate many ideas quickly, and if an evaluation topic follows, student or instructor judgment can be used to narrow the discussion to those elements necessary to the discovery.

Conversely, a teacher who operates from a more deductive or convergent strategy will find that a beginning topic in a unit will fall into the generalization–description dimension to be followed by many problem examples of the explanation–data dimension. Whatever particular strategy is followed by the teacher, it can be charted in the matrix and used to check on the teacher's own plans and progress. Further discussion of the use of these matrices in other fields is found in subsequent chapters.

EVALUATION

Mr. Jenkins was asked by a school-board member, whom he happened to run into one evening, whether or not there was any evaluation available of the modern math program that his school was using. He answered, "Yes and No. There has been no formal evaluation with tests that I know about, but the teachers have formed their own opinions on it and are very clear on their judgment. They like it and have decided to adopt it."

This is a very common situation that underlines the presence of two very different types of evaluation of school programs, one informal and the other formal. Although scholars tend to report only the formal type in their written reports, there is little doubt that informal reports are more influential in adoption and rejection of program materials at the school and teacher levels.

For one thing, formal reports usually come much later, after new program decisions, either pro or con, have been made. The great enthusiasm for the new math came with no evaluation data at all. For another, the informal approach stresses an overall judgment on the total program rather than atomistic test scores and thus tends to be trusted more by decision makers.

Here are some examples of the different types of questions asked in each of these approaches—first, informal evaluation:

Are the materials easy to use and comprehensible to students and to teachers?
Do the students appear to like the materials and are they learning from them?
Is the approach approved by noted authorities?

Second, formal evaluation:

Do students using new materials profit more than comparable groups of students using the old materials or programs?
Are there special subgroups (e.g., gifted) who seem to profit more or less under either method?

The informal evaluation method is in operation in every teachers' lounge, PTA coffee klatch, and professional meeting. If the answer to any of the key questions noted above in the informal list is a resounding "No," it is unlikely that any positive formal results would change the negative decision making we would expect to fall upon the program or materials in question.

It appears that one of the products of any revolution is a counter-revolution. Thus, one of the products of the mathematics revolution is a counterrevolution that criticizes the new math philosophy and procedures (see Kline, 1973).

Kline has pointed out that many of the new mathematics programs were spawned by an unusual collection of psychologists and university mathematics professors who did not feel any major obligation to apply the subject to science or to practical ends in general. He pointed out that only a small fraction of the students will be seeking a career in mathematics and that the rest will need diverse applications of mathematics that should form a major part of the curriculum, much more extensive than they get in the "new math" programs (p. 78).

> Of course mathematics is not an isolated self-sufficient body of knowledge. It exists primarily to help man understand and master the physical world and . . . the economic and social worlds. . . . It is because mathematics is extraordinarily helpful that it is in great demand and receives so much emphasis today.

Part of the criticism of these new programs comes from the inability of the new math proponents to teach teachers how to use these procedures sensibly. Over 1 million elementary school teachers are employed across the nation, and their puzzlement over the new math has been evident. Even the extensive efforts at teacher training apparently fell far short of what was really necessary to make a major change.

Part of the complaint about the new math is that it is too abstract in nature. It is puzzling to imagine why the schools feel that a potentially useful set of procedures (i.e., new math) must necessarily be applied to all children in the school. All the evidence on individual differences has apparently not yet penetrated the decision-making procedures of many school leaders.

Why mentally retarded or slow-learning children should be forced into the intricacies of probability or set theory is indeed mysterious. Nor is the situation changed by arguing that these children *can* learn these concepts. The fact that they can does not mean they should! As has been pointed out, teaching an elephant to walk on his hind legs is an impressive accomplishment for the trainer but adds little to the practical skills of the elephant to do what elephants do, except in a circus.

But the gifted student, who must understand science if not actually be a scientist, should have firm foundations in these areas so that later concepts of fields, modules, or other content areas such as statistics are more comprehensible. At any rate, we can raise the issue of evaluation and ask what the evidence is.

One of the most extensive attempts at a formal evaluation of mathematics curricula has been reported by Begle and Wilson (1970). The National Longitudinal Study of Mathematics Abilities (NLSMA) attempted to follow the performance of 110,000 fourth-, seventh-, and tenth-grade students from 1500 schools in 40 states over a three-to-five-year period. At periodic intervals an extensive battery of measures of arithmetic skills and abilities was administered and factors related to student performance were examined.

One of the key comparisons made was that between classes of students who were using "modern math" texts with classes using more traditional texts. As the reader should expect, such a study produced very complex results. Nonetheless, it seemed clear that the classes using SMSG (School Mathematics Study Group) texts appeared to produce mediocre results compared to traditional classes in the area of computation (as critics claim), but were superior in the comprehension of number systems and in their application and analysis, which was a major goal of SMSG.

However, the results showed no consistent advantage of modern math over the traditional texts. In some instances, where the modern texts appeared to be formal, abstract, and rigorous, the students did less well, whereas one traditional textbook group appeared to do quite well in all areas, including application and analysis. Furthermore, the older the student, the less the influence of the textbook altogether.

The analysis of the six Biological Science Curriculum Study classrooms by Gallagher (1967) reported in the chapter on science is instructive here. The curriculum, however ingeniously devised, must be delivered through, and is at the mercy of, the particular instructor utilizing it.

Aiken (1972) reviewed the massive research on student attitudes toward mathematics and arrived at some rather unsurprising findings—namely, that student attitudes are most influenced by teacher attitudes and that girl students have a more negative view toward mathematics than do boys.

These results seem to follow earlier efforts at evaluation that suggest that modern math students do as well as traditional students in arithmetic fundamentals and better in those areas of special "modern math" emphasis. This is especially true of the gifted students in such programs (Provus, 1960; Suppes, 1961; Mayor, 1967).

Few studies have covered the specific issue of performance of gifted students in the various curriculum evaluation efforts, looking instead at individual differences among students as a kind of afterthought. One exception to this was an extensive research project by Goldberg, Passow,

Camm, and Neill (1966), who studied the performance of over 1500 able junior high school students in twenty-five school systems over a three-year period. The students were compared over six different mathematics programs.

1. *Standard Enriched.* Social applications and traditional algebra beefed up with special units.
2. *Standard Accelerated.* Combined seventh- and eighth-grade material in one year and standard algebra program.
3. *School Mathematics Study Group Normal.* The regular SMSG program for junior high.
4. *School Mathematics Study Group Accelerated.* Four years of SMSG materials in a three-year sequence.
5. *University of Illinois Committee on School Mathematics–8.* The usual UICSM materials for these grade levels.
6. *University of Illinois Committee on School Mathematics–7.* Beginning two years earlier in program and ending with geometry.

A carefully selected battery of tests was chosen that measured mathematics achievement at the end of a three-year period. The order of findings for the various methods used with able students was (1) SMSG Accelerated, (2) UICSM–8, (3) UICSM–7, (4) SMSG Normal, (5) Standard Accelerated, and (6) Standard Enriched. Thus, the accelerated programs were usually superior to enriched programs and the modern math programs superior to the traditional ones.

In general, the higher-ability students seemed to profit the most from modern mathematics in the currently available evaluation studies. This is hardly a surprise, however, since these approaches do stress major abstract principles, plus an inquiry strategy that seems ideally suited to children of high ability.

SUMMARY

One of the basic educational objectives for gifted students in the area of mathematics is an improved understanding on their part of more abstract concepts and systems related to mathematics. This means the ability to master not just standard mathematical processes, as found in algebra and trigonometry, but a greater understanding of the conceptual fabric that comprises mathematics itself. A second objective is to aid the gifted student in understanding that mathematics is not a static subject area where everything is known and where the task is merely to master what has been previously attained. It is, instead, an area of adventure and potential creative accomplishment. It is an expanding field, dependent upon the creative and innovative ideas of gifted students, scientists, and mathematicians to keep the field growing.

The idea that there should be special mathematics content for the gifted is based not only upon their greater abilities to master such ideas, but on the different educational purposes to be achieved for different children. There is a genuine question as to whether students whose education will terminate at the secondary level should be subjected to Boolian algebra or set theory, as opposed to the mastery of interest rates and family budgeting. The gifted students are marked for further advancement in the educational system, should be preparing to master those higher mathematical levels, and need a strong early foundation to do so. Such content fields as set theory and probability seem to more adequately prepare the student for that goal, although there is current controversy about the full utility of the new math in such a regard.

Much of the controversy about mathematics seems to go back to the basic values of society and what it wants of its young people. There is little doubt that one of the inhibiting factors in mathematics, particularly at the elementary level, lies in the limited talents and knowledge of the elementary school teachers in this content field. If the demand is for greater complexity and understanding of mathematical systems, it is unlikely that that demand will be fulfilled by teachers who themselves have an extraordinarily limited grasp of the content field. Therefore, part of the innovative work in the field of mathematics is how knowledge of mathematics can be transmitted to the students, given these existing staff limitations. The use of computer-assisted instruction, programmed learning, and special mathematics clubs monitored by well-trained staff have been explored as alternatives to putting all the responsibility on the beleaguered elementary school teacher.

UNRESOLVED ISSUES

1. Where will teachers of gifted mathematics students come from? Currently, there is a kind of game of Russian roulette in which a gifted youngster is issued one of a million available elementary teachers, based primarily on the community he is in and on the school he is attending. The odds are strong that that teacher knows little in depth about mathematics. New procedures by which gifted students get a better mathematics preparation need to be pursued, such as team-teaching or mentor approaches.

2. We need to discover a great deal more about the essential conceptual linkages between early mathematical understanding on the part of students and their later mastery of more complex systems of mathematical ideas. Contrary to the usual assumption, very little systematic work has been done on such development, and thus unsolvable argu-

ments arise as to whether teaching set theory or probability at early ages is useful or not for later mastery of college mathematics.

3. Will the new social and intellectual freedom for women release gifted girls from the rather clear hesitation that has been observable in their approach to mathematics?

READINGS OF SPECIAL INTEREST

BEGLE, E., & WILSON, J. Evàluation of mathematics programs. In E. Begle (Ed.), *Mathematics education.* 69th Yearbook NSSE. Chicago: University of Chicago Press, 1970. Pp. 367–404.

An extended discussion of the methodology and procedures used in studying the relative effectiveness of differing programs of mathematics. The results from this major effort show no clear superiority for any system and emphasize the large number of individual and content factors that can influence arithmetic performance.

CAMBRIDGE CONFERENCE ON SCHOOL MATHEMATICS. *Goals for the correlation of elementary science and mathematics: The report on the correlation of science and mathematics in the schools.* Boston: Houghton Mifflin, 1969.

One of the more recent efforts to draw meaningful curricular linkages between the sciences and mathematics. A particularly important effort in view of recent tendencies for mathematics programs to sponsor mathematics for its own sake rather than see it in its traditional role as handmaiden for the sciences.

DESSERT, D., & FRANDSEN, H. Research on teaching secondary school mathematics. In R. Travers (Ed.), *Second handbook of research on teaching.* Chicago: Rand McNally, 1973.

A comprehensive review of available research on major topic in mathematics at the secondary level. Among the major topics included are current evidence on the "learning by discovery" controversy, ability grouping in mathematics classes, and computer-assisted mathematics programs.

KLINE, M. *Why Johnny can't add: The failure of the new math.* New York: St. Martin's, 1973.

A stinging indictment of the new math, questioning its goals, methods, and results. A clear antidote for uncritical acceptance of modern mathematics, though Kline's critical points are mostly applicable to the average student, who clearly needs to be able to apply mathematics to practical situations and is therefore less interested in or in need of advanced mathematical concepts.

5

Science for the Gifted

Most of the gifted children of the next generation will either be a part of the scientific community or will have to deal intimately with that community. It is extremely important, therefore, that education present as clear a view of science and its activities as possible to all children in the school program, and particularly to the gifted. Even talented art students should not be without a basic understanding of what science is and, perhaps even more important, what science is not. To accomplish this goal, much in the school program, and in the culture itself, may need to be modified.

Cranshaw had shown considerable interest and enthusiasm over science. Mr. Jenkins was reporting this fact in a conference with Cranshaw's mother and was startled at the negative reaction he obtained. His mother said, in effect, "I didn't raise my son to be a scientist." Her fears and anxieties about what would happen to her son if he became a scientist may very well influence his choice of occupations. Nor is Cranshaw's mother that atypical. There appears to be a deep current of antiscience as well as antiintellectualism identifiable in our culture.

The scientist has gained much prestige through the cornucopia of goods and services stemming from his work. The automobile, television, all manner and kinds of creature comforts, are linked to the scientist. But so are pollution and the energy crisis and, above all, the bomb, which hangs ominously over the heads of humanity. A new wave of students seems more interested in human services than in scientific theories, and thoughtful scientists have begun to wonder where the next wave of gifted scientists will come from.

One of the most dramatic changes in the past decade has been the growing social consciousness of physical scientists. Many of these scientists feel keenly their own role as well as the attendant responsibilities, in introducing the atomic age to mankind. The curriculum materials for science have begun to reflect this concern in a revived interest in the humanities. The Harvard physics program (Project Physics) has as one of its major goals the design of a humanistically oriented physics course (Rutherford, Holton, & Watson, 1970).

One dimension proposed in the Project Physics program is exemplified by the chart in Figure 5–1. Such charts allow the child to see the historical flow of great contributions in various areas in music, art, literature, and links these trends to science. These pictorial interrelationships give the student a chance to integrate knowledge across content fields and historical times. One can see by the chart that Bach is the contemporary of Peter the Great and Isaac Newton and that the electromagnetic discoveries of Maxwell are contemporaneous with the reign of Queen Victoria and the early life of Alfred Tennyson and Louis Pasteur.

Karl Marx had made his contribution by the time that Sigmund Freud had started on his discoveries on psychoanalysis, Monet was painting and Tchaikovsky composing music. The relationship of one major field of endeavor to another has never been an easy one to fix, and charts such as this, which the student himself can prepare, can help him grasp the interrelatedness of societies and various fields of endeavor.

The directors of Harvard Project Physics provide their students with an extended letter that describes the rationale for the study of physics. Mentioned first is the intellectual excitement of discovery and the practical benefits to society, although the authors point out that practical benefits do not come directly from basic science. Second, the study of physics as it relates to other fields and the study of physics as a science can be generalized to serve as a means of solving problems in life itself. This broader view of physics is presented in a quote from Nobel Prize physicist I. I. Rabi (1970, Preface):

> Science should be taught at whatever level, from the lowest to the highest, in the humanistic way. By which I mean it should be taught with a certain historical understanding, with a social understanding and a human understanding, in the sense of the biography, the nature of the people who made this construction, the triumphs, the trials, and the tribulations.

THE CHANGING CURRICULUM

There has been a strong move in the last decade to make major changes in both the *content* and the *process* of presenting science to elementary and secondary students, particularly the talented students. Why?

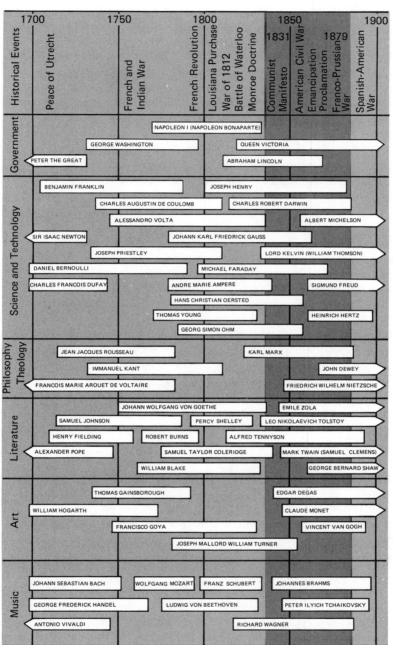

FIGURE 5–1.   *The Flow of History.   (From F. Rutherford, G. Holton, & F. Watson.   The project physics course.   New York: Holt, 1970, Unit 4, p. 109.)*

The inclusion, in previous decades, of large numbers of intellectually average and below-average students in the secondary school, together with a steadfast insistence against homogeneous grouping and the lack of knowledgeable teachers, led to some predictable trends. Among these was a lowering of the level of conceptualization at which the curriculum was presented. This reduced level of complexity was made necessary by the fact that the slow learner would be easily left behind by a curriculum placed at a high conceptual level that demanded a large amount of *prior knowledge* on the part of the student.

In addition, greater emphasis was placed on functional knowledge in the educational program. The practical knowledge of how a car operates or how a bank book is balanced has dual virtues. In the first place, such functional knowledge is of interest and practical value to many students who would not be continuing their education. It also demands little *prior* knowledge on the part of the student, who can learn most of the essentials in the self-contained unit. The teacher can also quickly familiarize himself with the topic without having an extensive background himself. This was an important feature when many science teachers had only minimal education in science in their own training program.

Scientists in the fields of chemistry, physics, and biology rebelled against the patchwork quilt of science textbooks and insisted on curricula that stressed the basic structure of the discipline and the nature of the scientific process.

They joined together in such programs as PSSC (Physical Science Study Committee), CHEM (New Chemistry Project), CBA (Chemical Bond Approach), BSCS (Biological Sciences Curriculum Study), and Project Physics, in a major attempt to rebuild science curricula through projects that stressed the team effort of scientists, educators, teachers, and psychologists and that developed texts, films, experiment kits, and so on.

The rationale for those changes in the new science curricula that are specially designed for talented students has been most concisely put by Bruner (1960, pp. 23–26) as follows:

> At least four general claims . . . can be made for teaching the fundamental structure of a subject. . . .
> The first is that understanding fundamentals makes a subject more comprehensible. This is true not only in physics and mathematics . . . but equally in the social studies and literature. Once one has grasped the fundamental idea that a nation must trade to live, then such a presumably special phenomenon as the Triangular Trade of the American Colonies becomes simpler to understand as something more than commerce in molasses, sugar cane, rum and slaves. . . .
> The second point relates to human memory. Perhaps the most basic

thing that can be said about human memory . . . is that unless detail is placed into a structured pattern, it is rapidly forgotten. . . . A scientist does not try to remember the distances traversed by falling bodies in ·different gravitational fields. . . . What he carries in memory instead is a formula that permits him . . . to regenerate the details on which the more easily remembered formula is based.

Third, an understanding of fundamental principles and ideas appears to be the main road to adequate transfer of training. To understand something as a specific instance of a more general case—which is what understanding a more fundamental principle or structure means—is to have learned not only a specific thing but also a model for understanding other things like it that one may encounter.

The fourth claim for emphasis on structure and principles in teaching is that by constantly reexamining material taught in elementary and secondary schools for its fundamental character, one is able to narrow the gap between advanced knowledge and elementary knowledge.[1]

The Science Style

Karplus (1969, p. 36) has summarized the essence of the new science courses (in a variety of fields from physics and chemistry to the natural sciences) that started at the high school level but have now spread to the elementary level as follows:

> The most valuable features of the new courses are their scientific integrity and an emphasis on science as inquiry, experimentation, evaluation of evidence, and construction of models and theories. Perhaps their greatest weakness is a lack of integration of science with the remainder of the school program, especially mathematics, reading, and writing.

The emphasis on abstract ideas and scientific models exactly fits the needs of gifted students, if not necessarily the needs of students of other ability levels. Karplus (1969, p. 37) summarized the secondary school science experience as follows:

> As might be expected, the gifted, scientifically oriented, high school student has derived the greatest benefit from the courses, because they provided a much more appropriate challenge for him than did traditional courses.

Morrison (1964, p. 6) points out the close relationship between the artist and the scientist. Both deal with symbolic representations of the world, and one of the kinships between the practitioners of art and those of science is direct experience with the world around them.

---

[1] Reprinted from *The process of education* (copyright 1960) by permission of Harvard University Press.

The experience is indispensible to art; in the style we hope to build for science, it is no less essential.   There is an aesthetic of pushing a lever or turning a crank or seeing a yeast cell bud or hearing the Doppler-shifted train whistle or tasting the diluted quinine or smelling the green mold colony or balancing on the swing or waiting for the precipitate to form jet black, which cannot be replaced by words or pictures.   We believe we deeply share this aesthetic with the artist; and we feel it ought to be strongest in the earliest experiences in science.

One of the clearest statements of the new instructional approach to science has been presented by Hawkins (1965).   He places special attention to "messing about," to the free and undirected observations of phenomena by students.   Science teachers, like all teachers, often feel the press of time and the need to cover a certain number of topics before the end of the year.   If teachers yield to that pressure, they will probably not allow their students time for exploration, for the discovery that comes spontaneously when necessary materials are available and events are allowed to happen. The various phases in Hawkins' suggested method of teaching are as follows (pp. 6–7):

Phase I: Exploration (Messing About).   There is a time, much greater in amount than commonly allowed, which should be devoted to free and unguided exploratory work.   Children are given materials and equipment—things—and are allowed to construct, test, probe, and experiment without superimposed questions or instructions.   I call this phase . . . *Messing About.*

Phase II: Elaboration.   If you once let children evolve their own learning along paths of their choosing, you then must see it through and maintain the individuality of their work. . . . there must be on hand what I call "multiply programmed" material that contains written and pictorial guidance of some sort for the student but which is designed for the greatest variety of topics, ordering of topics, etc., so that for almost any given way into a subject that a child may evolve on his own, there is material with a rich variety of choices for teacher and child.

Phase III: Synthesis.   Although different children had specialized differently in the way they work with pendula, there were common elements increasing with time, which would sustain a serious and extended class discussion.   This pattern of discussion . . . includes lecturing, formal or informal. . . .   Here we were approaching a question . . . of theory, going from the concrete perceptual to the abstract perceptual.

Hawkins uses the example of providing children with the material to construct a pendulum and then leaving them alone in the "messing around" stage as they explore the various phenomena that can be created through the random play or experimentation related to pendula.

He also makes the important point that just having this random experience with phenomena is not sufficient.   One must also experience the other two phases, where there is an opportunity for the students to follow through on some of their ideas and suggestions in a way that gives them a greater understanding of the phenomena. In Phase III, gifted students, particularly, will profit as they learn to understand the larger theoretical positions and generalizations that follow from the specific phenomenon that they originally observed.

One of the freeing experiences in working with gifted students is the reasonable assurance that they already understand the basic ideas and facts related to most phenomena normally taught to students of their age level. One is therefore not so tempted to cover every single bit of information or fact related to the phenomenon and the teacher is not under time pressure to cover a prescribed and very specific set of curricula facts to be delivered to the student. The student, freed of the obligation of learning specific facts that he may very well have learned before, can be allowed to explore, try out, and have an intellectual adventure that will stimulate him to pursue those larger ideas and important concepts that the teacher is really eager for him to absorb.

Science Topics

Table 5–1 indicates the classification of biological science topics into the curriculum analysis matrix presented in Chapter 4. Of course, similar topics could be inserted from physics, chemistry, and so on. Although it is common to think of the activities in these science classrooms as focusing almost exclusively on topics related to description and explanation, it does not necessarily have to be that way, and it is quite possible to include topics related to evaluation and expansion. It seems quite probable that those teachers who are described as exciting or interesting by the students periodically salt their lessons with topics such as the expansion topic described as "What would happen if there were no more photosynthesis?"

It is also clear that data topics are easily available in science classrooms because of the emphasis on specific experiments. Under these circumstances, the specific phenomena that are being observed are at the data level. The focus of the curriculum experts of science who address themselves to the education of the gifted point out that data topics can be used as a prelude and as a base for leading to larger ideas—or the larger idea can be presented in advance of that data, and the data can be used as supplementary or elaboration of information related to the basic idea, system, or generalization.

In either respect, and similar to the other areas of curricula, one would expect a major dimension in programs for gifted students to be topics at the generalization level of abstraction, including the dimensions of

TABLE 5-1. *Classification of Biological Topics.*

	DESCRIPTION	EXPLANATION	EVALUATION	EXPANSION
Generalization	The system of photosynthesis.	Show how the system of photosynthesis explains the change in leaves from brown to green.	Does this represent an adequate statement for photosynthesis? $CO_2 + H_2O \rightarrow [CH_2O] + O_2$	What would happen if the system of photosynthesis ceased functioning?
Concept	The definition of a heterotroph.	How do we know that the oxygen from photosynthesis comes from water?	Do you believe that it was essential for autotrophs to develop?	Contrast the autotroph and the heterotroph.
Data	What colors do you see in the spectroscope?	Describe in sequence the experiment by Calvin.	Was *our* experiment a success?	Compare black and white cloths in their ability to absorb light.

evaluation and expansion as well as the more traditional topics dealing with description and explanation. As revealed in the Gallagher analysis of biological topics taught in science classes (Gallagher, 1970), the teacher strategy that appears to be least desirable is a steady diet of concept level information. Instead, the concrete nature of experiments should be used to bring data topics to enrich such abstract concepts as "heterotroph," and the excitement in the synthesis of ideas that occurs in discussing generalizations should be encouraged.

Examples of how basic concepts can be presented to gifted children, and be received with enthusiasm by them, are given in the dialogues that follow. In the first instance, a teacher of biology at a junior high school is presenting the concept that the rate of growth of bacteria follows a mathematically predictable function. The students have just begun experiments of collecting various cultures from different sources, such as from a drinking fountain, freshwater, a table top, and a kiss. Such activities may be characterized as data—expansion in the topic system—a good way to get the students involved in a subject area. The next topic deals with factual information and may be called concept—description, but then the teacher brings the class to an important systems concept, and this topic may be characterized as generalization—explanation.

Mary: It says here—(reads from book) cholera bacterium reproduces at the most rapid rate. In 24 hours you have—I don't even know.

T: Read the numbers—with the—commas and so forth and then let me—(writes on blackboard)

Mary: 700, 000, 000, 000, 000—(laughs)

T: Oh, no!

Mary: 000, 000. Another one.

T: Another like that? Let's stop there. (number is 700,000,000, 000, 000, 000, 000) This would be millions and billions and trillions and quadrillions, and what comes after quadrillions? (name). . . . quintillions, wouldn't it? So those are the kind of numbers you would get from a cholera germ, which multiplies, I think, about every—about one every 20 minutes or a little bit less. And—that would be in how—in how long a time, Mary?

Mary: 24 hours.

T: In 24 hours.

Mary: It'd weigh 3000 tons.

T: It should weigh 3000—that many tons. All right now, the next thing is we want to—find out why this doesn't happen. The world would be embedded with bacteria, wouldn't it, if this happened. So we want to talk a little bit more about the growth and reproduction of bacteria where we were yesterday when the bell rang. We were talking about reproduction. And I want to put onto the board for you a curve. (draws on blackboard)

This is the growth curve—of a bacterial culture. What would this much of the growth curve indicate? Maybe that would rise just a little bit. But in the beginning there is a what?

Kevin: Little activity.

T:[2] There is only a little activity or—and sometimes this is called the *lag period.* There is a lag there until they get started. Then what happens? They increase very, very rapidly and that would be your 24-hour increase. And then the growth curve levels off, doesn't it? Here is the increase. Here it levels off, doesn't increase much and then what begins to happen to those bacteria?

Joe: They start to die.

T: They start to die, don't they and down here we get the—deaths. Now then, why does this happen? Why are these things that can multiply so rapidly—why do they an—in the end are they killed off? Do you have any ideas, Kevin?

Kevin: Well, maybe because they don't have enough food.

T: All, right, one reason is the—the lack of food. Pretty soon they eat up all the food, wouldn't they? Lack of food would be one reason. There's another good reason too. Name another reason they might all be killed off. Roger.

Roger: They're so many of 'em that they need much more warmth and they'll—

T: Well, they—they're pretty warm. All of 'em together and they're all (dependent upon) respiration. That's all right. That was a good try though.

Mark: Well, maybe they use up all of the moisture so—

T: All right. They might have used up the lack of moisture—There's another real good reason. Georgianne.

Georgianne: Well, their waste products—

T:[3] All right. Their waste products. Their metabolic products or their waste products accumulate in such quantity and those waste products prove toxic to them just as our waste products would prove toxic to us. (adds drawing)

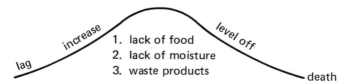

[2] In this instance the teacher is in a hurry to get his point across, so gives the students the explanation of what the curve means. It might be better to elicit from the students the relationships given here so as to be sure they really understand the curve.

[3] Notice that the teacher cuts off each of the students before he is finished. Al-

So here we have this growth curve. We go along and it takes them a little while to get started and then they increase very rapidly, level off, and then they begin to decrease and finally death occurs in this culture. Now, the same things happen with the yeast cell. The yeast cell we have growing in a sugar solution and it thrives very rapidly and seems to be growing fine and producing carbon dioxide and alcohol and energy for its own growth and then it—when it gets up to 14 percent alcohol the yeast cell dies. Because the alcohol is a—one of the—waste products of the yeast cell. Its own waste product kills it.

Notice how the teacher keeps the interest of the children by presenting them with a puzzle or problem. (Why don't the cells keep multiplying indefinitely?) The number of different children responding gives some indication of the interest of the group.

The teacher has also emphasized the *growth process* idea by relating the same properties to yeast as to bacteria, so that the students learn, not only the facts relating to bacterial growth, but also a more abstract concept of the life and death sequence that can have many applications in the future.

One of the key concepts in any branch of science is that of *measurement*. Few laymen realize that the character and limitations of measuring instruments often determine the amount and the direction of the growth of scientific information in a given area. This concept is rarely of concern if science is taught as functional applications or as a body of information to be memorized. It becomes important only when the teacher and students *are attempting to act like scientists*. The following excerpts from a class of sixth graders show the teacher taking the students through: (1) the relationship between rate, distance, and time; (2) the concept of direct measurement, and (3) the concept of indirect measurement.

T: At first I want to begin with you—I want to be sure that you people can work some of these problems that involve figuring out how far it is to a certain place if we know how fast something is moving to a certain place and how long it takes. For example, if I'm riding in a car 30 miles an hour and Kankakee was 60 miles away, how long will it take me to get to Kankakee? Margaret?

Margaret: 2 hours.

T:[4] All right now let's look at the other side of the problem. If I am going to Chicago at 30 miles an hour and it takes me 4 hours to get to Chicago, how

though this speeds up the class discussion, it may also discourage students from having flights of ideas and cause them to stick to relevant facts.

[4] By watching how the class responds to these problems the teacher can quickly discover if they have the basic knowledge of rate, distance, and time to enable the teacher to progress to the next concept, which depends on that knowledge.

131

far away is Chicago? You hold a steady speed and you don't stop for traffic lights. (laughter from class) Jeanne?

Jeanne: 120 miles.

T: 120 miles. (a few words unclear)—if I tell you how long it takes to get there, you can tell me how far it is, if you know the rate of speed. If you know the rate of speed and I tell you how far away it is, you can tell me how long it takes to get there.

How about these figures of 186,000 miles per second and—it takes—this is the speed of light—and we know that the moon is about 240,000 miles away, how long does it take light to get to the moon? I don't mean for you to work it out, just tell me what you would do to find out how long it takes light to get to the moon. Laura?

Laura: Well, you divide the 186,000 into the 240,000.

T: Yes, and this will tell you how long it takes for light to travel from the moon to us.

Having satisfied himself that this group of gifted children have these concepts in hand, the teacher proceeds to the next step, *direct measurement.*

T: How do we measure relatively short distances between two places—I'm going to stop here. If I wanted to measure the distance between me and Charles, what's the easiest way to do it? Wolfgang?

Wolfgang: The yard stick.

T: O.K., you'd use a yard stick. And then somebody figured out how long an inch is, how long a yard is and they put it out on a stick. And we got this information, and we know this is pretty accurate because we took this to Washington, compared it with their metal stick that measures one yard and it turned out to be just about the same as their metal sticks—so we know what one yard is and we can lay this out here and I can find out how far it is between me and Charles. . . . Okay, now we got the problem, of course, that you can't just take this yardstick and start measuring the distance to the moon —not yet anyway.

Note how the teacher brings in the concept of the standard measure in Washington, so as not to give the impression that we would accept *any* marked stick as a good measuring instrument. Now there is the logical development to *indirect measurement.*

T: So here is the problem. You've got to measure the distance to an object we can't get to, can't pace it off, can't use a yardstick, can't use a ruler. And yet there are ways of measuring these distances very, very accurately. Zelda, do you know something about this?

Zelda:[5] Well, wouldn't you first try to estimate it? And then you—you'd

---

[5] Zelda's desire to be recognized and to be a star student sometimes gets her into this kind of trouble when the question demands extrapolative thinking rather than memory work.

first try to estimate it—you'd estimate it if you could and then after you estimate it—Oh, I don't know how you'd do it but you'd have to estimate what
you thought it would be first.

T: Okay, Zelda, now how would you go about making an estimate—say,
how far it is to the moon. What would you want to know about the moon
first?

Zelda: Well, how big its orbit is . . . (trails off—obviously doesn't know.)

T:[6] You can estimate how far away certain objects are from you, for example, I'll hold up this eraser. Now each of you make an estimate of how
far away this eraser is from you. Now, try to think of the method you used
to estimate how far this eraser is. Wolfgang what method did you use?

Wolfgang: Do you want to know the measurement?

T: Did you make an estimate of this?

Wolfgang: Yes.

T: Well, how did you make it?

Wolfgang: Well, I thought about it in feet.

T: Oh—

Wolfgang: I estimated it about 10 feet.

T: 10 feet. Now, how did you get 10 feet? Why didn't you say 50 feet?

Wolfgang: Because 50 feet is a lot farther.

T: What did *you* do, Charles?

Charles: Well I estimated it with a grown person and of about 6 feet size
and it was a little over that, so it was about 7 feet.

T: You kind of mentally laid out a grown person here between you and
this eraser and how many grown persons—put one down on the floor and put
his feet on top the other one's head—(laughter from class) how many people
would you have to put on the floor in order to get to the eraser, okay. This
is one way—I guess a lot of people do it this way, they figure an adult man is
somewhere near 6 feet, and how many men standing on each other's head will
get up to the top of that building. . . . Now, I'm going to ask you to imagine
something else. I imagine that I hold up this eraser in a perfectly dark room,
the eraser is lit, let's say it's a flashlight, not a flashlight—let's say that it's
something that shines so that it has the size of the eraser. But the room is
perfectly dark. Can you imagine this so that you can't mentally lay out people on the floor to gauge the distance of that object? You don't see a thing
in the room except that object. Ricky?

Ricky: You could see how bright the light or how dim it was.

T: How bright or how dim, is there any other thing that would give you a
clue? Doug?

Doug: How large it was.

T: How large. I think these are all the clues you could get. How bright
it is and how large it is. And then you try to compare it to bright and large

---

[6] Note the use of concrete examples within this classroom to illustrate this concept
before taking it to the level of the stars.

things you may have seen. . . . Now this gets very difficult as we get out into space because if we try to see how large the moon is we can do this, we can take a coin or a small object and hold it at arms length and see what size object we need to completely hide the moon behind the object. Take a guess and what do you think I'd need? Ricky?

Ricky: A 50-cent piece?

T: How many think a 50-cent piece would hide the moon? Well whatever size the object turns out to be you'll find that exactly the same size object blocks out the sun. . . . You are starting at a point where you know the sun is very much farther away than the moon, yet they both appear to be about the same size. Brightness isn't much of a clue because the sun is very much brighter than the moon and you were probably thinking of bright things being closer. Now the way—in order to understand something of the way that you measure these distances it's necessary for us to know something about triangles. What's a triangle? John?

John: It is an object that has three sides connected at three corners. Straight lines.

Notice that the teacher patiently lets the students wander down false trails, much as they would in actual problem solving, before leading them in the fruitful direction. In terms of topics, the teacher goes from the data—explanation of the specific train problem to the generalization—expansion of finding a new form of indirect measurement.

Next the teacher develops the concept of angle, how it is measured, and how we can find all the necessary facts about the triangle. Once these are established, they are now ready to talk about measurements of distance in space. The experienced teacher can realize what would happen here in an intellectually heterogeneous group. The teacher would soon have to slow his pace drastically in order to teach patiently each concept in turn, thus irritating the bright students caught up in the excitement of ideas; or he might decide to cast adrift the slow learners and teach only the stars in the class. Neither choice is a very happy one.

SCIENCE TEACHERS AND THE GIFTED

One of the most revitalizing effects of the science curricular efforts in the 1960s was the attention paid to teacher training and retraining. Such attention was very necessary since changes in both the science content and the process by which it was taught were involved. Intensive summer workshops and inservice training programs were conducted so that the teachers could grasp the reorganization of the content and understand new scientific concepts in greater depth.

Even more dramatic than the change in content was the insistence on a change in the manner that material was to be presented. If one of the major objectives of the program was to help students to act like scientists and experience the joy and excitement of science, teachers had to be wooed away from didactic lectures and canned experiments and into more adventuresome and less predictable teaching procedures.

Joe was not impressed by the science "experiments" in his traditional textbook that he was supposed to carry out. "If you want to know what happens in that experiment, it is right in the back of the book," he advised his more naïve classmates. "Mr. Jenkins wouldn't do anything unless he knew it would come out right!" Joe's cynicism is unfortunate but not inaccurate. Many teachers of science choose only tried-and-true experiments for demonstration and create a predictable boredom, in addition to an image of non-risk-taking that is an unfortunate model to follow.

Student Participation

The attitude about student participation that the new-curriculum personnel wished to instill in teachers is summed up in the following ancient Chinese proverb (*Introduction to the elementary science study*, 1966, p. 2):

> *I hear . . . and I forget.*
> *I see . . . and I remember.*
> *I do . . . and I understand.*

But wanting to introduce such a style is one thing and doing it is often something else. One of the concerns of curriculum and project directors is that on any large project, such as Project Physics or Project CHEM, it is difficult, if not impossible, to ascertain whether the program that the curriculum innovators have suggested *should* go on in the classroom actually *does* go on in the classroom. Whether the basic innovative concept is built around "open education," the "new math," or one of the chemistry or biology programs, the hidden issue is often: Are the concepts and skills being validly presented in the program? After all, there are over 2,000,000 elementary and secondary school teachers and it is asking a lot for all of them to adopt new concepts *and* new teaching procedures.

For example, the Biological Sciences Curriculum Study (BSCS) has as one of its basic objectives the mastery of certain concepts in the curriculum field; it also subscribes to the basic notion of helping the student understand the role of the scientist. When student output is used as an evaluation index, it is often very difficult to interpret or compare one class with another with regard to these issues because of the many differences among classes, in teacher preparation, in student ability, in the content covered, and sometimes even in the subject area.

Gallagher (1967) conducted a rather unique comparison of classrooms in which most of these variables were controlled and examined the extent to which broad science curriculum objectives were being executed in the regular program. To do this, he chose six biology teachers and their classes of high-ability students, all of whom were studying the BSCS, Blue Version, *Molecules to Man*. All these teachers were instructing classes of talented students in suburban communities outside a metropolitan area, and all the teachers had recieved training in the BSCS concepts and how to present the program.

The purpose of the study was to tape-record three consecutive class sessions during the introduction of the concept of *photosynthesis*. Each of the classes had in common (1) a teacher trained in BSCS program and activities, (2) a class of high-aptitude students, (3) the use of the same general curriculum program, and (4) the identical concept to be taught.

The three consecutive days of classroom sessions were then analyzed by means of the Gallagher et al. topic classification system (1966), which broke the topics covered in the classroom into the model already familiar to the reader of description, explanation, evaluation, and expansion, plus the three levels of conceptualization—data, concept, and generalization. A third dimension was also considered that was most important to BSCS objectives. This was the distinction between topics focusing on skills versus content. The skills topics were those in which the basic thrust of the topic was to increase the students' abilities to carry out some kind of investigation or discussion of the scientific method, procedures by which data are obtained or analyzed, and the like. Content topics refer to those where knowledge and ideas are being discussed.

In the analysis, major differences were found from one classroom to another in terms of the content-skills dimensions and the level of conceptualization. For example, in one classroom, 30 percent of the total topics in the three days of analysis were taken up with skills, but in two classrooms, skills were mentioned in no topic at all. In terms of the level of conceptualization, in which we stress the importance of generalization for high-aptitude students, one classroom had as high as 16 percent of the topics in that area (a very high percentage), but two other classrooms had only 2 percent of the total three days at that high level of conceptualization and would seem not to be stressing that level of thinking.

As might be expected, the vast majority of the topics in this science classroom focused on description and explanation, with only a few adventures into the field of expansion and evaluation topics.

A further analysis of the specific topics that were covered during the three days reveals major differences between the styles of the various instructors. In one classroom, ten topics focused on the nature of life, whereas in two others no topics at all touched on that area. In one classroom, the teacher referred to no topic in any other chapters or to any other materials in other chapters in the book. In another classroom twenty-eight of the topics in the three days were focused on different topics related to other parts of the textbook.

Thus, despite the fact that the teachers were all teaching the same concept, to students of the same level of ability, from the same curriculum program, substantial differences were found in the amount of teacher talk, in the topics related to goals, and in the levels of abstraction. Gallagher concluded that "each teacher filters the curriculum materials through his own perceptions and to say that a student has been through the BSCS curriculum probably does not give as much specific information on his classroom experience as the curriculum innovators might have hoped" (p. 17).

Such results are not a plea for the uniformity or mechanical application of curriculum materials. It is often the excitement and uniqueness of interest in the individual teacher that stirs the student and commits him to seek similar adventures. But Gallagher went on to point out that some of the objectives, such as student participation and exploration, were clearly not visible in the recordings taken in the period of time in which the classes were observed, so that some of the essentials of the curriculum were not being implemented.

Teachers clearly influence the style of student thinking through the types of questions they themselves ask. If they wish to stimulate Expansion topics, such as shown in Table 5–1, they will ask questions like

How would our world be different at conditions of Martian gravity instead of Earth gravity?
What useful substitutions could be found if we ran out of copper?

If teachers wish to stimulate Evaluative Thinking topics, then they might use questions such as

Compare which metal would be better for space rocket shielding—zinc, iron, or neither?
Identify the best strategy for seeking an answer to questions about the proposed existence of extra sensory perception.

It is equally obvious that the teacher is not likely to be able to systematically do this without specific instruction. If benefits are to be obtained by teaching students certain styles of inquiry, then we must design such experiences as deliberately as we design the cognitive mastery of *photosynthesis*. (Chapters 8 and 9 will detail such methods further.)

An example of the almost unlimited curriculum choices available to the teacher in the realm of science is given by Smith (1966) and shown in Figure 5–2. In this example, Smith shows that by starting with the concept "tomato," one can move either horizontally to various fruit and vegetable concepts or vertically to major conceptual ladders, such as the

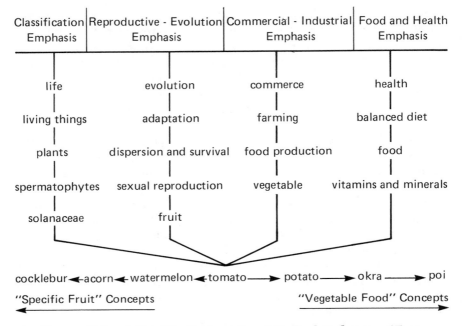

Classification Emphasis	Reproductive - Evolution Emphasis	Commercial - Industrial Emphasis	Food and Health Emphasis
life	evolution	commerce	health
living things	adaptation	farming	balanced diet
plants	dispersion and survival	food production	food
spermatophytes	sexual reproduction	vegetable	vitamins and minerals
solanaceae	fruit		

cocklebur ◄— acorn ◄— watermelon ◄— tomato ——► potato ——► okra ——► poi

"Specific Fruit" Concepts ◄———   "Vegetable Food" Concepts ———►

FIGURE 5–2. *A Possible Horizontal and Vertical Ordering. (From H. A. Smith. The teaching of a concept. Washington, D.C.: National Science Teachers Association, 1966, p. 9. Reprinted by permission.)*

reproductive–evolution dimension or the commercial–industrial emphasis, or food and health, and so on.

Naturally, there are major restraints on the teacher, not the least of these being (1) available time, (2) the knowledge base of the student, and (3) the knowledge base of the teacher. A teacher who knew that his students were only vaguely aware of such notions as solonacae or spermatophytes would think seriously about embarking on such a direction if the time available were not seen as sufficient or if the teacher were fuzzy on these concepts himself.

It is in the nature of gifted students that they have mastered, at some level, many of these concepts already and are ready individually, or as a group, to move higher up the abstractional ladder.

Therein lies the rub for the science teacher, for all teachers, of the gifted student. They must resign themselves to continue to be learners, to be perpetual students, because the gifted student will be forever pushing at the frontiers of the teacher's own understanding. If such pushing is invigorating to the teacher, working with gifted students will be a joy; if it is a frustration and continual source of embarrassment, that teacher would be well advised to seek some other group of students to work with.

Part of the desire of science educators is not just to have students learn the techniques of science but also to pick up some of the fire of inquiry and passion for the truth manifested by great scientists. Reading assignments in the biographies of scientists can provide a model, as illustrated by the following quotation (Dubos, 1960, pp. 20–21).

> Admission to the École Normale Supérieure was by competitive examination, and in 1842, Pasteur was declared admissible, sixteenth in rank. For anyone else this would have been a very satisfactory result, but not for him. In a gesture which is probably unique, or in any case extremely rare, he refused admission to the school and took up his studies again to prepare himself better. He competed again in 1843, was fifth in rank, and this time entered the school. The urge for perfection revealed by this detail was to remain one of the dominant traits of his scientific career.

One of the basic intuitive understandings one expects gifted students to obtain from the study of science is that the world is an orderly place and that things behave the way they do because of laws and principles, if we are only wise enough to understand them. As Morrison (1964) put it, students should learn that experiments always "work." Experiments may not turn out the way you expect but they are always following lawful principles. Some of the most exciting discoveries in science have occurred by following up on puzzling or unexpected results from experiments. Alexander Fleming's discovery of penicillin derived from some odd behavior of molds that required a new conceptualization.

Hans Selye's discoveries of the effect of stress on human beings (Selye, 1956) derived from a series of experiments that did not turn out as they were supposed to. Briefly, he found that inexperienced investigators kept getting one set of results from a series of experiments, whereas experienced and well-respected investigators got quite different results.

Selye, puzzling over this odd finding, discovered that the inexperienced investigators were using procedures that allowed impurities to get into the chemicals being tested. The experienced and more careful investigators did not allow this to happen. Therefore, it was not the substance itself that was causing the reaction, but the impurities! So the experiments did "work," and Selye started on a highly productive line of thought on the reaction of the body to invasion by outside irritants. Students need to have some experience at explaining the experiments that "didn't work" and to realize that it is the puzzling results that often stimulate new ideas and discoveries.

The great emphasis that was placed upon having the student learn science by acting like a scientist has brought the rather predictable counterreaction. One of the leading forces in that counterreaction is Atkin (1968), who points out that it's not just in the process of science that children need to be educated but in the conceptual frames of reference that represent new ways of looking at the universe. Atkin suggests that "the best way to teach process skills is not by aiming for them directly, but rather to use the processes of science while seeking to build general principles of science contact" (p. 14). In other words, not to study the tool, or the scientific method as an entity, but rather to study how to use the tool in the specific problem areas.

He states further (p. 13):

> Scientists don't usually study how to hypothesize or interpret data or make operational definitions in some abstract fashion preparatory to conducting research. I submit that children don't either. Children might well learn a few of the things scientists do, but their goal is not some specialized understanding of scientific process; their goal is understanding how the universe works. This latter goal is much more powerful motivationally for children than contrived exercises to improve their skill at observation or their ability to classify objects.

What we have then is a plea for the marriage of process and content in a more sophisticated science curriculum for gifted students.

ALTERNATIVE MODELS AND PERSONNEL

Not all reform need be tied into trying to modify traditional school programs by increasing the skill of the teacher. Other alternatives are available in different forms of delivering science education or in the use of different types of personnel.

One of the most organized and imaginative developments in strengthening science education has taken place in Japan, as noted by Glass (1966). He describes the establishment of science education centers that have as their central purpose the retraining of science teachers on a formal and mandatory basis. Teachers are released from classes for short courses a week long, or in some cases for longer courses lasting a full semester. The cost is shared by the school system and the Ministry of Education.

Each science education center has a permanent staff consisting of scientists and skilled teachers in physics, chemistry, biology, and earth sciences, who plan the courses and teach them in laboratories that resemble those with which the teachers are familiar in their own schools. And the emphasis in every course is on the acquisition of special skills and methods of science teaching, new and old, and upon the updating of the teacher's knowledge of the subject matter.

The development of such teaching centers would seem to be an extraordinarily important aspect of a total program for educating gifted students, particularly at the secondary school level. There is little doubt that teachers of gifted children need rather strong and consistent updating in their knowledge, or they will find themselves faced with students who know more about the subject matter than they do. Also, to experience the new methods by which the students can explore the area for themselves and to experience the excitement of learning that science is not a body of knowledge but a method of obtaining new knowledge is a highly desirable development and one that has been inadequately used in our current school systems.

One of the most innovative of recent methods of teaching, and one with great promise for the gifted student, is the utilization of high school students to teach elementary school science. This program, *Learning by Teaching*, initiated by Jerrold Zacharias (1966), capitalizes on a fundamental proposition that all teachers know very well. When one teaches a subject to someone else, the teacher often learns more than the person being taught.

For the gifted student, the opportunity to teach other younger children is an invaluable experience if he is carefully supervised and allowed to bring his experiences back for discussion with an experienced teacher. Some of the comments on this method of teaching Physical Science Study Committee curricula gives some of the flavor of the experience. Two comments by teachers were:

> Because of the natural enthusiasm and vitality of the high school students, this material was alive and fascinating to the elementary students.
>
> Our high school students gained in two ways; one, they reviewed a great deal about circuitry, and two, they had an exposure to teaching, which could lead to their consideration of a teaching career.

The high school students themselves were quoted as follows:

> As for my personal reactions toward the experiment, I can honestly say that it was one of the highlights of my high school studies. Beside the considerable amount of basic knowledge I acquired, I also achieved a completely changed outlook on teaching and the educational process. Never before this experiment had I realized the great amount of planning and psychology that a teacher must have to teach a class, especially one this young; not to mention the amount of patience needed.
>
> Teaching really tests the teacher's understanding of a topic. I found myself looking up in a chemistry book to see exactly how a flashlight battery works and was suprised to see all the misconceptions I had.

ACCELERATION OF THE CURRICULUM AND THE STUDENT

Perhaps the most significant change over the last decade and a half in the field of science education lies in the greater tendency to bring more and

141

more complex ideas and concepts to the elementary and primary levels of schooling. This movement, of course, coincides nicely with the needs of gifted students at those age levels.

Previously it had been thought that preadolescent children cannot think at the abstract and logical level necessary to the generation of high-level scientific ideas and principles, and that one therefore has to delay science instruction until the cognitive stage of what Piaget refers to as "logical operations." However, the new philosophy is that children of a young age can do many other kinds of thinking that are quite appropriate to establishing the scientific approach to problems. For example, they can become aware of the world around them or of distinctions between living and nonliving things. They can be taught the importance of measurement to scientific observation.

As Ennever and Harlen (1971) have pointed out, even a simple walk in the woods for 7, 8, or 9-year-old children can be translated into science education objectives. In collecting different pieces from varying trees, one can achieve the objectives shown in Table 5–2.

TABLE 5–2.   *Educational Objectives of a Walk in the Woods.*

INSTRUCTIONAL OBJECTIVE	STUDENT ACTION
1. Willingness to collect materials for observation.	1. Collecting samples of materials.
2. Appreciation of the need for measurement.	2. Comparing heights of trees.
3. Development of a concept of environment.	3. Considering differences between dense and open parts of the wood.
4. Awareness of change in living and nonliving materials.	4. Comparing the old fallen trees and rotting wood with the younger trees and wood.

Source: Adapted from L. Ennever & W. Harlen. *With objectives in mind.* Bristol, England: School Council Publications, School of Education, University of Bristol, 1971, pp. 37–42.

Thus, some of the activities that are carried on in everyday primary school can be adapted to the objectives of science if the teacher has these objectives carefully in mind and is able to direct the students' attention to the necessary observations. In a heterogeneous class, in which all levels of intellectual ability are present, the teacher can still give assignments to the gifted and advanced students that would stress the more advanced objectives for them, while saving simpler objectives for the less advanced students. However, elementary science programs need to be based on valid and important ideas just as the secondary programs do. Atkin and Wyatt (1962) pointed out that in astronomy instructions:

1. A child is given virtually no understanding of how scientists have arrived at the factual material presented in the children's books.
2. The child is given virtually no comprehension of the structure of our own galaxy of stars or of the physical universe and its component galaxies.

Most school children, and adults too, can remember interesting but highly inconsequential astronomical facts. The sun is approximately 93,000,000 miles from the earth; Mars has two moons; Saturn's rings are really a group of asteroids. Very little attention is ever given to *how* we were able to discover all these facts without leaving mother Earth, something to be emphasized with gifted children. Unless our curricular efforts lead to generalizations as well as interesting data, we overwhelm the student with specific information but give them little chance to generate ideas concerning the system as a whole.

EARLY ACCELERATION.   It has long been known that early precocity characterized the life histories of famous scientists. For example, John Stuart Mill, Blaise Pascal, Jeremy Bentham, and Karl Gauss, all showed outstanding early development, as reported by Cox (1926) in her classic study *The Early Mental Traits of Three Hundred Geniuses*. Although the conventional wisdom has been that school acceleration should be limited to a carefully planned one or two years, there are recent outstanding exceptions that should cause careful thought on the matter.

Norbert Wiener, the originator of cybernetics, completed high school at 11 and obtained his Ph.D. in mathematical logic from Harvard University at age 18. Michael Grost entered Michigan State University at age 10 and obtained a Master's degree in mathematics at age 17. John Bardeen, a two-time Nobel Prize winner, was advanced from the third to the seventh grade.

Keating and Stanley (1972) have reported on two outstanding science students who have been accepted by Johns Hopkins University in a special program. The first student, Dave, was accepted by the university directly from the seventh grade, with outstanding academic credentials and with the support of understanding parents. He has been performing at a superior level in college and looks forward to advanced study at the tender age of 17.

A second student, Bill, bored with junior high school requirements, was also admitted to the university. His own adjustment to his peer group was poor—he was quite unpopular and miserable. When admitted to the University, Bill really improved his adjustment. At Johns Hopkins no one thought that his long hair was funny or his intellectual interests peculiar. He has done honor work consistently and will receive his B.S. at age 17.

What do such studies mean? Certainly not that all high-aptitude students can or should be jumped from junior high school to university work.   But it does mean that we should consider carefully individual students with enormous precocity who just might profit by cutting four years off of an interminable educational ladder.   In science and mathematics, where early precocity is more easily noticed, we can stay alert for the Daves and Bills, who may be the Bardeens and Gausses of the next generation.

SUMMARY

In the view of many gifted scientists, the subject area of science is often distorted in its presentation to young minds.   In particular, stress is often placed on the products of science—jet planes, color television, new architectural models, and the like.   These scientists feel that it is important for gifted students to understand that the true nature of science is that it is a means or strategy for searching for the truth.   It is the careful procedures by which the truth is sought that are the essence of science.

The curriculum suggestions presented in this chapter are more those of the scientists themselves than of teachers of science in schools.   Consistent with that is the emphasis on active student participation in scientific experiments, plus attempts to provide the highest level of complexity and understanding that the student can master.

As in the chapter on mathematics, the objectives of science teaching would be different for gifted and slow-learning students.   With the slow-learning student, direct application of science is probably a more useful educational objective, but to the student going on to higher and graduate education, the firmest foundation that can be laid in understanding the true nature of science and of technology is more important, even if the gifted student never enters a scientific occupation.   As C. P. Snow (1960) points out, science has had a great impact on the world's culture in the past half century, and it is important that people holding key community or leadership positions understand the nature of science and its powerful impact on all our lives.

The final message from the scientists themselves is a much greater concern about the impact of scientific ideas on our culture and our values that was hardly noticeable only a decade ago.   No longer is any new scientific discovery automatically considered good or beneficial.   New knowledge is not automatically considered a good thing.   The atomic age has resulted in many second thoughts, and gifted science students as well as gifted scientists will have to grapple with many questions of ethics and values, as well as simple mastery of systems of biology, physiology, and chemistry.

The scientists themselves are apparently having sleepless nights as they try to determine the positive or negative impact of new scientific directions on a society that has been increasingly skeptical about science itself. These are arguments and discussions that the gifted student must hear in organized fashion in the classroom and not simply in the dormitory or on the street corner; concern for the ethical question is one of the important changes in the various science curricula.

UNRESOLVED ISSUES

1. We need better answers to such questions as whether the gifted student should learn important concepts in a fashion similar to the scientist, or whether he should be taught the necessary knowledge and scientific skills as a ready-made package. Much time is involved in allowing the student to learn inductively. Whether this type of learning is important to a proper attitude toward scientific inquiry, or even toward the mastery of the ideas themselves, remains an open issue.

2. The teaching of science has, at its advanced levels, been traditionally a master–apprentice relationship. This is hardly useful for those who are learning about the sciences from the standpoint of the consumer. Many gifted students entering such fields as politics, economics, and business need to know about the physical sciences and need to have a curriculum designed for that level of understanding.

3. Can we generate a more effective integration of current science topics, so that subject areas such as biology, chemistry, physics, and physiology become more properly blended? Their current isolated status puzzles and confuses the talented student who sees the glimmer of interrelationships but is unable, without help, to make the essential linkages among these scientific disciplines.

READINGS OF SPECIAL INTEREST

GALLAGHER, J. J. Three studies of the classroom. In J. J. Gallagher, G. Nuthall, & B. Rosenshine, *Classroom observation.* AERA Monograph Series No. 6. Chicago: Rand McNally, 1970. Pp. 74–108.
A report of a unique study comparing six BSCS biology classes of gifted students. All classes were tape recorded while teaching the same concept (photosynthesis) from the same BSCS curriculum. However, many differences were found related to individual teacher patterns.

KLOPFER, L. Evaluation of learning in science. In B. Bloom, J. Hastings, & G. Madaus (Eds.), *Handbook on formative and summative evaluation of student learning.* New York: McGraw-Hill, 1971. Pp. 559–642.
An interesting breakdown of the processes of scientific inquiry is presented.

Attention is paid to the affective and attitudinal domain. Enables the teacher to analyze both student and teacher performance and to assess science-teaching objectives.

POSTELTHWAIT, S., NOVAK, J., & MURRAY, H. *The audio-tutorial approach to learning: Through independent study and integrated experiences.* Minneapolis: Burgess, 1969.

A specially designed program of independent study in botany that allows the student to proceed independently at his own rate by using audiotape in specially arranged carrels. Research suggests that students using this approach can master concepts in much less time.

SHULMAN, L., & TAMIR, F. Research on teaching in the natural sciences. In R. Travers (Ed.), *Second handbook of research in teaching.* Chicago: Rand McNally, 1973.

A comprehensive review of the last decade of science education. Covers concepts such as the structure controversy, the discovery issue, programmed instruction, curriculum evaluation, etc. An excellent summary for teachers.

6

Social Studies for the Gifted

Zelda's parents have always been quite pleased with her work in social studies. She invariably comes home with high grades, and sometimes the parents are prompted to put her on exhibition because of the vast extent of her knowledge. Since her class is currently studying the South American continent, Zelda has an impressive array of facts regarding the imports and exports of each South American country and their major population centers, and can reproduce from memory adequate maps of the topography of the various countries.

But what does Zelda know about the people of other cultures, their behavior, and how they interact with one another? Very little—and there is no reason why she should. Such topics are not discussed, and sometimes they are systematically avoided in her classrooms. The notion that people act toward one another out of their fears, their hopes, their prejudices, and that many of our social interactions today are based on such crass individual and group motivations will remain a mystery to Zelda and to bright and average children alike, until the social studies curricula focus attention on those dimensions, as well as on the geographical dimensions, of social studies. As Harvey (1965) puts it, "The high school graduate who has been taught to expect regularities in the affairs of the physical universe will never have heard of the search for regularities in the affairs of men." Few children, no matter how gifted or talented, will be able to stumble upon basic generalizations of human behavior without specific guidance or instruction.

Many educators of gifted children view social studies as a curriculum area of great potential but also of some threat. Gifted children, with their penchant for exploring beyond facts and seeking explanations and value judgments, are liable to be both a joy and embarrassment to their mentors. Social studies, dealing as it does with the real world, may result in the gifted student's drawing some conclusions that the adult

world is not all that it seems.   When Zelda reads the Bill of Rights, she
may not stop at memorizing but begin to relate the concept of freedom
of the press to events in her own town and possibly create an awkward
situation for the teacher by asking for an explanation as to why we are
not living up to the Constitution.   Such a situation is unpleasant.   We
do not like to have pointed out to us that we adults are not living models
of virtue.

We have ways of protecting ourselves from such embarrassments.
One way is to avoid such discussions at all costs, by keeping our talented
students busy learning lots of nonembarrassing facts.   Another way is to
try to impress on them our version of the truth.   Neither of these subter-
fuges works entirely.   Unhappily, they work well enough so that those
of us who would succumb to the temptation of avoiding controversy
have some recognizable strategies.

HOW TO MAKE SOCIAL STUDIES BORING

One would think that the complex interrelationships present in social
studies, to say nothing of the presence of live and exciting persons of the
past and present, would serve to make this an area of inherent interest
to gifted students.   All too often, though, these very students find the
subject dull, stale, flat, and unprofitable.   How can one change such a
fascinating topic to a dull unit?   Two standard ways still too much
in evidence deserve some comment here.

The Holiday Curriculum

One method is to keep the discussions and assignments at a low conceptual level, with social studies being intertwined with drama, historical
stories of fact or fiction, recreation, and art, to such an extent that any
larger concepts of importance are forever lost.   One extreme example has
been referred to, satirically, as the "Holiday Curriculum."   This is in
honor of elementary school teachers who, after they get their classes
settled in the fall, head straight for Halloween with units on autumn,
seasons of the year, and perhaps little plays complete with witches,
pumpkins, and hobgoblins.   One need not have too much imagination
to picture the artwork during this period.

After Halloween, the teacher can swing full force into Thanksgiving,
with a unit on the Pilgrims, the Mayflower, the early Indians, and the
life of the early settlers.   This unit, too, often culminates with a play
celebrating the fine relationships between the new settlers and natives.

Why all those friendly feelings later deteriorated into hostility is rarely mentioned.

Once the turkeys and the tall black hats are put away, there can be only one goal—Christmas. Then the classroom can be filled with gay greens and reds and, if the teacher has a dramatic flair, there can be another dramatic production, involving the wise men, a stable, and assorted shepherds and angels.

After Christmas, there is that glorious triumvirate in February: St. Valentine's Day, and the birthdays of Lincoln and Washington. From these, one can set sail for Easter and Spring and, before one knows it, another year is gone.

The Grand Tour

Another problem faced by teachers of social studies at the intermediate grade level is the emphasis on physical geography in many textbooks. Although knowledge of physical terrain, crops, or the location of major cities is interesting, there is little that is "social" about such social studies.

Instead, such lessons or textbooks seem almost more related to a guided tour than to illuminating the complex forces operating on human beings. Just as the tourist must "do" the Continent in three weeks, so often the students leapfrog from the British Isles (four days), to France (three days), to the Benelux countries (one day), and so on, with little deeper understanding of the *common* economic, social, and political problems facing each country.

Units focusing on the grand tour are often rich in information regarding different lands and peoples, but do they really provide a conceptual structure for social studies? Until they start relating the conditions or happenings of one country to another, one people to another, one era to another, the generalizations that gifted children should be discovering will be inevitably lost in a swamp of details.

In a world tearing itself apart through the inability of one man to communicate with another, where many leaders of our society often are economic and psychological illiterates, it is a gross disservice to the growing generation not to give some better portrait of man and his problems to those who will be keystones of the next generation.

It might be mentioned in passing that the same advantages and disadvantages accrue to The Holiday Curriculum and The Grand Tour as they do to similar units in science and arithmetic. Such programs require little in the way of past foundations of knowledge on the part of the teacher. Each new country or new season can be started from scratch; if the child has missed the pertinent facts about Italy—well, he

151

has just missed a part of the tour and can join it again in France at a later date. This type of approach can be used in an intellectually heterogeneous class, since the dull child will not be embarrassed by his lack of foundation knowledge and the gifted child can spend his time on more and more detailed information on each stop. A teacher without background could also act as a "guide" on such a tour with a minimum of brushing up.

What is to be done? It is easy enough to tell the teacher that the curriculum needs to be explored in depth or at a higher level of conceptualization. The teacher has been told that many times before. What the teacher wants to know, and needs to know, before planning for gifted children effectively, is how he can do this and what "depth" actually means in regard to a given problem or topic.

In the not-too-distant past, social studies required little sustained effort or scholarship to grasp what little needed to be absorbed. It has been said that if a parrot were taught to say "supply and demand" to any question, he would be two thirds of the way to being an economist. If a student could learn that an unhappy adulthood was often spawned by an unhappy childhood, that frustration breeds aggression, and that sex seems to be involved in more aspects of our life than previously thought, then he had enough psychology to get by.

This era of superficiality has passed so rapidly that many persons still have not grasped the fact of its passing. Today the maturing sciences of economics, psychology, and sociology deal more with the handmaiden of science—mathematics—than with the crystal ball. Even the fields of anthropology and history require much more extensive scholarship and technical training in advanced methodologies. So the search for basic concepts in this field is not the forlorn one that the pessimist might depict.

INSTRUCTIONAL PRINCIPLES

In a previous chapter we listed some of the major principles for instructing the gifted as follows:

1. Teach to the highest cognitive level possible.
2. Teach gifted children to utilize all their thinking processes.
3. Teach important ideas about all aspects of their life and times.
4. Teach methods by which the gifted children can discover knowledge for themselves.

Table 6–1 shows these principles put into action in social studies. In looking at the cognitive levels of data, concept, and generalization, one

TABLE 6–1. *Social Studies Level and Type of Thinking.*

	DESCRIPTION	EXPLANATION	EVALUATION	EXPANSION
Generalization	In all colonial relations, the mother country exploits the resources of the colony.	Produce and justify a generalization on colonization.	Did the colonists have a better system of justice than we have now?	Predict our trade relationships with our Martian colonies.
Concept	The American Colonies' trading policies with the mother country.	Showing the sequence of events by which the goods were exchanged.	Which of the mother countries had the most lenient policies toward their colonies? Why?	Comparing trade policies of colonial days and today.
Data	A detailed description of the Pilgrims' journey.	Explaining why the Pilgrims felt they had to leave England.	Were the Pilgrims justified in leaving England? Why?	Suppose the Pilgrims had landed in Virginia; what might have happened?

can see how it is possible that an entire discussion of social studies or history can remain at a very low level of conceptualization. By following a narrative or story approach to history, one can fill a curriculum with specific data and never get to the level of generalization that is within the grasp of gifted students as early as the fifth- or sixth-grade level.

One can give a detailed description about the Pilgrims and what happened to them, or one can talk about those facets which are general to all *colonization*. It is the teacher who is the key to the level of complexity and thought considered in the classroom. The research by Gallagher et al. (1967) revealed clearly that children rarely deviate from either the level or type of thinking process that the teacher requests.

Following is a brief dialogue from a social studies classroom at the junior high level in which the teacher has presented the problem of what kinds of generalizations one can make about colonies, and, starting from the traditional discussion of the American colonies, has broadened it to help them think at the higher or generalization level on the general topic of *colony*, as illustrated by the table.

Teacher: If you were to describe to someone what a colony was or what this term "colonialism" means, going back to our first day's discussion, what would you say about the time element?   Mark?

Mark: Countries, that is, were beginning to desire to have land in this area, now that it had been explored, and they knew what it was like.   There was no certain time limit as the colonization period in (Africa?) started as soon as it was partially explored.   The same in North America.   The same in South America.

Cranshaw: Well—I think what you meant was that—to define a colony—a colony does not have to exist in any certain year or period of years to be a colony.   But—it seems to me that—colonies come in sort of waves. The Roman col-colonization, and now it's Europe—they colonized lots of these countries. And now the Soviet Union—it's a different type of colonization.   They're satellites, but it's definitely a type, because they control them.

Teacher: I think this is a very interesting notion.   This is sort of the Cranshaw Wave Theory of Colonization.   This is worth investigating further, Cranshaw.   And—see if you can pin down some—pin your theory down a little bit.

Leland:[1] Well, I think that the place is—I think—I don't think that the place in *itself* is important, but I think indirectly it's important.   It seems to me that the—places that the—colonies that have the—the best natural resources and have the climate, the closest to what it was in the mother country where the colonists came from, I think *these* were the ones where the colonists achieved independence the soonest.   Because the United States was one of the first colonies in the hemisphere to get its independence and we have tremendous

[1] This student has already shown advanced conceptualization of *colony* in being able to divorce it from a specific time and place.

natural resources. And gradually now the colonies that *don't* have such good natural resources are getting their independence. And I think natural resources definitely help, because if they don't have natural resources, they have to depend on the mother countries, so they *can't* really revolt and be successful.

Curtis: I'll tell you another thing that is important in colonization would be important natural habitats, but—like maybe if there was a lot of jungle animals or maybe a lot of dangerous malaria or mosquitoes and things like that, it wouldn't be ideal for a colony no matter what kind of geographical structure.

In addition to seeking a high level of generalization, the teacher would be interested in helping the gifted generate a wide variety of thinking processes. As stated in the earlier chapters, it is fairly common in all classrooms to include the operations of description and explanation but much rarer to find extensive use of the operations of evaluation or expansion (divergent thinking). The gifted need practice and guidance in making judgments on the relative importance, usefulness, and correctness of an event, as in evaluation. Sometimes the evaluation takes the form of judging whether a particular idea fits a set of criteria. In the case of this particular class the issue would be whether, once having reached a generalization, it can be tested or matched by comparing a specific instance matched against the generalization with a judgment made as to goodness of fit. The following is a brief dialogue along those particular lines.

Teacher: Now, we agreed that today we ought to take up this business of the economic forces affecting a colonial area. Now, I ran into this statement, and I would like you to consider it in the light of the information that you have found. A statement of the record is: The basic purpose of colonization is to increase the economic well-being of the homeland. (writes on board) Now, let's test this today by bringing together some data that you have. Who has a colonial situation that they've investigated that points to a contradiction of this statement? All right, Saragale.

Saragale: Well, Massachusetts isn't—it was started in 1620—and, well, for almost 50 years it had nothing or little to do with the homeland. And they backed it with mostly their own money. And then they finally took over. But, for a long time, it was almost like a separate country, and it's just a colony, more or less.

Teacher: All right. Now, why was the colony established? The colony of Massachusetts? Was it a commercial company or was it—

Saragale: Yes, it was a commercial company. They say that it has been overstressed—the thing about wanting to worship in their own way. It was basically for economic reasons, and, of course—of course, the things that they wanted was to worship freely, although they didn't give that right to other people.

155

Teacher: If they did have an economic purpose, apparently it doesn't match this statement then, that the people of Massachusetts were not concerned about improving the well-being of the homeland?

Saragale: No.

Teacher: Who else has a colony that you think is—presents an exception to this hypothesis? Bryan?

Bryan: Well—Greenland. Greenland does not help the homeland, but the homeland helps Greenland.

Leland: Well, with Greenland, we don't think there—there's anything there and there isn't anything much there that we can get to. But in a few years with the way science is moving—we still don't know what's under that ice. The way science is moving now, we could probably make things that could get underneath the ice—well, heat making it melt, or things like this. So I think they probably colonized Greenland just thinking that someday they might be able to get to use it.

Mark J.: In the 600's??? (dubiously)

Mark B.:[2] Well, I had New England—The Plymouth Colony. And the reason for settling there was purely for the freedom of religion. They, well, and also, they could have gotten—could have gotten freedom of religion over in Holland. But they wanted a place where they could keep their own—the same customs, where other customs and other manners couldn't influence their children and—and such. And so they came to America for these reasons.

Teacher: All right, let's accept that for the moment as a fact. Can we in any way stretch this, or *should* we try to stretch this to fall within the domain of this statement? Bill?

Bill: If there's somebody rich and they feed more people and they try to help a number of people leave England, so, you have to feed less, so the government gets more.

Teacher: If we look at this from the standpoint of the homeland, as you have, that perhaps they were glad to reduce the number of dissatisfied or unemployed, or something of that sort.

Bill: And also, you could cut down on the number of soldiers—soldiers you have just to keep these Puritans from leaving.

Saragale: Well, I have some conflicting evidence with this—purely that people came over for freedom of religion. 'Cause I read in this encyc-encyclopedia—I'm not saying that it's right or wrong—but I just read it. It said that it was probably overstressed a great deal and that it was probably just as much, if not more, economic reasons. Because there was colonizing groups.

Leland: Well, I had something to say about the freedom of religion (T: All right. Go ahead) being the sole reason. Well, if this was the only reason— the freedom of religion, then why didn't Great Britain want to give the colonies their freedom when we asked for it? Why did they just line so many

---

[2] In the process of trying to answer this basic question the students have absorbed many facts—but it is not fact-gathering for its own sake, but, rather, the use of facts to solve a problem.

of their soldiers and try to put down the revolution when they could have just let us go anyways, unless they had some reason of their own?!

Such discussions can then culminate in an assignment where the students try to present the broader meaning of colonization, as shown in Table 6–2.

Table 6–2.   *Student Ideas About Colonization (Excerpts from teacher assignment to present the broader meaning of colonization).*

1. Colonization is a time and place where a section of land is under the control of a larger country. This period is not usually more than 100 to 150 years long. It is usually a period in which the colony has very little or nothing to say and has few rights in governing itself. These people sometimes have to give a large section of their earnings to the country which rules them. There is no specific era to which colonization is confined. Colonies can be made at any time.

2. Colonization is an establishment in an undeveloped land brought about by help from a country toward finance and support. If people in the colony do not like its system of government or other things, they can rebel. The colony has many undiscovered natural resources and dangerous diseases or hostile natives. Sometimes it is inhabited by convicts or people seeking a land of free religion.

3. Colonization is when a country takes possession of unclaimed or claimed land and rules it. Where the colonial land is located does not matter as long as it is ruled by a country. A colony can be made any time. Most colonies were founded because of something that the mother country could get out of it—such as crops, mineral wealth, escaping religious persecution, etc. The colony usually was governed by the mother country or one man appointed by the mother country. The mother country usually got some of the benefits of the economy.

4. What makes a colony is that a group of people from a certain country go to a new, partially unsettled, country and build their homes and a community in a certain place. As they build their communities, they form ways of living, farming, mining, etc. and build a settlement. The government can be self-ruled, or ruled by the mother country. The economy depends on how it is ruled. If it is the mother country, the products are liable to be exported to her.

Just as interesting to students is the consideration of what would happen if conditions were different, or what the future might be like if the ideas they have developed are applied. This stimulates use of the knowledge available to them and creates in them excitement and enthusiasm as they exercise their own intellectual abilities. Suggestions as to the expansion of ideas, which in effect is a divergent approach, are illustrated in Table 6–1. Expansion can be based on either the data, the concept, or the generalization level.

Emphasis on the level and the kind of thinking process covers two of the general instructional principles. The third principle focuses on teaching important ideas in all aspects of life and times relevant to the child. One of the most difficult of such topics involves instructing students in the domain of human relationships. This is not just because this area has been less thoroughly investigated than the physical sciences, but because it also involves ourselves and the world we wish to portray to our children. The world that the adult generation traditionally wishes to pass on to their children is a world where hard work achieves good results and where rational thought, justice, and fair play are the guiding lights of society.

Gifted students, being more perceptive than other students, are able to see the lack of relationship between what adults say is true and what actually happens. In effect, they are able to make an evaluation of the goodness of fit between the ideas that we have presented and the events that are occurring. When the gifted see that they don't fit, they begin to ask difficult and embarrassing questions. One common adult strategy is to avoid and ignore such issues or to point out the relative immaturity of the child and say that he will understand when he gets older. Such an approach misses the mark, as gifted students often comprehend, from about the age of 11 or 12, about as much as the average adult and lack only experience to bring them up to adult competence.

Therefore, the challenge of the educational system is to start introducing concepts of human behavior that are more realistic and more in line with what we now understand. One fundamental concept would be the role played by self-interest and the fact that power is used in human relationships to maintain self-interest. Until the basic rule of self-interest is recognized in human affairs, much of what goes on is puzzling and unexplainable to children.

THE PROPER STUDY OF MANKIND

One of the themes of this book is that the instruction of gifted students should focus on the major ideas, the large generalizations that they have the capability to grasp, for to them clouds of facts are hardly more illuminating than just two or three facts. One can learn the campaigns of the Civil War with dates, battles, and characters without learning anything about why wars are fought between friends, or what ideas can be generalized to other conflict situations. It is the large idea, the big truth as we know it that we should be seeking to deliver. Bruner (1960, pp. 12–13) states the following:

The basic ideas that lie at the heart of all science and mathematics and the basic themes that give form to life and literature are as simple as they are powerful. . . . The early teaching of science, mathematics, social studies, and literature should be designed to teach these subjects with scrupulous intellectual honesty, but with an emphasis upon the intuitive grasp of ideas and upon the use of these basic ideas.

Bruner, in a major effort to practice what he preached, put together an important and comprehensive curriculum, entitled *Man: A Course of Study* (1970), in which he attempts to bring major ideas to young and inquiring minds. *Man: A Course of Study* is organized around three questions:

What is human about human beings?
How did they get that way?
How can they be made more so?

In this curriculum effort, which is available with numerous booklets, films, and readings, he tries to contrast and compare man with animals (baboons and salmon) and with primitive tribes so that with such visual and written experiences the young student will begin to think on the issue of "What is a man?"

If the proper study of mankind is man, then such provocative comments as the following are worth some study (Bruner, 1966, p. 113).

The single most characteristic thing about human beings is that they learn. Learning is so deeply ingrained in man that it is almost involuntary, and thoughtful students of human behavior have even speculated that our specialization as a species is a specialization for learning.

Or in a discussion on man and seals (Beals, 1967, p. 2) . . .

Man and seal are both warm-blooded mammals. . . . The seal is smaller and has slightly less brain tissue per pound of body weight. The flesh and blood and bones of a seal are much like those of a man. . . . The seal observes the world around him and learns all of the basic tricks of survival. The man also observes and learns. Both animals learn complicated routines, do tricks, and appear in circuses. . . . What is it that man has and the seal lacks?

Or to use poetry as a means for opening discussions on such profound ideas and questions:

Dreams
Hold fast to dreams
For if dreams die
Life is a broken-winged bird
That cannot fly.
Hold fast to dreams

159

For when dreams go
Life is a barren field
Frozen with snow.

LANGSTON HUGHES[3]

Whether or not the intensive study of the baboon, the salmon, or the Eskimo will make learning about mankind easier for elementary school students in general is an open question. To some educators it is dubious that such large conceptual leaps can be made to tie modern man to these diverse subjects, especially for slow-learning children with limited capacity to generalize. But to the child who is gifted, who enjoys the intellectual exercise of conceptual broad jumps, such as Bruner encourages, there would seem to be little doubt that such a curriculum program carries with it precisely the elements that one would like to see in curriculum programs for gifted students.

Primitive Man

On the shelf in Cranshaw's bedroom there exists, in unwitting juxtaposition, carefully constructed models of a prehistoric Brontosaurus, a moon rocket, and a World War II Spitfire. To dismiss this unlikely combination by saying that Cranshaw has broad interests is to not do justice to the significance of these models. Cranshaw, through his intellectual talents, has the ability to transport himself to other times and other places.

His ability to use verbal symbols as tools to create, in his imagination, past events or future possibilities or the never-neverland of fantasy enables him to be responsive to adventures that take him traveling from the present to the past, to the future, or to pure fantasy.

The more intelligent the student, the more likely it is that he will speculate upon man's origin and what it is like to live in other places and times. Not surprisingly, he will be intrigued by such subjects as early history or anthropology and will be thrilled by the detective story-like assemblage of clues about our early origins. The integration of such material is illustrated in the experimental units produced by the Anthropology Curriculum Study Project (ACSP), which has the goals of teaching (1) the investigatory skills of the social sciences, and (2) some basic conceptual understandings that may have broad general application. It combines some of the advantages of the unit approach with the conceptual depth of the new curricula.

[3] From *The dream keeper and other poems,* by Langston Hughes. Copyright 1932 and renewed 1960 by Langston Hughes. Reprinted by permission of Alfred A. Knopf, Inc.

Although the ACSP curriculum developers were committed to no single instructional strategy, the inductive approach gets considerable attention (see the chapter on "Discovery"). For example, the students may first be introduced to a map of an archeological digging which reports the position of the discovery of artifacts, and the nature of the artifacts. The students are then expected to speculate upon their possible meaning. One such digging and its artifacts are shown in Figure 6–1.

Students are asked to think about what new data are needed to reach valid conclusions in terms of knowledge of climate, water supply, and so on. Additional information is then provided the students via slides that describe the physical environment surrounding the Kalahari Desert. Putting these bits of information together, students might come forth with the following:

They existed in small family groups which survived on hunting and mongongo nuts.
They hunted with bows and arrows and spears.
They made objects of the bones and shells.
They ground meal of sorts with mortars and pestles.
They had some religious ceremonies and dancing.

Further information is then provided with a slide tape of what is already known about the Bushman in the Kalahari. The additional data force some revision of the earlier guesses or hypotheses, a useful antidote to bright students, whose ability to spin off plausible answers to puzzles sometimes outruns their devotion to seeking data to prove or disprove their hunches.

Some of the basic ideas to be grasped by the student in his study of anthropology would be

1. The environment is very important as a limiting factor in determining and controlling cultural characteristics, especially of hunter-gatherers.
2. The beginning of the idea that cultures are adaptations to circumstances.
3. An idea of the limits of archeological interpretations reached in the consideration of artifacts unless their symbolic meaning is understood and they are viewed in context with other data.

Beyond School Walls

Lake (1973) describes an exciting illustration of how a few gifted students can expand the boundaries of their educational setting to the world. With the cooperation of the U.S. Office of Education, Office of the Gifted and Talented, the Explorers Club, and Educational Expeditions International, awards were given to over 150 gifted students that allowed them to participate in summer expeditions with noted scientists around the

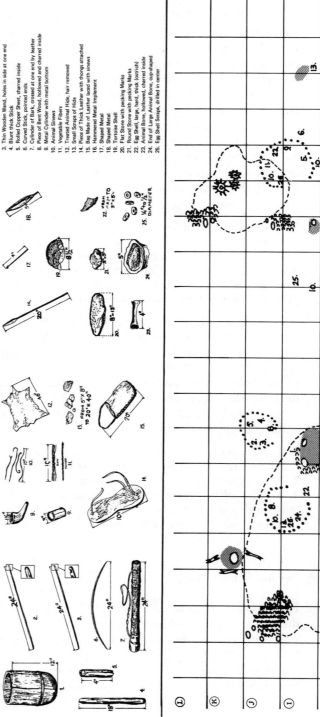

1. Wooden Bowl, thick bottom
2. Thin Wooden Wand, polished on one end
3. Thin Wooden Wand, holes in side at one end
4. Blunt thick Stick
5. Rolled Copper Sheet, charred inside
6. Curved Stick, pointed ends
7. Cylinder of Bark, crossed at one end by feather
8. Piece of Bent Wood, hollowed and charred inside
9. Metal Cylinder with metal bottom
10. Animal Sinews
11. Vegetable Fibers
12. Treated Animal Hide, hair removed
13. Small Scraps of Hide
14. Piece of Thick Leather with thongs attached
15. Bag Made of Leather laced with sinews
16. Hammered Metal Implement
17. Shaped Metal
18. Shaped Metal
19. Tortoise Shell
20. Flat Stone with pecking Marks
21. Round Stone with pecking Marks
22. Egg Shell, large, hard, thick (ostrich)
23. Animal Bone, hollowed, charred inside
24. End of Large Animal Bone, cup-shaped
25. Egg Shell Scraps, drilled in center

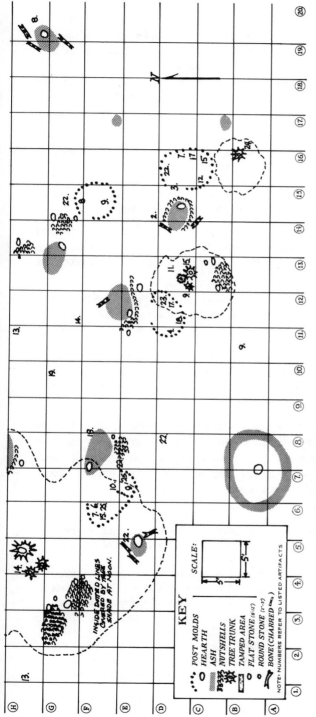

FIGURE 6-1. *Kalahari-1 Site and Its Contents.* (*From Anthropology Curriculum Study Project, History as Culture Change: An Overview,* 1968. Reproduced by permission of the American Anthropological Association.)

world studying anthropological digs, glaciers, volcanoes, and the like. In the summer of 1973 students in the Exploration Scholarship Program traveled to places in Africa, the Middle East, Europe, Asia, South and Central America, Iceland, and the United States.

Both the students and scientists were highly enthusiastic about the experience. One scientist reported on studying the effect of DDT on crustaceans in Cape Cod Bay, and the role these teenage gifted students played (p. 12).

> They were treated as graduate students, where they were responsible for a lot of self-initiation. The students selected one animal that they would study. They were free to go and collect their own samples, and were responsible for designing their own experiments to discover what they could about feeding, breeding and swimming behavior.

This increased level of responsibility was noted in all the experiences and is best expressed by the comments of the students themselves. One of the students, 18-year-old Rebecca Miller from Texas, remarked as follows (p. 14):

> Everything had crystalled in my mind concerning the goals which the scientists of prehistory had achieved in the Near East and those which they were still working towards. I am now structuring my studies toward a degree in either anthropology or Near Eastern archaeology. I can only hope that my education in a college situation will be as rewarding as the priceless wealth of knowledge and educational experience which I have gained in my all too short visit with prehistoric man at Ubeidiya.

Important ideas can be stimulated through the preparation of exercises and experiences that will elicit some of the larger ideas in such fields as economics. Instead of grocery-story, simplistic economic exercises, organized curricula such as the one developed by Senesh (1965, p. 139), can allow the gifted student at the elementary or junior high level to understand the following ideas:

1. All people and all nations are confronted with the conflict between their unlimited wants and limited resources. The degree of the conflict may vary, but the conflict is always present.
2. From the beginning, men have tried new ways and means to lessen the gap between unlimited wants and limited resources. Their efforts to invent new machines and improve production processes are evidences of the desire to produce more, better, and faster.
3. In all countries the basic questions to be answered are: what goods and services will be produced; how much of these will be produced; how will they be produced—that is, with more men or more machines or more raw materials; and who will receive the goods and services?

164

4. In the United States what and how much will be produced, how it will be produced, and for whom are largely determined by the free choices of the American people, either as consumers or participants in the production process.
5. Through their political process the American people sometimes limit their individual free choices in order to increase the general welfare.

One Source or Many?

The ability to present a balanced judgment on history, and those men and women who make it, is not given to many writers. How often does one find a statement that places even our opponents in calm perspective— for example (Johnson, 1964, pp. 12, 14):

> Karl Marx was a philosopher, and a great one. He looked at the way the world was run in his time, and he saw much that he thought was wrong and much more that he thought was foolish.
> All of us have wondered why things happen as they do—why one man works hard and gets richer and his neighbor works just as hard and gets poorer. But most of us stop with wondering. We decide that the problem is too hard, and give it up. Karl Marx never gave it up. Through a long life he kept studying, and he discovered a great deal. Some of it has turned out to be wrong but not all. Much that he discovered is true, and that is why wise people regard him as a great man.

It is much better to depend upon a collection of views in which the biases of the varied contributors will balance out. To depend on one book, or one source of knowledge, is to leave yourself at the mercy of the biases of that one source. If gifted children learned nothing else in their education but that one fact, they are well on their way to being educated persons.

There once was a famous lecturer who carried a small ball around with him. He would take this ball out of his pocket and hold it up to the audience and ask them what color it was. The audience would shout back the ball was red. The lecturer would then say, "Oh, no, you're wrong. It is white!" They would react with injured surprise and insist indeed the ball was red. In fact, the ball was half red and half white so that both the audience and the lecturer were right from their limited viewpoints, and the lecturer had made his point about the importance of seeing both sides of an issue.

This has always been a goal of teachers of gifted students, but rarely have they had the opportunity to provide just this kind of experience. Figure 6–2 shows two different views of the same event, the Boston Tea Party. These excerpts from the English viewpoint and the American viewpoint can make the talented student pause and reflect. It is not

FIGURE 6–2. *Two Views of Same Act.* (*From Wolff, 1966, p. 119.*)

American Newspaper
PARLIAMENT'S TEA ACT ATTACKS TRADE
TAX ON TEA REMAINS

American colonies, Summer 1773: News has arrived that Parliament has passed a new Tea Act. The Act, which became law on May 10, lowers the price of East India Company tea and keeps the despised three-cent import tax per pound of tea. There is no question why Parliament's evil design to use the East India Company, which can now sell tea cheaper than anyone else, to undercut colonial merchants and eliminate them from the tea trade. At the same time, Parliament will use the low-priced tea to trick the colonists into paying a tax without the consent of their legislatures.

British Newspaper
PARLIAMENT'S TEA ACT GOES INTO EFFECT—
EAST INDIA COMPANY TO BENEFIT

London, May 10, 1773: Today Parliament's new Tea Act becomes law. The Act will help the East India Company, which is almost bankrupt and has millions of pounds of unsold tea in its warehouses. The Act allows the Company (1) to ship the tea in its British warehouses to America free of any British export duty, and (2) to ship tea directly from India to the American colonies. The Act keeps the American import duty of three cents per pound of tea, which Parliament had placed on tea in 1767.

Because this new Act removes export duties and allows the direct shipping of tea, the East India Company will be able to sell its tea cheaper than anyone in America. By being in such a good position, the Company should be able to improve its financial situation.

FIG. 6–2 (*Cont'd*)

American Newspaper

BRITISH LEAVE COLONISTS NO CHOICE—TEA DUMPED

Boston, December, 16, 1773: Tonight a group of "Mohawk Indians" boarded three ships lying at anchor in Boston harbor. They carefully took the ships' cargoes—chests of East India Company tea—and emptied them into the water, without the least damage to any other property on the ships.

This drastic action was taken only when the townsmen knew that they had no other choice. Ever since November, they had made it clear to the local British officials that they could not permit the landing of the East India Company's tea. To do so would be to submit to the tea tax without the consent of their colonial legislature. In addition, they tried every course of action to convince both the customs officials and Governor Hutchinson that the ships and their cargoes of tea should be allowed to return to Britain. But, both customs officials and the Governor refused to give the ships clearance to sail. The townsmen, knowing that if the ships remained in the harbor a few more days the tax on tea would be collected, made their decision—the only one possible. They destroyed the tea.

British Newspaper

BOSTON MOB DESTROYS TEA, DEFIES TEA ACT

London, January 22, 1774: News has arrived that the tea exported to America by the East India Company, under an Act of Parliament passed last year, has produced a wave of anger throughout America.

The town of Boston, which has been so long obnoxious to the British government, was the scene of the first outrage. When three ships carrying tea arrived in the harbor, the Bostonians demanded that they return to Britain with their cargo. British officials, not willing to be dictated to by a mob, refused to give the ships clearance to sail. Then a mob of angry Bostonians, disguised as Mohawk Indians, boarded the ships on the night of December 16th. In less than four hours the mob hurled into the sea 342 chests of tea, valued at 18,000 pounds.

By their violent and outrageous proceedings, the Bostonians have destroyed the East India Company's property and defied the law and authority of Parliament.

hard to get him to see modern-day applications of this situation and to have him devise many examples of his own. News stories from the Israeli and Arab newspapers could be obtained that describe the same event in the Middle East. Or pro- and antiadministration newspapers could be studied for their reporting on a single news event.

One of the great difficulties in instructing talented and average students is to provide them with practice so that they can distinguish fact from feeling, or fact from supposed motivation. Most conclusions are given as though they were fact, particularly in ordinary textbooks, and it is easy for the unreflective student to accept them in the same vein. The fact of the matter in the situation described in Figure 6–2 was that tea was dumped in the harbor by some men dressed as Indians. However, the reasons leading up to that act and the evaluation of its rightness or wrongness need to be considered separately.

If the sequence of events leading up to a particular confrontation such as the Boston Tea Party is studied, then it is also possible to study the suggested ways of intervening before the final confrontation. It is very clear in the world today that we cannot afford the luxury of too many eyeball-to-eyeball confrontations, and it is up to talented students and adults to learn, not just how to have a successful confrontation, but preferably how to avoid them altogether, if at all possible.

One device for teaching youngsters the difference between behavior and implied motivation is the creation of a robot who has some peculiar characteristics, the most important of which is that the robot can report only behavior, but he cannot infer motivation. The robot cannot say, "He was angry"; he can only say, "He curled his hand up tightly and shook it at me rapidly." He cannot say, "She was happy." He can say, "She bared her teeth at me and hopped up and down clapping her hands together."

The students quickly see that the statement "He was angry" is not really a statement about behavior but a statement about inferred motivation.

This point can be made in reverse order by giving motivation and asking the students to provide the statements that the robot might make to situations like these:

1. Teacher has it in for Jerry.
2. Mike wants to be president of the class.
3. Linda's feelings were hurt.

Once the students get into the habit of distinguishing between statements that describe inferred motivation and statements that describe actual behavior, they have provided themselves with the foundations for avoiding many of life's most difficult situations.

Games Used to Study Human Relations

For many years, when children became freed from the formal demands of the school program, they would enthusiastically engage in game playing. It has only been through recent advances in the field of mathematics that the fun of games has advanced to the point where it now appears obvious that games are important learning situations. They provide not only recreation and relaxation for individuals, but, because of their structure and organization, a potential opportunity for certain kinds of learning. This is particularly true if one is attempting to teach a high-level conceptual system such as trade relations, government institutions, or family relations. The concept behind this approach is that a person best learns "systems" or large generalizations by becoming involved personally in them. Instead of studying them from afar, he or she learns them through personal contact.

All games have certain characteristics in common: (1) there is a contest, (2) there are adversaries, (3) the adversaries operate under certain rules, and (4) there is a payoff, or victory. Although we are used to thinking of games in terms of baseball or football, it is obvious by this definition that marriage is a game; the classroom is a game; business is a game; and war is certainly the most exciting and dangerous game of them all.

One of the useful instructional objectives that the device of games can be put to is the exploration and understanding of human motivation so that gifted students can gain greater insight into their own, and others', otherwise mysterious behavior. Berne (1970) has presented a format that is attractive and easily usable, particularly in secondary school classes, to provide a base from which teacher and students can explore and expand on the type of "games" we all play with one another.

Table 6–3 shows two such games that we all can recognize. In the first game the aim of the player is to cause some damage and social disruption but to escape from personal blame or censure. A sample type of dialogue follows:

Joe: I just saw Pete and told him what a great time we had at the rock concert last night.

Mary: But, Joe, you know I had told Pete I was going to study last night and I just changed my mind at the last minute when you called. Now Pete will never speak to me again.

Joe: There I go again. I forgot all about that, I was just so excited about the concert. I always seem to mess things up.

Mary: Oh, it's not your fault, Joe, I am the one that changed my mind. I'm responsible.

Sample dialogues like that can be the stimulation for more detailed discussions about what Joe's motivation might have been and what

TABLE 6–3. *Games and Human Relationships.*

GAME	THESIS	AIM	ROLES	MOVES
1. I Am Sorry I Cause So Much Trouble (the schlemiel).	I can be destructive and still get forgiveness.	Absolution	Aggressor; victim	1. Provocation → Resentment. 2. Apology → Forgiveness.
2. The "Yes, But . . ." Game.	See if you can present a solution I can't find fault with.	Reassurance	Helpless persons; advisors	1. Problem → Solution. 2. Objection → Solution. 3. Objection → Disconcertion.

Adapted from Berne, E., *Games People Play.* New York: Grove Press, 1964, pp. 114–122.

170

alternative solutions there might be to avoid playing such a destructive game. Once the style of the game is established (i.e., thesis, aim, roles, moves), it is easy enough to ask students to identify other kinds of games that include people interacting together and then to ask them to explore alternative solutions to the problems presented.

The second game noted in Table 6–3 is a game with which we can all empathize since it is one of those standard interactions played between teacher and pupil or parent and child. A sample of the "Yes, But" game dialogue is reproduced below.

Zelda: I can't finish my history assignment on time. The teacher gave us too much to do and it is all unfair.

Mother: But you have the whole weekend to do the project, if you just get down to it.

Zelda: Yes, but you told me I would have to clean up my room and that will take a half day all by itself.

Mother: Well, maybe I can help and we can get it done sooner so you can get at your project.

Zelda: Yes, but Aunt Sally is coming for dinner tomorrow and you wouldn't want me to be impolite and not spend some time with her. Besides, my other teachers have given me other assignments so that I won't be able to finish in any event.

Talented students are very good at creating dialogue and role playing in such situations. The eventual instructional goal is greater honesty in interpersonal dealings, and this approach can result in a clearing of the air as we become more conscious of the little deceptions and ploys we use on one another every day. Also, a genuine attempt to create ways out of the traps that are laid for us in such interaction games can result in valuable insights for each student that can be of long-term utility. The series of books by Stephen Potter on *Oneupmanship* (1962), *Gamesmanship* (1948), and the like provide another humorous approach to the topic that can be used as a basis for classroom discussion. As previously noted, the subject of people, as individuals and as groups, should form the core of a social studies curriculum for gifted students and—to the extent possible—for the slow and average student as well.

SUMMARY

This chapter, like the previous ones in science and mathematics, suggests a curriculum for gifted children that focuses on the depth of understanding of important concepts, rather than on a superficial breadth of coverage that consists of a collection of huge amounts of unconnected facts. In addition, there is a strong plea for modifying the emphasis of content now used in social studies for the gifted and for all students. The major advances and discoveries in psychology, sociology, anthropology, and economics are poorly represented in the current elementary and secondary programs provided in traditional public schools.

In this chapter, distinguished social scientists have made the point that the proper study of mankind is man. This is particularly true for gifted students, whose future position of leadership will often bring them into influential contact with the lives of many people. If they do not understand the basic concepts of economics, of sociology, or of psychology, the damage that they can wreak will be much more devastating than that which the average citizen might cause.

One of the major barriers to more adequate presentation of ideas in the social studies field lies in its relatively greater controversial nature. Although few people would argue against the presentation of conflicting points of view or theories in physics or chemistry, the presentation of similar conflicting views in social studies, affecting as it would current politics and community affairs, is often approached with great caution on the part of public schools.

However, it is important that gifted students not only be introduced to conflicting ideas but be provided the tools by which they can analyze them, find additional information, and make up their own minds as to which seems to be the most valid. When citizens understand that the basic objectives of such a program are not to indoctrinate these students in a particular viewpoint, but rather to allow them to see the arguments more clearly, such a program usually receives support by the general public.

Each of the content areas has the objective of deeper understanding endangered by the limited talents and understanding of the teachers. Special afterschool clubs, released time projects, monitored independent study, all try to bring the gifted student in closer contact with talented and knowledgeable adults.

UNRESOLVED ISSUES

1. Can elementary school gifted students, who are cognitively mature but socially and emotionally relatively immature, be brought to some understanding of complex human motivation? For example, can a gifted child of 10 years truly understand the passions and drives of adult human beings, or study with understanding the impact of an issue such as the role of approaching death on the decision making of aging national leaders?

2. In what way can we most effectively bring into the schools the most recent ideas of economists, historians, psychologists, and sociologists, so that gifted students can be up-to-date in these rapidly growing fields without waiting for fifteen or twenty years for the new concepts to filter down through the usual curriculum development process?

3. To what extent are we able to integrate subject matter across fields in the social studies so that there is greater understanding of human beings, their behavior, and the ways in which these human sciences interact with complex social areas such as economics and political science? The gifted child cannot, without aid, make such complex integrations on his own.

READINGS OF SPECIAL INTEREST

BRUNER, J. *Man: A course of study. Seminar for teachers.* Cambridge, Mass.: Education Development Center, 1970.

A valuable rationale for the development of a curriculum with man at its center. Discusses various teacher strategies for stimulating student thinking and provides the basis for inclusion of particular subjects in the curriculum.

JOHNSON, G. *A history for Peter.* New York: Morrow, 1960.

A trilogy on the history of the United States written for Johnson's grandson. Highly readable, focusing on the human as well as the noble characteristics of great men. A fine supplementary book for preadolescent gifted and adults who like their history filled with human beings.

JONES, R. *Fantasy and feeling in education.* New York: New York University Press, 1968.

A critique of the "new social studies," particularly that proposed by Bruner, on the grounds that it is too cognitively oriented. This author wishes to bring more of the affective and emotional feelings into the experience of students. He shows how this can be done, using Man: A Course of Study *as an example.*

TOFFLER, A. *Future shock.* New York: Bantam, 1971.

A challenging discussion of the problems caused by the rapid and continual change in the institutions and society around us. The thesis is that rapid change itself causes anxiety and tension. Should provoke stimulating discussions with gifted students.

7

Language Arts for the Gifted

Language arts appears to be a favorite subject of gifted students. Of our four gifted students, Zelda and Cranshaw are very fond of language arts and look forward to it in the school day. Even Joe will express a relative liking for the subject, as compared with such areas as mathematics and science. Only Sam finds the area uninteresting and would much rather study mathematics than engage in language arts activities. Although Zelda and Cranshaw both express highly positive attitudes toward language arts, their reasons are very different and underscore the impression that language arts is such a broad and comprehensive field that it has a little something for everybody.

Zelda likes the structured nature of grammar and linguistics and is intrigued by the revelations of hidden systems and order in literature and in poetry. She feels at home in most structured situations and, since her vocabulary and linguistic skills are very high, she is able to perform excellently with little effort. On the other hand, Cranshaw likes language arts because it gives him the opportunity to use his imagination and his creative bent. He particularly likes to write short stories and poems and feels that this is one place where he can cease being a passive learner and become an effective expresser of ideas.

Joe likes language arts for quite a different reason. In this area there is not the same pressure for daily output and sustained academic work that one finds in classes on science and mathematics. It is true that there can be an assignment for a book report two weeks from now, or a theme to write, but these are in the future, and Joe is an expert anyhow at postponing such tasks beyond their deadlines. So he likes the class discussions and genuinely likes to read some literature.

On the other hand, Sam, with his limited background in language and his different cultural and family background, finds the fascination on the part of other students with words a puzzling thing. He does not get joy out of manipulating words or finding complicated puns in the humor selections. Since he does better in mathematics than he does in subjects with a strong verbal character to them, he does not look forward to this subject matter.

This consensus of positive opinion on the part of our four youngsters is sustained by research conducted by Rice and Banks (1967). They reported on the opinions of over 100 gifted students in the San Diego program who expressed highly positive judgments toward the area of language arts. Students voted strongly for flexible schedules that would allow for individualized programs but also made an emphatic plea for more literature courses, fine arts, music, and dramatic offerings.

Another interesting point is that the gifted students spoke strongly in favor of intradisciplinary seminars and discussions that would tend to relate the sciences to the social sciences and to literature. The talent of the gifted student for interrelating ideas is seen in these types of interests. Above all, the gifted students felt strongly the need to create something, to be active learners and producers rather than passive absorbers of knowledge. And it is that emphasis on student activity that underlies most of the suggestions in the special curriculum ideas for the gifted in language arts.

LANGUAGE ARTS OBJECTIVES

In order to decide what type of curriculum should be provided for gifted students in language arts, it is useful to review what the expected objectives are for that broad and amorphous subject area. Table 7–1 gives some sample objectives taken from Endres, Lamb, and Lazarus (1969), who have developed a comprehensive series of objectives, using the five major dimensions: perceiving, listening, speaking, reading, and writing. Table 7–1 indicates some of these objectives that seem particularly appropriate for gifted and talented students of middle childhood and older. The ultimate goal of the authors is to move the student from a consumer-assimilative posture to that of the producer-creative. A worthy goal, but very difficult to attain.

As seen in Table 7–1, the objectives in language arts fall into the broad categories of receptive abilities, expressive abilities, and integrating or associative abilities. Many of the objectives require student judgment to be applied to the information that he is receiving. The gifted student, as well as other students, is expected not merely to accept the information that comes to him at face value but to be concerned about the intention of the sender and to recognize that a person communicating with him may have more than one intention. It is often surprising to observers

Table 7–1.   *Selected Objectives in the Language Arts.*

I. *Perceiving*

1.1 To develop an awareness of self—physically, emotionally, socially; to perceive oneself as an individual person.

1.8 To realize that the sender's primary intention is usually not the most apparent to the receiver (sometimes not even to the sender himself); to recognize primary and secondary intentions.

1.11 To perceive motivations behind emotional appeals on billboards, radio, television, etc.; to be able to identify rationalizations and double talk.

II. *Listening*

2.5 To listen to others' ideas with an open mind and to extend to others the courtesies in listening which one expects when speaking.

2.7 To acquire skills of critical listening: i.e., listening for ideas and supporting data: to avoid being swayed by propaganda.

2.15 To develop critical taste—e.g., to prefer the authentic and the imaginative over the stereotyped and contrived in movies and TV and other media.

III. *Speaking*

3.2 To speak spontaneously and easily with others; to speak freely when there is something significant to be said.

3.7 To express oneself, or to express one's interpretations, in play acting, story telling, poetry reading, ballad singing, etc.

3.10 To apply the conventions of general American-English usage, put to use whatever function variety of language is appropriate to the occasion.

IV. *Reading*

4.4 To recognize the nature of meanings of what is read; to make of reading a question-asking, problem-solving process; to realize that language *suggests* more than it says.

4.9 To value the literary tradition of one's culture; to be able to identify folklore and allusions.

4.14 To apply, in reading, certain techniques of critical listening: to distinguish between report and propaganda; between less slanted and more slanted news.

V. *Writing*

5.1 To produce written signs and symbols with a sense of exploration and discovery.

5.7 To develop an awareness of writing styles and to improve one's own writing as a result of continuous exposure to literature.

5.9 To enjoy writing prose and verse; to enjoy writing various genres and modes (haiku, free verse, stories, fables, skits, etc.).

Source: Adapted from M. Endres, P. Lamb, & A. Lazarus. Selected objectives in the English language arts. *Elementary English,* 1969, **46**, p. 419–425.

in education that gifted students, who can be extremely sophisticated in their knowledge of the laws of the physical world and of mathematics, can be unbelievably naïve when it comes to interpreting the motivations of other individuals. A strong language arts program in this area should help that student to become more sophisticated regarding the purposes and directions of others, as well as more aware of himself.

In addition, the gifted student should be encouraged to express himself with imagination, to develop original and unusual ideas, and to learn the skills that will provide him with the mechanisms for more effective expression. In the areas of both communication reception and communication expression, the gifted youngster can be expected to learn early to communicate his own needs and ideas to others, and also to carefully interpret the information he is receiving from others.

Is there any real difference between language arts programs for the gifted and those for the average student? Isn't a description of a program for the gifted merely a description of a good program for an average classroom? Evidence on what actually happens in language arts programs in heterogeneous classrooms and in classrooms that are grouped for ability has been provided by House et al. (1972). House and his colleagues conducted an extended evaluation that involved classroom observation in programs where gifted students were found attending classes with students of high ability and in classes in which there was a wide range of ability.

Some of the key distinctions between the two programs are shown in Table 7-2. As House points out, there is a higher proportion of talk by the teacher in the average program, the textbook seems to be followed rather rigidly, and all assignments are clearly stated. These assignments do not necessarily reflect the teacher's wishes in such matters, but reflect more the teacher's feeling of responsibility that students who have not learned basic skills should be in the business of practicing them until they become learned. However, when there are thirty-three students in a given class, it requires a remarkably energetic teacher to provide full stimulation for the few students at the top, while fulfilling his responsibility to the many students who are still struggling with imperfect skills and inadequate knowledge.

In direct contrast to these programs, House reports that in the programs where students are grouped for ability in language arts, there is a greater freedom to encourage creative and reflective thinking on the part of the student. The techniques described in much greater detail in the chapters on creativity and problem solving are found in these classrooms, together with a greater student independence to proceed at his own rate. As House et al. point out, there were a number of gifted students in the normal program as well, but those gifted students did not have the opportunity to proceed as easily because of the responsibilities that the teacher felt for the total range of ability that he had to work with.

178

TABLE 7–2. *Distinction Between the Gifted and Normal Language Arts Program.*

GIFTED PROGRAM	NORMAL PROGRAM
Daily for an hour 12 students meet with their teacher in a sixth-grade language arts class which attempts to encourage creative and reflective thinking.	Daily for an hour 33 eighth graders meet for a language arts class supposedly centered on composition and creative writing—in which the teacher talks 75% of the time.
Through brainstorming and other techniques the teacher hopes to develop the students' self-confidence in producing and using their own ideas.	The text is followed rigidly and all assignments are totally prescribed. Most emphasis is on the ways things are said rather than the ideas.
They are expected to develop skills in writing and speaking and to learn how to focus on a problem. No tests or grades are given.	Students are irritated with the many small nit-picking assignments and are frustrated to be receiving grades lower than they could earn in the regular class.

Source: Adapted from E. House, T. Kerins, & J. Steele. *Illinois gifted program evaluation.* Urbana, Ill.: Center for Instructional Research and Curriculum Evaluation, University of Illinois, 1972, p. 127.

A LITERATURE PROGRAM FOR THE GIFTED

Since many gifted students possess an unusual aptitude for reading and for devouring books and papers at an enormous rate, it is no surprise that literature programs are often referred to as a means of additional stimulation for gifted students. Providing a balanced literature program for talented students is no easy matter. The students' interests, themselves, appear to run in streaks. That is, when Cranshaw was interested in space travel, he would read nothing else but books on outer space, science fiction, and the like, to the almost complete exclusion of any other topic. When he then became interested in animals and the ecological cycle, he went through one book after another on animal stories and nature. There is certainly nothing wrong with such spurts of interest on the part of the student as long as, over a period of time, some kind of balance is introduced into the selection.

Table 7-3 shows a series of suggestions for a specific literature program for gifted students at various grade levels, from the California State Department of Education (1971). These suggestions are based upon a wide range of experiences in special programs for the gifted in that state. The program suggests that the children at the earliest primary grade level already take an active role in writing or rewriting a story, rather than accepting passively the author's point of view.

TABLE 7-3. *Literature Program for Gifted Students.*

Goal: Literature offers an economical way to learn of the achievements, failures, and aspirations of a race. For the gifted, literature can serve as a high speed vehicle to realms far beyond the ones we have known.

GRADE LEVEL	OBJECTIVES	SUGGESTED ACTIVITIES
1-3	The enjoyment of literature and realization that stories are a time-space machine to transport them from the present.	Children can end a story differently from the way the author ended it. Discuss what would happen if a character in a story had made a different choice.
4-6	To learn about cultural values held by mankind in a cross-section of countries. Appreciation for language: i.e., knowledge of writing techniques, a deeper understanding of subtle meanings of words.	The study of myths, folk tales and fables used to study historical, cultural and geographic similarities and differences among people. Study of biographies as information about people, their motives, values and accomplishments.
7-9	To lead the gifted child away from the easy answers of childhood to the consideration of adult issues. To develop a thematic approach of major youth-adult conflict themes such as heroism, temptation, and situational ethics.	Compare legendary heroes of the past with modern heroes of books, television, and movies. Study of a series of stories with the Faust theme can help the student gain insight in the multivaried nature of temptation. The Prometheus legend can serve as a keystone to discussion of the nature of rebellion against authority—a theme surely of interest to the gifted.
10-12	Students at this level should be provided the tools for intellectual inquiry and involved in the processes of defining, question asking, data gathering, observing, generalizing, etc. Four organizational approaches to language can be explored: history and chronology; textual analysis (structure, style, and meaning) and theme.	Historical—a study of a particular literary tradition, i.e., to study authors and their periods to show that literature is not written in isolation. The study of propaganda and its nature can focus on textual analysis so that the difference between reporting and propaganda can be delineated. Themes that underlie literature of varying periods—such as the search for immortality and the meaning of life—can allow the gifted to generalize some of the major themes of mankind.

Source: From California State Department of Education. *Education of mentally gifted minors.* Sacramento, Calif.: CSDE, 1971, pp. 51-57.

At the upper elementary level, a broader appreciation for different cultures and an initial understanding of the structure of the language itself are stressed.   In particular, the study of biographies is a strongly suggested program for the gifted, on the very sound grounds that some degree of identification and career interest may be stimulated when a particular biography hits a particular youngster just right.

At the junior high level, very deliberate attempts are made to help the youngster toward self-examination and to note the beginning of social conflict between individuals and larger groups within the society.

Finally, in grades ten to twelve, the program suggests that gifted students should be deeply involved in learning the tools for intellectual inquiry—how one collects data, organizes data, and reports them.

The emphasis placed throughout on the careful analysis of propaganda or advertising, or the study of information when there may be ulterior motives on the part of the communicator, is a strong one and suggests that students who will be in leadership positions cannot afford to be easily gulled by the first easy talker who comes along.

To know others and their feelings and emotions, one has to know oneself; and literature, poetry, and songs all provide a very strong opportunity for the gifted to explore his own psyche.   One example of a poem that can begin interesting discussions is the poem "Envy," by Edgar Kramer. This poem, tracing as it does the very human characteristics of envy or "the grass is greener" approach to life, can be used to begin extended discussions in classes about the nature of envy.

Envy[1]

I have a brother
   Who has not seen
The white foam flying
   Where tall ships lean;
For he is plowing
   The fields at home,
While I am faring
   The trackless foam.
But while he labors
   Where grass and tree
Are trembling beauty,
   He envies me.

I have a brother
   Whose footsteps turn,
When dusk is falling
   And candles burn,
To where a lassie
   And laddie wait
To hear him open
   The garden gate.
And while I wander
   Far ways and dim,
Though dreams are calling,
   I envy him.

EDGAR DANIEL KRAMER

Similarly, popular songs have lyrics that often go past adults but that are very meaningful to teenagers and others who are struggling to find some medium of expression for their own rather confused feelings and

[1] From J. Abramowitz & W. Halliburton, *Searching for values*.   New York: Globe, 1973, p. 219.

emotions. The song "Both Sides, Now," by Joni Mitchell, which talks
about the ups and downs of loves and life, is very real to sensitive teenagers, who can take the general concept of "Both Sides, Now" and creatively interpret for themselves the pluses and minuses, the ups and
downs, of their own life situations.

Both Sides, Now[2]

Moons and Junes and ferris wheels,
The dizzy dancing way you feel,
As ev'ry fairy tale comes real,
I've looked at love that way.
But now it's just another show,
You leave 'em laughing when you go.
And if you care, don't let them know,
Don't give yourself away.
I've looked at love from both sides now,
From give and take and still somehow
It's love's illusions I recall;
I really don't know love at all.

In Table 7–3 one of the objectives was to suggest that one should value
the literary tradition of one's culture, but what is *the* culture in a diverse
and culturally pluralistic society such as the United States? Obviously,
the culture of Cranshaw is not the same as the culture of Joe, and neither
is the same as the culture of Sam. Of all the youngsters being discussed,
Sam probably had the least appropriate introduction of materials in language arts and, as a consequence, did not really enjoy the time spent in
this area. This is both because his abilities did not go toward the verbal
or semantic dimension and because the content of the materials did not
seem appropriate or interesting to Sam. In his earlier readers he ran
across many stories that had to do with a farmhouse and a white picket
fence, talking farm animals, the slim happy mother and father, and he
knew that these had little to do with him or his background or his cultural
heritage. It was as different as if the books were talking about some
Egyptian or Eastern European culture.

Much more appropriate to Sam and his needs would be stories that not
only deal with important issues of authority and concepts such as life and
death but also provide a setting and characters that are recognizable and
real to Sam's experiences.

Having Sam read a section of Wright's *Black Boy* can bring forth his
interest and recognition of the problems. In one chapter the story is told
of the angry father demanding quiet so he can get some sleep and railing
against a kitten that is meowing. The boy in the story proceeds to draw

a noose around the animal's neck and kill it, leading to the following exchange.

> My mother hurried toward me, drying her hands upon her apron. She stopped and paled when she saw the kitten suspended from the rope.
> "What in God's name have you done?" she asked.
> "The kitten was making noise and Papa said to kill it," I explained.
> "You little fool!" she said. "Your father's going to beat you for this!"
> "But he told me to kill it," I said.
> "You shut your mouth!"
> She grabbed my hand and dragged me to my father's bedside and told him what I had done.
> "You know better than that!" my father stormed.
> "You told me to kill 'im," I said.
> "I told you to drive him away," he said.
> "You told me to kill 'im," I countered positively.
> "You get out of my eyes before I smack you down!" my father bellowed in disgust, then turned over in bed.
> I had had my first triumph over my father. I had made him believe that I had taken his words literally. He could not punish me now without risking his authority. I was happy because I had at last found a way to throw my criticism of him into his face. I would never give serious weight to his words again. I had made him know that I felt he was cruel and I had done it without his punishing me.[3]

This is a very different kind of story from that found in the usual readers, although stories from different cultural backgrounds are becoming more and more available. Youngsters like Sam can identify with the heroes of such stories because the heroes' predicaments are recognizable and important to these youngsters.

The basic message is that no single textbook or single book of any kind can satisfy the rich literary talents or needs of the average youngster and certainly not of the gifted and talented. There has to be a diversity of materials and diversity of program efforts to match in some regard the diversity of abilities, cultural backgrounds, and motivations of youngsters in a heterogeneous neighborhood and school.

On the other hand, popular songs and the messages that they include have a more universal appeal, and one can present for analysis and careful study the phraseology of those songs where there is a depth of understanding and feeling.

A further set of suggestions of specific language arts activities for the gifted is given by Bachtold (1966) is Table 7-4. These activities follow the same general patterns of communication expression or reception but

[3] R. Wright. *Black boy.* New York: Harper & Row, 1945, pp. 10–11. Copyright 1937, 1942, 1944, 1945 by Richard Wright. Reprinted by permission of Harper and Row, Publishers, Inc.

183

Table 7–4. *Language Arts Suggestions for Gifted Students.*

Communication Skills

Prepare a chart with six columns titled: Love of Family, Self-Interest, Thrift, Health, Fear, and Keeping up with the Joneses. Study advertisements on television and radio, in newspapers, in magazines, and on billboards. Record each advertisement in the column or the category to which the advertiser is appealing.

Purposefully listen for gossip and rumor for one week. Each time you hear gossip, try to determine whether it is malicious, idle talk, or simply an attempt to raise one's own prestige by lowering another's. . . . Write a theme on "Gossip as a Form of Communication."

Many speakers use "glittering generalities." This technique works in a fashion similar to name-calling, but in this case the labels are likely to illuminate the speaker's cause and to place anything or anybody supporting it in a favorable light. Examples of such labels are *freedom-loving, democratic, American, patriotic,* and *friend.* Such words often fill the listener with good feelings so that he accepts the speaker's propositions without reasoning them out. [Such propaganda techniques should be taught and well understood by gifted students.]

Encourage Development of Values and Philosophy of Life

What is a philosophy of life? Do we need one? Do we always have one whether we are aware of it or not? What are some of our basic beliefs? What are some of our guiding principles? What would you like to contribute to our society?

"Liberty is a boisterous sea. Timid men prefer the calm of despotism"— Thomas Jefferson. What did Jefferson mean by this statement? What are the implications for people today?

Discuss the making of a great man, Abe Lincoln, and ask whether or not today's children could adapt themselves to his early environment. The influence of time and necessity are also factors for discussion in *Abe Lincoln Grows Up,* by Carl Sandburg.

Expressive Fluency

Different things bring a feeling of happiness or pleasure to different people. Happiness can be expressed in a number of ways: for example, happiness is the sound of a silver dollar clanking in a piggy bank, or the smell of a rose on a spring breeze. How many similar expressions can you make regarding things that give you pleasure?

Rewrite each of these statements in as many different ways as you can without changing the meaning:

There is more power in the open hand than in the clenched fist.

A chip on the shoulder usually indicates a block of wood close by.

We may not be always rewarded for our deeds, but we are sure to be judged for our misdeeds.

On the Tell-el-Amarna tablets was recorded the diplomatic correspondence

Table 7–4 (*Cont'd*)

between the Egyptian king and the Babylonian, Assyrian, and Hittite nations. What problems do you think might have been discussed?   Do similar problems exist today?

Source: From L. Bachtold. *Counseling: Instructional programs for intellectually gifted students.*   Sacramento, Calif.: California State Department of Education, 1966, pp. 58, 61.   (ED 011 124)

for slightly older youngsters.   The student is encouraged to take a skeptical view of messages from those who have other motivations, such as advertisers and politicians.   Bachtold also encourages a concern for values—the active consideration of guiding principles, of the essence of greatness, and of the responsibilities of liberty.

An increasing number of authors have been making specific suggestions on how to stimulate the expressive abilities of gifted students.   Most of these ideas fall into the following categories: (1) seeking multiple answers, (2) thinking about common objects or ideas in uncommon or unique ways, and (3) encouraging playfulness in dealing with words.

Arnold (1962) suggests a variety of ways of thinking about the use of language, some of which are presented here.   When this type of exercise is tried, the teacher can be struck by the enthusiasm and wonderment of the students, which is evidence enough that they had not given any consideration to such alternatives on their own.   In teaching the gifted student this type of approach, the teacher can be assured that he is doing something for the gifted child that the child cannot do for himself, the essence of a good educational program for the gifted.

The following is a list of general questions (adapted from Arnold, p. 254) that can be used to spur students' thinking during brainstorming sessions using common objects as a basis for thought.

Other Uses
> *Can it be put to other uses as is?*
> *Can it be put to other uses if it is modified?*

Adaptation
> *What else is like it?*
> *What other ideas does it suggest?*
> *What could you copy?*
> *Whom could you imitate?*

Modification
> *What new twist could be made?*
> *Can you change the color, size, shape, motion, sound, form, odor?*

Magnification
> *What could be added?*
> *Can you add more time, strength, height, length, thickness, value?*
> *Can you duplicate or exaggerate it?*

Minification
> Can you make it smaller, shorter, lighter, lower?
> Can you divide it up or omit certain parts?

Substitution
> Who else can do it?
> What can be used instead?
> Can other ingredients or materials be used?
> Can you use another source of power, another place, another process?
> Can you use another tone of voice?

Rearrangement
> Can you interchange parts?
> Can you use a different plan, pattern, or sequence?
> Can you change the schedule or rearrange cause and effect?

Reversibility
> Can you turn it backward or upside down?
> Can you reverse roles or do the opposite?

Combination
> Can you combine parts or ideas?
> Can you blend things together?
> Can you combine purposes?

A similar exercise can be derived from the EDC curriculum on *Baboons* (1968), where the issue of language—what it is, and what differences there are between anthropoids and man—inevitably comes up. Some of the elements of linguistics and what they allow us to do is contained in the following list from *Baboons* (p. 36).

Describe things that have already happened:	I took a bath yesterday.
Describe things that haven't happened yet:	It will be difficult to live on Mars.
Describe situations that don't really exist:	She likes to make believe she is an actress.
Argue or disagree:	You're wrong to say that baboons live for hundreds of years.
Ask questions:	Who is the best player in the club?
Think of things that are fanciful:	The giant had three eyes right on top of one another like a traffic light—only one was blue, one was orange, and the middle one was the color of dried blood.
Think of things out of sight:	My sister is at band practice.
Humorously think of double meanings:	Our eggs can't be beaten.

Finally, some useful word games presented by Renzulli (1973) that are designed to stimulate linguistic expressiveness are presented in Figures 7–1, 7–2, and 7–3. The first of these is a word tree game that can encourage the interrelatedness of words and language. The second game —Making Words with Prefixes and Suffixes—focuses the attention of the student on the multitude of words with standard prefix and suffix terms. The third game—Word Boxes—can encourage, with a crossword puzzle format, use of the reservoir of words that the gifted student maintains. Each one of these activities could serve as additional exercises or "enrichment" for the gifted students who have completed their assignments. They can easily design and carry out such activities with a minimum of teacher supervision.

THE DEVELOPMENT OF VALUES

It is in language arts classes that some degree of discussion of values and judgment is expected to come into play. In the fields of science and mathematics the emphasis is on *how* to obtain the answer rather than the social usefulness of the answer. Social studies too often becomes a factual recounting of past events. If issues related to what is "important," "valuable," or "proper" do not get raised in the language arts curricula, they are unlikely to appear elsewhere.

One day in class, Zelda suddenly became very upset during a discussion of the plight of Vietnamese children. She broke into tears and for a period of time was inconsolable. It was clear that she felt very deeply about the injustice of innocents' being hurt. The other children looked at her strangely and were, in their own turn, upset that a peer would show such intense emotion over something that was happening so far away.

It was then that the teacher realized the special burden felt by those talented and gifted students who had a more highly developed ability to empathize and to relate to faraway places and faraway times. Such ability can bring delight, when imagination carries one to adventures in

FIGURE 7–1. *Word Trees.* (*From* New Directions in Creativity—Mark 1 *by Joseph S. Renzulli. Copyright © 1973 by Harper and Row, Publishers, Inc., New York.*)

FIGURE 7–2. *Prefixes and Suffixes.* (*From* New Directions in Creativity—Mark 1 *by Joseph S. Renzulli. Copyright © 1973 by Harper and Row, Publishers, Inc., New York.*)

FIGURE 7–3. *Word Boxes.* (*From* New Directions in Creativity—Mark 1 *by Joseph S. Renzulli. Copyright © 1973 by Harper and Row, Publishers, Inc., New York.*)

Name _____ Date _____

21 Word trees (a)

What words can you think of to complete the following
Word Trees?

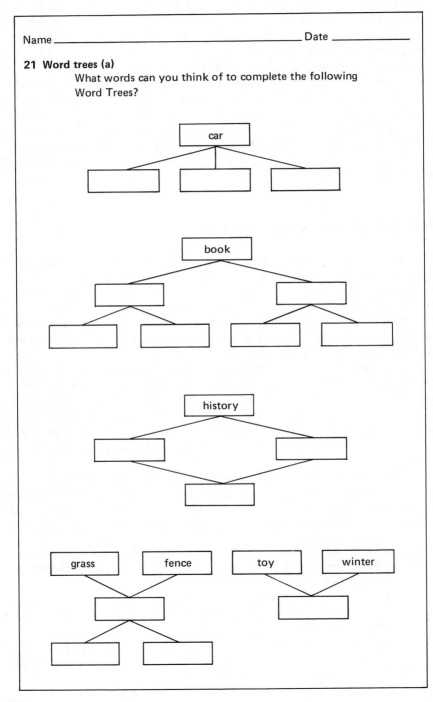

Name_____ Date_____

9 Making words with prefixes and suffixes (a)

A prefix is a letter or group of letters that is put in
front of a word to change the meaning of that word.
For example, if the prefix *un-* is put in front of *clear,*
the word becomes *unclear,* which means the opposite
of *clear.* We can increase our vocabulary and make
our language more interesting by learning how to use
prefixes.

See how many words you can make, using the following
prefixes. Use the back of this page if you need more space.

un *happy*   re *copy*   dis *obey*
un *clear*   re *build*   dis *like*
un _____   re _____   dis _____
un _____   re _____   dis _____
un _____   re _____   dis _____
un _____   re _____   dis _____

A suffix is a letter or group of letters that is placed at the end of a word to alter
the meaning of that word. For example, if the suffix *-en* is added to *dark,* the
word becomes *darken;* and its meaning is different from but related to the word
dark.

See how many words you can make by adding the following suffixes to words
you already know. Use the back of this page if you need more space.

_____ *kin* ship _____ *American* ism _____ *happi* ness
_____ *penman* ship _____ *human* ism _____ *soft* ness
_____ ship _____ ism _____ ness
_____ ship _____ ism _____ ness
_____ ship _____ ism _____ ness
_____ ship _____ ism _____ ness

Name _____ Date _____

16 Word boxes (a)

People who write crossword puzzles must think of words that will fit into a certain number of spaces and that will have certain letters in common with other words. In this activity, try to complete the Word Boxes below by thinking of words that fit in the spaces provided.

distant places and distant times, but it can bring deep concerns about issues like justice and morality that do not seem to be within the comprehension of the child of average ability at the preadolescent age.

Zelda's teacher also has something else to concern her. Who will instruct these talented youngsters in the areas of values or ethics or morality? The churches in this town, as in many others, have become of decreasing importance in the lives of the citizens. The schools, nervous about offending members of the community by injecting themselves into controversial issues, become jittery at the very thought of having a full-fledged discussion of the rights of citizens. There have been days and weeks where a full-fledged discussion of the Bill of Rights, to say nothing of population control or war and peace, could get the incautious teacher in a great deal of difficulty. Where, then, can Zelda go for instruction? To her parents, whose own search for what is "right" is hardly more coherent than Zelda's? Who will provide them with the bedrock of evaluative concepts that will carry them through the difficult and important decisions that lie in front of them? There is perhaps no more important question that the schools have to ask themselves than that.

It is a rare student who has heard a vigorous discussion in the public schools over rights of property versus civil rights, or the rights of employers versus the rights of employees—two of many issues about which many citizens are today seeking guidance. The reasons for this ethical vacuum are not hard to find. The schools, highly sensitive to partisan criticism, have tended to shun controversy as the easy way out. Another reason that keeps the public schools from more effective action is the philosophy that the school's primary mission is to pass on information and job skills, not values.

The focus of a typical unit or a discussion in the schools is "What is the *right* answer?" But suppose that there is no one set of correct answers but only a large number of answers, depending on the values each person holds. How does a teacher finish a topic under those circumstances?

Since many ethical issues are so open to debate characterized by highly charged emotions, the easiest thing to do is to ignore them, to say that these are the problems of the church or the family, or to rationalize them away on the basis of the supposed mental immaturity of the student.

We may be told that 10-year-olds have not had enough life experience to be able to make such decisions or to think clearly on such matters. Later on, much later on, perhaps they will be able to take up the discussion of these issues! And so they probably will—in the informal atmosphere of the dormitory, where few discussion topics are avoided because of the fears of a nervous adult society that the younger generation will learn too much, too soon.

One drawback to the schools' becoming involved in discussions on values and ethics may be the very real fear that such lessons on values

could easily become indoctrination by teacher or school. This is a justified fear, but there is a way around the dilemma. The school can concentrate on *how* the child can make value decisions rather than the nature
of the conclusion he arrives at. By focusing on the *process* by which such
decisions are made, the school need not take positions on such controversial issues as capital punishment, freedom and responsibility of the
press, and the like.

The Martian Expedition

The author once conducted a brief adventure into the ethical judgment
of a group of gifted children, some of which is reproduced here. (Gallagher, 1966a). The purpose of the study was to determine whether a
group of fifth-grade, intellectually superior youngsters from middle- and
upper middle-class homes could meaningfully discuss ethical concepts
and arrive at some resolution to problems presented to them. These
children were seen for one hour a week in a group of ten to sixteen children.

For a period of seven weeks, these youngsters were taken on an imagi-
nary trip to Mars as adult members of a first expedition to this planet.
This theme allowed for the introduction of many problems that needed
to be solved by the class; these were presented to the group for their discussion and resolution. The teacher maintained a neutral attitude and
did not express his own opinions on the problems or eventual decisions.

The students were told that they were going to make an expedition to
Mars. As the teacher, I would be the captain of the voyage; each of the
students was given the opportunity to create the character that he or
she would play in this expedition. The choice of characters in itself was
most interesting. The majority of the children chose a scientific role,
such as geologist, physicist, or biologist. Two of the youngsters chose to
be doctors, while many others picked pilot or assistant pilot. Such free
choices can tell you much about the children. One of the boys, who
seemed the most insecure, chose to be a corporal in the security force.
By implication, the lower the rank, the lower the duties or responsibilities expected of the individual. One of the girls in the class rejected
the traditional feminine role by taking on a masculine character as her
alter ego during the trip.

THE FOOD SHORTAGE PROBLEM. The members of the expedition were
informed that our spaceship had crashed on Mars and that it was likely
to take about eleven months to repair the ship so that we could return
to Earth.

The first problem presented to them was that we had only four months of food supplies and, thus, a serious difficulty in the distribution of this food. The students' approach to this problem followed a pattern repeated often in the weeks to follow. First, they tried to avoid making the difficult decision of how to divide the food supply. This would represent the normal reaction of adults in this situation—to solve the problem in a way so that the grinding and difficult ethical decision really doesn't have to be made. This could be done by finding edible plants on the planet, obtaining food from the natives, or even making artificial food; all these were suggested by the students.

In order to keep the problem as a real ethical issue, the captain rejected all of these possibilities, at least for the immediate future, and forced them into making some kind of a decision as to what should be done with the limited food. Eventually, after much discussing, they agreed by majority vote that the food should be equally rationed among all members of the expedition. They rejected the notion that the captain should get more than his just share because he was the captain, or that the head scientist should get more because of his status or position. The concept of equality of treatment was clearly established. The alternative concept that special persons should obtain special rewards was rejected.

THE DYING CREWMAN PROBLEM. Another rather difficult problem that was presented to the youngsters was that one of the members of the crew had been seriously injured and that both of the expedition doctors reported that he would surely die very shortly. The ethical question presented to the students was whether the food, which was already in very short supply, should be given to this person or whether it should be withheld on the grounds that he was going to die anyway and those who were living would need all the food they could get.

This problem brought out more ingenuity in the group in their attempts to avoid the central issue. The majority had no trouble coming to a conclusion that the person should obtain food, *but* the basis for the decision was that the doctors might not be right! Since doctors have been wrong before in their diagnoses, it would be wrong to withhold food and deliberately kill the person when he might have a chance to remain alive.

No one, in this instance, suggested that the person should receive food, even though he was going to die anyway, merely on the basis of his membership in the human community. The decision was not unanimous, and there were quite a few suggestions that the person should be allowed to starve to death on the basis that the other people needed the food more.

THE ARTISTIC CREWMAN PROBLEM. An interesting example of the rather finely developed sense of compromise of these gifted youngsters was revealed in another problem presented to them. One crew member was

193

supposed to be working on the repair of the ship but instead was so entranced by the beauties of the Martian countryside that all he wanted to do was to go off and paint Martian landscapes. He would be neglecting his duty by going off and doing this, even though his paintings were quite beautiful.

These students were loath to forbid completely this kind of activity and reached a compromise solution in which the artist would be allowed to continue his painting but would be encouraged to do it in his off-hours. He would be allowed then to work on the night shift where his other skills would be demanded by the emergency situation. If he would agree to this, he would be encouraged to continue his painting, but if he did not agree and completely avoided his other responsibilities, he could be punished by having his painting materials confiscated.

THE NATIVES' RIGHTS. Two additional problems presented to the children probably represented the most serious challenge to the youngsters' senses of right and wrong. They were told that we were in luck! One of our scientists had found some metallic deposits of the type necessary to repair the spaceship; but there was one problem. The only place that we could find this metal was in the holy ground of the natives. According to them, any outsiders coming into that ground would desecrate it. We would therefore have to do serious insult to the religious feelings of the natives if we pursued the metal we needed. Should we do it?

For the first time, the students came face to face with the conflict between abstract standards and direct human needs. Although they all felt that the natives' religion should be respected, in the end the consensus was that we should take the metal. The guilt feelings of the students were manifest. They would take only so much metal as was absolutely needed. Furthermore, they would return that amount of metal plus payment for damages when they returned to Earth.

It should not be concluded from the lively discussion held over this question that these talented children now had insight into *why* some people transgress against standards that they hold in high regard. The most single striking observation of these students is that whereas they had a well-developed sense of right and wrong, they had little or no understanding of the motivation of the transgressor. In most instances, he was "bad," or dismissed casually as "nutty."

The conclusion drawn from these discussions was that intellectually superior children in the elementary grades were quite capable of conducting vigorous and spirited discussions of "right" or "wrong" behavior. Their own inexperience in dealing with such issues was also apparent, however. None had raised such questions before in school or in their families, and they were eager to discuss among themselves and with others what the resolutions might be to issues of deep and worrisome concern to children such as Zelda and Sam.

Additional Teaching Techniques

A number of options, techniques, and procedures are available to the teacher interested in stimulating greater student interest in the area of values. One such device is referred to as the *value sheet* (Raths, Harmen, and Simon, 1966). This value sheet consists of a provocative statement and a series of questions duplicated on a sheet of paper and distributed to the class members. The purpose of the provocative statement is to raise an issue with value implications and carry each student through the value-clarifying process.

Raths et al. suggest that it is important for students to work on their own values on an individual basis and without classroom discussion, which may tend toward argumentation, or a strong pressure toward consensus. One such device is the use of a stimulating or provocative quotation such as the following from Gustave Flaubert:

> Nothing great is done without fanaticism. Fanaticism is religion; and the eighteenth century "philosophers" who decried the former actually overthrew the latter. Fanaticism is faith, the essence of faith, burning faith, active faith, the faith that works miracles.

After making sure that the class understands the quotation, the teacher might proceed with some questions to spur the discussion on—for example:

1. Are *you* a fanatic about anything?
2. What groups of people in our society seem fanatical to you? Why would you or wouldn't you join them in their efforts? What is better about *your* alternative?
3. How did you arrive at your decision about what to do?
4. Have you done anything lately about what you believe?

Once the topic of values is open, the number of stimuli or devices that can be used to help the students clarify their own values are unlimited, such as pictures without captions, a small scene from a play or a movie, role playing, and so on. In all these situations the attempt is to help the students clarify their own values and not to impose a particular set of values from the standpoint of the teacher or the school. This is the kind of philosophy that would seem to be essential for any values program that would survive in the public school setting. The role for the teacher is summarized by Raths et al. (p. 149) by three major principles for the teacher:

1. Unconditional acceptance of the student and problem.
2. No advice given even when that is requested but extensive use of clarifying questions and comments so that the array of alternative decisions and their consequences are made available to the student.
3. Look at the issue from the vantage point of the values of the student and not of the teacher.

What this approach relies on is that given the proper set of alternatives and a clear view of the consequences for each of the decision alternatives, the student will tend to make the sensible and ethical decision.

ROLE PLAYING.   More and more teachers have been considering the advantages of role playing in bringing forth from students a greater appreciation of their own values and an understanding of various alternative decisions and their consequences.   Basically role playing is a group problem-solving method that involves a variety of techniques—discussion, problem analysis, and definition.   The teacher often begins the role playing with a story that introduces a variety of characters and a theme or conflict situation.   The students are then asked to continue or complete the story by spontaneously reacting in a dramatic or stage-play setting. The actions of the various characters are then discussed at some length. According to Shaftel and Shaftel (1967, p. 10), the major elements of role playing are as follows:

1. Initial enactment of proposals (taking on of roles).
2. Observer reactions to the enactments (discussion).
3. The drawing of conclusions or generalization and decision making.

As in the other techniques noted here, role playing provides a means for children to make their own discoveries and make better decisions because of their increased awareness of alternatives and consequences. One of the criticisms of this approach has been that it tends toward group conformity through the group discussion process.   But it doesn't have to be this way, as shown by this example from Shaftel and Shaftel (pp. 108–109):

> Thus in the story "Sacrifice Hit" Danny faces a difficult choice; his ball team votes to buy a present for a man who has helped them. . . .   But Danny has been saving his money to buy glasses that he badly needs . . . and that his parents cannot afford to get for him.   If the role playing group can see that, in this instance, Danny's need outweighs the group's purpose they are acquiring judgment. . . .   And if they can appreciate what a struggle this is for Danny, how difficult it is for him to stand against group pressures . . . they are acquiring sensitivity to others' feelings.   Moreover the teacher can help the group to recognize that they can support an individual rather than function only to coerce him into group conformity.

Role playing is, after all, just one more tool that the teacher can use to enlarge the experience and knowledge of his students.   Like other tools, they are only as good as those who use them.   If role playing or any other technique is used without sufficient knowledge, training, or understanding, it will serve little purpose in a quality educational program.

A task reported by Dodder and Dodder (1968)[4] encourages students to accept the inherent value of many different kinds of persons. Each child is given a list of people, for example:

your brother	a baby	a musician
a teacher	the President	a minister
your best friend	a crippled child	a fisherman
a sick man	a sailor	a writer
your parent	an expectant mother	an astronaut
an orphan	a Communist doctor	you
a policeman		

He is then asked to imagine the following: You are marooned on a desert island and in the midst of a terrible epidemic. The doctor has serum for only seven people. Which seven would you innoculate if you wished to:

1. Create a new society on the island.
2. Have an enjoyable stay on the island.
3. Conduct scientific experimentation.
4. Ensure the continuation of democracy.

The students will grasp rather easily that different people are valuable in different circumstances and that everybody is valuable for something —a useful lesson for gifted students who may tend to be contemptuous of talents other than their own.

No greater error could be made than to assume that the gifted child, by virtue of his precocious intellectual development, will necessarily be a law-abiding or moral person. The distinction between perceiving what is right and doing it is not only worth keeping in mind from the standpoint of the educator, but worth presenting to the gifted student as well, since some gifted students seem to equate intellectual superiority with overall personal superiority.

From the limited research that has been conducted on the development of morals in children, several points are worth keeping in mind. The work by Bandura (1969) has contributed a great deal to the understanding of the development of concepts of identification through social imitation. It is fortunate that the child can learn entire patterns of behavior through imitation, since trial-and-error learning would be a fantastically inefficient procedure.

As Bandura's research shows, the child does not imitate everyone around him, nor all the adults around him. Instead, the child tends to imitate those adults around him who appear powerful and able to get necessary things done. This is true even when the child may not express great affection for the powerful adult. The work of Whiting (1960) lends

[4] From *Decision Making* (Boston: Beacon Press, 1968). Reprinted by permission of the Unitarian Universalist Association, 25 Beacon Street, Boston, Mass. 02108.

substantial support to the concept that the child's self-control has its roots in his fear of the loss of parental love. Guilt feelings that lead to self-control seem to develop if the child has an investment in keeping the parents' affection and at the same time is relatively uncertain about gaining that affection. It is the parents' power to withdraw needed affection that represents the strongest influence on the development of moral attitudes and behavior, and Whiting has found this characteristic to be present across many different cultures.

If the intellectually gifted child does not receive this kind of parental or parental-surrogate relationship, he is no more likely than the intellectually average child to perform in moral ways. The mere understanding of what is the right and proper thing to do is not likely to change his performance, although it may help the gifted child to broaden his applications.

Thus, the intellectually gifted child can grasp early the concept that all mankind has much in common, regardless of individual differences in culture and background, and that being fair with one is equivalent to being fair with others. Whether, when he is an adult, he will support actions that, for example, would reduce starvation in other parts of the world depends on other facets of his development and on his own needs. In this regard, you may recall the students' choosing to take the metal from the sacred ground even though they accepted that it was wrong to do so.

SUMMARY

In this chapter we have repeated the theme of the previous three chapters that gifted students should be allowed the opportunity to understand ideas of greater complexity and systems of knowledge in the content field in question. In particular, there is a plea to go beyond the rather sterile presentation of grammar and syntax and to use literature as a means to instill appreciation of past cultures. Such devices as novels, songs, poems, and biographies can be used as a stimulus or jumping-off point for discussions about feelings, emotions, and values and can lay the foundation for a better understanding of the self.

The generally greater gifts that the gifted student has for language and for the understanding of complex ideas provide him with a stronger base for a study of values and the beginning of a base for making intelligent judgments of conflicting ideas.

The generally less important educational role being played in the society by organized religion has thrust additional responsibilities on the schools to help the children develop a sense of who they are and how they can live with others in a diverse, and not very secure, world.

Most educational programs rather carefully avoid the discussion of values, lest they be accused of attempting to indoctrinate the students with one set of values when the diversity in the American culture calls for a plurality of values. However, this chapter points out that values can be studied in the classroom without the teacher's being committed to any particular set of values that he then imposes on the students. Instead, what is taught are the techniques and means by which value statements can be judged and evaluated, thus giving the gifted student more tools with which to be independent of propaganda and of unfair persuasion. The study of values can be crucial to the gifted student and receive wide community acceptance, if prior explanations of the goals of the program are provided to the public.

A possible limitation to investing in a program that focuses on values may lie in the teacher's own uncertainties and lack of background. As in all the other content fields, major efforts at staff inservice training, organized professional support, or technical assistance seem necessary to help the teachers of the gifted interact as a team so that they can call upon those skills and resources of other members of the team that they themselves do not possess.

UNRESOLVED ISSUES

1. The creative and expressive student in language arts rarely finds instruction at the elementary or junior high school level that is the equal of his own talent. The freewheeling intellect of the creative student can intimidate and frighten a less talented teacher, who may invoke grammatical rules or some set of standard procedures as a means of regaining control of the situation, to the detriment of the student. How can this be avoided?

2. Can we find ways for the public schools to feel freer to discuss controversial issues and to teach the nature of value systems and social systems unlike our own as a means of increasing the sophistication of gifted students, who must eventually deal with such systems in their adult life?

3. Can we devise programmed learning sequences or computer-assisted instruction programs to teach the gifted students the mechanics of language arts so as to allow these students more time to be expressive and interpretive?

READINGS OF SPECIAL INTEREST

ABRAMOWITZ, J., & HALLIBURTON, W. *Searching for values: Pathways to the world of English.* New York: Globe, 1973.

A variety of selections from literature, poetry, and the popular sciences to stimulate student exploration of values. Provides the stimulus for student exploration.

LYON, H. *Learning to feel, feeling to learn.* Columbus, Ohio: Merrill, 1971.

Presents a strong personal argument for greater inclusion of humanistic education in the classroom. Many references are provided to other books and films that present this point of view.

SHAFTEL, F., & SHAFTEL, G. *Role playing for social values.* Englewood Cliffs, N.J.: Prentice-Hall, 1967.

Provides a sound basis for the use of role playing with elementary and junior high school students. Many examples give a firm understanding of the basic arguments and mechanisms used in role playing in the schools.

TURIEL, E. Stage transition in moral development. In R. Travers (Ed.), *The second handbook on research in teaching.* Chicago: Rand McNally, 1973.

An updated description of available knowledge in the development of moral thought in young children. Presents the proposition that there are regular stages of development through which children pass. Gifted children will naturally reach these levels at an earlier age.

SECTION III

Stimulation of Productive Thinking

In Section Three we deal with one of the most puzzling and exciting areas of education. Namely, how does one enhance the problem-solving and creative-thinking skills of gifted students through the educational program?

The ability to generate new information through the internal processing of available information is one of the most impressive and valuable skills of mankind. Information is available not only through observation in the environment but also as information stored in the memory of the thinker. It is the ability to recombine the bits of this information into new meanings that sets mankind apart from the animals. It is the ability to perform these thinking processes well that sets the gifted student apart from the student average in ability.

This section is divided into two chapters: problem solving and creativity. At first glance this might seem to be an artificial distinction because many of the same thinking processes are involved in both these operations. It is my belief, however, that there are real differences between problem solving and creativity in terms of teacher and student expectations, the learning atmosphere necessary for these processes to flourish, and the procedures one follows to reach a productive thought.

In problem solving we are faced with the equivalent of the detective story in literature. One is confronted with a series of elements that relate to a puzzle or to a need to reach a solution that is not immediately available. Someone, the teacher or a textbook, has created the problem and knows what the answer should be, in most cases. It is the students' role, then, to discover how to put the available elements together to reach a reasonable solution.

In short, they need to call upon certain available thinking strategies or heuristics that they have at their disposal and apply them in the appropriate manner to reach the desired solution. The work reported by Covington, Crutchfield, and Davies (1966) in Chapter 8 actually follows a detective story format as they attempt to stimulate the understanding of mental rules that the students can follow in problem solving.

Creativity refers to a mental process where the expectation is that something new and original will be produced. That is, a new and unique combination of existing elements will produce a product that was not wholly predictable by either teacher or student when the process began. We are not maintaining that the term creativity or creative process can be used only when the thinking processes create a product truly unique to mankind. This would be too stringent a criterion for a child, or for adults for that matter. What is required is merely that the producer of the creative effort be ignorant of the exact same product having ever been produced before. The exhilaration at producing something that no one else ever has (to his or her knowledge), whether a poem, story, scientific invention, or painting, is part of the joy of creative work and quite different from the feeling of quiet satisfaction at finally solving a puzzle or problem created specifically for him or her by someone else.

This is an extraordinarily important topic for teachers of gifted students because a student with great facility in these thinking skills has achieved a type of declaration of independence from teacher and textbook. He can learn on his own rather than wait for learning to be shoveled into him.

Cynics have noted that student intellectual independence does not always rank high as a teacher or school goal. Schools have not been noted for extensive educational programming for creativity, and probably deserve only passing grades for their emphasis on problem solving. The next two chapters bring together many of the new bits of evidence or recently developed techniques for stimulating these thinking abilities in gifted students. It is an area ripe for further development.

8

Problem-Solving Strategies
for the Gifted

When is a gifted child ready for the discovery of new ideas, for independent searching, for inquiry? Sometimes it seems as if a student must wait until graduate school before he is allowed or expected to carry out independent inquiry. It is true that in the modern world there are more and more things to learn, but if education consists merely of cramming these ideas into a receptive cortex, then through what miracle will the idea gatherer become the idea producer?

Worse still, students can become comfortable in the role of fact absorber and are uncomfortable when asked to solve problems on their own. Zelda, for example, has been rewarded so often for her encyclopedic knowledge that even when the opportunity to do independent work or problem solving appears, she retreats into mastery of factual material, as in the following example:

T: What might have happened if Lincoln had lived?

Zelda: I read where Lincoln was alive for several hours and some people had hopes that he might pull through. The plotters planned to assassinate the Vice-President too, etc., etc., etc.

Notice how Zelda sidesteps the adventurous question and slides back into the rote memory where she is comfortable and secure.

Education should ask more of gifted children than that they be walking memory banks. They must also be problem solvers and creative thinkers, and they will not reach that goal by passively soaking up more information. Intellectual independence is a hard-won prize, and it must be practiced diligently and with skill.

Several methods of accomplishing this goal are presented in this chapter. All these methods are harder on both teacher and pupil than lecturing and note taking, but they are also more exciting. In addition, they contain the seeds of an active pedagogy that is more likely to produce citizens who meet problems head-on rather than merely catalogue them.

Much useless debate can be stimulated by asking which is more important, the structure of the content, or the pedagogical methods of presenting content? This is like asking whether the left leg is more important than the right!

Many of the supporters of the "new curricula" lean toward the "discovery" approach, since it seems to resemble the type of activity engaged in by scientists or scholars in their search for knowledge. It is no coincidence, therefore, that discovery methods have enjoyed much popularity at the same time that these extensive curriculum revisions were being developed.

There are many persons who seem to subscribe to the general proposition that "There is nothing new under the educational sun." No sooner does some innovation in education appear, such as the "discovery" method, than numerous persons, alert to educational history, protest. Schultz points out that the same method was used by Count Wolfenstein in the Alsatian schools in 1892. Rosselli notes that this method was used by Caberenni in the Sicilian schools in the early 1700s. Chang asserts that it was the same as that applied by Lao Tse Hung in the Northern provinces in China in 300 B.C., and so it goes. Although these particular references happen to be fictitious, such reminders are useful in giving perspective to current views; but it is also true that each time the idea returns, it is added to and modified according to the needs of the times.

TEACHING FOR DISCOVERY

The work of Piaget (1970), well-known child psychologist, has had an increasing influence on American psychologists and, through them, on educational psychology. His major point of interest to us is his concept of stages of intellectual development. He believes that children's thought processes and operations go through distinct changes at various age levels. These levels are shown in Table 8–1.

Let us suppose that we have four children ages 3, 7, 10, and 15, all of whom are of average intellectual ability. What would Piaget's stages mean in terms of their reaction to various situations—for example, watching a tea kettle whistle?

The 3-year-old might say, "It is singing a song to me," thus revealing the egocentric and preconceptual thinking of his age. The 7-year-old

TABLE 8–1. *Stages of Intellectual Development.*

APPROPRIATE AGE LEVEL	THOUGHT PROCESS
1½ to 4 years	Development of symbolic and preconceptual thought.
4 to 7 or 8 years	Intuitive thought leading to the threshold of the "operation."
7 or 8 to 11 or 12 years	Concrete operations are organized. These are groupings of thought concerning objects that can be manipulated or known through the senses.
11 or 12 years through adolescence	Formal thought is perfected and "its groupings characterize the completion of reflective intelligence."

Source: From J. Piaget. Piaget's theory. In P. Mussen (Ed.), *Carmichael's manual of child psychology.* Chicago: Rand McNally, 1970, pp. 703–732.

might say, "When the kettle is on the fire and it has been there for a while, then the kettle begins to whistle." One can see in this statement the beginnings of logical association, but further inquiry would probably reveal that the essentials of the situation still escape the child at this age.

The 10-year-old might say, "The stove heats the water, which makes stem which pushes against the opening and makes the kettle whistle." This certainly makes more logical sense, but it still lacks depth and larger organization. The 15-year-old might say, "Heat causes expansion of the molecules and thus an increase in pressure." This is generalizing the situation beyond the immediate and the observable, and is the mark of the adult intelligence.

Naturally, the kind of response a child gives depends not only upon his age but also on his intellectual ability and his previous experiences with the situation.

It has been a common observation of American educators and psychologists, as well as of Piaget, that children below the chronological age of 10 or 11 cannot produce the formal structure of thought required for the *traditional* exposition of complex mathematical or physical concepts. This has led to the erroneous conclusion that, since formal thought cannot be elicited at a young age, the ideas themselves should not be presented to children before the age of 12, or thereabouts.

Advocates of new curricular programs have pointed out that, although young children cannot *produce* the formal language necessary for exposition, they can effectively *operate* on the ideas. The results of this line of reasoning are sometimes quite amazing. They lead to teaching primary-aged children the elements of set theory, geometric theorems, and complex physical concepts, such as the attraction of bodies and time–space continua.

This is possible because the children are not being asked to present the material in logical structure but, rather, they are enabled to operate on the information through problem solving. Important generalizations can be introduced in social studies and language arts in the same fashion. It remains a possibility that different types of instruction might improve the young gifted child's capacity even for formal logic.

Another goal of those who propose the use of the discovery method is to train gifted children to adopt a set or attitude about the search for knowledge itself. The proponents complain that the average textbook is not organized according to the way in which the scientist or scholar actually performed the experiments or thought through the problems. Textbooks are usually arranged in logical order, proceeding systematically from one point to the next, whereas the actual thinking processes of the scientist or scholar himself are often chaotic, intuitive, and occasionally incoherent. By presenting material in a carefully organized structure, it is possible for the student to gain understanding of that structure without being equipped with the set or attitude necessary to the discovery of further knowledge.

Learning or Mimicry?

Too much emphasis cannot be placed upon the importance of the set or attitude that the teacher establishes in students by the manner in which he approaches a topic. Two major teaching strategies can be identified by observing in most classrooms. A teacher can take the general attitude that "Truth in all its ramifications is yet to be discovered." The alternative strategy is presented by the teacher with the set or attitude that "Truth will be revealed to you in due time." Such strategies, presented day after day over a considerable period of time, can steer the students in predictable directions. If the teacher holds to the second strategy—that truth will be unfolded step by step—the natural student strategy would be to find out what it is that the teacher has in mind. Thus, the student's main job would be to get inside the structure that the teacher has in mind, rather than to attempt to build a structure of his own.

However, student strategy is quite different if the first strategy is adopted. If the truth is still considered relatively elusive, then it is up to the student, as much as to the teacher, to discover as much about this phenomenon as possible. In the process of doing so, the student is forced to develop a structure or organization of the subject himself, rather than merely to attempt to mimic the teacher's structure.

Discovery in Science

Teachers and educators of gifted children must come face to face with the central fact that one of their goals is to stimulate an attitude or approach toward the world, as much as to provide an infusion of knowledge of specific content. If teaching methods and the educational program are effective, one would expect the gifted child to come forth from that program not only with large bodies of information but with an enthusiasm for "questing," for searching out new knowledge. Somehow in this experience, a child should gain a love for the "hunt," a desire to search for knowledge with the same kind of enthusiasm that prior generations of youngsters had for the hunt for wild animals.

How can this attitude or motivation be engendered by the teacher? There are strong suspicions that certain types of teacher behavior in the elementary schools are not very conducive toward the building of such an attitude. It has been found that, in typical classrooms, teachers will ask from eight to ten times as many questions as will the children. Theoretically, it should be the children who are searching, questioning, and inquiring into new ideas. Should it be the teacher's role to be continually testing the extent of knowledge of the children?

Suchman (1965) presented a sequence of inquiry training in which the goal was to establish within children a systematic approach for discovering information on their own. This is demonstrated by a movie portraying an unusual physical phenomenon to the children.

Figure 8–1 illustrates one type of situation used by Suchman, in which he presents the standard physics experiment of the bimetallic strip. The elementary school children, most of whom had not had any prior contact with the experiment itself, are genuinely amazed when they see the strip bending *upward* under conditions of heat.

Suchman shows the film to the students and then announces that he will answer "yes" or "no" to questions about the phenomenon; the children's task is to try and arrive at the physical principle that will explain the phenomenon observed. Without specific training, the children seemed confused and uncertain as to what to do or to how to go about solving such a problem. Perhaps this is some reflection on the uniqueness of the task as far as the children are concerned. Many of them seem never to have been forced into a situation where they themselves had to think and reason out the answer to a question, as opposed to one where they could look for someone in authority to answer it for them. An example follows of a typical exchange between an adult and a child, in which the child is confused about what he has just seen.

Examiner: What made it go up? I'm here to answer questions.
Mark: Yes, I know. I can't think of any to ask.

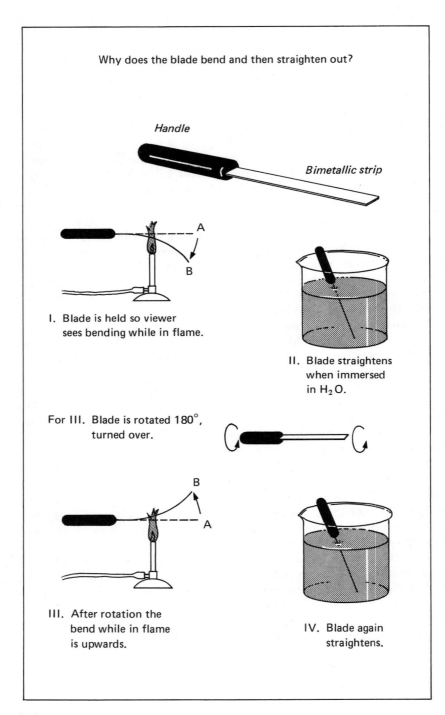

Why does the blade bend and then straighten out?

Handle

Bimetallic strip

I. Blade is held so viewer sees bending while in flame.

II. Blade straightens when immersed in H_2O.

For III. Blade is rotated 180°, turned over.

III. After rotation the bend while in flame is upwards.

IV. Blade again straightens.

Examiner: I see. Think. Try.

Mark: [Pause]   Well I can't think of any questions.

Examiner: What is it you want to know?   What would you want to know?

Mark: Why it bended upwards.

Examiner: What could you do to find out what things were necessary?

Mark: Try it.   Ask someone who knew.

Examiner: Yes, you could ask someone who knew, but that would just be getting somebody else to tell you, wouldn't it?   I mean finding out for yourself.

Mark: Just try different things.

Examiner: What?

Mark: Well, you could get the materials and things, and then trying holding the thing at a different angle.

Examiner: What do you think would happen?

Mark: I don't know.

Despite the fact that Mark is a bright youngster, he is genuinely confused and stumped as to how to begin.   Another type of response to this situation could be described as the pseudointellectual approach, in which a gifted child faced with such a task will try to throw together as many long words as he knows which could be vaguely related to the situation itself.   An example of this type of interchange is shown in the questioning of Henry by the examiner.

Henry: Did it straighten in the water because the atoms of the heat molecules on the knife changed?

Examiner: The atoms on the [Interrupted]

Henry: Changed from a minus to a plus.

Examiner: How could you possibly find that out?

Henry: Well, it would be kind of hard, unless you did it with a telescope or microscope.

Examiner: I can't answer that question then.

Henry: It seems that this is just another fact of science, even though it's amazing, but sometimes it takes weeks to figure out answers. I'll do the best I can to find out an answer. Did it straighten because of the quick change of temperature?

In this interchange with Henry one can see a fine example of an intellectual bluff put on by some gifted children.   Although the words have a ring of authenticity and importance, it is clear that Henry really does

---

Figure 8–1. *Bimetallic Strip.* [*From R. Suchman. Inquiry and education. In J. Gallagher (Ed.)*, Teaching gifted students: A book of readings. *Boston: Allyn and Bacon, 1965, p. 219.*]

not know the essentials of the situation. It is just as clear, however, that Henry has successfully used this technique many times in the past with teachers who would comb through all of this chaff to get at a nugget of golden thought, or what they think is a nugget, in Henry's ideas. The teacher would then take the ideas, reform them, explain them in the proper way, and perhaps come to the conclusion that Henry understood the situation but wasn't able to express himself clearly, when the truth was that Henry really understood very little. As long as the teacher takes the responsibility for presenting the major ideas, Henry stands a very good chance of getting away with such a performance. But whenever it becomes the students' responsibility to solve the problem, Henry, and the children like him, become revealed for what they are—clever intellectual malingerers.

Suchman conceives of three stages of inquiry that youngsters can follow to solve such puzzles. The first stage he calls *episode analysis*. At this point the youngster learns that his primary task is the verification of the facts observed in the film. The example of a child's response following this type of training may be seen in the following interchange between Steve and the examiner. Notice that Steve is trying to lay out dimensions of the situation itself in order to form a basis for further thought processes.

Steve: Was this plain water in the tank?
Examiner: Yes.
Steve: Was this a special kind of a flame?
Examiner: No.
Steve: If you had used a wood flame, would it work?
Examiner: Yes.
Steve: Was the blade hot when the film was going on?
Examiner: When it was being heated, certainly.
Steve: Did it melt?
Examiner: No.

The second goal of inquiry is the *determination of relevance*, which, in effect, means the isolation of relevant and necessary conditions. A second goal of this stage is the identification of the conditions necessary for the outcome of the experiment. In this stage the child is encouraged to think up kinds of verbal experiments, in which he changes the situation and then asks the examiner to comment on what might happen. A short example of this kind of hypothetical reasoning is seen in the interchange below.

Steve: If this had been left to sit for five days, would it work?
Examiner: Yes.

Steve: Could this have been made—was this made any different way than any other knife you would think it would be like?

Examiner: Yes.

Steve: Did that have any effect on it?

Examiner: Surely.

Steve: Was there some chemical in the metal that did it?

Examiner: No.

The final stage Suchman labels the *induction of relational constructs,* which represents the realization that different metals expand at different rates under heat. The intellectual jump from stages one and two to stage three is of major proportions, and it is still not clear why some youngsters are able to make it and others are not.

Although the teacher himself may not be in a position to carry out precisely this type of operation, he is in a position to have the children take a more active part in inquiry into a field of knowledge, whether it be science or social studies. The teacher, to use these ideas in his own circumstances, must think up examples of how these stages can be elicited from students. For instance, the students might be shown a strange map and asked to discover, through a similar procedure, as much about it as possible as a stage-one operation. Stage two, the determination of relevance, could be attacked by asking the students to use their knowledge to place cities or the kind of crops to be raised on the map.

Discovery in Social Studies

In the area of social studies, it is not possible to isolate a part of the conceptual structure in the same way that it can be done in mathematics or science. Thus, the "discovery" of the students will not be nearly so predictable in social studies as in the more quantitative fields. The teacher has to adapt his methods to the development of the topic. For instance, a teacher could introduce his topic as follows:

T: Do you know that there has just been discovered a new island in the Pacific Ocean? I am fortunate enough to have some maps of that island right here today. (Said with mock secrecy while passing out maps of Island *X,* shown in Figure 8–2.) The mysterious sailor who sold me this map did a thorough exploration of the island, and you can see that it has some interesting features: a mountain range that runs down to the sea on the West and South; a major river running down to the sea; and a broad, flat, fertile plain on the Eastern coast with forest areas to the North. (This description ensures that all the students in the group have been informed of the major physical characteristics of the island.)

213

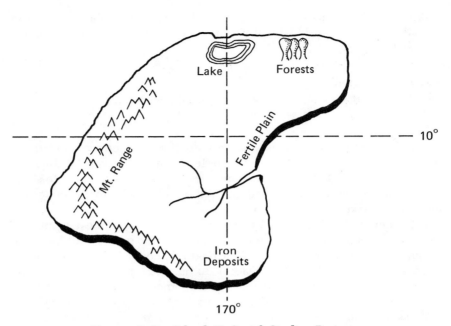

FIGURE 8–2.   *Island X—Social Studies Project.*

Mary: Are there natives on the island? (Here is a sticky question. Introducing further complications of a native population would ensure the class's getting involved in questions of dominant versus weaker cultures, possible physical threat from the natives, or the clash of cultural values. The teacher wisely limits the issue to the effect of physical surroundings on the colonists.)

T: No, Mary, no natives. Now, class, our problem is to try to decide in advance where the settlers that will come to the island will live and what they might do. Cranshaw?

Cranshaw: Well, there will be some farmers who will want to settle in that plain—

Pete: Some mining engineers will come and make some camps up where those iron deposits are.

Juan: What kind of climate does this place have?

Mary: It could be anything!

Josie: No, it couldn't. Look, we have the latitude and longitude. That'll tell us something.

Joe: It tells us it will be plenty hot—that's almost on the equator.

Mary: No hotter than Hawaii. That's almost on the equator, and those sea breezes make the climate very nice.

Mike: (Insight) Tourists! There will be lots of tourists there. I bet they'll go to that lake there.

214

T: If you had to guess where the largest community would be, where do you think?

Mike: On the lake. A vacation resort.

Carol: No—It will be where the river meets the sea because the tourists will have to land there, and the miners will send the iron to be put on ships.

Steve: Yeh, and the farmers will send their produce for export there.

(And so it goes. Notice that with a group of gifted children the teacher can let the students "carry the ball" to a much greater extent. The students also have a tendency to build on the ideas of other students to enhance and modify their own.)

The teacher could give further assignments, asking the students to draw in the major railways and roads—later, he might even ask them to write a fictitious history of the first ten years of colonization.

While the students have not been asked to state the concepts that form the base of their judgments in formal terms, their ability to defend their positions and ideas will rest upon the validity of specific concepts in their own minds.

Similar exercises can be used, with the discussion relating back to our own continent. For example, suppose that an argument ensues between Mike and Carol as to who might be right. The teacher might then ask how we could make a judgment. One of the students would almost surely suggest that our own continent was settled in a similar way, and we could readily see where the largest cities had been situated.

The essence of *guided discovery*, then, can be stated in the following points:

1. The teacher has in mind a general principle that has to be learned by the student. This is an essential and limiting requirement in itself. It means that the teacher has already conceptualized, in his own mind, the topic to be discussed.
2. The teacher then constructs examples, each one of which would illustrate some elements of the concept.
3. These problems are then presented to the students with the number of examples varying according to the needs of the particular group. In some instances, one or two examples might be sufficient, whereas, in others, it might demand maximum ingenuity and patience to illustrate the concept.
4. Students are encouraged to demonstrate their understanding through the application of ideas or problem solving, rather than through verbalization. The case against verbalization is based on two factors: (a) too early verbalization of the principle would tend to short-circuit the other students' discoveries, and (b) too early verbalization tends to be poorly stated, and organized in such a form that attention must then be paid to the preciseness of the verbalization itself, often resulting in loss of the concept and its meaning.

215

All this presupposes a teacher flexible enough to veer from the point he had in mind to others to which the students' inquiry might lead. It matters little in what order the anchor points of a conceptual structure of mathematics or social studies are discovered, so long as they are all present at the end.

The prime limiting factors in the successful use of this technique are the intellectual flexibility of the teacher and the teacher's own conceptualization of a content area. Fortunately, both these factors are trainable to a large extent. It seems entirely likely that increased knowledge of an area in itself can lead to increased flexibility in the teacher, just as lack of knowledge can lead to rigidity.

Evaluation of the Discovery Method

Kagan (1965, p. 560) presents four major arguments in favor of the discovery method as a desirable teaching technique.

1. Studies of both animals and young children indicate that the more active involvement required of the organism the greater the likelihood of learning. . . . A major advantage of the discovery strategy is that it creates arousal and as a result maximal attention.
2. Because the discovery approach requires extra intellectual effort, the value of the task is increased. . . . It is reasonable to assume that activities become valuable to the degree to which effort is expended in their mastery.
3. The inferential or discovery approach is likely to increase the child's expectancy that he is able to solve different problems autonomously. . . .
4. The discovery approach gives the child more latitude and freedom and removes him from the submissive posture ordinarily maintained between teacher and child.

These arguments are based on solid educational and psychological principles. Nevertheless, it would be more reassuring if there were direct experimental evidence as to the value of the technique.

The discovery method, despite its inherent attractiveness, is not without its cost. Perhaps the largest cost of all is that of *time* and increased teacher preparation. Guided discovery means careful teacher preparation in choosing the examples to be used to attain the concepts. In addition, there is the time required for the student to follow the path to the expected discovery. Thus, a principle that could be quickly stated, along with several cogent examples by the instructor in a formal presentation, must be evoked from the students through the discovery method, which might take four or five times as long. Eventually, the decision has to be made as to whether the gain obtained is worth the cost involved.

In the author's opinion, the discovery method generates obvious enthusiasm and excitement in preadolescent children that is not obtained through more formal presentation. The discovery that is useful, however, is not random discovery but the discovery within an organized and structured framework that the teacher already has in mind. This does not mean that the children will not come up with some surprising associations that even the teacher had not considered, but it is important that the teacher of gifted children—those who most likely will be dealing in the world of thought in their adult life—be able to use this pedagogical technique effectively whenever it seems appropriate.

PROBLEM-SOLVING PROGRAMMED INSTRUCTION

There are few materials available that instruct students in the process or strategies of problem solving itself. Most of the time the student is supposed to gain problem-solving skills through intuition or through imitation of a good problem solver, perhaps the teacher. Rarely does he get a chance to focus on the essence of the thinking process itself or how he can arrange his own strategies to maximize his performance.

Covington et al. (1966) provided one such set of materials in the form of a series of puzzles faced by a preadolescent boy and girl, Jim and Lila. They solve a set of sixteen mysteries through the careful application of problem solving. Each of the sixteen lessons, presented in a comic-book, programmed-learning format, starts out with a mystery, such as a mysterious message related to a man's will left for them to decipher, as follows:

ROUND AND ROUND IT GOES
THIS WAY, THAT WAY
AS IT BLOWS

Jim and Lila systematically make a list of all the meanings that this message might have, and they test each of them, as shown in Figure 8–3.

The student is expected to follow along and become interested and excited about the puzzle, since he can participate in the search too, until the answer is obtained. The list of techniques presented by the authors for attacking a problem is also given in Figure 8–3. These principles represent sound strategies, and a gifted student who grasps them can apply them in many other situations.

How well does this type of exercise help to stimulate problem-solving ability? A research study that tries to answer that question will be reported later in the chapter.

217

FIGURE 8–3. *Exercise in Problem Solving. (From M. Covington, R. Crutchfield, & L. Davies.* The productive thinking program. *Berkeley, Calif.: Brazelton Printing Co., 1966, pp. 5–15. Reprinted by permission of the author. A revised version was published in 1974 by Charles E. Merrill Publishing Co.)*

Figure 8-3 (Cont.)

Uncle John is right. The guides for good thinking that you, Jim, and Lila have been practicing in these lessons are valuable in *all* kinds of problems -- both in school and out. So, try to use these guides:

Be planful in your work on the problem.

> Before diving in, get clear just what the problem is all about. Get the facts well in mind. Decide on a good way to start.

Keep an open mind. Don't jump to conclusions.

> Often, we decide too quickly that our very first idea is the right answer. Give yourself a chance to think of other possibilities.

Try to think of MANY ideas. Don't be afraid of unusual ideas.

> One good way to think of many ideas is first to make a list of all the important things in the problem -- every object and person. Then, think about each of these things, one at a time, and see what ideas it may lead you to.
>
> Another good way is to ask yourself what are all the MAIN kinds of ideas that might be possible. Then see what *particular* ideas each of these main possibilities makes you think of.

Check your ideas against the facts.

> Decide which ideas can be thrown out because they don't fit all the facts, and which ideas seem the more likely ones to follow up.
>
> Go back and review all the facts to see whether you missed something before. Decide what further information you need in order to check on your ideas.

FIGURE 8-3 (Cont.)

220

When you get stuck for ideas, don't give up. Try to look at the problem in a new and different way.

One way is to *just suppose* that a certain possibility is the right answer, no matter how unlikely it may seem. Often, this will force you to take a whole new view of the problem.

Another way is to suppose that the *opposite* of what you have been assuming is really true. This will also help shake up your thinking.

Keep your eyes and your mind open to the things around you.

All sorts of things in your surroundings can start a new train of thought going in your mind and can remind you of possible ideas.

And often, too, you will find odd and puzzling things that may turn out to be clues to the solution.

When you observe a puzzling thing, think about it and try to explain it.

This is one way you can find your own problems to solve, and some of the best fun in thinking comes in working on the problems which you yourself invent.

When there are lots of puzzling things you are trying to understand in a problem, look for a *single idea* that will explain all of them together.

Good thinking to you!

These principles represent sound strategies and a gifted student who grasps them can apply them in many other situations.

FIGURE 8-3 (Cont.)

The general lack of challenge facing many gifted children in their schools and the difficulty of finding or retraining personnel to meet their challenge has led some to look for alternative ways of stimulating the gifted. The areas of programmed learning or computer-assisted instruction have in common the presentation of materials that have been prepared by outside experts and are likely to be conceptually valid. Are these techniques to be considered desirable alternatives for educating the gifted? The answer, disappointing to those seeking simple certainty, is that it all depends! Depends on the situation, on the task required of the student, the degree of flexibility allowed the student, the readiness of the student to grasp the ideas, and so on.

Programmed learning has a number of clearly identifiable features. It consists of a systematic presentation of materials in which the student is provided with a series of questions he must answer, sometimes by a computer and sometimes just in a workbook, as in the stories with Jim and Lila. The student receives immediate feedback on the correctness of his answers, then progresses to the next question.

The potential advantage of such a technique would be that the gifted students can progress alone and at their own rate on materials that are sometimes not in the teacher's domain. For example, Figure 8–4 shows a typical page from a programmed-learning textbook entitled *Applied Logic, An Introduction to Scientific Reasoning* (Scriven, 1965), a subject not often tackled or raised by upper elementary or junior high teachers, yet one of substantial interest to many gifted students.

The book attempts to help the student see the differences between the scientist and an astrologer in terms of concepts, such as evidence, prediction, probability, and other concepts necessary for the student to feel comfortable in the land of the scientist, whether as a resident or as just a visitor.

There are mixed feelings about whether such approaches can be useful. Again, one can say that it all depends! It depends on the importance of the topic, on the way the programmer has organized the learning, and the interest that the program elicits in the student.

Crutchfield and Covington (1965, pp. 8–10) have identified five ways that programmed instruction *could* be harmful to creative development of the gifted.

1. It may lead to *undesirable uniformity or homogeneity in content and ways of thinking,* because of the high degree of pre-structuring and close guidance of the learner through the steps of the program.
2. The highly *structured and controlled* character of programmed instruction may render it less able to account for *many distinctive and idiosyncratic* ways in which the individual thinks.
3. The very characteristics of a good program may result in learning which is too effortless, too much centered in the program and too

222

little in the learner. Thus the program may mitigate against the pupil's creative *development*.

4. The efficiency and effectiveness of the programmed sequence may instill in the learner a sense of deference to the program's authority, with no opportunity for questioning, dissent, or even rejection of content.

5. One of the cardinal aims of programmed learning is to achieve the utmost of clarity and precision in the learning task, whereas one of the essential characteristics of the creatively gifted children appears to be the ability to tolerate ambiguity, complexity, and lack of closure.

These are serious drawbacks that need to be considered. Certainly programmed instruction will not likely enhance creativity, but then it is not supposed to.

There are other techniques available for the stimulation of creative thought (see Chapter 9). If programmed learning is done well, it represents one type of independent activity that can be accomplished by the student with minimum teacher supervision.

Feldhusen, Treffinger, and Elias (1969, p. 8) suggest some dimensions that need to be present if a programmed learning lesson is to be appropriate for the gifted.

1. A teacher's manual stating objectives in terms of *advanced thought processes* should be present.

2. The learning outcomes for which the program was designed should be revealed to the gifted student.

3. The material itself should have a higher reading level and call for more complex verbal responses with a minimum of repetition and review. It should be possible to administer the program individually and to proceed at individual rates.

The possible utility of programmed-learning material depends, in a large measure, on whether the programmed-learning sequences are part of a total instructional program. Thus, while the teacher is trying to stimulate Cranshaw's class with a wide variety of imaginative and creative problems, Cranshaw can be spending a part of this time with a programmed-learning sequence mastering particular sets of information that provide the necessary factual basis upon which to make more creative and imaginative solutions.

Treffinger and Ripple (1971) commented on the nature of programmed instruction that was necessary to increase effectiveness of programmed-learning materials. In this case, they were using the productive-thinking program presented earlier in this chapter. For the instruction to be effective, the interaction of the teacher and the general instructional program must be correlated to the productive-thinking materials.

If the teacher participates extensively in the presentation of the program, *if* the materials are spaced rather than concentrated so that there is

138.   In science, we are mainly interested in factual informa-
        tion. In order to decide how much FACTUAL output an
        informant is giving you, ask yourself what would make
        his output FALSE. If an astrologer says that you have
        no brothers or sisters, you can easily say what would
        make his output false. Such output would be false if
        you had at least one brother or _____ sister.   one
                                        (number)
        Would this output be false if you had two sisters and no
        brothers? _____   yes
                    yes/no

139.   If the astrologer had said that you have no brothers, then
        his output would be _____ if you had at least one   false
        brother, regardless of how many sisters you have.

140.   Now suppose the astrologer said: "Either you have at
        least one brother or you don't." Notice that this output
        would be _____ in all cases. In other words, if you   true
                 true/false
        have at least one brother, the output _____ true.   is
                                              is/is not
        On the other hand, if you do not have at least one
        brother, then the output would also be_____   true
                                               true/false
        Would this output be false if you had a sister? _____   no
                                                        yes/no

141.   Output that can't be FALSE can't give FACTUAL
        information. In other words, the output "The door is
        either open or it is closed" _____ give you   does not
                                     does/does not
        factual information because it would be true in _____   all
                                                        some/all
        cases.

time available for additional synthesis and practice, and *if* the criteria used to evaluate the effect of this material are similar to the objectives of the material itself, there is evidence that such materials can be useful in stimulating the thinking abilities of the student.

Such results remind us again that no materials, however cleverly designed, can be effective unless they are integrated into the instructional program, and that the teacher using such materials cannot, in effect, walk away and expect that the materials by themselves will create a favorable result. The hard evidence is that a teacher has to become involved in a programmed-learning program if it is to be effective.

INDUCTIVE-THINKING STYLES

There appear to be many misconceptions about the proper role of the teacher in providing gifted students the freedom to think broadly and to search for new ideas with a sense of freedom of exploration. To some, the teacher's role should consist of an ability to nimbly step out of the gifted student's path and let him explore on his own, with a minimum of teacher interaction. This is an appealing approach to teachers who are, as are we all, just a trifle frightened of this expanding intellect before them.

But such a laissez-faire approach does not fit into our knowledge of classroom interaction very well. If the gifted child could in fact learn all these important ideas on his own, there would be no need for a teacher in the first place. The sad and painful fact is that more, not less, is required of the teacher whose objective is to extend the sense of intellectual excitement in the child. The teacher needs to know how to sequence topics and assignments so as to lead the child through the necessary stages of thought so that he will at last discover major ideas on his own.

The following description of one such sequence is taken from work done by Taba and Hills (1965) in an integrated social studies text. The students are expected to learn a large generalization: "Civilizations change when they meet a new culture." In Table 8–2 the steps suggested by these authors begin with a learning of specific facts (not dissimilar to Suchman's initial episode analysis), their distinguishing features in different cultures are found, and, in the third stage, the student is expected to explore the possible reasons for the difference.

Table 8–3 represents a brief discussion between teacher and students based on the proposition in Table 8–2 that America has just discovered

Figure 8–4. *Programmed Learning Sequence on Science.* (*From M. Scriven,* Applied logic: An introduction to scientific reasoning. *Palo Alto, Calif.: Behavioral Research Laboratories, 1965, p. 28.*)

Table 8–2.   *Steps in the Formation of a Generalization.*

Goal: Understand the generalizations:
      CIVILIZATIONS CHANGE WHEN THEY MEET A NEW CULTURE
             and
      UNEVEN DISTRIBUTION OF RESOURCES CREATES NEEDS
        FOR DIFFERENT TECHNICAL SKILLS, LEVEL OF EDUCA-
        TION AND PATTERNS OF LAND OWNERSHIP

Specific content: Study of Bolivia, Argentina, Mexico

  Step 1: *Learning Facts About Various Countries*
    Sample Teacher Questions:
      What is the climate like where the Aztecs lived?
      What are major trade items for this country?
      What are the proportions of European, Indian and other populations?
    Sample Assignment:
      Make a map and chart showing centers of populations and chief exports
      and buyers, education, major work of the people, etc.

  Step 2: *Discrimination of Unique Elements in Various Cultures*
    Sample Teacher Questions:
      What differences do you notice among these different civilizations?
      How do you account for these differences?
    Sample Assignment:
      Write a short story of a Mexican child visiting Argentina. Emphasize
      all of the things he or she might see that would be different from
      his own experience. Try to explain the reasons for the differences.

  Step 3: *Drawing Inferences About Differences*
    Sample Teacher Questions:
      Suppose explorers from a different part of the world (i.e., Japan) landed
      in Mexico or Bolivia; how would life be different there today?
      Suppose the climate of these countries got twenty degrees colder.
      What changes would we notice?
    Sample Assignment:
      Find three or four elements in present day culture that can be traced
      back to the original explorers.

  Step 4: *Finding Generalizations About Cultures*
    Sample Teacher Questions:
      What common things can you find in all of these cultures? (Govern-
      ments, education, trade, etc.)
      Are there certain kinds of things we would expect to find in any other
      culture we would have studied? What would they be?
    Sample Assignment:
      Rewrite the short story of the Mexican child. This time you will con-
      centrate on the things he would see and experience that would be
      familiar to him or her.

  Step 5: *Generalization Application*
    Sample Teacher Questions:
      Can we see how the kind of influence the discoverers had on Bolivia,

TABLE 8–2 (*Cont'd*)

Argentina, etc. was reproduced here in our own country?

How does our current government reflect the nature of our colonizers?

What is likely to happen if we meet a more primitive culture when we land on Mars? What changes would we expect to see in that culture?

Sample Assignment:

Respond to the following proposition:

Suppose that America suddenly discovered a large beautiful island out in the Pacific Ocean close to California, inhabited by rather primitive people who were farmers. What would happen?

Create a cognitive map of all of the possibilities that emerge from discussions and research on above issue.

Source: From H. Taba & J. L. Hills. *Teacher handbook for Contra Costa social studies, Grades 1–6.* San Francisco: San Francisco State College, 1965, p. 103.

TABLE 8–3.   *Exercise in Logical Reasoning.*

OPERATION	CONTENT	SPEAKER	COMMENT
Prediction	Tools	S	They don't know how to make tools.
Informational support		T	All right. How are most of our tools made?
		S	By machines.
Prediction	Machines	T	Do you think that they would have machinery as we have it?
		S	No.
Support by logical reasoning		T	Why do you think that they wouldn't?
		S	Because they wouldn't have schools.
		S	Electricity would run the machines.
Prediction	Electricity		They probably don't have electricity over there.
		T	Why do you think they wouldn't have electricity?
Support by logical reasoning		S	Well they don't know about electricity.
		S	But they can still have machines if they knew how to use water power.
Prediction	Water Power	T	Do you think that perhaps they would know how to use water power?
Support by logical reasoning		S	Maybe.

227

an island of farmers off our West coast. It is likely that most of the major dimensions will be spontaneously brought up by students, but the teacher can open the door with other questions, such as, "What changes would we see in the education of the natives?" The students' predictions of what would happen are followed by the teacher's asking for logical support.

Figure 8–5 gives a description of the cognitive map that can be produced from the problem presented here. Starting from the specific consequences noted at the first level of the chart (i.e., we would attempt to take them over), we can make larger and larger generalizations by moving up the chart. Here again students of differing levels of ability can

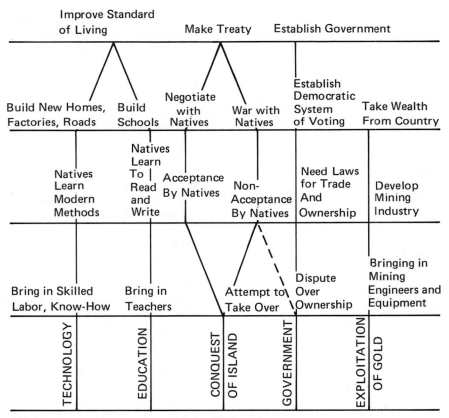

Focus of Discussion

Suppose that America Suddenly Discovered a Large Beautiful Island Out in the Pacific Ocean Right Close to California, Inhabited by Rather Primitive People Who Were Farmers. What Would Happen?

FIGURE 8–5. *Cognitive Map of Content in a Fifth-Grade Discussion.*

operate on different parts of the chart, with the gifted students focusing on generalizations and applications of generalizations.

This is only one of a number of possible ways to approach the introduction of abstract concepts to children. What is important is that the teacher have clearly in mind what the goal is and what the desired sequence of activities would be to reach the goal. Introducing stage 5 questions in stage 1 can lead to student confusion and chaos.

It is clear that students cannot generalize or apply major ideas unless they have some type of background facts and information. They need to compare and contrast differing situations so that the major ideas come clearly into focus. When the student obtains a generalization through this procedure the teacher can justifiably feel proud of his own role. He has been the guide who has led the intellectual tenderfoot to the right place at the right time.

SUMMARY

The theme of this chapter is that one of the three major dimensions of special programming for gifted children should focus on teaching them skills for learning that will help them become independent of their teachers and instructors. Perhaps an efficient strategy can be devised once educators admit that the facts they present today will inevitably be replaced by the discoveries and inventions of tomorrow, and that more attention must therefore be paid to teaching the child to seek knowledge on his own. All students, not only gifted students, should be able to solve problems and seek answers using search skills in the jungle of facts and ideas similar to the search skills they would need to survive in the natural jungle.

Several organized approaches to problem solving have been presented that will accomplish this instructional goal—notably, discovery learning, which has often been integrated into the total curricular program of recent science efforts. Although there are a number of logical and rational arguments for such an approach, the evidence for or against is extremely scanty.

The proponents say that it encourages more student involvement, strengthens the student's confidence in his own skills, and thus eventually leads to more independence on the part of the student. Opponents point out that searching takes a great deal longer than mere factual exposition, and if you have a lot of important material to cover and a limited time in which to do it, you may not be able to afford the student time to "mess around" searching for new ideas. They also tend to dismiss the proponents' argument that in discovery-learning the student is acting as a scientist acts in his own discovery process. Evidence is needed on both sides.

Almost everyone appears to agree on the fundamental point that it is possible to teach gifted students certain broad general strategies that can enhance their ability to meet problems successfully. Such strategies as, first, assembling facts and key relationships; then, speculating tentatively about possible causes or answers; and then, testing the answers for validity seem sound enough to teach students, either through direct teacher instruction or through supplementary educational devices such as programmed learning or computer-assisted instruction.

Since the topic of problem solving has rarely been accorded special attention or consideration, the various methods suggested here constitute a mere beginning; much more needs to be done to make this area a major emphasis in educational programs for gifted children.

UNRESOLVED ISSUES

1. Can the various skills related to problem solving be taught by teacher surrogates, such as programmed-learning series or computer-assisted instruction, and then applied by the gifted student in the regular instructional program?

2. Can we identify the essential characteristics that comprise a consistent problem seeker, the person who is able to discover and choose the problems worth attention rather than merely solve problems already chosen for him?

3. Can we organize problem-solving strategies into a more consistent set of skills that can then be part of a special curriculum taught directly to gifted students, rather than hope, as at present, that the student will come upon them through random experience?

READINGS OF SPECIAL INTEREST

FINK, D. *Computers and the human mind.* New York: Anchor Books, Doubleday, 1966.

A brief and readable description of the functioning of computers, relating them to the operations of the human mind. It focuses attention on such issues as "Are machines intelligent?" and "Can machines create?" Interesting for both teachers and gifted students.

GETZELS, J., & DILLON, J. The nature of giftedness and the education of the gifted. In R. Travers (Ed.), *The second handbook of research on teaching.* Chicago: Rand McNally, 1973.

A rather comprehensive overview of the available research in the field of the gifted with a definite emphasis on the area of creativity and productive thinking. Discusses the broadening definition of giftedness and the correlates of productivity.

MEEKER, M. *The structure of intellect: Its interpretations and uses.* Columbus, Ohio: Merrill, 1969.

An imaginative attempt to translate the Guilford structure of intellect model into educational activities and exercises that can be used for all types of students, but particularly the gifted.

WILLIAMS, F. *Classroom ideas for encouraging thinking and feeling.* Buffalo, N.Y.: Dissemination of Knowledge, Publishers, 1970.

A valuable source book of teacher suggestions on how to stimulate productive thinking. Attention is paid to affective as well as cognitive behaviors.

9

Creativity in the Gifted

During the past decade there has been a "creativity" boom in education. Probably more articles and books have been written on the subject in the past ten years than in all the accumulated educational literature written before that time.

Guilford (1968) reported in his presidential address to the American Psychological Association in 1950 that less than 1 percent of all of the psychological literature up to that time had dealt with creativity, despite the fact that it is one of the most complex of human behaviors and should be of great continuing interest to psychologists. Guilford's own work since that time has played a major role in changing that situation.

The reason for this great interest in creativity is not hard to imagine. In a rapidly changing culture, with whole new fields of study coming into existence in the space of five to ten years, while other occupations are going out of existence, the preparation of the young for their role in such a dynamic society becomes more complex. If we teach them specific facts alone, we face the very real problem that by the time the child spends twelve years in a school program those facts are no longer needed or the occupations they were prepared for no longer exist.

The situation is well put by one of education's more severe critics, Silberman (1970, p. 114).

> To be practical, an education should prepare a man for a work that doesn't yet exist and whose nature cannot even be imagined. This can be done only by teaching children how to learn and by giving them the kind of intellectual discipline that will enable them to apply man's accumulated wisdom to new problems.

The transformation of old information to solve new problems is the definition most often used for creativity. As Barron (1969, p. 10) puts it,

> Creativity may be defined quite simply as the ability to bring something new into existence. . . . Since human beings are not able to make

something out of nothing, the human act of creation always involves a re-shaping of given materials whether physical or mental. The "something new" is a form made by the reconstitution of, or regeneration from, something old.

Four elements need to be present to generate an educational boom. The first of these is a clearly stated need understood by both educators and the public. Second, a new conceptualization of intellectual or cognitive processes leading to a new look at the dimension involved must be present. Third, there must be new ways of measuring the characteristic or dimension involved. A variety of "creativity" tests, newly designed, have become available to fill this criterion. Finally, the ideas and concepts that are being discussed must be capable of new and easy translation to the educational process and program. All four of these key tests have been met and thus explain the popularity of creativity at this time.

STRUCTURE OF THE INTELLECT

The conceptual model that has undergirded much of the educational effort to measure and educate for creativity is Guilford's *structure of the intellect*, previously presented in Chapters 2 and 3. He used the statistical technique of factor analysis to generate as many different kinds of mental abilities as could fit into the model seen in Figure 9–1.

The structure is a three-dimensional cube consisting of intellectual *operations*, *products*, and *content*. This model assumes that there are a total of 120 possible cognitive abilities.

Content

The first of these dimensions, content, is illustrated in Table 9–1. The *figural* type of content refers to material that can be distinguished by form, size, shape, color, or texture. Although there is no meaning to this material, it is possible to present problems in this area for the student to grapple with intellectually.

The *symbolic* area essentially consists of figural elements to which some meaning has been attached. The prime example of symbols is the number system, but other material such as chemical formulas, highway signals, or even combinations of letters or words can be thought of as symbols. As noted in Table 9–1, the same type of task can be presented in all three of the content areas. It is necessary only to change the form

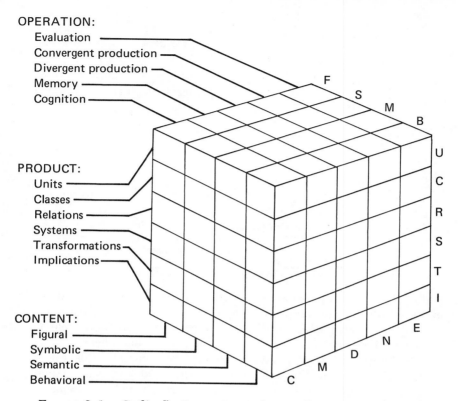

OPERATION:
Evaluation
Convergent production
Divergent production
Memory
Cognition

PRODUCT:
Units
Classes
Relations
Systems
Transformations
Implications

CONTENT:
Figural
Symbolic
Semantic
Behavioral

FIGURE 9–1. *Guilford's Structure of the Intellect Model.* (*From J. P. Guilford.* The nature of human intelligence. *New York: McGraw-Hill, 1967, frontispiece. Reprinted by permission.*)

in which they are presented. How would you change the following task requiring figural skills into a semantic or symbolic form?[1]

The reader is encouraged to practice with such transformations until he feels familiar with the content areas.

The important role that semantic content has played in school performance is clear. If anything, because of the emphasis on semantic con-

---

[1] Some possible solutions would be:

Semantic				*Symbolic*			
gallon	half gallon	quart	_____	16	12	8	_____
national	state	county	_____	chat	hat	at	_____

TABLE 9–1. *Guilford System by* Content.

FIGURAL	SEMANTIC	SYMBOLIC

FILL IN THE BLANK.

[figure: two rectangles] is to   Orange is to Fruit   ½ is to 1

[figure: half-circle shape]

    as   *as*   *as*

        is to____   Celery is to____   10 is to____

WHICH ONE DOES NOT BELONG?   Chair   Sofa   25   49
[figure: triangle, square, pentagon, diamond, circle]   Table   Bed   81   14
                                         Refrigerator   64

tent in IQ tests, it is possible that we have underestimated the importance of the symbolic and figural content areas. Guilford presents a fourth content area, *behavioral*, which covers such content as the development of social skills but which is not well developed at this time.

The differentiation of students' abilities by content skills can help explain why a student can be a crackerjack in social studies and language arts, or even certain mathematics courses that are highly dependent on semantic content, but still be mediocre in shop work and art courses, which depend on figural skills that the student has not developed to such a degree. There is no necessary assumption here that these skills are inborn, or that they could not be modified through experience.

Products

The second Guilford dimension is that of intellectual products. Table 9–2 indicates the various subdivisions under the general area of products. Examples are given for both semantic and symbolic approaches. In terms of desirability, there is little question that a teacher would prefer to have his students expressing themselves in the last three categories, rather than in the categories involving simple units, classes, and relations. But the categories of transformations, implications, and systems merely represent a more complex interrelationship of the simpler products. Thus, the example for systems, "Chicago is the center of a network of trade and transportation serving the entire Middle West," is made up of numerous units, classes, and associations—all put together in interaction

236

with one another to create a system. In a similar fashion, the transformation item, "What would 12 be in a base system of 7?" first demands knowledge of certain basic thought units and classes before the student can handle the more difficult transformation.

It is necessary for the reader to approach these categories actively in order to feel comfortable with them. Here are some simple tasks that the student might carry out for this purpose. Start with the following statements or propositions, and then construct a table similar to Table 9–2, creating the other examples yourself.

Relations:	*Lions are more dangerous than gazelles.*
Classes:	*Lions, gazelles, giraffes, and leopards are all mammals.*
Implications:	*A continued population growth will lead to serious over-crowding.*
Relations:	*The more people there are, the greater the need for food.*
Systems:	*Even numbers added or multiplied always give even numbers.*
Classes:	*4 24 42 108 are all even numbers.*

Remember, there is no limit to the number of possible correct answers to such exercises. It is important for you to try to do some of them, even if you are not too sure of the definitions of the categories themselves.

The intellectual skills that we would like gifted children to exercise

TABLE 9–2. *Guilford System by Products.*

SUBDIVISION	SYMBOLIC	SEMANTIC
Units	2.	Chicago.
Classes	2 is an even number.	Chicago is a large city.
Relations	2 is to 4 as 4 is to 8.	Chicago is smaller than New York.
Transformations	What would 12 be in a base system of 7?	If rail transportation disappears, Chicago will lose much business.
Implications	If we were living with a number system in base 7, what would happen to 8 and 9?	The diverse nature of its population makes conflict between subgroups more likely.
Systems	The series of laws relating to even numbers.	Chicago is the center of a network of trade and transportation serving the entire Middle West.

more are those of implication and transformation. These skills, which demand the ability to change existing circumstances to different forms or structures, have obvious implications for preparing gifted children for a flexible approach to the present, and a predictive posture for anticipating the future.

Intellectual Operations

Table 9–3 gives the third of the Guilford dimensions, intellectual operations. Whereas the category *content* provides the form in which the thinking will take place and that of *products* the result of the thinking, the category of intellectual *operations* concentrates on the means by which the product is reached. Guilford has found five general dimensions of intellectual operations: cognition, memory, convergent thinking, divergent thinking, and evaluation.

COGNITIVE MEMORY.[2]   Cognitive-memory activities deal with the reception and reproduction of material. In the case of *Hamlet*, for example, cognitive memory skills would be activated first by having the students read the play and then by asking them questions about it that would have to do with facts or ideas presented within the play itself. Any kind of interpretative statements or ideas would not fall under the cognitive-memory category, which covers what happened, not why it happened.

So much emphasis is often placed upon the stimulation of the higher thought processes that the impression is sometimes given that the collection and reproduction of facts is not very important. It is, of course, the irreplaceable foundation for advanced thought. It is first necessary to know what Hamlet did and said in order to make an evaluative judgment on his wisdom, to produce alternative courses of action, or to reason through the impact of his behavior on his mother.

TABLE 9–3.   *Guilford System by Intellectual Operations.*

OPERATION	EXAMPLE
Cognitive Memory	Whom did Hamlet kill by mistake?
Convergent Thinking	Explain why Hamlet rejected Ophelia.
Divergent Thinking	Name some other ways Hamlet might have accomplished his goals.
Evaluative Thinking	Was Hamlet justified in killing his uncle?

[2] In the classroom the distinction between cognition and memory is blurred. In applying this classification system to the classroom, Gallagher et al. (1968) combined the two into cognitive memory.

CONVERGENT THINKING.   Convergent thinking refers to the process whereby the student takes a large number of facts or associations, and puts them together in certain predictable combinations to come out with the one right possible answer.   The clearest academic illustrations of convergent thinking can be found in arithmetic reasoning problems, where the student takes a variety of facts and pulls them together to come out with the right answer.   All instances of deductive reasoning involve convergent thinking.

Although convergent thinking has been most often identified with the sciences and mathematics, it is found quite regularly in other subject areas as well.   Any problem that has a large amount of given information and that requires close logical reasoning to reach a valid conclusion calls for convergent thinking.   The question in Table 9–3 "Explain why Hamlet rejected Ophelia" is of this type.   The student must follow some type of deductive reasoning, such as:

> *Hamlet was disillusioned with all women.*
> *Ophelia was a woman.*
> *Therefore, Hamlet rejected Ophelia.*

Of course, this is not the only possible interpretation, but it is typical of the logical process that the student must follow to arrive at a reasonable explanation.

DIVERGENT THINKING.   Divergent thinking, on the other hand, represents a much more free and open type of intellectual operation, in which the distinguishing characteristic is the large number of possible associations or problem solutions.

The teacher who is interested in stimulating divergent thinking could pose the following problems: What other ways could Hamlet have used to trap the King? What other courses of action might have been open to Hamlet's mother? Suppose that Polonius had not been killed; how would that have modified or changed the eventual outcome of the play? All these questions attempt to make the student become more fully aware of alternative paths of action and of the development of the play itself. By considering such alternative lines of action, one gets a more thorough understanding of the particular sequence chosen by the author.

EVALUATIVE THINKING.   Almost any play or story will offer a rich field of discussion related to evaluative thinking. Evaluative responses require the student to establish some value continuum and then to weigh various alternative actions or persons against these values. For example, the statement "Was Hamlet's plan to revenge himself moral or right?"

requires the student to draw a value dimension of rightness or morality and then to place this particular act or plan somewhere on this dimension. While it might not be possible to prove directly which student's answer might be more correct, it is always possible to indicate the implications that could follow from certain decisions. For example, the teacher could point out that revenge breeds counterrevenge and that various feuds between families, clans, and nations are kept boiling through this mechanism.

The teacher could take a quote such as "There cracks a noble heart" and raise the issue as to how noble Hamlet really was. In a similar way, one could question the motives and approaches of each of the characters. More time could be allotted to such discussions with a gifted group, since a lesser proportion of time would need to be spent on cognitive-memory aspects, the teacher being reasonably assured that the necessary facts have been absorbed.

Much of the stimulation of evaluative thinking can be tied to convergent thinking; for example, the teacher can ask the question "Was Hamlet morally right in his revenge plans?" If we can imagine the student saying, "Yes," we can further imagine that practically any teacher would follow this reply with the question "Why do you believe this?" In this case, the student would be required to present a reasoned argument demanding convergent thinking, such as "Hamlet was only doing to his uncle what his uncle had previously done to his father." In other words, the logical sequence could be evoked: (1) People who do wrong should be punished; (2) Hamlet's uncle did wrong, and the only one in a position to punish him was Hamlet; (3) Hamlet, therefore, was justified in punishing his uncle through his plans for revenge.

The reader is warned that this Guilford conceptual system cannot be learned merely by passively reading from the printed page. It requires sustained practice and use. However, the results of such practice are almost surely to give you a better appreciation of the various forms of mental processes used by both students and teachers.

Once one has mastered the relations among the elements of this system, it is possible to identify entire units of classroom performance that fit into the model.

No classroom can escape a certain amount of cognitive-memory operations, since any thinking process must use certain facts and ideas that have been previously learned. It is a boring and uninteresting classroom, however, that confines itself mainly to this kind of activity, rather than using it as a prelude to other kinds of thinking performance.

In the instance of the class just described, the teacher used the facts that were established earlier to trigger some divergent thinking on the part of the students. The following sequence illustrates the teacher's approach and the students' response:

DIVERGENT SEQUENCE. During the first twenty minutes of class, Leslie, Kit, Sandra, and Nancee—in that order—deliver reports from their groups on facts and data they have found relating to problems agreed upon by the class, such as those which might be encountered if they stepped from a time machine and became the first settlers at the mouth of the Amazon River, Brazil, in 1500 A.D. After brief comment and discussion of the reports, T makes a change to a new topic and a new approach to discussion.

T: Now I'm going to be a combination Atlas, Hercules, Paul Bunyan, Pop-Eye, and Pecos Bill! I'm going to pick up a continent, and *move* it! (T picks up a rubber-wire outline map of South America which has been matched to the outline contours of South America as depicted on large, world wall map at front of room. T "moves" South America south and westward, over toward the area of New Zealand.) *Now—how would South America be different if it were moved over there?* (T sticks wire outline of South America to new spot. Class shows rousing interest; buzz of comments begins, many hands go up.) All right, Leslie, what do you think?

Leslie: Well, a lot of it would be cold that's hot now.

Kit: Part of it would still be in the tropics—it would still be hot.

T: Would it change the Amazon basin?

Class: Yes!

Jeannie: Maybe it wouldn't be discovered when it was. And maybe if it was, it'd be by different people.

Dan: There'd be some swell winter and summer resorts! (Some chuckles from class)

Leslie: The Indians'd maybe come over from Australia instead of coming down from Greenland (*sic*).

Sandra: Australia would probably be considered an island instead of a continent, compared with a big continent like South America next to it.

Katy: Australia'd still be a continent!

Dan: Magellan's straits would be a lot different. They'd run right into the South Pole. He could have had a short cut.

Cathy: Simón Bolívar, or—and Pizarro—they couldn't do much. They might not even *have* been there!

Katy: There wouldn't have been a Panama Canal—there'd be no need for one, really.

Leslie: Probably there'd be a lot more oriental people on this (South America at New Zealand spot) continent, and English settlers rather than Spanish—from Spain, which is so far away.

William: The Indians would probably come in down through the Philippines and some of those other Pacific islands.

Sandra: The theory of Africa and South America being connected earlier—that theory wouldn't exist.

One of the distinguishing features of divergent thinking in the classroom is the wide variety of ideas it stimulates, as can be seen by this exchange. The absence of a "correct" answer also seems to free the children from the inhibiting bonds produced by the fear of making a mistake; they become enthusiastic and excited by the ideas presented.

Most class sessions are a complex mixture of various kinds of thought processes. The teacher can plan to bring forth certain combinations of thought processes, such as the evaluative and convergent operations in the sequence that follows. This is a common combination. The teacher will first ask the students to weigh or judge certain facts or ideas (evaluative), and will then ask them to justify their ratings (convergent).

EVALUATIVE–CONVERGENT SEQUENCE. The children have just returned from their fifteen-minute recess. Earlier in the morning, the class had been discussing some of the proposed solutions to problems they might encounter if they stepped out of a time machine and found themselves the first settlers at the mouth of the Amazon River in 1500 A.D. The class has been dealing with these problems for several days, both in small group work and in class discussion.

T: The driver in our time machine told me that I could take three things back with me to Brazil in the time machine. So I decided to take—(Writes on the board as below; then turns back to class and asks) *What do you think of my choices?* Jesse?

(on board) { Tray of ice cubes
             { Automobile
             { Rubber ball

Jesse: (chuckling) Pretty bad!

Katy: Well, I think they're pretty poor choices. There are other things you could use than a ball.

Henry: I don't see how a car—a *car* wouldn't be useful. It'd get rusted down there in the jungle, and the jungle's all full of weeds and heavy undergrowth—the car couldn't go through it, and so the weeds'd just grow all over it. (Some laughter; other commenting; general amusement over T's obviously poor choices.)

T: Well, let's see what else I could take. (Writes on board as below; many hands up.)

(on board) { Billfold full of money
             { Bicycle
             { Jug of water

Cathy: I don't think money would be any good—what are you gonna buy?

T: Jeannie, you seem to have an opinion on this—*What do you think of my choices?*

Jeannie: Well, I think I'd better start to go down the list. First of all, if we were *first* settlers, what'd we need money for?   Number two—the bicycle—you couldn't ride.   There'd be mountains and hills, and there'd be too much undergrowth on the plains.   And then, with the jug of water—you could just as well take the ice cubes and let them melt.

William: Keep your jug!

T: Why wouldn't water be good to take (along in the time machine)?

Sandra: It'd get too hot.

Rhoda: Couldn't you put the jug down in the Amazon River—tie it to a tree with a rope or a vine and let it down into the river—to keep it cold?

THE CREATIVE PERSON

One approach to trying to understand more about the quicksilver nature of creativity is to examine closely the special nature of those persons who seem to use these talents or skills in abundance.

Who are the most healthy citizens in our society?   Who are the citizens most able to use all their human potential and what are their special traits or characteristics?   This is an interesting question and far from the usual questions, which tend to focus more on those children and adults who have special problems in adjusting to our society.

When we ask ourselves how we would define "healthy," we discover that it is often defined as the absence of something.   That is, "mental health" is the absence of "mental illness."   Physical health is the absence of sickness.   However, that is neither a satisfactory description nor a useful approach.

The psychologist Abraham Maslow (1970) took a different approach in studying the "self-actualizing" person; that is, a person who appears to be using all his talents and gifts.   He tried to study a group of the most outstanding self-actualizers through historical biographies or, in the case of contemporaries, through direct interview.   Examples of people who fit Maslow's criteria of self-actualization would be Abraham Lincoln, Thomas Jefferson, Albert Schweitzer, Eleanor Roosevelt, Pablo Casals, Pierre Renoir, and Benjamin Franklin.

In his studies, Maslow tried to identify those characteristics that seem to be possessed by all these people in greater or lesser degree.   First, there was a lack of artificiality and a certain simplicity and naturalness about their approach.   They appeared to have solved the basic needs that plague other human beings and were thus freed to use their abilities without straining for social prestige or placing a protective or defensive veneer over their real feelings.   The subjects generally seemed to feel safe and unanxious, accepted, loved and loving, and to have basically worked out their philosophical and religious attitudes toward life.

243

Another definitive characteristic was their ability to focus on problems that lie outside themselves. They were concerned with larger issues, and their concern extended to mankind rather than to more selfish or limited concerns. There was a quality of detachment in their ability to stand apart from the problems and the issues that concerned them, and they positively liked and sought solitude and privacy for a time so that they could intensely concentrate on their work.

Above all, Maslow found one characteristic in particular to be common to all the people studied—a special kind of creativity, originality, or inventiveness. The level of psychic health reached by these individuals allowed them to be freed of the usual barriers and frustrations, and permitted them to produce with freshness and spontaneity. As Maslow well realized, such descriptions make these individuals seem almost unreal and unhuman. He hastens to remind the reader that these self-actualized citizens are not free from the failings of human beings. They are vain, they are prideful, show temper, and sometimes their psychic strength enables them to get over crises such as family death or divorce with such dispatch as to be almost shocking. Whether or not we agree with Maslow on all of these dimensions, we can certainly agree that "the study of crippled, stunted, immature, and unhealthy specimens can yield only a cripple psychology and a cripple philosophy" (p. 234). The careful and intensive study of self-actualizing people must be the basis for a more universal science of psychology.

The Creative Person in Action

Three of our gifted students, Sam, Joe, and Zelda, would not seem to be likely candidates for high-creative performance. In each case the reason would be slightly different but the nonproductive result the same.

Parnes (1972) has given two general principles for the stimulation of creative potential. In analogous terms, he says that we should "(1) feed his brain the fuel required for it to operate at full capacity and (2) remove the brakes that stop his associative mechanisms from functioning naturally" (p. 21). What Parnes is referring to, naturally, is the richness of experience that the child has (the fuel) and the degree to which inhibition prevents him from fully exploring the problem space (the brakes).

Sam, for example, has been fed limited fuel and needs to be made more fully aware of his own talents and his own perceptions. Sam's teacher could be working with him on an assignment to "see something unique on your way home from school, something beautiful or ugly you hadn't seen before." The ability to perceive one's own world has been one of the prerequisites of creative performance.

With Joe and Zelda, the story is somewhat different. Zelda has a great desire to succeed, to please her parents, but that desire shows itself in the great need to look good to others, to be a "good student." What does a good student do? Zelda, in observing teachers and other students, has seen that the good student always has a hand up ready to answer the teacher's question and that the teacher seems pleased with such quick response.

Yet from Parnes' viewpoint, one of the essences of creative thought is the delayed response, the ability to inhibit the impulsive first reaction and allow the gifted student to let the associative thought flow without having to reach an immediate answer. One challenge to our educational program is how do we convince Zelda that it is better to delay responses, to meditate or mull over a problem, than to always try to be first with the right answer?

Joe's problems are different again. His own sense of failure and his inability to take risks that would open his sensitive self-concept to possible criticism create brakes of a very personal sort for Joe. Even when the teacher encourages, pleads, exhorts for unique ideas or the unusual association, Joe's self-censorship protects him from possible humiliation or failure. The price of such "protection" usually comes high. Joe has protected himself against derisive peer laughter, but he has shut himself off from the genuine excitement and self-expanding ego that comes from genuine production or creative thought. Anyone who has seen a child radiant from the production of a well-received poem or theme will never fail to recognize the inherent motivating force of creativity. But in Parnes' parlance, there isn't much trouble keeping the engine running once it turns over, but sometimes we have very cold creative engines that require a great effort to start.

Mr. Brooks. the school counselor, received a rather unusual visit from Zelda's mother recently. Her mother is an intense, serious woman who is extremely ambitious for her daughter. Perhaps it is not surprising that she holds a very low opinion of the school and its personnel, who never seem to do enough for her daughter. She had been recently reading in the popular magazines and books about creativity and now wanted to know what she could do at home to enhance Zelda's creativity.

Although Mr. Brooks had become used to thunderous attacks on the school curriculum as outdated, or even that the school was paying more attention to the handicapped than to the talented, he was somewhat taken aback by this parental request for assistance. Unfortunately, he didn't know what the accumulated research had to say on this matter, because the important literature that summarized the available data was in journals far from Mr. Brooks' ken.

The most effective reviews of the correlates of creativity have been done by Dewing (1970), Wallach (1970), and Dellas and Gaier (1970).

All these reviews have concluded that creativity is linked to personality characteristics and, to a lesser extent, some intellectual characteristics that seem rather consistent and long-term. Dewing, in reviewing those family traits that relate to creativity, identified three major characteristics that seem to persist in various studies. The first is permissive child-rearing; the second is a wide-ranging, diverse, and strong intellectual interest on the part of the parents; and the third is a sense of emotional detachment from the child on the part of the parents. There were few warm or close relationships found between the children who will eventually become creative adults and their parents. This kind of result is hardly to the liking of Zelda's mother, who has an extremely close relationship with her daughter. It underlines an important fact: Major changes in personality styles, to be significant, have to involve fundamental changes in the patterns and life-styles of the individual and are not easy to initiate or maintain.

There is no exercise that can be done for fifteen minutes a day to improve the creativity of children. It is a life-style, a way of life that has to be adopted, and that means that no educational gimmicks will do. As we look at the parental characteristics that seem to be associated with creativity, we see that the lack of emotional attachment and the permissive child rearing allow the child to have a certain lack of commitment to his family and social past and to be free to strike out in new directions. The diverse intellectual interests of his parents allow him to explore along intellectual dimensions without fear of repression or parental disapproval.

In the Dellas and Gaier article, a number of similar personality characteristics are identified in the synthesis of both adult and child creative persons. One of these is an openness to stimuli, whether they be taboo or not. Part of the artist's reputation for bizarre or unusual behavior comes from his free acceptance of feelings of violence, sex, or other taboo subjects. Also, the willing acceptance on the part of the gifted individual of traits often identified with the opposite sex makes the male creative person appear somewhat feminine and the female creative person appear somewhat masculine (Barron, 1969). It does not appear that the males are necessarily less masculine in reality, but only that they do not reject or repress those feelings that are identified as belonging to the opposite sex.

Another strong and consistent finding is that the gifted individual is independent in attitude and social behavior. He does not follow the crowd nor is he swayed by the crowd, because he has a strong self-concept and sense of personal identity, which allows him to go his own way. Finally, there is a strong intrinsic motivation and interest that sustains the creative individual through inevitable periods of frustration.

At the same time that these characteristics provide part of the recipe of creative development, they may also cause difficulties for the teacher. Because creative people do not repress taboo subjects, they are likely to be embarrassingly frank. Because they are independent in attitude and social behavior, they are more difficult to control in a group. Because they have strong intrinsic motivation to pursue their own bent, they may resist attempts of the teacher or other persons to mold them in certain directions.

It is thus that even Cranshaw, with his favorable adjustment and acceptance, is sometimes seen by some teachers as being difficult. He is difficult because he will go his own way, regardless of the wishes of the teacher. Because he is Cranshaw, he does this with some diplomacy and thus keeps out of serious trouble, but not all creative persons are interested in keeping out of trouble. Indeed, some enjoy disorder and social complexity as well as cognitive complexity.

If Zelda's mother were to review carefully the general characteristics that seem common to creative persons, she might well conclude, "If that's the way a person has to be to be creative, maybe I don't want my daughter to be creative." And maybe she doesn't! For each personality characteristic there are pluses and minuses; there are no perfect individuals. The cost of being creative is sometimes being lonely, sometimes being out of step, sometimes being surprised that others will deny or twist experiences that are perceived in embarrassing correctness by the creative individual. In each instance, one totes up the cost and decides "Is it really worth it?"

As has been previously suggested, the characteristics of the creative person from an attitudinal or personality standpoint would seem to have a great deal more to do with creative functioning than do any of the cognitive operations previously discussed. It is useful to think about the creative person and how he performs by returning to our friend, the computer. Newell, Shaw, and Simon (1962) have described the intellectual performance of a computer that has been taught to play chess.

Some of the computer programs have now become so complex that only the most skilled chess masters can defeat the computer in its operations, but it is a useful task to think about how one would "teach" a computer to play chess. One first has to have all the available plays at the computer's disposal, which is quite an array in itself. Some judgment then has to be made as to which one of these plays would be the most powerful to use under a given situation.

Thus, the total range of possible plays has to be made available to the computer as well as some rules, or heuristics, that tell it which plays are better than other plays. This set of rules or heuristics has its analogies in human behavior. One can observe creative persons and imagine what some of the rules are that have been provided for their memory. Some basic scanning rules by which creative individuals search their own past experience would likely be as follows: (1) Consider all associative link-ages with the prime stimulus, no matter how ridiculous, (2) do not put special weight on social consensus as to the proper answer, and (3) if the first search yields no favorable answer, change the rules or seek more information.

These appear to be the rules that are followed by most creative individuals when they are in the process of creating. In addition, they have other personal characteristics to support them—in particular, a strong ego that enables them to withstand pressures from their social or peer group and to continue in their quest through clouds of ambiguity and frustration.

Is the climate ripe for the development of creative abilities of children in this country? Many people do not think so. Included in this group is the noted historian Arnold Toynbee (1968, p. 1), who commented,

> To give a fair chance to potential creativity is a matter of life and death for any society. This is all important, because the outstanding creative ability of a fairly small percentage of the population is mankind's ultimate capital asset.

He feels, however, that there are two adverse forces currently operating in the Western world to combat creative abilities: first, a kind of wrong-headed egalitarianism, which makes it an offense to be different from one's neighbors, and second, a benighted conservatism. On this point Toynbee states that America rose to greatness as a revolutionary community, following the lead of creative leaders, who welcomed and initiated timely and constructive changes, instead of wincing at the prospect of these.

Just as the child is embedded in the family and owes much of his own development to that relationship, the family is embedded in its own subculture, and the school embedded in the total society. The school can no more deviate sharply from that heritage than can the individual child, without causing great concern and disruption. So if one tends to attack the schools for their unimaginative and lockstep programs, a sustained look at the society that spawned them might be in order.

Creative Women

The rapidly changing role of women in our society has focused more attention on the nature and dynamics of development of creative women. One study, by Schaefer (1970), studied ten exceptionally creative adolescent girls, chosen from a larger group of 200 creative girls in an urban area. Each of these girls had been nominated by their teachers as having produced one or more creative products and had scored above a minimum cutoff on some of the Guilford tests related to creative abilities.

All these girls tended to come from rather comfortable home situations, with seven of the mothers continuing to combine a career with marriage, while all the mothers had worked full- or part-time outside the home since marriage. In addition to the mother as a role model in this regard, many of the fathers also provided their daughters models of creative ability, and there is some evidence that the daughters were identifying at least in part with the father.

Other information about this group of girls suggested that they felt somewhat aloof from their parents and rarely engaged in family group activities. This is very similar to the lack of intense emotional closeness or intimacy that has been noted by MacKinnon (1962) and Roe (1952).

These girls reflected a number of traits common to the creative person, including openness to change, impulse expression, imagination, a sense of autonomy, and emotional sensitivity. But such talent does not come without a price. In this case, the price is a confused sex role identity and unresolved conflicts of dependency versus autonomy. The girls seemed torn between their desire to be feminine and socially acceptable and their yearnings for independence and high achievement.

It is likely that these high school girls will continue to carry with them both the fruits of increasing acceptance of women in creative roles in our society and the basic conflict between the more socially acceptable feminine roles and the ones that they would like to follow.

THE CREATIVE PROCESS

Whereas trying to study the creative person, himself, is one strategy, another approach is to try to understand the *process* by which one creates. Those who create, and those who study creative persons, practically all agree that there are processes or a sequence of stages through which a creative person passes in his production. Although many different terms are used to describe these stages, those suggested by Wallas (1926) have probably received the most widespread usage. He proposed the following four main stages in the creative process:

1. *Preparation.* This is the stage in which the problem is investigated from all directions and is primarily a problem-identification and fact-gathering period.
2. *Incubation.* In this stage the person is not consciously thinking about the problem. There is some kind of internal mental process which associates new information with past information. Some type of re-organization of the information seems to be going on without the individual being directly aware of it.

3. *Illumination.* This is the stage during which the "happy idea" occurs. It has been referred to as the "Aha Phenomenon!" In this stage, the creator suddenly sees the idea, concept or solution to the problem.

4. *Verification.* This is the stage in which the idea which has been obtained through the first three stages is put to the test to see if it has validity or not.

Although these stages are commonly observed, it does not mean that they must invariably occur in each instance, or that they occur in a set time sequence. One stage might represent months or years of planning or study, whereas, in other cases, it could occur in one day.

Educational programming has never been too successful in helping a student be more effective in the stages of incubation and illumination; it has concentrated most of its operation on stage 1, preparation, and stage 4, verification. Educators can present facts as the groundwork for the individual's learning about a particular problem or subject. Much of the school curriculum can be identified as stage 1 activity. Then the student may be taught how to evaluate an idea once it is available—a stage 4 type of operation.

Table 9–4 represents the author's concept of different expectations that teachers need to consider for the different stages of the creative process. We are all familiar with the teacher whose predominant evaluation of a composition seems to be in terms of neatness and well-organized form. On the other hand, there is also the teacher who feels that excessive emphasis on form might interfere with richness of content. As Table 9–4 indicates, it would seem that neither teacher is entirely wrong or entirely right. If the task required is that of gathering facts or laying

TABLE 9–4. *Expectations for Different Stages of the Creative Process.*

STAGES OF CREATIVE PROCESS	EXPECTED FORM	PREDOMINANT THINKING OPERATION	PERSONALITY FACTOR OR ATTITUDE REQUIRED
Preparation	Neat Well-organized	Cognitive memory	Studiousness Sustained attention
Incubation Illumination	Sloppy Often confused Incoherent	Divergent thinking	Intellectual freedom Risk taking Tolerance of failure and ambiguity
Verification	Neat Well-organized Clearly stated	Convergent thinking Evaluative thinking	Intellectual discipline Following of a logical sequence

the groundwork for a problem, then one would want the material neat, well organized, and well stated. The individual has very little of a personal nature to add to the situation and has only to collect data which other people have organized for him. Similarly, the material should be well organized, clearly stated, and reasonably neat whenever the person is trying to prove a point through verification. The very basis of verification is an orderly, step-by-step presentation of proof or disproof.

It is, however, in the period when the creative act depends on incubation and illumination that the teacher should expect the material to be sloppy, confused, and incoherent. The individual not only has to collect the material but must produce new ideas or organization. Any new idea or organization of ideas can hardly be expected to be in neat order or in clearly outlined form. So, in answer to the general question "Should a child be expected to have neat, well-organized papers?" the answer would seem to lie in the purpose of the assignment itself.

Similarly, if we could trace the predominant thinking operation required at each stage of the creative process, we would see that, in the area of preparation, the predominant mental operation is that of cognitive memory. The person who is studious, sincere, and highly motivated can show his mettle by collecting large amounts of facts and information from such sources as reference books and encyclopedias.

In the incubation and illumination stages, the predominant thinking operation seems to be divergent thinking. Here the individual is trying to get a new slant on the material that has been collected, a new way of organizing it, a uniqueness that has not been perceived before. This requires the individual to have flights of ideas, not to be afraid to make mistakes, and to live with the realization that every problem does not need to be solved before the end of the day.

In the verification stage, on the other hand, a closely organized and well-reasoned approach to a problem is required; here a person who has strong talents in the convergent thinking area can show his talents and ability.

We can expect that the truly creative–productive individual has significant talents in all these areas and knows *when* to use which skills. Yet, if we think for a moment, we can find, in our classroom, youngsters who have gained reputations as specialists in one area or another. The student who is a specialist in the area of preparation often seems to gather facts just as a squirrel gathers nuts. His cheeks are puffed with facts that he is pleased and proud to spout forth upon request.

Zelda is a fine example of the cognitive-memory specialist. She dotes on facts and absorbs information like a sponge. Her dislike for divergent thinking stems from the same personality dynamics. Her need to be right, and to be approved, fences in any tendencies she might have to give unusual or unique answers that may be off the track. The risk of looking foolish (something that must be accepted by the divergent thinker) is too much for her. She compromises by collecting only facts, a very safe and approved way of gaining a certain intellectual status.

The student who specializes in divergent thinking, to the exclusion of the others, is likely to be somewhat of a nonconformist, one who derails the orderly process by coming up with unusual ideas, sometimes for the sensational effect they might have on the class, but more often for the sake of self-expression. At the same time, he may bring forth many fascinating possibilities about the project or problem at hand that would not otherwise have been discerned.

The student who specializes in convergent thinking is one who continually must have his ideas well organized and well considered. Oftentimes, he seems to be a cautious individual who plays the diligent "ant" to the divergent thinker's frivolous "grasshopper." He cautiously and systematically takes care of the knowledge presented to him, while the grasshopper seems to fritter away such information in a nonsystematic, but sometimes highly illuminating way.

The specialist in evaluative thinking feels the need for judging ideas and persons. There is some reason to believe that such a person may not turn out to be too creative. MacKinnon (1962) refers to Jung's concept that mental functioning consists either of perceiving (becoming aware of something) or judging (coming to a conclusion about something). He concludes (p. 493):

> Everyone perceives and judges, but the creative person tends to prefer perceiving to judging. Where a judging person emphasizes the control and regulation of experience, the perceptive creative person is inclined to be more interested and curious, more open and receptive, seeking to experience life to the full. Indeed, the more perceptive a person is, the more creative he tends to be.

Ideally, one would look for students who have strength in all these areas, but there is some reason to believe that excessive attention to any one of them is likely to inhibit the development of talents in the others. For example, high talent in convergent thinking is likely to lead the individual to hesitate to make statements unless there is solid proof for them or unless a closely knit and logical argument can be developed for a position. The student who habitually responds in this way will certainly not develop the personality or attitude necessary for the risk taking required of the divergent thinker. Similarly, the person who specializes in divergent thinking may develop enough intellectual sloppiness so that he is unable to, or is uninterested in, following through any of his unique ideas to see if they have any real validity. What we especially seem to need are methods by which we can strengthen the skills of the youngster in any one of these areas that would seem needed at any given point in time.

In many ways, the personality factors and attitudes (shown in Table 9–4) required to perform well in stages 1 and 4, seem almost opposite to those needed in stages 2 or 3. The strong intellectual discipline necessary for verification might seem to be at odds with the risk taking to be used in incubation. To be able to suspend one of these talents in favor of the other requires an unusual person indeed—perhaps this is why the truly creative person is a *rara avis* in our culture, or in any other culture.

The real question for educators is whether or not the various processes or stages of creativity can be enhanced through instruction. Can gifted children be taught rules or procedures to make their productive talents more efficient? We thus return to the role of the teacher and the school.

THE ROLE OF THE TEACHER AND OF THE SCHOOL

Many persons, seeking ways of improving the conditions for creativity in the school setting, have wondered whether sizable gains might be made if the teachers' attention could be called to any actions of theirs that inhibit creative expression. The assumption of ignorance on the part of the teacher in this regard does not seem justified, however.

One of the more illuminating experiences of the author has been to ask groups of teachers to pretend, for a moment, that creativity is a very bad quality for a child to show, and that it has to be stamped out at any cost. These teachers are then asked for suggestions as to how this obliteration could be accomplished. No group of teachers has failed to arrive quickly at a large number of suggestions, among which they easily recognize some of their own teaching practices. Some of the major ways often mentioned by teachers to stamp out creativity are as follows:

1. *Establish a rigid curriculum, together with a limited time in which this curriculum is to be presented.* When there is a large amount of required material to cover, the teacher is almost always less tolerant of unusual ideas or apparently off-the-track statements, no matter how interesting. Also, there has not been sufficient recognition of the tyranny of time and its limitations on teacher behavior. The end of the month or of the school year sometimes approaches with the speed of a jet plane, and the conscientious teacher is filled with a desire to cover the necessary or required material. This, too, has the effect of less tolerance of error or diversions.

2. *Teach in content areas in which the teachers are not well versed.* Teachers recognize that ignorance or lack of knowledge on their part is a powerful inhibitor of student freedom. Many teachers are concerned about allow-

ing too much freedom when they themselves lack the ability to evaluate the unusual or different thoughts that occur.

3. *Accept one source as valid, and only one.* Having a required textbook is one method that teachers consider as inhibiting creativity. No consideration should be given to contradictions or conflicts among textbooks. Only facts, not ideas, should be considered.

4. *Do not allow discussion or evaluative statements on the part of the students.* The only act of student participation allowed should be the answering of factual statements or the regurgitating of the teacher's own ideas. Make it clear to the students that there is only one right way to do something. This will effectively discourage any imaginative approach by the students and should, if continued over a long period of time, effectively inhibit any creative impulses.

Teachers generally show considerable awareness of these problems, and often give strong expressions of guilt and exasperation when they find themselves trapped into behaving in a way that they know to be unconducive to productive student performance.

This suppression of creativity, as recognized by teachers, calls for certain obvious modifications in administration and programming. Many times, the responsibilities for such changes lie in the hands of the administrator rather than in those of the teacher.

Several desirable changes suggested by the teachers who have recognized these problems are as follows:

1. *Organize and base the curriculum primarily on the teaching of concepts, rather than of facts.* This would allow a large number of possible approaches to children, with a range of individual differences. Thus, a concept such as "democracy" can be presented in different ways, and at different levels of abstraction, for the gifted and nongifted students. This recommendation implies that the teacher has a firm grasp of the basic concepts to be taught and of the necessary methods of pedagogy to implement them.

2. *Allow more individual assignments of projects under competent supervision.* The key term, "competent supervision," suggests that the student be allowed to develop his own ideas, without having to limit his performance to group activities and group designs. Considerable supervision time must be allotted to carry out the proposed individual projects. These projects can be effective only if they are done under close supervision, wherein the student would be able to refine his ideas and thinking based upon the feedback he obtains from the supervisor.

3. *Bring the students into contact with the maximum talent and knowledge available in the teaching staff.* Most school systems have at least one excellent teacher in each of the various subject areas. The task of the administration is to get that teacher and his ideas in contact with as many gifted children as possible. Whether this is done through closed-circuit TV, team teaching, or some other device, it should be a major goal of the creative administrator.

4. *Follow the general philosophy that "Truth is something to be sought for,*

rather than something that will be revealed." One of the most presumptuous ideas that could be presented in any society is that we now have all the truth that needs to be passed on to succeeding generations. Teachers would be much better-off to accept the position that much of the truth about man's affairs and his surrounding environment remains to be discovered. This would mean that the teacher's role would not be one of an authority, but, rather, of a fellow seeker after truth, albeit a more sophisticated one.

5. *Provide more competence in content and pedagogy in teacher training.* In the area of teacher training, we need to establish, first of all, a greater competence in content areas, as well as more knowledge of thought processes, of how these develop in gifted children, and of how they can be stimulated.

The Teacher's Values

One of the more provocative questions regarding teaching for creativity in American schools is whether the essential inhibition to greater effort in this area is based on a lack of technical skills on the part of the teachers or runs counter to the basic values of the teachers. Torrance (1965, p. 228) reports on opinions and judgments obtained from over a thousand teachers in the United States regarding what characteristics they found most desirable and appealing in their students. The ten most highly thought of values are

1. Consideration of others.	6. Curiosity.
2. Independence in thinking.	7. Sincerity.
3. Determination.	8. Courteousness.
4. Industriousness.	9. Doing work on time.
5. Sense of humor.	10. Healthy.

Torrance points out that conspicuously missing from this list are such matters as courageousness of one's own convictions, independence of judgment, unwillingness to accept the judgment of authorities, and a variety of other qualities characteristic of the creative child. Since it is in the nature of such characteristics as originality or creativity that they are open-ended and hard to control, the teacher who is nervous about his own capabilities in handling such exercises can easily fall back into the more routine exercises in the class and avoid such anxiety-producing efforts.

Torrance pointed out that the student in an educational setting is quite potentially responsive to teaching skills. Students who have been instructed to be original in their essays or written stories will tend to be more original. If instructed to be fluent (i.e., give many different answers), they will do so. Such results, which show classroom intellectual activity to be highly responsive to teacher initiative, provide great opportunity and great responsibility. The teacher can encourage creative and imaginative thought, but he can also subdue or discourage it by the kinds of tasks he proposes and the style and manner that he adopts in the classroom.

Before we get too deeply into the popular game of "Blame the Teacher" for educational faults, it is wise to remember that the responsibility for proper training for teachers lies with teacher-training institutions and the responsibility for upgrading their skills lies with the educational administrators in their school system.

The three-dimensional model presented by Guilford has apparently stimulated others to think in similar terms. For example, Williams (1970) presents a complex model (see Figure 9–2) that is designed to aid the teacher to modify tasks in the classroom along the dimensions of curriculum, pupil behavior, and teacher behavior.

Williams introduces an affective layer of student behavior in addition to the cognitive layer usually identified. In this layer the teacher can design items that test such dimensions as risk taking, curiosity, and imagination as well as the more traditional productive-thinking dimensions as fluency and flexibility. By providing a set of eighteen different types of teacher behavior—from use of paradoxes, to search skills, to creative listening skills—Williams encourages the teacher to consider the use of a greater variety of behavior than is often used in the classroom.

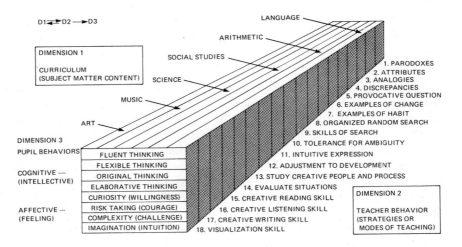

FIGURE 9–2. *A Model for Implementing Cognitive–Affective Behaviors in the Classroom.* (*From F. Williams,* Classroom ideas for encouraging thinking and feeling. *Buffalo, N.Y. 14214: Dissemination of Knowledge, Publishers, 1970, p. 203.*)

An example of three tasks designed to tap curriculum, pupil, and teacher behavior is given in Table 9–5. With the help of this three-dimensional

TABLE 9–5. *Tasks to Stimulate Thinking Abilities.*

IDEA NO. 190
TO ENCOURAGE: FLEXIBLE THINKING AND CURIOSITY
THROUGH: Language Arts
USING: Strategies No. 3—Analogies
                No. 9—Skills of search

The children were asked to select a word that they did not know the meaning of from a story they were currently reading or from the weekly spelling list and look up a synonym for it in dictionaries or thesaurus. Each child had a turn to state his or her word and its synonym to the rest of the class. *This activity developed a great number of different words which were new to the class. They learned to appreciate the many different possible ways of expressing words* and aided in building *vocabulary.*

IDEA NO. 191
TO ENCOURAGE: ORIGINAL THINKING AND RISK TAKING
THROUGH: Art
USING: Strategies No. 11—Intuitive expression
                No. 18—Visualization skill

To provide a freer atmosphere for original expression, a special table of odds and ends (papers, scissors, paste, tape, etc.) were arranged next to the supply cabinet. Here children, especially those who were introverted or insecure, were able to sit and construct anything they liked. *They were encouraged to create any new form or design they could think of.* Some who never had the courage to try anything before produced art work of great sensitivity. All items created were placed so the other children could see their work on the bulletin board.

IDEA NO. 192
TO ENCOURAGE: IMAGINATION AND COMPLEXITY
THROUGH: Social Studies
USING: Strategies No. 4—Discrepancies
                No. 6—Examples of change
                No. 14—Evaluate situations

The class was asked to use their imaginations and think ahead to the year 2000, to think of how old they will be then, and to try to predict as many changes as they can that will have come about by then. They were asked to discuss in detail how their lives would be affected by changes in food, clothing, automobiles, transportation, places to live, work, leisure activities, etc. *After they had made their predictions, they were to test these against the facts by establishing some basis or evidence for their predictions.*

Source: From F. Williams. *Classroom ideas for encouraging thinking and feeling.*
Buffalo, N.Y. 14214: Dissemination of Knowledge, Publishers, 1970, p. 107.

model any teacher or group of teachers can create a wide variety of tasks designed to stimulate the thinking abilities of gifted children.

Instructional Techniques for Stimulation

To give teachers advice on what to do to increase creativity is presumptuous. But research has discovered certain cognitive factors that do seem related to creative output. The cognitive component parts of creativity that appear most consistently are *ideational fluency, originality,* and *flexibility.* These *are* factors that a teacher can get his teeth into and try to stimulate further. Thus, if the teacher would rephrase the question to ask, "What can I do to stimulate cognitive abilities that appear to relate to creativity?" some tentative answers can be provided.

FLUENCY. One common method applied in group situations, such as that of the classroom, to stimulate greater fluency of ideas has been *brainstorming.* This technique has been publicized in management and industry, and many adaptations of it have been made to fit differing situations and purposes. One essential element involved in the method is to have a group focus on a particular problem such as: how to bisect an angle; how to improve our relations with Latin America; or how to avoid an unpleasant task in the proper way (as Tom Sawyer did). The students are then invited to give as many ideas as they might have for possible solutions to the problem. There are some very important ground rules that need to be observed if this technique is to work.

1. *No criticism allowed.* Nothing smothers the free flow of ideas like the sharp critical remark, or even sharper guffaw of scorn, of a peer or of a teacher. The temptation to point out a faulty answer is very strong and needs to be quickly checked. The students need to know in advance that no critical comments will be entertained for the moment. Evaluation comes later.
2. *The more the better.* The students can accept the proposition that the greater the number of ideas presented, the more likely the chance is that a good one will be among them. A premium could be placed on unusual or unique ideas.
3. *Integration and combinations of ideas welcomed.* The students can be alerted to the possibility of combining or adding to previous ideas.
4. *Evaluation after all ideas have been presented.* The teacher can judge when the fluency or inventiveness of the class is lagging. At that point, he should encourage evaluative thinking on the part of the students.

Now they can judge the relative merits of the ideas. The reader may well ask, "Doesn't criticism even at this point dampen the fluency of the group or the individual?"   The distance in time between the original utterance and the criticism dulls its effect.   There is the additional possibility that the original thought has been added to or changed by other thoughts, and is no longer identified as the production of any one individual.   Let's see how it could work.   First we need a problem.   We may presume that the teacher has already established the ground rules.

T: Class—Let's do some brainstorming on a very mysterious problem.   What do you suppose happened to the lost colony of Roanoke?
Pete: I think they got on their ships, went out to sea and a big storm came and sank it—everybody died.
Ruth: I think they got struck by a terrible epidemic and all died of some disease.
Henry: A band of Indians swooped down and massacred them.
Jim: If what Ruth and Henry said were true, why didn't. . . .   (T interrupting)
T: Remember, Jim, no criticism while we are "storming."   (Class laughter at the "storming")
Cathy: I think they got a disease like Ruth said and then they panicked and went on their boat to get help and all died and the ship eventually sank.

Note how Cathy combined previous responses to get a new one; also how the T intervened to preserve the rule of "no criticism," and protected Jim from criticism by a humorous reference to the process.
Are there any disadvantages to this procedure? Yes! Most important is that something *meaningful* must be done with the results of the brainstorming.   The final decisions on the lost colony must fit into the curriculum and the concept to be taught.   Otherwise, this procedure can be considered merely an interesting game that has little or nothing to do with learning or with important school goals.
The stress on fluency can be emphasized by the teacher's seeking multiple answers and rewarding children who can give them.   Instead of asking:

"What category do kangeroos fall into?"

Ask students to:

"Name as many marsupials as you can."

Instead of asking:

"Students, complete this unfinished poem."

Ask students to:

"Make up as many different endings as you can for this poem."
(Give credit for as many different endings as can be given by one person.)

259

Instead of asking:

"*What happened to Lincoln's killer?*"

Ask students to:

"*Make up as many different plausible stories as you can about Lincoln's killer's fate.*"

REDEFINITION.   One of the dimensions of thinking operations that seems related to creativity is the skill of *redefinition,* or the ability to find ways of improving existing products or processes.   One of the approaches to such improvement is to analyze the nature of the object or process to be made better.   If one is asked how to improve a screwdriver, it would be a useful first step to consider just what a screwdriver and its operation does (Guilford, 1967b).   For example, an analysis of a screwdriver might look like the following (p. 339):

It has a round steel shank.
It has a wooden handle riveted to the shank.
It has a wedge shaped end to enter a screw head.
It is manually operated.
Torque is applied to achieve a twisting movement.
Pressure is exerted to keep the end in the slot.

Given this list of attributes, attempts to improve could focus on changes of one or a combination of these factors.   Similar, if more complicated, types of analysis can be tried for such entities as *public education, mass transit, modern marriage,* or *how to improve toys.*

Although most of the exercises that have been used as illustrations have the element of play or game to them, one does not have to reach too far to take subject areas of deadly seriousness.   The students respond to topics that smack of the real world and in which they have had some contact, however fleeting.

ORIGINALITY.   The gifted and creative student is often challenged and excited by the opportunity to produce the unique response rather than just the correct response. Such requests can be made in any subject matter from language arts to science—for example:

1. The teacher can establish a game whereby words are presented for association to key words by the teacher.   Responses judged correct or reasonable *and* unusual receive two points.   For example, if the stimulus is RED, responses such as *fire, pencil,* and *blood* will get only one point, whereas responses such as *spectrum, ultraviolet,* or *China* might receive higher credit. Such training exercises result in at least temporary improvement in student ability to think of the unusual response.

2. A more complex task would be to find a new way to communicate with one another by long distance if the phone bug chewed through the long-distance lines and made them unusable.

TABLE 9–6.   *Consequences in Political Science.*

Problem 1

As a result of a remarkable scientific breakthrough by an Irish physicist, Ireland alone of all countries in the world has at her disposal virtually unlimited supplies of nuclear energy at little cost.   What could be the consequences?

Problem 1 (solutions)

A gradual but cumulative development of industry which would transform the economy.   Ireland would rapidly become a powerful economic force.

A gradual development of agriculture through heating of soil and provision of food in processed form for animals.

Control eventually of weather through ability to create or retard precipitation.

Development of scientific education to allow greater use of the atomic resources.

Scientific attainment would help tear down the "Green Curtain."

Ireland would become a World Wide Retirement Center, and we'd still have all the greenery we are famous for.

Destruction of Irish culture with excessive foreign capital and emphasis on material wealth.

Problem 2

Genetic changes produced by increased nuclear radiation prove to be sex-linked for intelligence alone, and it is specifically the intelligence of women that will undergo an increase in magnitude.   In Ireland, what would be the consequences?

Problem 2 (solutions)

The gradual elimination of male dominance in decision taking, in business, in government.

Emphasis on physical beauty by women, to cover their greater IQ.

Disillusion with intelligence as an indication of general ability.

Gradual female take-over of the initiative in partner selection for marriage.

Fall in population.

Homes would be better planned and better organized and equipped.

Children would get better home education.

Unlikely to affect traditional relationships, e.g., women not likely to become leaders in home with even a 15 percent increase in intelligence.   Tradition and religion would discourage women as leaders.

Change in educational patterns as more women take graduate courses.

Incursion of women into Government.

Source: From F. Barron. *Creative person and creative process.* Holt, Copyright © 1969 by Rinehart and Winston, Inc. Reprinted by permission of Holt, Rinehart and Winston, Inc.

TABLE 9–7. *Teacher Stimulation for Divergent Production.*

DIVERGENT PRODUCTION OF SEMANTIC IMPLICATIONS (DMI) is defined as the ability to produce many antecedents, concurrents or consequents of given information.

Tests

Planning Elaborations. Add those detailed operations needed to make a briefly outlined plan succeed. (37)

Occasionally mechanical aptitudes tests require answers to items similar to the Possible Jobs test; the *Stanford Binet* has several questions which tap DMI.

Curriculum Suggestions

The requirement of producing many consequents, concurrents, or antecedents makes this an open-ended task which can be used for almost any teacher-determined subjects. There is a non-structuring in the possible answers, which gives the exercise a quality of flexibility in answers for solving the task; that is, the answer lies in the student's searching for possible precedents.

PRIVILEGED NEIGHBORHOOD

In a privileged neighborhood: Robert came home from school. His big sister came home at the same time and read a note to him from their mother. It said to have a snack and play until she got home. She had gone with a neighbor to see a sick friend. Robert had a peanut butter sandwich and grape juice and then went to the garage to get his bike. When he got there he noticed that the car lights were on and getting dim and the car doors were locked. Why do you think they were on? How could he turn them off? (Say nothing about windows or extra car keys since these are alternative suggestions.) What might happen if he did not turn them off?

UNDERPRIVILEGED NEIGHBORHOOD

In an underprivileged school district: Robert was sitting on the curb watching the big kids play in the street. It was quiet for a moment, and then he heard water dripping. He followed the sound inside the apartment house and saw water trickling down the stairs from an apartment where the door was locked and no one was at home. No one was at home in his apartment either. What do you think happened in the apartment? What could Robert do? What would happen if he did nothing?

Source: From M. Meeker. *The structure of intellect: Its interpretation and uses.* Columbus, Ohio: Merrill, 1969, p. 99.

3. If one were suddenly faced with running out of petroleum, what could be the variety of other sources of energy available to us?

Consequence Tests provide not only an excellent measure of fluency and flexibility in the domain of divergent thinking but provide a basis for seeking unique solutions to very real problems. Barron (1969) reports the use of "consequences" to stimulate business leaders in Ireland on problems of real or probable happenings that should be thought about in advance of their arrival (see Table 9–6).

Table 9–7 provides an example from Meeker (1969) of how to translate the cognitive skill of implications into curriculum suggestions with differentiated tasks for privileged and underprivileged neighborhoods. Similar suggestions are available for each of the thinking processes in workbooks by Meeker and Renzulli (1972) and Williams (1970).

SUMMARY

One of the special emphases of current pedagogy for the gifted student is the stress on teaching for creativity. The need for new solutions to meet the conditions of a rapidly changing world is manifest, so the strategy is to reduce the emphasis on the collection of unrelated facts and to train, if possible, the gifted student in the techniques necessary to become more creative and original so that he is a problem solver rather than a problem stater.

Such a move is stimulated by the emergence of new models of intellectual performance, such as the *structure of intellect*. With this model as a guide, specific and direct instructional techniques can be devised that would have easy application to educational programs for the gifted; a number of these have been presented in the chapter.

There have been two major strategies adopted by those who wish to lift the curtain on the mysterious nature of creative behavior. One strategy has been to study the creative person and discover how, and in what way, he is different from less talented or productive persons. There do seem to be consistent findings related to the distinctive personalities of creative individuals.

In general, they seem to be less bothered by societal pressures and taboos and more open to all kinds of stimuli. They are inwardly directed and do not have close or intimate relationships with their parents or with others around them. They seem caught up in the nature of the task they are working with. They are characterized by strong egos, not easily swayed. In this regard, recent studies show that creative women exhibit similar characteristics to those of creative men.

The second major strategy has been to try to understand the process or sequence of steps by which an individual creates a new idea or product. There seems to be a complex set of behaviors ranging from careful and conscious planning and verification behavior to free association at the unconscious, or at least unplanned, level. Some suspension or self-evaluation for a time seems critical for the production of tentative or unique ideas.

Teachers often seem to know more about how to stamp out creativity than how to enhance it.   This may be because standard teaching techniques lean toward group learning and social processes in the classroom rather than toward the stimulation of individualistic behavior that lies at the heart of creativity.   However, teachers can and should systematically encourage student intellectual independence and reward playfulness, expressions of humor, and original thought.

There are a growing number of systematic suggestions for teachers as to how to stimulate some of the assumed components of creativity, such as fluency, flexibility, and the drawing of implications.   It seems likely that this area of creative thought will continue to be a fruitful area of activity for both the researcher and the curriculum specialist for the foreseeable future.

UNRESOLVED ISSUES

1. If the key to personal creativity is the individualistic personality, or the person who goes his own way relatively resistant to societal pressures, then how will such creativity be preserved when the increasing interacting organization of the society will bring greater and greater pressure for some degree of social conformity?

2. Can we design an inservice training program that prepares teachers not only to use the techniques of creativity but also to become more open and free in their own expressiveness and thus create a model for creative and productive thinking, as opposed to a model of more sterile fact accumulation?

3. How can we release the term "creative thinking" from its current, almost exclusive association with the performing or creative arts?   A person can be a creative historian, scientist, or plumber.   "Creativity" is not something one does in a given time period during the day but is an attitude, a philosophy of life, that imbues and affects the whole scope of the educational program and of the life of the individual.

READINGS OF SPECIAL INTEREST

GHISELIN, B. (Ed.)   *The creative process.*   New York: New American Library, 1952.

A collection of personal statements and recollections from outstanding creative scientists and artists about their own efforts in creative work.   Einstein, Van Gogh, Jung, Wolfe, Lawrence, and others all have their say on why and how they were productive.   Since they are insightful people, the readings are quite intriguing.

Gowan, J.   *Development of the creative individual.*   San Diego, Calif.: Robert Knapp Publishers, 1972.

A summary of existing material on the nature of the creative person with emphasis on developmental stages.   Explores social and family factors related to creativity.   Theories of Freud and Maslow considered in explaining the process and development of the creative individual.

Koestler, A.   *The act of creation.*   New York: Macmillan, 1964.

A serious, often introspective account on the mysteries of the creative process and the creative person.   Provides useful insights from the perspective of the author himself on how the process operates.

Torrance, E. P.   *Creativity.*   Belmont, Calif.: Dimensions Publ. Co., 1969.

One of the most creative and imaginative of educators presents a series of suggestions for parents and teachers of preadolescent children, discussing ways to stimulate more creative thinking in the child.

SECTION IV

Administration and Training for the Gifted

Previous sections have dealt with the problem of providing differential content or methods to the gifted child in an educational setting. The chapters in this section deal (1) with the problems faced by administrators and program directors for the gifted, and (2) with the nature of special training for educators who are planning to work in this field.

Program directors are faced with such questions as "Should gifted students be moved ahead or accelerated in school?" "Should the school spend some of its resources for a screening program to identify talented youngsters?" These are some of the issues dealt with in Chapter 10 on administrative changes. Whereas the previous discussions have focused mainly on the individual teacher–child interaction, we are dealing now with matters of total school policy, and the acceptance or nonacceptance of gifted programs in the community have a great deal to say about whether any special provisions are made for these students at all.

In Chapter 11, "Training Educational Personnel," a variety of information is presented on the nature of special training programs for educational personnel. There are many personnel in the educational system, in addition to the classroom teacher, who should receive some kind of specialized training. In particular, the importance of supervisory personnel has been increasingly noticed in the past few years. In this chapter we address such issues as "Are there special personality or cognitive characteristics of teachers for the gifted?" "What is the nature of a reasonable training program to prepare a teacher for working directly with high-producing gifted youngsters such as Cranshaw and Zelda?" and "What different kinds of training need to be provided for those personnel who would be focusing mainly on low-producing youngsters, as typified in this text by Joe and Sam?"

10

Administrative Changes
for the Gifted

In this chapter we will be concerned with the third method of adapting educational programs for gifted children—changes in the nature of the learning environment. There is no law that says that all three of the possible adaptations—curriculum, learning style, and learning environment—cannot be included in a single program. Indeed, there is good reason now to believe that attempts to change the learning environment *without* taking advantage of the opportunity to also change the program elements is a substantial missed opportunity and runs the risk of creating the image or picture of a special program when, in fact, very little has changed.

Ask yourself how much difference would be created if you took the eight or nine most intelligent and highly motivated students in each of three fifth-grade classes and put them all together in the same class? If the teacher assigned to such a program has no special training, if there is no change in the material to be covered or in teacher planning except that everything will naturally move faster, why should we be surprised if evaluations reveal little improvement in measurable attainment for the new program, as compared with the more heterogeneous setting?

What are the most important elements that educational experts consider to be crucial to programs for gifted children? Renzulli (1968) asked twenty-one experts to list what they felt to be the crucial elements in gifted programs. The three elements selected by these judges most frequently were the teacher, with both selection and training seen as major issues; the curriculum, and how it can be made purposefully distinctive; and student selection procedures for the particular program in question.

269

Such a result could probably be obtained by taking any twenty or twenty-five judgments at random from people who have had experience with programs for gifted students. What is also clear, however, is that despite the general consensus among experts that the teacher and the curriculum need special attention, relatively little effort has been expended on either, and the primary allocation of scarce state and local resources remains in the support of excess cost funds to local communities in order to provide additional educational personnel.

This is not to say that educators are deliberately ignoring issues such as curriculum development or special training—it is just easier, given the way education is structured, to provide the local school district some extra funds from the state level to conduct a "gifted program."

There are a number of pitfalls that await the enthusiastic but inexperienced administrator as he tries to develop special plans or programs for administrative readjustment for the gifted. One such pitfall will be the assumption that the parents of Cranshaw, Zelda, Sam, or Joe will be wildly enthusiastic about a suggested change.

Assistant Superintendent Campbell happened to meet Cranshaw's parents at a social gathering recently and talked to them enthusiastically about the new program for special classes for talented children that he is thinking of instituting. To his surprise, he got a very cool and reserved reception, with Cranshaw's parents raising all sorts of possible objections or problems. Will he be happy? Will he have too much work piled on him? Will it affect his grades? What will other students think of his being singled out this way?

Parents of gifted children who are doing reasonably well are in exactly the opposite position of parents of handicapped children when the consideration of a special program is requested. For the parents of the handicapped child, any new effort is likely to be received with enthusiasm. Their child is probably not doing too well in school now, and any change is almost certainly going to be for the good.

A gifted child, however, is likely to be doing quite well in the existing program. A new program carries with it the risk of things going wrong, of unanticipated problems, of possible loss. That is why the parents of gifted children often are grateful but cautious about possible changes in existing programs for their children.

Teachers also should not be expected to cheer and throw their hats in the air at the prospect of a special program for the gifted. These teachers assigned to the special program can picture themselves spending many more hours preparing for such a class; the teachers who will have the remainder of students may well feel that they are being robbed of the only students that made life worthwhile to them. So there will be a respectful hearing of Dr. Campbell's proposal, but he is not likely to

270

be carried off on the shoulders of a cheering throng at the next PTA meeting. Here, as everywhere else in this book, the matter of values, self-interest, and intent loom large even when they are not immediately apparent.

The objectives for embarking on some type of administrative changes for the gifted are fairly straightforward:

1. Reduce the *range* of talent and achievement in a group to allow the teacher a better opportunity to focus his efforts.
2. Reduce the amount of time that the gifted child, student, and adult must spend in the total educational process.
3. Bring the best-prepared personnel into touch with these students.

The establishment of grouping or special classes for the gifted student, either in general placement, or in special academic areas such as mathematics, is usually done with the first objective—reducing the range of ability—in mind.

The notion of ability or achievement grouping, to a teacher such as Mr. Jenkins, makes a great deal of sense, since he realizes that if the administrator does not group students by class, Mr. Jenkins will have to group *within* the classroom. It is just not possible to challenge a student with a tenth-grade reading level and satisfy the needs of a student reading third-grade material, at the same time, in the same group.

Nevertheless, the idea of grouping, to the lay public, is not an entirely popular one. It raises images of favoritism, such as giving the best teachers to the fast group, or creating an intellectual elite. It must be said that such notions are not entirely without foundation. The public *should* be annoyed if grouping becomes merely a means of dispensing favors to influential citizens and their children, rather than being part of an integrated program concerned with the education of the slow and average learner as well as that of the high-aptitude child. These objections from the lay public have undoubtedly played an influential role in the limited number of school systems in the United States that use "grouping."

In terms of local popularity, Rice (1966) reported the following distribution of programs for gifted pupils in California, a state with a very active program: enrichment in regular classroom, 52 percent; special classes, 25 percent; special counseling or programs outside the classroom, 10 percent; and advanced classes or acceleration programs, 10 percent. For states that are active in this area, the proportions are roughly indicative of the range and approximate incidence of various kinds of program elements for the gifted. Even in the active states, only one in four or one in three is likely to establish special administrative provisions.

271

CASE-STUDY APPROACH

It is, of course, not always possible to have an organized total school pro-gram for gifted children, and the question always arises, what can be done under circumstances where a community has not developed a special program? A teacher may find himself in a rural area where the organ-ization of grouping programs for gifted children is quite difficult. One approach found effective in individual cases has been the *case-study* method. This involves gathering as much information as possible on a gifted youngster from as many different sources as are available.

This information is then shared in a staff meeting, to which might come the teacher, principal, director of curriculum, director of special education, or other personnel who have come or could come in contact with the youngster. At this meeting, the information about the youngster is reviewed on the basis of information already available; then a general agreement is reached as to a plan of attack appropriate for that school system. Naturally, such a plan would vary considerably, depending on the particular child and upon the resources of the school system. An example of this kind of approach has been reported by Gallagher, Green-man, Karnes, and King (1960), who have described the range of deci-sions which could be made through such a committee or case-study procedure (p. 411):

1. One child was moved to another school where he could receive more intellectual challenge and stimulation.
2. Three children were accelerated after special planning with present and future teachers.
3. Classroom committee assignments and revised seating assignments were given to some students with a view toward improving their so-cial acceptance.
4. Children were, in a few instances, referred for special treatment of speech and emotional problems.
5. Special projects were given to some children in an area of their known interests in an attempt to stimulate greater motivation and interest in school.
6. Special activities were suggested for children who did not seem to show sufficient creativity or originality. Such activities included completing unfinished poems, and creating stories out of imaginative themes. (What would have happened if Lincoln had not been assassinated? What would be the feelings of the first man to land on Mars? Suppose there were no more winters, what would happen?)

This investigation showed clearly that there were some children who profited from case studies and others who did not. Below is given a short synopsis of two youngsters who seemed to be aided by such a pro-cedure.

Tim. Tim was the most intelligent child in the present study (Binet IQ 205) and was doing very well on initial status in reading achievement. He had many self-doubts about his competence, especially in the area of sports. Tim used his high intelligence to bolster his sagging physical self-image by showing the other students how smart he was. Although his academic performance was quite adequate, it did not reveal creative thought or the unusual talent expected of a child of this ability level. The recommendations of the case-study committee were that the parents should be asked to aid in building his self-confidence in physical skills. The teacher spent a considerable time strengthening Tim's self-confidence in the classroom so that he would not feel it necessary to belittle other children.

At the end of the project, Tim was reported by the teacher as improving greatly in self-confidence, especially in the physical area. He was more confident and poised in giving reports. He moved from the most unpopular one fourth of his class in social standing to above average in social standing. Tim showed greater awareness of his own problems by judging himself as less than ideal in all areas of personal adjustment on the self-rating scale. There seemed little doubt that the increased interest in Tim's problems taken by the family, as well as the work of the teacher, played some role in this improvement.

Carl. Carl's problem was that, although he was doing moderately well in his school work, he was extremely sensitive to the feelings and attitudes of his classmates. Further, in his home school, his classmates were not interested in high academic achievement beyond their grade level. With the parents' consent, Carl was moved to another school where he received much greater intellectual challenge. The intellectual atmosphere of the home was improved by the purchase of books. The parents had always given Carl, an only child, much attention and affection. This attention took on a more intellectual flavor as a result of the study.

At the final rating, Carl was adjusting very well to school. After two years in the new school, he was one of the best achievers in the room, was well-liked, and held class offices. Moving Carl into a more adequate and challenging intellectual environment seemed to pay important dividends, as did similar moves in the three or four other cases where such a change in school environment seemed called for by the individual circumstances.

As can be seen here, Carl seemed to be in an unfortunate environment for the development of his talent, which received little recognition at home—not because the parents were not interested but simply because they hadn't been aware of their child's talent. Thus, changing the environment produced a very noticeable change in Carl's performance and attitude toward school.

In Tim's situation, his low self-concept in the physical area was causing him to behave in ways that made him socially unpopular. By giving

273

him greater confidence and experience in using physical skills that were basically not below average, one found the obnoxious behavior disappearing. Such habits, if not corrected, however, could solidify year by year and produce real trouble at a later age.

However, not every case turns out successfully, and sometimes we can learn as much about our procedures by closely examining our failures as we can by rejoicing in our successes. Two such cases are produced below.

Alfred. Alfred was a 10-year-old child who was markedly overprotected by his parents. Although his average academic achievement was high, he was slow and languid in accomplishing routine school work. He accepted the parental overprotection without protest, and exerted himself only in very restricted areas of intellectual problems. In the beginning of the study, he seemed to be fairly well-accepted by his particular group.

The program designed for Alfred tried to (1) encourage him to relate his interest in arithmetic to mechanical devices, inventions, and science; (2) encourage responsibility by placing time limits on his work in class rather than allow him to continue indefinitely through procrastination; (3) discuss with the parents the possibility of increasing his responsibilities in the home.

Follow-up interviews with the teacher revealed that Alfred was manifesting the same types of behavior as had been reported at the beginning of the study. Two quotes from the teacher's follow-up a few months after the program began were "Alfred's work habits have not improved," "He prolongs every assignment 'til he has to be kept after school to get his work finished."

Four months later the comments were much the same: "Alfred has had many opportunities to do creative writing but he continues to do mediocre work." "He continues to be effeminate." The two largest problems remaining at the end of the study according to the teacher were (1) his inability to work to capacity in areas aside from science, and (2) he shies away from physical activity. The recommendations for action did not touch the central problem, which would seem to lie within the family interrelationships.

Wanda. Wanda was a conscientious and compliant 9-year-old whose major difficulty seemed to be lack of originality and creativity. She came from a family that adhered closely to rural midwestern values and that did not place a high value upon intellectual excellence in girls. Wanda's mother was a dominant and aggressive woman who was active in community and church affairs and seemed to overshadow her three daughters.

Although Wanda did well on the achievement tests in school, her originality and creativity were quite poor and her reading interests were extremely immature. These interests centered around comic books and

274

detective stories. The television programs she watched were typical of those that interest younger children.

The program planned for Wanda attempted to broaden her interests, introduce her to areas of intellectual activities that she had previously been unaware of, and help her to improve her creative writing. A specific attempt was made to gain the parents' cooperation for this program.

The objective test scores, the parents, and the teachers all agreed that Wanda did not show improvement during the time she was observed. The reason for this lack of change seemed to be that the parents were not interested in cooperating with the school's recommendations, and that Wanda was too closely dependent upon the parents' good will to go against their wishes.

Here we see the limitations of such an approach. If the child has deep-seated and continually irritating emotional difficulties, such as Alfred, no manipulation of the school program that falls short of dealing with the source of the problem is likely to produce changes.   In Wanda's situation, there seemed to be basic value differences between the parents and the school; the child, being dependent upon the family, could not break away from them.

Another important limitation of this technique is the necessity to collect meaningful information on the student involved. What is his social adjustment? Who are his friends or enemies? What are his ambitions? Often, these kinds of questions cannot be answered through teacher observation, as numerous studies have shown that teachers may have a distorted notion of the social structure in their own classroom. Thus, unless a sociometric device of some sort has been given to the students, in which they are asked their choice of friends, and these friends have been tabulated and identified as such, the teacher may not have the information needed to answer crucial questions.

Information should be available regarding the student's own feelings and attitudes before the child is accelerated. Certainly his own feelings and attitudes should be taken into account. Unless one has some instruments or ways of answering these questions, then any decisions reached are based upon inadequate information.

If sufficient information is obtained to allow the committee to have reasonable confidence in the determination of the child's problems, the limitations in the facilities of the school system must then be considered. Any suggestions for improving the classroom situation by stimulating more productive thinking must rely upon the skills of the individual teacher. If the teacher knows how to enrich the curriculum and has the opportunity to do so, these recommendations can be very useful. If the teacher has neither the opportunity, the background, nor the outside aid, in terms of curriculum help or help from supervisors, not much accomplishment can be expected.

The recommendations made in this study as to what action should be taken by the schools are probably applicable to other schools (Gallagher et al., 1960, p. 422):

1. Additional psychological help [should] be employed to give necessary diagnostic service.
2. A curriculum specialist [should] be employed who can help supplement the skills of the teacher in certain content areas.
3. A program of grouping [should] be instituted to aid those children who are in a position of relative intellectual isolation.
4. Plans [should] be developed to enlist more effective aid from the parents in relation to the total school program.

Whatever the form that administrative change takes, such action must always be viewed in its proper perspective. It should be part of a team action that reaches its fulfillment in the touching of mind-to-mind in the teacher–learner relationship. If improvement in the teacher–learner relationship is not facilitated by the administrative change, no organizational chart, no printed curriculum, or no flowery report can make up for that deficit.

ADMINISTRATIVE ADAPTATIONS: ELEMENTARY

A close examination of the situation at the elementary level has led many people to believe that an adequate education for children of all levels of intellectual ability requires dramatic changes in the structure of the program itself. The problems that seem to weigh most heavily in the present situation are the lack of depth in content training of the teacher; the impressive range of intellectual ability in the heterogeneous elementary class, with the consequent heavy demands for multiple planning by the teacher; and a limited amount of time to work at the high conceptual level of the brightest children in her group.

Although the educational system has been under severe criticism and attack by a large number of people in the past decade, it should be clear that this problem exists independent of critics. It is a problem inherent in our present state of knowledge and in the philosophy of the American educational system that all children are worthy of an education. If all the critics who are now irritating educators throughout the country were placed on a large boat and shipped off to Madagascar, the problems would still remain to plague the elementary school teacher.

Many revisions of the elementary school structure have been under consideration; Table 10–1 summarizes presumed advantages and disadvantages of three approaches to the education of gifted children.

TABLE 10–1. *Advantages and Disadvantages of Administrative Adjustments for Gifted Students.*

APPROACH	ADVANTAGES	DISADVANTAGES
Group students by subject aptitude.	Teachers can concentrate on subject areas in which they are strongest. Reduction of the range of achievement in a given area, such as mathematics.	Teacher might have contact with over a hundred students and lose personal contact with students. Teacher might have to repeat material in different sections and lose needed enthusiasm. Lose chance for integration of subject matter.
Group students by general intellectual ability.	Can integrate subject matter at a high conceptual level. Can focus on such processes as inquiry and creativity.	Demands a highly intelligent and skilled child. Will not reduce the spread of performance as much as content grouping.
Team teaching or open classroom.	Can arrange for small group or individual study activities for gifted. Can bring teacher strengths in content areas to the gifted students.	Requires cooperative teamwork and planning on part of teachers. Amount of planning and teacher work load appears to increase.

The Open Classroom

The last decade has seen few major innovations that represent more than token changes from the older models described previously. The constant turmoil surrounding issues of desegregation and school busing plus the need to do more definitive planning for culturally different children has absorbed the energies of school personnel.

One administrative device that has been introduced that has possible merit is that of the open classroom. (See Featherstone, 1968; Yeomans, 1967.) This device creates a large open space for forty to eighty children and a staff team of teachers and aides. Although there are about as many versions of this concept as school systems using it, the essence of the open-classroom program seems to be

1. The creation of various student learning stations or centers where the student can go to concentrate on a particular type of activity, such as science or art.
2. A flexible schedule that allows students to spend time on activities of their own choosing.
3. Organizing teaching staff activities to use the particular talents and interests of the staff to provide a broader adult input and talent to the students.

The potential of this approach for gifted students seems manifest. It makes the design of independent study projects and independent student research a more practical possibility and can allow the gifted student to move more at his or her own pace. Whatever stigma is attached to being singled out for a special program for the gifted would also be avoided. However, such an approach does depend on staff interest and supervision. If the science station has the same tired, old, fifth-grade books and the teacher interprets student freedom to mean that she doesn't have to supervise and aid the student, not much can be expected to happen.

The Society Is the Schoolroom

The definition of education as something that happens only in the confines of certain buildings and that is provided by certain full-time paid staff of the public school system has inhibited many possibly useful efforts for the gifted.

Since one of the primary problems in planning a program for gifted children is the limited range of knowledge and talent of the teacher, it is only natural that thought be given to the introduction of outside experts who can present material at greater depth for gifted students. This seems to be particularly appropriate in communities of reasonably large size, where an impressive collection of knowledge remains untapped for potential use in the educational program.

Occasionally, it is possible to enlist the long-range aid of such persons in establishing Saturday seminars, or in a circumstance such as the one described by Sklarsky and Baxter (1961). There, use was made of a substitute teacher with a doctorate in science, who spent one period a day with students in the area of language arts. Because of the special interest of the teacher, the language arts project was centered on a science topic, "The Microbe and I." Extensive use was made of field trips, such as a visit to a large microbiology laboratory in the city. Experiments were carried out on bacteria, yeast, and molds, and the students were required to make reports and to write up experiments in much the same way that a scientist would. Additional guest speakers, acquaintances of the teacher, were brought into the classroom; oral presentations were made; and reports were written at the end of the program.

The authors claim that such extensive investigation of one area convinced the students that it takes time to do good work. They found that the assignments for the research class could not be hastily put together the night before they were due. This is a difficult fact for many gifted children to grasp, accustomed as they are to breezing through lessons. Some have never had to face the experience of writing and rewriting a paper in order to polish it and produce more effective communication.

Although the content for this kind of program can be varied, depending upon the skills and talents of the particular expert, the excitement, the increased effort, and the motivation that seem to accompany contact with the person who knows this subject area thoroughly and is enthusiastic about it, can positively color the students' entire attitude toward school and education.

Most school systems rarely have staff resources in such special areas of the curriculum as science, where teachers, particularly in the elementary school, have little knowledge and sometimes not much motivation for the subject.

Ryder (1972) describes an innovative program for young gifted children in a community with rich resources, San Francisco. Here the resources of the California Academy of Sciences, the Steinhart Aquarium, and the Morrison Planetarium are made available, and the gifted fifth graders are trained by the museums' staffs of experts to be *docents,* or volunteers, who guide visitors through art or natural science exhibits. The "docents" study the museum exhibits with purpose and enthusiasm since they may later serve as guides to these programs for their peers. In addition, they have opportunities to go on field trips, do independent studies, and so on. Parents are encouraged to participate in that program with weekend nature walks and the like.

Before the reader dismisses this approach on the grounds that his or her town is no San Francisco, he might consider what resources there are that could allow for an application of the docent idea there. Even in rural areas where skilled staff are in short supply, ingenuity and motivation can pay dividends. Morris (1957) describes a seminar that was conducted twice a week after school for high school students, in an attempt to give bright students a chance to integrate their knowledge and to clarify and deepen their concepts. The seminar itself followed the interests of the students, although it centered on the general theme of communication. The students read poetry aloud, listened to records of poetry, read such books as *Patterns of Culture,* by Ruth Benedict, and *Language in Thought and Action,* by Hayakawa, and conducted discussions on these experiences.

As Morris points out, one of the discoveries made by conducting such a seminar was that talented rural high school youth have serious questions to ask but have not had adequate opportunity to ask or answer them. The comments by the students themselves are indicative of the kinds of things that they appreciate, together with some implied criticism of the program in the regular high school curriculum (p. 33):

> "This is entirely different from anything that we have had in our schools."
> "We have the opportunity to think aloud and develop our thoughts orally without fear of criticisms."
> "It made me think more deeply on subjects I didn't think were important."
> "In regular classes, the answer is right or wrong—but in seminar you examine what everyone says."

None of these special attempts is without its personal cost. Generally, the organization and administration of such programs are wearing on the participants, whose satisfactions come from the appreciation of the youngsters and from the students' realization of doors that had not hitherto been opened.

ADMINISTRATIVE ADJUSTMENTS: SECONDARY

There are numerous differences between the elementary and secondary programs for the gifted which make many of the suggestions above applicable to the elementary level only. The reader should remind himself of the following:

1. There are no self-contained classrooms at the secondary level. Instead of having one teacher for all subject matter, the student has different teachers for five or six subject areas.
2. There are differences in training and philosophy of the instructional staff.

At the elementary level, the teacher is usually child-centered and is trying to adapt the curriculum to the individual. Teachers at the secondary level have probably received much more intensive instruction in their chosen subject area and also see many more children in a day than will the elementary teacher.

3. There are larger differences in ability and achievement at the secondary level. Some students will be taking calculus while others are doing remedial arithmetic. This increase in variation and the compartmentalization by subject matter makes grouping by subject aptitude or general ability much easier and much more necessary.

American Comprehensive High School

All these differences must be kept in mind in considering the development of differential programs for gifted children at the secondary level. One other important consideration is the phenomenon of the American comprehensive high school. This is an attempt to provide for the educational needs of children of all levels of ability from age 14 to 18. This type of high school has three main objectives: (1) to provide a general education for all future citizens; (2) to provide good elective programs for those who wish to use their acquired skills immediately on graduation; and (3) to provide satisfactory programs for those whose vocations will depend on their subsequent education in a college or university.

The United States has not always held to the principle of universal education at the secondary level. In the first decade of this century, a mere 50 years ago, only one out of every ten young people of high school age was in school, but at the present time approximately eight out of ten children from age 14 to 18 are enrolled in secondary schools, most of them in comprehensive high schools.

Passow (1956, p. 147) summed up the criticisms against the comprehensive high school as follows:

1. The secondary schools fail to get many of the brightest people to go on to college and advanced training. The Commission on Human Resources and Advanced Training reported that fewer than half of the upper 25 per cent of all high school graduates ever earn college degrees and only six out of ten of the top five per cent do.
2. Guidance and educational procedures fall short in motivating able youth, judged according to two criteria: first, the number of gifted children who are working up to capacity and, second, the number who will go to college. The lack of desire for college training is second only to inadequate finances as a reason for by-passing college.
3. The educational processes in American schools lack the quality found in European education and, as a consequence, gifted youth suffer. American secondary schools are accused of failing to revive intellectual rigor and to sustain scholarship.

4. The comprehensive high school program is watered down, frag-
mentized, and incohesive. Critics have charged that standards have
been lowered or abandoned, rigorous examinations eliminated, and
intellectual mediocrity accepted.

Although Passow recognizes the legitimacy of some of these objections,
he also provides us with some partial rejoinders. First of all, even if
50 percent of our most able youth are not going to college, this still is
not good reason to believe that they are not making a meaningful contribution to our society. Passow also points out that motivation for going
to college has, in many cases, little to do with school itself. Finally, an
educational program should be judged on the basis of whether it attains
its accepted goals. American youth should be judged not only on ability
in science and mathematics but also on effective citizenship, group membership, ethical values, and other traits which our culture seeks to encourage in our youth.

Conant Report

The Conant report (1959) on the status of the American high school contained a large number of recommendations on how to improve secondary
schools, and once again proved it is easier to propose changes than to
carry them out. Conant's recommendations were generally in terms of
modifications of existing programs, rather than elimination or drastic reorganization of them. The one exception to this general rule was his
recommendation to eliminate the small high schools that graduated
classes of 100 or less. He believed that it would be impossible to provide a comprehensive program, especially for the academically talented,
with this small number of children, where the classes would become ab-
normally small and the total cost per student extremely large. One general criticism of the high schools was of particular concern (p. 40):

> The academically talented student, as a rule, is not being sufficiently
> challenged, does not work hard enough, and his program of academic
> subjects is not of sufficient range. The able boys too often specialize in
> Mathematics and Science to the exclusion of foreign languages and to the
> neglect of English and Social Studies. The able girls, on the other hand,
> too often avoid Mathematics and Science as well as the foreign languages.

The recommendations in the Conant report were quite well-received
in most educational circles. A series of recommendations relating to the
upgrading of the conceptual level of instruction and to the introduction
of certain inherently important subject matter into the life of the student
follows (pp. 49–85).

1. *Ability grouping.* In the required subjects and those elected by students with a wide range of ability, the student should be grouped

according to ability, subject by subject. For example, in English, American History, 9th grade Algebra, Biology, and Physical Science, there should be at least three types of classes—one for the more able in the subject, another for the large group whose ability is about average, and another for the very slow readers who should be handled by special teachers.

For the purpose of developing an understanding between students of different levels of academic ability and vocational goals, home rooms should be organized in such a way as to make them significant social units in the school. To this end students should be kept together in one home room for the entire senior high school course, and care should be taken to have home room a cross-section of the school in terms of ability and vocational interest. . . .

2. *Academically talented.* Four years of mathematics, four years of one foreign language, three years of science, in addition to the required four years of English and three years of Social Studies; total of 18 courses with homework to be taken in four years. This program will require at least 15 hours of homework each week.

For the highly gifted pupil some type of special arrangement should be made. If they are too few in number in some schools to warrant giving them instruction in a special class . . . a special guidance officer should be assigned to the group as a tutor and should keep in close touch with these students throughout their four years of senior high school work. The tutor should see to it that the students are challenged not only by their course work but by the development of their special interests as well.

3. *English.* Time devoted to English composition during the four years should occupy about half the total time devoted to the study of English. Each student should be required to write an average of one theme a week. Heavy emphasis should be placed on English composition.

4. *Foreign languages.* School Boards should be ready to offer a third and fourth year of foreign language no matter how few students enroll. The guidance officer should urge completion of a four-year sequence of one language if the student demonstrates ability in handling foreign languages.

5. *Science.* All students should obtain some understanding of the nature of science and scientific approach by a required course in the physical sciences or biology. This course should be given in at least three sections grouped by ability.

6. *Social studies.* In 12th grade a course in American Problems or American Government should be required. Each class in this course should be a cross-section of the school: the class should be heterogeneously grouped. Teachers should encourage all students to participate in discussions. The course should develop not only an understanding of the American form of government and the economic basis of our free society, but also mutual respect and understanding between different types of students.

7. *Counseling*.   There should be one full-time counselor or guidance officer for every 250 to 300 pupils in the high school.   These counselors
should have had experience as teachers but should be devoted virtually full-time to counseling work: they should be familiar with the
use of tests and measurements of the aptitudes and achievements
of pupils.
  It should be the policy of the school that every student have an individualized program; there will be no classification of students according to clearly defined or labeled programs or tracks such as
"college preparatory," "vocational," "commercial."   In advising the student to an elective program, the counselor will be guided by the minimum program recommendations for the academically talented. . . .
8. *Grading*.   At the end of each marking period, a list shall be published
of the students who have elected courses recommended for the academically talented and have made an average grade of "B."   On
graduation, a notation might be made on the diploma of the student
that placed on the academic honors list for all four years.
9. *Acceleration*.   If enough students are available to provide a special
class, these students should take in 12th grade one or more courses
which are part of the advanced placement program.   Under the program, a student in 12th grade may take such courses as college mathematics, college English, or college history and after passing suitable
examinations, may be given college credit for the courses and also
sophomore standing in these subjects.

These recommendations seem to have been substantially forgotten in
the general uproar about desegregation, school busing, and other social
issues that have preoccupied and paralyzed educators for a decade in the
late 1960s and early 1970s.

Mentor Approach

Another approach growing in popularity is called the *mentor approach*
and refers to a procedure by which the gifted student leaves school for a
period of time, perhaps two or three afternoons a week, and comes under
the supervision of some specialist in the community who is an expert in
the area of the gifted student's particular area of interest.

If the gifted student is a bug about computers, the school will arrange
for him to work part-time in one of the electronics laboratories in town.
If she looks forward to a career in medicine, she can spend some time
working in the laboratory of the local hospital.   A talented girl in the
performing arts can spend some time under the tutelege of a professional
dancer in the local ballet.

Satinsky (1971) describes a special program established at Hahnemann
Hospital in Philadelphia, where a large number of gifted children from
the secondary schools in Philadelphia come to the medical school, take

284

special seminars, conduct experiments in the laboratories of the hospital, and generally get a realistic taste of the life of the medical scientist, an experience that would be impossible to obtain in the four walls of the local high school, no matter how willing or interested the staff might be in such an outcome. Since the gifted students have already mastered the essentials of the high school curriculum, one cannot accept the notion that they are missing out on some valuable educational experience by going into the community. This approach has been infrequently used not because of strong counterarguments but because it is administratively awkward.

Acceleration

Another technique used primarily to shorten the long period of time that gifted students find themselves in an educational setting has been acceleration. Its basic purpose is to move the child or student more rapidly to the end of his apprenticeship and launch him into a career. The methods for doing this are widely varied and the results almost always the same— success. One should not suppose, however, that because the evaluation reports are favorable the practice is either widely used or widely accepted. The need for such a move can be best illustrated with facts everyone knows about but still forgets from time to time.

As Table 10–2 shows, the gifted student who anticipates being a physician is faced with the problem that he will be 18 years old by the time he finishes high school, 22 by the time he finishes college, 26 by the end of medical school, and by the time he finishes an internship and residency —to say nothing of other special training he might receive—he will be 30 years of age before starting productive work in his profession or career. Similar requirements can be found in many of the other professions and sciences. Therefore, any educational readjustment that would reduce this extended period of time by at least two or three years could be of

TABLE 10–2. *Age of Completion of Educational Benchmarks.*

SCHOOL PROGRAM	EXPECTED AGE AT COMPLETION
Elementary school	12
Junior high school	15
Senior high school	18
College	22
Medical school	26
Internship	27
Residency	29

great benefit to the individual and to the culture, even in the absence of changes in the actual educational program that the youngster receives. We should remind ourselves that by the end of the sequence just noted, the student has been physiologically mature for 15 years and that many of his age mates have been gainfully employed for ten years or more. Yet the gifted remain dependent through the most physically vigorous part of their adult life.

For many years, most of the public and many educators have felt that acceleration and grade skipping were synonymous terms. As a matter of fact, grade skipping is considered one of the least desirable methods of accomplishing acceleration of gifted students. Table 10–3 shows the various methods of acceleration of gifted children open to the teacher and the school administrator at practically all levels of the educational program.

At the primary level, this includes admittance to school before the usual beginning age of 6 years. Another method that has gained increased popularity in the last few years has been the ungraded primary system. This provision enables a group of bright students to remain with one teacher, who will attempt to accomplish the goals of their primary years in less than a three-year period. This technique also allows slow learners more than three years to complete the primary level, if that seems desirable.

The junior high years can be shortened by reducing the three-year program to two years, while the senior high program can be reduced either by early admittance to college or by inclusion of seminars in various subject areas which would qualify for college credit. The Advanced Placement Program has become a popular method of stimulating high-aptitude students in high school. Even in college, the student may take tests for course credit without having to sit through the course itself; this also represents a type of acceleration.

TABLE 10–3. *Methods of Acceleration of Gifted Children.*

GRADE LEVEL	TYPE OF ACCELERATION
Primary (1–3)	1. Early admittance to school
	2. Ungraded primary
Intermediate (4–6)	1. Ungraded classes
	2. Grade skipping
Junior High (7–9)	1. Three years in two
	2. Senior high classes for credit
Senior High (10–12)	1. Extra load
	2. Seminars for college credit
College (13–16)	1. Early admittance to college
	2. Honors programs

What is needed to make acceleration for gifted children work is a thorough knowledge of the needs and abilities of the individual person and of the administrative organization, together with sympathy for this type of action, so that it is accomplished with the minimum personal dislocation of the students.

There is always the question as to whether *every* gifted child needs or benefits from acceleration. The answer is a resounding NO. Let's consider for a moment the four children Cranshaw, Zelda, Joe, and Sam. Sam, with his deficiencies in language development and his motivational problems, probably would not be benefited, and might be harmed, by any ill-advised attempt to accelerate him to a higher educational level. The same thing may be said for Joe. His inability or unwillingness to cooperate, or to work even at his present level of ability, makes it unlikely that putting him in an even more difficult competitive situation would stimulate him to more extensive action. We must remember that it is only the winners who love competition. Losers do not, and Joe has been a loser throughout his entire life.

Acceleration does seem to be reasonably feasible for Zelda and Cranshaw, as they are both doing well in their school work. Zelda's personal problems, however, would remain, regardless of whether she is accelerated or not. Some educational action would need to be taken on these problems, in addition to any possible acceleration. In this regard, it is worth noting that "acceleration" should never be considered as a *substitute* for other action but merely as a supplement to it. It will probably solve only the problem of the extended school program. Other problems will have to be dealt with in other ways. Since both these children are probably headed for professional work, the total time they spend in the educational system should be considered carefully.

Previously we mentioned research results on the effects of acceleration. A few summary statements plus some recent studies will give the flavor. Terman and Oden (1947, p. 281) suggested, as a result of their follow-up study:

> It is our opinion that nearly all children of 135 IQ or higher should be promoted sufficiently to permit college entrance by the age of 17 at least, and that the majority of this group would be better off entering at 16. Acceleration of this extent is especially desirable for those who plan to complete two or more years of graduate study in preparation for a professional career.

Gallagher (1966, p. 100), in summarizing research on the topic, reported:

> The recent research on acceleration has done nothing to change the generally favorable portrait of these methods for moderately shortening the educational career of talented youth. The advantage of saving a year or

two from a long investment in educational time does not seem diluted by social or emotional difficulties.

Reynolds, Birch, and Tuseth (1962), in reviewing research on evaluation of early admittance programs, commented as follows (p. 17):

> It may be concluded, from the research . . . that early admission to school of mentally advanced children who are within a year of the ordinary school-entrance age and who are generally mature is to their advantage.   There are few issues in education on which the research evidence now available is so clear and so universally favorable to a particular solution.

A recent study of early admittance by Braga (1969) is typical of the kind of study and the general findings. The purpose of this study was to determine the effect of early admission on sixty-three children in the first, third, fifth, and seventh grades in terms of academic and non-academic achievement, social and emotional development. Subjects admitted to school early were compared to normally admitted subjects, and late-admitted subjects matched for IQ and sex (early-admitted subjects therefore had lower mental age). The elementary school training for all three groups was exactly the same in that they attended the same regular school classes—there was *no* special program for the early-admittance children.

Information was gathered from (1) achievement tests (MAT and Iowa Test), (2) permanent school records, (3) parent and teacher questionnaires, and (4) a specially devised teacher-rating instrument. Results showed that there were no significant differences between early-admitted subjects and their non-early-admitted peers. Parent and teacher questionnaires showed that, in general, teachers were opposed to early admission and that parents of early-admitted subjects were in favor of early admission, whereas parents of non-early-admitted children were not.

This result would seem to speak well for a policy of early admission, especially in view of the fact that early-admittance subjects were comparable on all variables with their classmates of higher mental ages. The gifted child who was admitted early will now leave his total educational program a year earlier, with no observable academic or emotional harm.

In 1963, the State Department of Education in California initiated a program that they called Project Talent (Plowman and Rice, 1967). The purpose of this project was to demonstrate a variety of educational adjustments to the program of gifted children, one of which focused on the issue of acceleration. Ten projects were established around the state to illustrate this particular set of practices, and a total of 522 pupils have been accelerated through a variety of means—in particular, through a summer school program that allowed the skipping of third grade.

The criteria accepted in the California study for these students were

(1) that their mental ability be in the upper 5 percent of the general population, (2) that they have maintained a consistent record of high academic achievement with school marks at B or higher, (3) that they have a social–emotional adjustment of normal or higher, and (4) that their height, health, and general physical characteristics be average or higher. Thus, we can see that Cranshaw and Zelda might be considered for acceleration in this program but not Joe and Sam. Acceleration is not for every gifted child.

The total results of the project should be extremely useful and instructive to educators concerned with programs for gifted children. Of the 522 youngsters who were actual accelerants, only 9 have been reported to have serious problems after their placement in the higher grade. In all nine of these cases, questions were raised during the initial placement with regard to their possible acceptance.

Despite this record of successful accomplishment, there are continuing strong negative feelings on the part of both teachers and parents—strong enough to suggest that only half these programs in acceleration will be continued in the school systems where they were established. In addition, each of the school district programs has undergone serious criticism from the community.

As Plowman and Rice (1969, p. 51) report, "Neither the research nor this study has fully identified the main obstacles to the establishment of acceleration programs. It has been seen that 'successful programs' by any meaningful academic or professional standards are abandoned because they are exposed to incessant pressure from teachers and parents who do not agree on emotional grounds with the aims, functions, and benefits of acceleration."

In other words, the real reasons for the strong opposition to acceleration that one finds in school systems lie not in the actual research data, which are highly favorable, but in some hidden concerns or anxieties of both parents and teachers regarding this practice. One possible reason that has been suggested is the premature thrusting of the child out of the parental nest. After all, a child and a parent have only so many years together. Acceleration really means that the child will leave home one year earlier. This, however, does not explain the concern of teachers for this procedure; we can only agree with Plowman and Rice that this is an area of major potential study and investigation.

But educational administrators are concerned more with *operational feasibility,* or the ability to put a good idea into effective action, than with the research literature. As just noted, it is well established in the literature that early admittance to school, or admitting youngsters at the age of 5½ or even 5, who have the requisite emotional, intellectual, and social development, does them no lasting harm. It has the advantage of cutting a year off their total educational program without their missing any of the curriculum. Hiskey (1962, p. 50) commented, "Would that we could be assured that as many of our regular entrants would adjust and progress as well in school as the early entrants do." Nevertheless, very few school systems have adopted this procedure because of this problem of *operational feasibility*.

In order to put this provision of early admittance into effect in a school system, one must have some method of screening the 5-year-olds in the community to find out which of these have the necessary characteristics. This requires such expense in terms of professional time and diagnostic testing that it has been considered not feasible by most school systems.

One of the ritual statements made by educators is that students should be allowed to progress at their own rate. When we check this philosophy against actions in the case of acceleration of gifted, we find a puzzling contradiction. Despite the evidence in favor of it, hardly anyone does it. Why not? Wouldn't life be boring if the next generation of students had no problems left to solve! This is one they are willed for free!

PROGRAM COSTS

Recent interest in educational accountability, of demonstrating the tangible worth of a program, has focused interest on costs and program evaluations. Are programs for the gifted really beneficial? They do cost more money than the general per-pupil cost of an ordinary program.

The excess or additional costs of programs for the gifted have never been considered high, especially when compared with the costs of other special programs. A recent survey completed by Rossmiller, Hale, and Frohreich (1970) indicated that special programs for the gifted student cost less than $100 per child over the average expense. Comparative figures for other special programs are presented in Figure 10–1.

There are very strong reasons for support of remedial or supportive programs, and we do not suggest that money should be transferred from handicapped programs to gifted programs. One clear message is that the society can find money for programs it feels are necessary; therefore, the expense of a program for the gifted would hardly seem to be one of the more serious problems to be overcome. Much more serious are those myths and anxieties of decision makers that stand as barriers to more effective educational help.

PROGRAM EVALUATIONS

On the other side of the coin we find the benefits, and to analyze these we need to look at the outcome of various programs. Later in this

290

CATEGORY OF
EXCEPTIONALITY

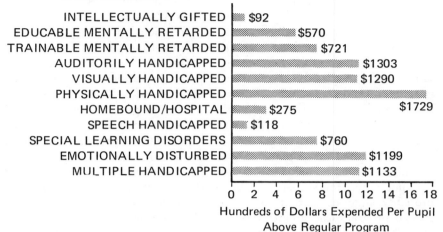

Hundreds of Dollars Expended Per Pupil
Above Regular Program

Figure 10–1. *Expenditures in 27 Model Districts in Five States (California, Florida, New York, Texas, Wisconsin) with Superior Programs for Children with Exceptional Learning Needs: Excess Beyond Regular Program. (From R. Rossmiller, J. Hale, & L. Frohreich. Educational programs for exceptional children: Resource configurations and costs. Washington, D.C.: National Education Finance Project, 1970, p. 127.)*

chapter we evaluate in great detail a total state program, but in this section we will concentrate only on the results of specific programs.

One of the questions often asked in educational circles is "What is the impact of ability grouping?" One of the most comprehensive studies was carried out by Goldberg, Passow, Justman, and Hage (1965).

Within the New York City public schools, eighty-six fifth-grade classes in forty-five elementary schools were arranged in various patterns of ability grouping and maintained this status for two years. A wide variation of broad-range and narrow-range ability groups were evaluated on the basis of achievement, self-attitudes, social acceptance of deviant children, and teacher ratings. The results of the study indicated no advantage for the narrow-range ability-grouped, highly talented children. In some instances, there seemed to be more gains made by the broad-range groups. Few differences were obtained among ability groups on attitudes or interest measures as well.

The authors concluded that merely changing the ability grouping within the class *without* changing the curriculum or the manner in which the children were taught cannot be expected to produce any substantial changes. As Goldberg (1965, p. 41) has commented, "Ability grouping is by no means a sufficient condition insuring greater academic achievement at any ability level. At best, it provides a framework within which enhanced learning may be more effectively planned and executed." A similar study reaching similar results was completed by Borg (1964).

In most of the numerous evaluation studies from the California State program, Robeck (1967) reported on the academic performance of samples of gifted children who participated in various types of special programs when compared with gifted children who did not receive the special program and were assigned to a control group. The results of these studies are summarized in Table 10–4, which indicates that the Saturday Special Class and the full-time Special Class programs for gifted children resulted in a significant gain in standard achievement measures for these elementary school students. The same amount of improvement was not noted for students in the part-time interest class. What this probably suggests is that the more definitive and more intensive the special program, the greater the chance of getting measurable improvement in the performance of the gifted students.

One of the concerns that parents have, and sometimes do not share frankly with the educator, is whether the creation of a special program will single out their youngster for identification as an "egghead" or as a strange individual, will cause them to lose their friends, and so forth. These are legitimate concerns and need to be answered as straightforwardly as possible with a minimum of rhetoric and a maximum of facts.

Martinson (1972) summarized for the U.S. Commissioner of Education the results of a wide variety of evaluation studies done in Ohio, New

TABLE 10–4. *Pupil Achievement Gains in State Study—STEP Tests Grades 5 and 6.*

	0	5	10	15
Theoretical Gain	▬▬▬▬▬			
Saturday Class				
Experimental	▬▬▬▬▬▬▬▬▬▬▬▬ **			
Control	▬▬▬▬▬▬▬▬			
Part-time Interest Class				
Experimental	▬▬▬▬▬▬▬▬▬			
Control	▬▬▬▬▬▬▬▬			
Special Full-time Class				
Experimental	▬▬▬▬▬▬▬▬▬▬▬ **			
Control	▬▬▬▬▬▬▬▬▬			

Source: M. Robeck. Special classes for intellectually gifted students. In P. Plowman & J. Rice. *California Project Talent.* California State Department of Education, Sacramento, California, 1967, p. 99.

York, Los Angeles, and Illinois and came to the following conclusion (p. 102).

> Conclusions derived from these studies generally agreed that participants did not develop personality or social problems, did not become conceited, or did not suffer health problems because of pressures; rather, participants showed improvement not only in academic areas but also in the personal and social areas.

In a specific study of the impact on social relationships, a group of fifth- and sixth-grade talented pupils who came from rural schools and who engaged in a program of Saturday classwork attained significant gains in social status within their regular classroom, despite the fact that their peers were unaware of the special work that was going on. In addition, a detailed psychological inventory of the gifted pupils at the junior and senior high school levels in the California program suggested that participants in special programs gained in personal and social maturity compared to equally gifted nonparticipants. The total evidence significantly suggests that gifted pupils participate in special programs without damage and with a reasonable expectation of enhancement of personal, social, or psychological factors.

Gallagher (1965b) compared a group of gifted students from a university laboratory school with a similar group in a public high school on attitude and self-concept. All these students had originally applied to the laboratory school for admittance and those attending the public school had been *randomly* selected, so that there was good reason to believe that the two groups were relatively equal at the beginning of their junior high school period.

Four years after this selection, a total of 249 students who had been through these programs (over 90 percent of the available students) were retested and compared on the basis of productive-thinking measures, measures of self-concept, and attitude. The major differences discovered between the two groups lay in the attitudinal dimension. The laboratory school gifted students showed a gain in self-concept in the senior high school, accompanied by a reduction in their positive image of their families. Also, a greater number of the students in the university laboratory school expressed negative feelings about school or doubts about their own ability to do well. This was generally considered to be the result of the stronger competition found among these students, and also because of a single dimension of success in the laboratory school where only academic performance appeared to count for status.

The gifted students who attended the public high school seemed to have a more positive self-attitude, partly as a result of a variety of possible avenues of achieving acceptance and success, if not in academic areas, then in the area of social acceptance or in achievement in the arts or athletics.

Which program is better? We have to respond, better for what? The study did not answer that question, because there seemed to be advantages and disadvantages to both school settings. The laboratory school students had the advantage of being exposed to the newest in curriculum advances and also completed their total junior and senior high school program in five years instead of the customary six. On the other hand, the public school children seemed more at ease with the school and with themselves. Depending upon the value system of the observer, one may be considered better than the other. What the study *did* show is that different educational environments can create significant differences in self-concept and attitude in gifted students.

Although a wide variety of such studies attests to the various merits of special programs for the gifted, it would be interesting to the teacher to get some perspective on what the students themselves felt about such programs. Barbe (1955) asked over 400 graduates of the Cleveland Major Work (ability-grouping) classes to evaluate their experience in the program.

Forty-seven percent of the respondents (a 77 percent return of all contacted was achieved, which is a good return figure for questionnaires) approved of the program with enthusiasm, 37 percent responded with some reservation, and 8 percent disapproved or strongly opposed the program. The specific nature of their attitudes is shown in Table 10–5.

TABLE 10–5. *Evaluation by Graduates of Major Work Classes, Cleveland.*

	BOYS (N = 210)	GIRLS (N = 237)
Best-liked aspects of program	1. Opportunity to express individuality 2. Enrichment procedures 3. Freedom from regimentation	1. Foreign language 2. Enrichment procedures 3. Opportunity to express individuality
Least-liked aspects of program	1. Attitudes of other students and teachers 2. Lack of social contact with other pupils 3. Foreign language	1. Lack of social contact with other pupils 2. Attitudes of other students and teachers 3. Not enough attention to skill subjects
Suggested changes	1. None 2. More mixing with other pupils 3. Better-trained teachers 4. More acceleration	1. None 2. More mixing with other pupils 3. Vocational guidance 4. Better-trained teachers

Source: Adapted from W. Barbe. Evaluation of special classes for gifted children. *Exceptional Children,* 1955, **22,** p. 61.

The opportunity to express individuality was highly valued by both boys and girls as was the opportunity to take part in the enriched program. In addition, the boys liked the greater freedom from regimentation in the Major Work program, whereas the girls valued highly the foreign language experience in the Major Work program. The boys, however, listed French as one of the least-liked aspects of the program. The negative aspects of the program that were most often perceived were (1) negative attitudes of other students and pupils toward them, and (2) lack of social contact with other students. Barbe reports that there was a reduction in the percentages of response in this area from 1940 to 1950, which suggested that these aspects of the program have been improved.

Over half the students responding suggested no changes at all. Those changes which were requested followed expected lines. The students would have liked more opportunity to mix with other students and also requested more effectively trained teachers.

Although program evaluation has not been given a major emphasis in gifted programs, the results now available suggest that where definable programs with clear goals are instituted the results are generally favorable.

STATE AND FEDERAL PROGRAMS FOR GIFTED

It is increasingly obvious that more and more of the resources for education will come from the state and federal level and less from the local level. Thus, the central resources for initiating and keeping programs for gifted and talented students in effect will probably rely as much on decisions made in the state capital and in the national capital as in the local school board. Recently, nationwide hearings on the education of gifted children were held in the ten different Department of Health, Education, and Welfare regions around the country. Testimony was taken from a variety of school persons, parents, students, and educators, and a variety of surveys were conducted about the current status of education of the gifted.

One such survey (Gallagher, 1972) explored the scope and depth of state actions for the gifted. Was there an identifiable state program? Were there leadership personnel in the state department of education clearly responsible for such a program? If no program now existed, were there planning commissions or study commissions working to generate such a program? The results of that survey are summarized in Figure 10–2. At the time of the survey in 1971, twenty-one states had legislation providing special resources or incentives to local school districts to increase their program efforts on education of the gifted and

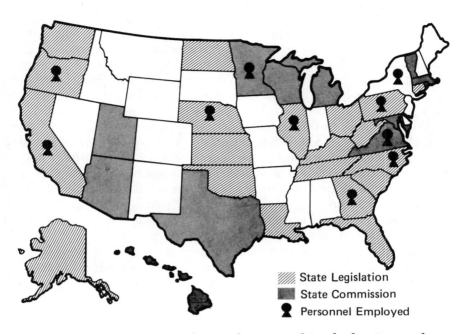

State Legislation
State Commission
Personnel Employed

FIGURE 10–2. *State Legislation, Planning, and Leadership Personnel for the Gifted.* (*From J. J. Gallagher et al.* Analysis of hearings held by Regional Commissioners of Education on education of the gifted. Education of the gifted and talented. *Report to the Congress of the United States. Washington, D.C.: GPO, 1972, p. 164.*)

talented. A quick glance at the figure will show that these states are scattered throughout the country and not grouped in any one particular region. Furthermore, there were ten additional states that had study commissions, suggesting that even more of the states would be considering legislation in the near future.

But legislation, when it is passed, usually represents intent, the desire to accomplish some goal. How fervently that desire is carried out depends on what extent the resources in that state are allocated to this program. Although state legislatures have recognized the needs of the gifted, as is manifested by special legislative action, the limited resources actually applied to the program suggest a strong lack of urgency. For example, only ten of the states had leadership personnel at the state department of education level who could provide key direction for the program in that state.

The amount of funds allotted to the gifted are miniscule when compared with other special education programs. The state of California, long recognized as a leader in this field, still provides less than $100 per pupil above the normal program cost for the gifted.

State personnel were asked what were the major barriers to state action for the gifted; the results are summarized in Figure 10–3. It is clear that insufficient financial support and a lack of a high priority were the key elements in most states and the rest of the problems follow from that lack of priority. What is wrong? Is the need not recognized? The witnesses in the hearings again and again made it quite clear that the problem was that the allocation of resources at the state level is practically always made on the basis of crisis and immediate problems. Those youngsters who are dropping out of school, who are a physical threat to the teacher, or who are so slow as to cause great problems to the teacher—all would take precedence over the gifted, who can survive without creating great daily crisis in the classroom itself. What this neglect does to the long-range status of our nation was eloquently stated by some of the witnesses at the regional hearings. A few quotes will tell the story.

> In other words, the longer that any talent or set of talents remains dormant and unused, the more confidently can it be predicted that the persons will never really use such potential talent in their entire lives. (Taylor)

One obvious reason for giving our gifted and talented children an optimal

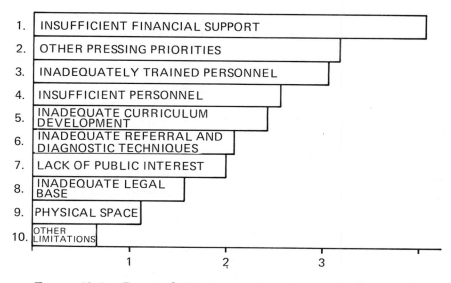

FIGURE 10–3. *Perceived Barriers to State Action for the Gifted.* (*From J. J. Gallagher et al.* Analysis of hearings held by Regional Commissioners of Education on education of the gifted. Education of the gifted and talented. *Report to the Congress of the United States. Washington, D.C.: GPO, 1972, p. 167.*)

chance to develop their maximum potential is that now, and in the fore-seeable future, we need leadership. (Olson)

Follow-up studies of the gifted indicate that they are the persons who make our great scientific and medical discoveries, write our great music and books, and help us to solve our social problems. To shortchange these potential contributors is not only state and national suicide, but conceivably a harbinger of global atrophy. (Rothney)

Although a number of states have mounted interesting innovative pro-grams, among them California, Connecticut, Georgia, North Carolina, and Nebraska, we have chosen to describe one state program since it pro-vides a variety of rather specific provisions for gifted children and also has made the most comprehensive evaluation of that program of any in the fifty states. It is possible to see not only what was intended by the state when it set up these proposals but to get some measure of judgment as to whether it worked or not.

TABLE 10–6. *Components of Illinois State Program for the Gifted.*

SECTION	RATIONALE FOR SECTION
I. Reimbursement	Provides support through formula or personnel method for a wide variety of special services for gifted students, the particular nature of which is determined by local needs.
II. Demonstration Centers	Provide centers that would demonstrate excellent educational programming for gifted students so that visitors would become aware of new developments, could decide whether such innovation fits their school, and could receive help for developing talent in their own system.
III. Experimental Projects	Research support given to program development efforts such as curriculum innovation and to efforts to evaluate or investigate the impact of the various programs for gifted students.
IV. Training	Provides support for summer workshops, in-service training programs, year-round fellowships and scholarships to provide competent professional personnel to staff other elements of the program.
V. State Staff	Provide administrative leadership for program, coordinate the various elements of the program, and provide consultant help for school systems on program development for the gifted.

Source: J. Gallagher. *Research summary on gifted child education.* State Department of Public Instruction, Springfield, Ill., 1966, p. 135.

Table 10–6 summarizes the five essential components of the state program in Illinois as designed in 1965. The first dimension was a provision for general *reimbursement* of school systems, where each school system was allowed to spend a small amount of additional money to help the programs in its own area. The second major component was that of a provision for the establishment of *demonstration centers* designed to make visible the newest in educational programming in hopes that visitors would observe these programs and take them back to their own communities.

A third area of the state program was *experimental programs,* which attempted to encourage new program development activities that would strengthen the other parts of the program, particularly the demonstration and reimbursement centers. The fourth part of the program was *training* to provide special support for summer workshops, inservice training programs, year-round fellowships, and the like. A fifth part of the program provided for state department of education *staff,* which provided administrative leadership and also technical assistance to local school systems upon request.

Not only was this program unique in conception but also unique in setting up a most comprehensive evaluation program (House, 1972). A wide variety of checks were attempted to gain a portrait of the program's effectiveness. For example, attempts were made to obtain the anonymous responses of children and teachers in the program, visitors to the demonstration centers were asked what they had done with their observations and new knowledge, direct observations were made in the gifted classrooms to see what was actually happening, and so on. Following is a summary of the results of that evaluation effort.

EVALUATION: ILLINOIS PROGRAM FOR THE GIFTED

Reimbursement

The initial purpose of the reimbursement section of the Illinois state program was to provide local school systems with small amounts of resources to conduct whatever services they felt were appropriate for gifted and talented students. The evaluation, then, had to do with what the outcomes of such activities were and whether, in fact, an increased number of gifted students received services locally as a result of this small amount of stimulation.

It was found that the number of districts participating increased dramatically during the period of time reviewed and that almost one third of the districts in the state (which, however, enrolled over 80 percent of the student population) had participated in developing programs for gifted children as a result of the reimbursement program. In an attempt to evaluate the quality of the program, some 10 percent of the districts were randomly chosen and asked to name the best programs that they had operating, and these programs were studied in detail. It was found that small school districts had a difficult time providing adequate services for their talented students but that medium and large districts could and, in fact, did establish medium- or high-quality programs that included more productive and stimulating classroom activities and a positive and appropriate climate for learning.

One of the questions asked by curious persons regarding programs for the gifted is "If gifted students all are assigned to the same program, does anything different happen in that classroom?" One indication that something different does happen can be seen in Figure 10–4, where a variety of variables are compared with gifted students in average classrooms, in classrooms where some reimbursement was provided for gifted students,

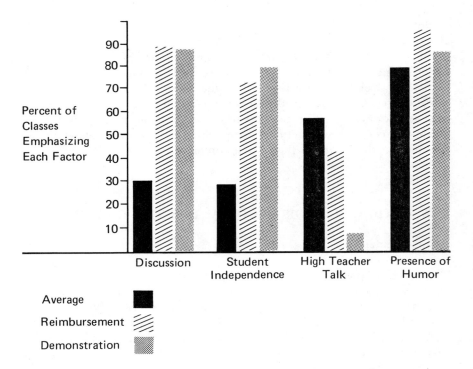

FIGURE 10–4. *Illinois Evaluation of Gifted Classes: Difference in Focus and Climate.* (*Adapted from J. Steele et al.* Instructional climate in Illinois gifted classes. *Urbana, Ill.: Center for Instructional Research and Curriculum Evaluation, 1970.*)

and in special demonstration programs for the gifted in the state of Illinois. There was a tremendous difference in the amount of discussion taking place in the gifted classes versus the average class, and in the range of student independence allowed compared to the average. Another consistent finding was the remarkably high percentage of teacher talk, particularly in secondary classes, despite all efforts of curriculum specialists and supervisors to modify it.

In this instance it is clear that, at least in those gifted classes that had demonstration programs, the lesson had been learned. Only 6 percent of the gifted classes were identified as having high teacher talk, whereas over half the average classes were identified in this fashion. It was suspected that the presence of humor might also be more characteristic of classes of talented and gifted youngsters, but this did not turn out to be the case. As seen in Figure 10–4, humor seemed to play a large part in most of the classes, regardless of the origin or type of student attending. Nevertheless, the overall impression is one in which a great deal more informality and student participation can be found in programs designed specifically for gifted students than in the average program, and this would be in line with the expected philosophy in such programs.

The overall weaknesses of the reimbursement programs were as follows: They tended to be established only at certain levels, for example, at the elementary school level, rather than throughout the whole range of the age continuum. Small districts had not been able to produce quality programs; and special provisions for gifted underachievers or extremely gifted children were not really provided. Furthermore, and perhaps more serious, some districts responded to the pressure to do something for the talented by continuing or instituting high-pressure courses that represented not innovations, but rather the worst of traditional schooling, accelerating fact-gathering and memory-type tasks.

Experimental Programs

These experimental projects were designed to stimulate curriculum innovation or to evaluate the impact of various programs locally on gifted students. Although some interesting projects were supported, the assumption that they would be disseminated to many other schools or that the excellent experimental projects developed in one district would be transferred to another did not occur. However, within the originating district, very good results were obtained and represented some of the best programs in the state as a whole. This apparently means that experimental programs are good for the local district but that major change in the method of delivery of new ideas has to be considered before the state, as a whole, would profit.

301

Demonstration Centers

The demonstration centers did not live up to the very high expectations everyone had of them. It was hoped that the demonstration center would provide a base for illustrating excellent educational programming and that visitors would be inclined to take these illustrations and use them in their own local situations. The evaluation concluded that the demonstrations themselves were quite well done. The content of the classes was good and the visitors did respond positively to what they had seen. However, after a year or less, only 29 percent of the teachers visiting the demonstration center were able to give any example of how they had changed their own situation, as a result of their visit.

One of the most pertinent bits of information was that, with both teachers and administrators, adoption of the new practice had little to do with the degree to which either teacher or administrator thought the demonstration was valuable. Instead, the key element in adoption was the nature of the local circumstances from which the visitor came. It was concluded that in order for these change agents, as the demonstration centers were seen, to be effective, they must work within the local framework of the teacher and the administrator they are trying to help. In recognition of this fact, what had previously been labeled demonstration centers are now being called "area service centers," where specialists go out *from* the demonstration center to work in the local area and with greater cognizance of the local area problems and situation.

Training

Of all the elements that were part of the Illinois program, the inservice training and the intensive summer institutes for leadership personnel had the most tangible impact on the total program. In these intensive summer institutes, teachers and administrators were allowed to try out new practices and to evaluate them with videotape replay, which allowed them to explore their own competencies and shortcomings in both instructional content and methods.

An important element of the whole program was that the more educators that a school district sent to a summer institute, the more likely it was that the local district would be influenced by the results. In other words, sending an isolated teacher who could return to her own school district but not have much influence on program direction was infinitely less desirable than sending a team of people who could, upon their return, reinforce and draw strength from one another to try to continue the innovative practices that they had discovered in the summer program.

This total program evaluation of the Illinois program was impressive not only for its comprehensiveness but because it reveals what everyone in education really understands: that no program, despite its press notices, ever turns out exactly the way it is supposed to, nor produces all of the great results that its proponents suggest.

What the Illinois program did reveal was that training was extremely important to the development of the entire program and that "demonstration centers" really need to become "technical assistance centers" with a variety of personnel devoted to providing assistance and help to local districts within the framework of the local districts' definition of the problem, rather than to try to demonstrate a predigested program of excellence that may work only for the district that is being illustrated. The final judgment of the evaluation is worth quoting (House et al., 1968).

> The Illinois plan for education of gifted children has been a bold, innovative, and successful program. Compared to the high expectations for sweeping educational reform entertained in the early 60's, it has had its share of disappointments. Nonetheless, it has effected measurable and, in many cases, dramatic accomplishments. While it has discovered some of the premises on which it was founded not to be true, it has subjected itself to intensive critical examination and has taken broad adjustments on that basis.

FEDERAL LEGISLATION

With the exception of the Sputnik scare in 1958 when a frightened Congress put large sums of money into the curriculum development programs of the National Science Foundation and in the National Defense Education Act with the explicit purpose of preventing the Russians from beating us in the space race and in overall scientific capabilities, little national attention has been paid to the issues of educating gifted and talented students.

Most of educational legislation that was created at the federal level in the 1960s seemed focused on major crisis areas in education, on issues such as "inner-city schools" that threatened to crumble the edifice of public education. Since the gifted do not create major and immediate trouble in the schools if their educational needs are not met, their problems were put off until another day. Little attention has been drawn to the long-range problem of neglecting the national reservoir of talent, to the slow and steady erosion of national talent and human resources, until recently.

In the Elementary and Secondary Education Act of 1975 there exists a special provision to provide modest resources for educational purposes that the Congress felt were of special priority. Among these priorities were the education of gifted children. Some funds have thus become available to accomplish some of the following objectives noted in the legislation:

Establish a National Clearinghouse on Gifted and Talented Children and Youth to obtain and disseminate information to the public on gifted children and youth.

Provide grants to each of the states to aid them in the initiation, expansion and improvement of programs for the education of gifted from preschool to secondary school levels.

Provide grants for a program of training personnel who will be teachers, supervisors, or leadership personnel for educational programs for gifted children and youth.

Support research, demonstration, dissemination, etc., specifically devoted to improving educational programs for the gifted.

A few million dollars spread over the entire country will not, of course, solve all of the problems, nor will it establish the special programs noted in this text. What it can do is to serve as a catalyst to demonstrate to local and state educators what benefits can be obtained by only a small investment in these students.

SUMMARY

In this chapter we have discussed administrative changes, or learning environment modifications, in the school program for gifted children. When a change or modification in the educational environment occurs, some visible and public change takes place in the school system.

A sudden announcement of special programming for the gifted is often greeted with ambivalence by many citizens, and open hostility by a few. This is because such programming does not carry the positive aura of aid to students in special trouble as does special programming for the handicapped, which is more easily justified. To many an ordinary citizen, such programs for gifted students look like one more effort to create "special privileges for special people," and such feelings are intensified if practically all the children within the program happen to come from the most wealthy and influential families in the community. Special efforts need to be made to explain to the public the nature and needs for such programs and to assure that talented children from all socioeconomic levels and cultural subgroups of the community are given a fair chance to participate in the program.

The administrative desire to develop some type of special learning situation for the gifted is usually based on three fairly straightforward objectives: first, to reduce the range of talent and achievement levels that a teacher must face; second, to reduce the tremendous time, often over twenty years of his life, that the gifted student must spend in the educational system; and third, to try to meet the special talents of the students with the special talents of the instructional staff.

The process of *acceleration*, or speeding the gifted student's progress through the system, can be accomplished in innumerable ways, from early admittance to school to taking course credits by examination in graduate school. Research and evaluation studies of acceleration and its effects on gifted children are invariably positive, but the concept itself is not well institutionalized or accepted. This suggests that there is something deep in the American set of values that is antagonistic to the idea, but few convincing arguments have been heard as to just what that might be.

There seems to be some evidence that the particular nature of the learning environment does make a difference in the attitudes and self-concepts of the gifted student and that, in fact, different teacher and student behaviors do occur in specialized settings designed for the gifted. There is also rather convincing evidence that just grouping gifted students together in special classes, or separate content sections, does not seem to produce strongly positive effects. It now seems likely that major changes are most likely to occur if the learning environment is modified, *and* the content is upgraded, *and* the methods of teaching are adapted appropriately for the gifted.

There is a current trend to start doing more and planning more for the gifted student at the state and the federal levels. Some of this increasing public concern probably relates to a desire to begin conserving our intellectual resources, which are no more unlimited than our rapidly dwindling natural resources. Whatever the motivation, such moves mean that more resources will be made available to allow educators to set up special programming for gifted and talented students.

UNRESOLVED ISSUES

1. One of the most conspicuous forms of intellectual waste involves keeping gifted students in the educational track for twenty to twenty-five years of their lives. In what ways can we shorten that time so that these talents can be used more productively to their and society's benefit?

2. Can we find a way to modify public policy, which is traditionally geared to reacting to major crises, so that it can pay some attention to the long-range but gradual erosion of intellectual resources represented by our inadequate educational planning for the gifted?

3. We need more innovative ideas on the design of environmental settings to adapt standard programs for productive gifted students so that they will maintain enthusiasm and a sense of excitement in learning. Similarly, we need a variety of special settings for the underachievers who do not utilize their high intellectual talents.

READINGS OF SPECIAL INTEREST

KEATING, D., & STANLEY, J. *From eighth grade to selected college in one jump: Case studies in radical acceleration.* Baltimore, Md.: Johns Hopkins University, 1972.

A report on the acceleration into college programs of young teenagers, a technique not approved of by many educators but apparently successful in the cases of extraordinarily gifted students. Possible disruptive effects of such radical acceleration are discussed and discounted in these cases. Challenging to basic concepts of educators.

PLOWMAN, P., RICE, J., & SATO, I. *Education of mentally gifted minors.* Sacramento, Calif.: California State Department of Education, 1971.

A variety of contributions and program suggestions coming from the active and extensive California program. Legislation for the gifted has been available in California for over a decade, and this publication shows the gains in sophistication that have been made with the base of minimal state support.

RICE, J. *The gifted—Developing total talent.* Springfield, Ill.: Charles C Thomas, 1970.

A book that focuses on organizational and administrative issues in programs for the gifted. The long experience of the author in program administration has generated sensible planning ideas.

STEELE, J., HOUSE, E., LAPAN, S., & KERENS, T. *Instructional climate in Illinois gifted classes.* Urbana, Ill.: University of Illinois Center for Instructional Research and Curricular Evaluation, 1970.

An imaginative approach to evaluation in which classes for gifted children are compared with average classes on such dimensions as amount of teacher talk, level of thought processes expressed, and general classroom climate of acceptance of student ideas.

11

Training Educational Personnel for the Gifted

Earlier chapters have stressed the three major ways in which one can modify the school program to meet the special needs of gifted students. We can change the knowledge delivered, *the content;* the way in which the knowledge is handled, *the learning style;* or the setting in which the learning takes place, *the learning environment.*

The first two of these require changes in the interaction of the student and the teacher and imply different teacher preparation. The reason for the emphasis on teacher training is summarized by Martinson (1972, p. A65):

> Successful programs show that special preparation of teachers is mandatory. Teachers who have such preparation tend to be sympathetic to the gifted and talented, and to provide them with necessary learning opportunities. This preparation should be extended to the total educational profession and to the public at large so that the gifted and talented may be widely encouraged to use their abilities. The result would be greater numbers of gifted political leaders, inventors, creative artists, educators, medical personnel, and others contributing to society and working on its problems. The result would be a better future for all Americans.

Although practically everyone would subscribe to the general intent of the Martinson statement, there are major questions to be answered. What is the distinctive nature of the training of the teacher or other personnel to maximize the education of the gifted? How can the relevant institutions (i.e., universities or school systems) change their existing programs to include these training programs?

If special programs are going to be developed to assist the educational development of gifted students, it is clear that some type of personnel modifications are going to have to be made. But what? Are we going to retrain the elementary and secondary school teachers in special content areas, unique instructional techniques, or both? Should there be special training programs for teachers of the gifted? Should there be special workshops or institutes for educational administrators? Which? How much of each? This is a puzzling issue that remains to be answered.

In December, 1970, hearings sponsored by the Department of Health, Education, and Welfare on the education of the gifted and talented were held in twelve cities. An analysis of the testimony of the 265 witnesses at these hearings and the over 400 letters from others wishing to be heard revealed a significant consensus of opinion (*Education of the Gifted*, 1972). Whether the witness was an educator, a parent, or an administrator, there was general agreement as to educational needs.

Forty-seven percent of the witnesses spontaneously stated that there was a need for better-prepared teachers, while 37 percent commented on the need for additional specialized personnel, such as curricular specialists, psychologists, teacher consultants. A much fewer number of persons felt the need for administrative personnel or federal leadership persons. (See Figure 11–1.) Some specific witness quotes can give the flavor of the tone of the hearings.

> One of the things that concerns me is that practically none of the teachers we have been able to hire have had any preservice experience either in courses for the gifted or experience with talented groups. (McGuire, Region VII)
>
> You simply cannot teach this kind of child, especially in the high school and junior high school, the same way you teach other children. Ordinarily a good teacher will try hard and do very well, but she will need special training. (Baler, Region I)
>
> Teachers need more planning time, teachers need additional supportive staff, counselors are needed, school psychologists are needed. (Perkins, Region X)
>
> Many teachers want to do well by the gifted . . . but they simply don't know how. (Houck, Region X)
>
> I don't think you can take the average teacher and have him teach the gifted child. I think you need a very special teacher. I think you need a teacher trained specially in methodology, a teacher that is very well equipped in content areas. (Cross, Region VII)

It is worthwhile doing some simple arithmetic as we see the scope of the task we are charting for ourselves. The National Center for Educational Statistics has estimated that there are over 1.2 million elementary school teachers in the country and about 800,000 secondary teachers. The task of retraining any substantial amount of this huge force is staggering. Let us suppose that we wish to hold summer workshops to retrain teachers in special educational techniques particularly applicable for gifted students. Let us imagine further that we wish to reach 100,000

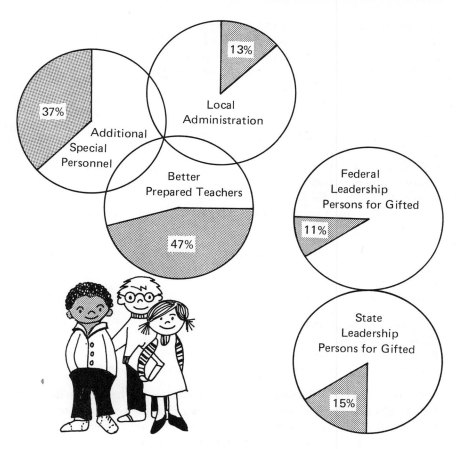

FIGURE 11–1.   *Perceived Personnel Needs for the Gifted.* (*Adapted from* Education of the gifted and talented. *Subcommittee on Education, Committee on Labor and Public Welfare, U.S. Senate, March 1972.*)

teachers, about 5 percent of those now employed. With about 40 teachers per workshop, this would require 2500 workshops. If each workshop cost $3000, the total cost would come to 7.5 million dollars.

Even if some odd set of circumstances should arise whereby 7.5 million dollars would become available to support such activities, there is the additional problem as to where one would find 2500 specialists capable of holding such workshops. Such a retraining effort would then have to be continued over a couple of decades to retrain even a majority of teachers. Even assuming that the training model of summer workshops was sufficient, a dubious proposition, the cost and investment of personnel time would be so tremendous as to be totally out of the question.

It is no wonder, then, that prudent professionals are looking for some meaningful alternative to direct teacher training. One such alternative is to focus our interests on *leadership training,* hoping that an increased supply of competent and knowledgeable persons in leadership or training positions will help train others to educate the gifted.

THE TEACHER: DESIRABLE CHARACTERISTICS

One of the favorite pastimes of some educators is to set down long lists of desirable characteristics of teachers of the gifted. These lists can have a rather paralyzing effect. A casual reading of them can give the impression that no human being can live up to such a set of characteristics, for example:

Good health and physical superiority
Versatility of interests
Creativeness and originality
Unusual proficiency in teaching subjects
Participating member of the community
Clear and consistent philosophy of education
Knowledge of theories of learning
Excellent sense of humor
Abundant physical energy

Anyone who could identify with that particular list has few self-doubts. One might add that the list omits one other characteristic, a complete ignorance of practical economics. Anyone with an abundance of the above characteristics ought to be able to achieve a position at the highest executive or professional level of our society.

There is probably more nonsense and less evidence dispensed about the needed characteristics of the teacher of the gifted than almost any other single issue. Our list of the all-encompassing virtues of teachers of the gifted is a good example. One study that used student opinions to choose successful teachers of the gifted, and then studied a group of thirty such teachers intensively through interviews and tests, revealed the following summary of traits (Bishop, 1968).

The successful teachers were found to be mature, experienced, and superior intellectually. It is, in fact, hard to believe that a teacher of average intellectual ability could present the kind of content and pedagogical program that has been discussed in this book.

Bishop found further that the successful teachers were more interested in literature, the arts, and culture, had high personal achievement needs, and were seeking their own intellectual growth through teaching. They tended to be more student-centered, stimulating in the classroom, and, not surprisingly, were supportive of special educational programs for the gifted.

The current view on the kinds of teacher characteristics that fit the needs of creatively gifted children is given by Bruch and Torrance (1972, p. 72):

1. Teachers should care about their pupils. It is not important that teachers be highly intelligent or good-looking (though they should dress neatly), but it is very important that they be interested in and assist and guide young people.
2. Teachers should be honest. Admission of mistakes, rather than bluffing as infallible experts, is desirable.
3. Teachers do not have to be strict. Although firmness is rated as "fairly important," the notions of the "tight ship" strictness, "tough" disciplinary methods, and a quiet classroom are rejected.
4. Teachers should trust their pupils. Pupils apparently realize that adults need to have confidence in the young person's ability to act responsibly.

The Training of Teachers

A recent survey of 239 experts in education of the gifted strongly advocated specialized teacher preparation, continued professional study, and frequent contacts with other teachers of the gifted. These experts recommended subsidies for training, university training centers, and in-service preparation for those already in the profession. This emphasis on inservice training included not only teachers but administrators and such auxiliary personnel as psychologists and counselors.

Who's Afraid of the Gifted Child?

The answer to the question is "Just about everybody." The high level of critical or creative thinking occurring early in the developmental processes of these children sometimes comes as a shock and a threat to the educator. It is not hard to see why some educators do not actively encourage free-wheeling thinking on the part of these youngsters.

It is unlikely that any of us can truly be of help to the gifted student if we do not come honestly to grips with our own feelings about them. It *is* an exciting experience to see their flights of imagination, to follow the grace and skill with which they swoop down upon a problem. But isn't it also somewhat unsettling in the same way that a champion tennis player is unnerving to those of more modest abilities, or a gifted speaker is to those who wish only to keep their audiences conscious?

> *Breathes there a man with soul so dead*
> *Who never to himself hath said,*

"I hate my neighbors all three—
They grow grass better than me."

Not great literature, perhaps, but perceptive. We are all, not just observers, but participants in the most free and open competitive society in the world. But if the teacher enters into competition with his gifted students, instead of helping them, he opens himself to frustration, and the student to a puzzling experience, since the student never quite knows why the teacher takes such an attitude toward him.

It is an act of sublime maturity when a parent can turn loose of his or her children and allow them to go off into the world without invoking guilt feelings or maintaining dependent ties. Similarly, the teacher who can allow the gifted student's intellect to fly higher than the teacher's can ever hope to soar, and to take joy in that effort, has earned a special badge of maturity. For those of us who cannot quite make that goal, we can at least understand our own feelings of jealousy and envy, and not let them rule us.

THE TEACHER'S ATTITUDE TOWARD THE GIFTED. When we investigate teachers' attitudes toward gifted students, we are partially in the realm of facts and partially in the personality and emotional life of the teachers themselves. For example, both individual experience and research studies (see, for example, Sister Josephina, 1961; Wiener, 1960; Rothney & Sanborn, 1968) present us with a portrait of hostile feelings of teachers toward the gifted student. That hostility is too often shown in giving the gifted student more work (the "That will show Mr. Smartypants" syndrome).

Where does such hostility come from? We would have to assume that it is a reaction to threat. What kind of threat is the gifted student presenting to the teacher? Such a student will challenge, often innocently, the teacher's role of master authority and will reach or exceed the teacher's knowledge in certain fields. Such a teacher is bound to fear and worry about what new indignity this troublesome child will visit upon her tomorrow. The thought of bringing together twenty-five or thirty of these children in one class can only qualify as a nightmare. From such sources springs the hostility of many teachers to special programs.

For example, Miss Walker, Joe's teacher last year, was telling the class one of her favorite stories about "The Lost Colony" and what might have happened to the colonists who mysteriously disappeared. In the midst of her presenting her theory that disease or a plague might have been the cause of the disappearance, Joe popped up with the information that he had read some books that said the plague theory really didn't hold water. Miss Walker was taken aback since she had not heard of the books that Joe mentioned, and she somewhat lamely brought the discussion to a halt, meanwhile noting to herself that while Joe rarely read his assignments, he did like to pick up all sorts of odd facts through reading on his own.

Counselors and school psychologists (Wiener, 1968) also have reacted hostilely to the gifted, presumably on the same basis as the teachers. In contrast, when teachers have experienced inservice training programs or special preparation (in other words, when they have become more comfortable with their own abilities to deal with these students), their attitudes are significantly more positive.

A PROGRAM FOR PENNSATUCKY

In order to understand the variety and complexity of personnel training problems, we might first imagine a mythical state, Pennsatucky, and think about how training efforts might be planned to help implement a program for the gifted in that state.

Pennsatucky is a state with many diverse and conflicting forces. It has one major metropolitan area, a major city, with several other cities of substantial size. Most of these are devoted to a diverse set of heavy industries and major commercial enterprises. On the other hand, Pennsatucky also has a substantial part of it total area still devoted to agriculture and rural small towns, though not as much now as in the immediate past.

Because legislative reapportionment has not yet caught up with population shifts, the state legislature still reflects the careful and conservative rural ethic of its recent past. They are for education but suspicious of "frills" and new programs. In this situation a combination of educators, interested legislators, and influential citizens have convinced the legislature to establish a small program to improve education of talented children. Much of the limited funds will be spent on training and retraining of personnel. What would be the nature of the program and what kind of training should the personnel receive?

HIGH-PRODUCING GIFTED

Table 11–1 indicates some separate needs for personnel dealing with high-producing gifted students (i.e., Cranshaw and Zelda) and low-producing gifted (i.e., Joe and Sam). Three levels of personnel are viewed as necessary for the program; the teacher, the program coordinator or consultant, and state leadership personnel.

TABLE 11–1. *Suggested Program for High-Producing Gifted in Pennsatucky.*

PERSONNEL	SPECIAL SKILLS NEEDED	STATE SUPPORT
Teacher	More extensive content knowledge More knowledge of methods of stimulating productive thinking Ability to analyze student and own performance	Scholarships and fellowships for advanced training Support for teacher-training institutions
Program Consultant	Extensive curriculum knowledge Teaching experience Tests and measurement background Knowledge of stimulating productive thinking Supervisory training Ability to conduct inservice training program	State reimbursement to local communities for a large part of the salary of the consultants
State Director	Ability to administrate state program Catalyzer for community action Ability to help local communities get programs underway	Full financial support for staff positions at state level

The Teacher

In certain large communities in Pennsatucky, it has not been uncommon to group students according to mental ability or according to aptitude in a given subject area. In these situations, certain teachers have the responsibility for these accelerated groups. What additional skills do such teachers need to have? What unique characteristics need they have to enter the program?

Some programs for the education of the gifted include a diversity of teaching arrangements, such as team teaching, open education, and the like. These may require a number of different skills and procedures not in the training or experience background of the teacher. A teacher who is given casually the responsibility for team teaching, or supervision of independent study, without some additional training has a right to protest, and so has the student.

PREPARING FOR INDEPENDENT STUDY.   One type of pseudosolution to the problem of providing a stimulating situation for gifted students is to enroll them in "independent study." All too often, independent study means giving the gifted child free time to go to the school library and write an unsupervised paper about some topic that the teacher knows so little about that she or he cannot adequately evaluate the material once it is produced.

For example, Zelda was once given that freedom by her teacher. She was told that she had been doing so well in her work that she would be allowed to do an "independent study" project. The teacher asked Zelda what topic she would wish to study. Having just read about President Andrew Jackson and his troubles with the courts in his administration, Zelda said she would like to write on presidents and their troubles with the Supreme Court. The teacher said whatever Zelda was interested in was all right with her and to go ahead.

The only trouble with that approach was that there was little material available in the school library (or community library for that matter) on that topic. The teacher was little help since she did not know the first thing about the courts versus the presidency, nor did she have any useful suggestions about where to go for help. The whole project fizzled, and Zelda, who started the project with some enthusiasm, retreated back into her fact-gathering style, convinced that this independent search activity was not for her.

It has become painfully clear that teachers need to be trained in the sequences and skills in the direction of independent study just as much as in their skills in teaching subject matter. One of the necessary dimensions of independent study that needs to be taught is the *gradual* release of the student from adult supervision. Any student, gifted or not, who has spent years in a school system where everything was directed and decided for him is likely to be uncertain and unprepared to fly on his own. It does these students no favor to abruptly turn them loose and tell them they now have the "freedom to work on their own." That kind of freedom cannot be useful unless accompanied by careful guidance and supervision.

Lonnon (1966, p. 253) reported on an independent study program and the sequence that a teacher might follow in such gradual release of control.

1. When a student first indicates an interest in doing work independently, we have found that it is usually best for the teacher to structure his early efforts to some degree. Independent study is an entirely new and foreign area to most students after several years of dependency upon a teacher, and we cannot expect any significant results if we merely say "Go independent study."

    a. This structure usually takes the form of some type of class outline or study guide.

    b. The student is usually released from the time schedule and encouraged to progress at his own speed. . . .

    c. Early in this experience, the teacher and student will hold regular conferences to discuss problems such as finding appropriate materials, and how to evaluate progress.

2. As the student becomes more familiar with his new situation, the teacher then encourages him to select his own line of study. At this point, one will see teacher structuring gradually dissipate. . . . The teacher is still responsible for the evaluation of progress and work, and regular conferences are still held.

3. The ultimate goal is to have the student assume complete responsibility for his educational program. He will select his own areas of study, establish his own materials and evaluate his own progress, the teacher serving as a consultant and resource person only. However, only a few students are equipped to function at the highest level. . . . Most students will function in stages one and two.

Lonnon suggested that a summer institute designed to demonstrate the successful use of independent study as a desirable training tool can assure that teachers using independent study know what they are about.

An independent study seminar program for highly gifted children (about 148 IQ) has been described by Martinson, Hermanson, and Banks (1972). They described the essential parts of the program as follows (pp. 422–423):

1. *Extensive study and guidance data.* A collection of test and school records and personal interviews on the gifted student.

2. *Individual planning.* Course of study is decided jointly between student and faculty advisor.

3. *Open curriculum guide.* Selected student could choose from large bibliography of literary and philosophic work. Seminar discussions focus on major themes and significant questions.

4. *Range of resource people.* University professors come into schools to guide discussions or matched with local experts, the student works on individual projects.

5. *Advanced placement.* Students have the chance to take college courses for credit plus the opportunity to pass courses by examination.

Such a program of independent study can provide great diversity of experiences for the gifted student, but unless the program directors and teachers have the program well organized and the resources available, it could be just one more promising disappointment.

INSERVICE TRAINING. Educators who have worked long in the field of gifted child education might wish that the universities and training centers around the country were pouring forth legions of teachers and educational specialists highly trained and committed to special education for the gifted. We know that it is not so, and cannot be so. The manpower arithmetic noted earlier in the chapter has told us how silly such a notion is.

So what is to be done? One move is to focus on leadership training so that a few highly trained specialists can spread their knowledge over a large area. Another move is to try to upgrade the skills of those competent teachers already at work in the schools of the country so that they are able to better deal with the gifted children in the regular program, or in a part-time special program.

Inservice training programs or summer institutes can focus on particular skills and knowledges that would seem to be most worthwhile. Several areas seem to be popular topics for inservice training (Rogge & Stormer, 1966).

ANALYSES OF STUDENT AND TEACHER BEHAVIOR. By closely reviewing the behavior of both students and teacher, the teacher can see what is happening in the classroom and can take specific steps to modify the atmosphere or discussion to be more in line with his teaching objectives.

Self-analysis on the part of the teacher has become a tool more and more frequently used to aid teachers in upgrading their skills in the classroom. Such self-analysis has been made more possible by the increasing availability of audio and video tape recorders, allowing the teacher to replay a class session in a fashion similar to the replay of football films, so that one can analyze what went right and what went wrong. Along with these technical advances has come a wide variety of coding or classification systems that allows for reasonably easy analysis of instructional objectives. Over eighty such systems have been published in a fifteen-volume set, *Mirrors of Behavior* (Simon & Boyer, 1967). The choice of which system to use or adapt depends on the educational objectives most important to the teacher.

Table 11-2 shows the ten-category system developed by Flanders (1967) and focuses on the way in which classroom interactions are conducted, as well as the general atmosphere of the teacher–student interaction. It is not concerned primarily with the content of the discussion. An observer can sit in the classroom and check one of these ten categories every ten seconds and there can be charted a very clear portrait of the interaction over a given period of time. If there is a long string of checks in category five, we know that the teacher is spending much of the time lecturing. If there are 4s, followed by 8s, followed by 3s, we then have some evidence that there is teacher–student interaction and that the teacher is doing some listening. If there is an excess of 7s, we know that there is a lot of criticism and defensiveness in the teacher's behavior.

A teacher can start out with a pattern of behavior that he or she would

TABLE 11–2. *Flanders' Categories for Interaction Analysis.*

TEACHER TALK	**INDIRECT INFLUENCE**	1.* *Accepts feeling:* accepts and clarifies the feeling tone of the students in a non-threatening manner. Feelings may be positive or negative. Predicting or recalling feelings are included. 2.* *Praises or encourages:* praises or encourages student action or behavior. Jokes that release tension, not at the expense of another individual, nodding head or saying "um hm?" or "go on" are included. 3.* *Accepts or uses ideas of student:* clarifying, building, or developing ideas suggested by a student. As a teacher brings more of his own ideas into play, shift to category five. 4.* *Asks questions:* asking a question about content or procedure with the intent that a student answer.
	DIRECT INFLUENCE	5.* *Lecturing:* giving facts or opinions about content or procedure; expressing his own ideas, asking rhetorical questions. 6.* *Giving directions:* directions, commands, or orders to which a student is expected to comply. 7.* *Criticizing or justifying authority:* statements intended to change student behavior from non-acceptable to acceptable pattern; bawling someone out; stating why the teacher is doing what he is doing; extreme self-reference.
STUDENT TALK		8.* *Student talk—Response:* a student makes a predictable response to teacher. Teacher initiates the contact or solicits student statement and sets limits to what the student says. 9.* *Student talk—Initiation:* talk by students which they initiate. Unpredictable statements in response to teacher. Shift from 8 to 9 as student introduces own ideas.
		10.* *Silence or confusion:* pauses, short periods of silence and periods of confusion in which communication cannot be understood by the observer.

* There is *no* scale implied by these numbers. Each number is classificatory, it designates a particular kind of communication event. To write these numbers down during observation is to enumerate, not to judge a position on a scale.
Source: A. Simon & E. Boyer (Eds.). *Mirrors for behavior.* Vol. 2. Philadelphia: Research for Better Schools, Inc., 1967.

like to attain for a given class session. A later comparison of the actual session against original expectations can give the teacher needed feedback into how close the actual class sessions are matching her own intentions.

The advantage of this type of classification system is that it is very easy to teach and learn and can be applied in almost any classroom immediately. Some other systems require more extensive training, as in the one reported by Gallagher et al. (1967). Their system focuses on cognitive behavior and the particular thought processes being used in the classroom. Some of the major categories are seen in Table 11–3. A

Table 11–3. *Gallagher–Aschner Categories for Teacher–Student Interaction.*

The primary classification categories in the present study were cognitive memory (CM); convergent thinking (CT); divergent thinking (DT); evaluative thinking (ET); and routine (R). A brief description of the first four areas follows:

1. *Cognitive memory* represents the simple reproduction of facts, formulae, or other items of remembered content through such processes as recognition, rote memory, and selective recall. (Although Guilford separates cognition and memory in his model, they are combined here because of the difficulty in differentiating them in class interaction and because both represent, from our point of view, nonproductive thinking operations.) Examples of cognitive memory performance can be seen in the following:

    T: What planet is closest to the sun?

    Bill: Mercury, and it doesn't rotate either.

    T: What were some of the main points covered in our discussion about mercantilism?

    Mary: One of the things we learned was that there was an attempt to keep a favorable balance of trade.

    T: Does anybody remember who was the sixteenth President of the United States?

    Bob: Abraham Lincoln.

    These teacher–student interchanges do not require the student to integrate or associate facts; the questions can be handled by direct reference to the memory bank and selection of the appropriate response from a store of remembered items. While factual information is indispensable to the development of higher thought processes, it is a sterile and uninteresting class which never moves into the challenge and excitement of more complex operations.

2. *Convergent thinking* represents the analysis and integration of given or remembered data. It leads to one expected end result or answer because of the tightly structured framework through which the individual must respond. Some examples of convergent thinking follow.

    T: If I had 29 cents and gave John 7 cents, how much money would I have left?

    Bob: Twenty-two cents.

    T: Can you sum up in one sentence what you think was the main idea in Paton's novel, *Cry The Beloved Country?*

    Pete: That the problem of the blacks and the whites in Africa can only be solved by brotherly love; there is no other way.

    Thus, convergent thinking may be used in solving a problem, summarizing a body of material, or establishing a logical sequence of ideas or premises—as, for example, in reporting the way in which a machine works, or describing the sequence of steps necessary for passage of a bill through Congress.

3. *Divergent thinking* represents intellectual operations wherein the individual is free to generate his own ideas within a data-poor situation, or to take a

TABLE 11-3 (*cont'd*)

new direction or perspective on a given topic.   Some examples of divergent thinking are:

T: Suppose Spain had not been defeated when the Armada was destroyed in 1588 but that, instead, Spain had conquered England.   What would the world be like today if that had happened?

Sam: Well, we would all be speaking Spanish.

Peg: We might have fought a revolutionary war against Spain instead of England.

Tom: We might have a state religion in this country.

These examples represent teacher stimulated divergent thinking, but it need not always be teacher generated.   In a discussion of the spoils system a student may generate the following:

Pete: Well sure, the spoils system might be a good thing when a political party is getting started, but what about when there's no party system—like in the United Nations?

Here the student reveals his ability to take off from an established fact or facts and see further implications or unique associations that have not been requested, or perhaps even thought of, by the teacher.   Instances of self-initiated student behavior would also fall under the general category of divergent thinking.

4. *Evaluative thinking* deals with matters of judgment, value, and choice, and is characterized by its judgmental quality.   For example:

T: What do you think of Captain Ahab as a heroic figure in Moby Dick?

Bob: Well, he was sure brave, but I think he was kind of mean the way he drove the men just because he had this crazy notion of getting back at Moby Dick.

T: Is it likely that we will have a hard winter?

Mary: Well, I think that the pattern of high pressure areas suggests that we will.

In the first example the student is asked to construct his own value dimension, what he considers heroic, and then to make a judgment as to where he would place Captain Ahab.   In the second response, the student is asked to give a speculative opinion or assessment of probability.   A third possibility, not illustrated here, involves entering a qualification or disagreement which modifies a prior judgment by another student, or stating a counter judgment which directly opposes the statement of the previous speaker.

Source: J. J. Gallagher, M. Aschner, & W. Jenné. *Productive thinking of gifted children in classroom interaction.* Council for Exceptional Children Research Monograph Series B5. Arlington, Va.: Council for Exceptional Children, 1967, pp. 19–20.

teacher using this system might decide to code only her own questions rather than an entire script.   In similar ways, classification systems designed for research can be simplified for practical teacher use.

Even in gifted classrooms much of the emphasis is on the thinking process of cognitive memory and convergent thinking statements and questions (Gallagher, 1965a). It is in questions by the teacher that the key appears to lie for classroom discussion and stimulation. If the teacher aspires to make evaluative thinking a major part of the discussion, she must ask evaluative-type questions. A question such as "Is it right for a few countries to control the world's resources while other countries are in poverty?" will certainly yield evaluative thinking, whereas a request for the relative gross national products of various nations will not. (See Chapter 9 for a thorough exposition of the use of these categories.)

CONTENT SOPHISTICATION. Teachers who work with gifted students often complain that the students will soon surpass the teacher in knowledge. Courses offered in summer institutes, however, can send teachers back into the classroom with renewed confidence that the gifted student will not embarrass them with more accurate or up-to-date knowledge than they themselves can provide.

In the previous chapters on content and curriculum, the suggested changes have been brought about primarily through intensive summer workshops for teachers in which they have been able to focus on physics, the new math, new approaches to economics, and so on. The reports from such training have been invariably positive.

Program Consultant

Discussions about personnel for the gifted almost always center on the teacher. Yet in most modern schools the teacher is only one member of a professional team, albeit the most important one, that blends a variety of skills and backgrounds into a total educational program. The importance of personnel auxiliary to the teacher is best seen when such personnel are absent.

Some states and local communities, particularly with large rural populations, still have few school psychologists, curriculum specialists, inservice training programs, travel funds for teachers to visit other programs, and so on. Under these circumstances of bare-bones programming, the chances for a fine program or rich opportunities for gifted students are not very high. An analogy to athletics makes the point. Suppose that a visiting expert on basketball is called in by the school system and given this problem: There is no one on the team over 6 feet tall, there is no gym in which the team can practice, and there is no money to hire a full-time coach. Under these circumstances, how could you build a championship basketball team? The answer, of course, is that you cannot. The key to any good educational program is well-trained personnel and the proper administrative structure in which to put their training to maximum use. Without such appropriate background and training, all else is meaningless and a sham.

This brings us to the touchy subject of *money*. In constructing a budget request, educators have been conditioned over long periods of time to ask for the possible, rather than the necessary. They have learned, through bitter experience, that funding agencies, particularly those responsive to the electorate, tend to choose the least expensive alternative first and will continue on to the more expensive one only if time proves the first one to be inappropriate. However, the full program of services outlined in previous chapters requires a modest increase in financial support of school personnel and of the training programs that produce them.

No rejuggling of administrative staff on paper will produce more effective education for these children unless more highly trained personnel are given the opportunity to use their special talents to work with these youngsters. There is no reason to suppose that the educational system is exempt from the precept "You can't get something for nothing." To improve the system, money must be spent. It should be spent judiciously and with an eye toward value received, but it must be spent.

Rice (1970) has provided an overall description of the general personnel needs of the gifted program as follows (p. 264):

1. Full-time or intermittent supervising teachers with the following qualifications—one or more academic majors at the master's degree level; six school hours or more graduate level course work on the psychology and education of the gifted;
2. School psychologists who, in addition to full pedagogical training, are experienced in identifying the gifted and are capable of advising teachers on learning theory as applied to program construction;
3. Curriculum specialists in all major academic areas, persons who can really write curriculum and demonstrate its application;
4. Lists of community experts from as broad a spectrum of professional backgrounds as possible; these experts should be available for personal student interaction as well as curriculum construction;
5. School counselors possessing special training in conducting group seminars and counseling counselors who understand and relate to the unique personal problems of the gifted; and
6. Overall coordinators capable of orchestrating all the variables toward the end of total talent development.

The question is not only what do we need but how do we go about getting it?

Supervisor or Consultant Training

Would the training of the consultant be different from that of the teacher? Although there would be many similarities, as pointed out by Jackson and Rogge (1965), there are some differences as well. Jackson and Rogge

(1965) have presented a model of inservice training programs for teachers, consultants, and supervisors for gifted children. This program, presented through summer institutes, relies upon the following four major assumptions:

1. Teachers, consultants, and supervisors should engage in vigorous self-assessment of prevailing practices. (This would include analysis of examination questions, student–teacher interaction, and student description of the classroom.)
2. Models of the goals must be provided, not just statements of the goals. (This means that the presence of demonstration classes, use of video-tapes of classrooms, etc. are available for such a model as part of the training program.)
3. Teachers, consultants, and supervisors must have an opportunity to practice while still in the inservice program.
4. Teachers, consultants, and supervisors must have opportunity to continue the processes of self-assessment after the close of the inservice program.

Gallagher (1966b) described a leadership training program that might prepare a supervisor for effective performance. These skills could either be brought to the program by the individual or provided in inservice, summer, or year-long training. The components of the program included knowledge of the following (pp. 4–6):

Individual differences. Certain experiences in the area of tests and measurements should be required, not so much to establish professional skills but to experience firsthand the measurement concepts, without which the person cannot have a full understanding of the term "giftedness."

Content specialty. It seemed important that the student have a grasp of at least one of the many areas of content. . . . No fewer than two units of graduate credit were required in a content specialty (math, economics, science) chosen by the student and advisor.

Pedagogy specialty. The consultant needs to be intimately aware of how such information can be organized and best presented to stimulate independent and productive thinking on the part of the gifted student.

Administration and supervision. It is essential . . . they have some grounding in the foundations of supervisory and administrative procedures. Courses and field study opportunities were provided.

Directed independent study. It is important and necessary for the student to have the freedom to explore problems of special interest under competent supervision. Just as we stress the necessity for greater independence in the gifted students, we must allow trainees the necessary freedom for exploration of their own.

Field experience. While the student was obtaining the theoretical and practical knowledge which forms the heart of this program, supervised visits and systematic observations at demonstration centers for gifted aided some integration to the most abstract concepts met during the academic portion of the training program.

State Director

What kind of experiences or training program is needed for personnel who would have leadership positions at the state education level? The training would have to be intensive and brief.

One of the new and promising training efforts in this regard is the National/State Leadership Training Institute on the Gifted and the Talented that was designed to develop, in participating states, a team of educators committed to the establishment and extension of programs for gifted and talented children and youth. Sato (1973) presented the major objectives of the Leadership Institute as follows (p. 1):

1. To establish and maintain a working communication network among Central Office of Education, Regional Offices of Education, States, and local educational agencies.
2. To formulate and initiate regional team activities involving unique planning and program development for the gifted and the talented.
3. To train selected individuals both nationally and regionally at regular training institutes or workshops (of sufficient duration).
4. To develop, reproduce, and disseminate some appropriate documents, publications, and media products on the gifted and talented through sponsored workshops and institutes.
5. To increase public consciousness, awareness, and knowledge about the gifted and talented.

The possible achievement of any of these objectives would be a substantial move forward to the professionalization of this subgroup of educators. No matter how many teachers are trained, we will need leadership persons to understand, at the very least, what the teachers are trying to do.

The author has experienced the inhibiting influence of educators who do not understand the program objectives. Following a summer workshop on teaching productive thinking, the author contacted the teachers who had attended and asked how they were doing. One teacher, and she was not the only one to have this experience, stated in tears that her principal did not understand any of these ideas or methods taught in the workshop, and ordered her not to use them in "his" school. We can expect that the expertise and understanding arising from leadership training experience will greatly stimulate program activities for the gifted and talented and encourage adventuresomeness in educational leaders who hold positions of influence in educational hierarchies.

LOW-PRODUCING GIFTED

Only a few years ago, the type of program for gifted children just described would have been the envy of any state. Training these specialists

326

and placing them in the school program would have been considered the epitome of planning for gifted children in our schools.

In the last decade, there has been substantial concern for the educational programming of such youngsters as Joe and Sam, whom we have called *low-performing gifted*. Now, a comprehensive program for gifted children must include a plan for these youngsters, along with the more fortunate ones described above. The research evidence suggests that children with a reasonably long history of inefficient performance are often having problems in the areas of motivation, emotional disturbance, or attitude. Furthermore, these kinds of problems, found in gifted children such as Joe and Sam, are very similar to those of the low-producing child at any level of ability.

In other words, there seems to be little difference between the dynamics, or reasons, for the low motivation of a child with an IQ score of 140 and those for the equally poor motivation of a youngster with an IQ score of below 100. The programs for these children should not require personnel with new talents and new skills. What is needed, rather, is a reorganization of existing personnel in such a way that staff members with established professional skills can be brought into contact with these gifted children.

The personnel suggested for the kind of program that Pennsatucky might support are shown in Table 11–4. If the school systems already employ diagnostic and remedial personnel, why can't these people handle the problems of gifted youngsters without the necessity for the reorganization suggested here? To understand why gifted children of this type are often untreated, it is necessary to understand that most school systems operate on a "crisis" basis. The three major problems that seem to motivate school personnel to act quickly on a child's difficulties are

1. He or she is failing in school so badly that he or she is causing instructional difficulties to teachers.
2. He is actively threatening to disrupt the educational environment through misbehavior.
3. He is so manifestly disturbed and unhappy as to motivate the school to take some remedial action.

As the reader will recall, the evidence in the chapters on characteristics of the gifted suggests that few gifted children, even low producers, would qualify on any of the three counts. Such children as Joe and Sam are not likely to fail courses, although they may be getting lower grades than might be expected of them. The chances are that they will not be actively antisocial or so manifestly disturbed as to call attention to themselves.

Thus, because few schools have enough special personnel to take care of all the problems waiting to be met, it is a virtual certainty that Joe's

TABLE 11–4. *Suggested State Program for Low-Producing Gifted in Penn-satucky.*

PERSONNEL	SPECIAL SKILLS NEEDED	STATE SUPPORT
Teacher	Ability to work with groups of culturally different	Fellowships and scholarships for further training
	Ability to encourage a learning set, i.e., a desire to learn in children	Partial reimbursement to local school districts for expense of program
	Teaching experience	
	Extensive curriculum knowledge	Inservice training support
Counseling Specialist	Extensive knowledge of tests and diagnostic procedures	Partial reimbursement to cover special assignment to gifted program
	Remedial skills with individuals or small groups	
	Counseling background and abilities	
	Knowledge of cultural diversity	
State Director	Ability to administrate state program	Full financial support for staff positions at state level
	Catalyzer for community action	
	Ability to help local communities get programs underway	

and Sam's names will be at the bottom of the referral list. The school year will be over before the psychologist or counselor has a chance to get to their problems. These specialists will be busy dealing with the much more immediate crises posed by other children. In the long run, it may be more serious for our community and our nation to suffer the talent waste represented by the inadequate performance of these gifted, low-performance youngsters, but few school administrators feel that they can afford to think in these long-range terms.

The Teacher: Desirable Characteristics

Since the types of problems represented by the underachiever are very diverse, a wide variety of skills is needed, and the problem should be attacked on a team basis. One inevitable member of any education team would be the *teacher* (see Table 11–4). In this instance, the teacher who works with gifted children would still need background in advanced curriculum content and in pedagogy. In addition, he would need intensive knowledge of children with special motivational problems and an understanding of the social background of the culturally deprived.

In this instance, the number of children brought together in a group would be smaller than the ordinary class, since they would require more individual attention by the teacher. The teacher's major goal, however, would be to stimulate a desire for knowledge rather than merely presenting any specific body of ideas or facts. The teacher's problem, in other words, is to rekindle in these children the desire to learn, the spark of which, for a variety of reasons, has been dimmed.

Sisk (1970) describes a university training program specifically designed to prepare teachers to work with culturally different gifted children. This masters level program includes special features (pp. 11–12):

Trainees are given first hand experience with disadvantaged children and young people during their entire training. These experiences may include:

1. Observing groups of disadvantaged children.
2. Working with one child and assisting a classroom teacher.
3. Working with small groups of children in either remedial or enrichment sessions as a co-teacher or team teacher.
4. Teaching enrichment sessions or remedial sessions with the responsibility of the classroom teacher.
5. Doing demonstration teaching.
6. Assisting in various administrative capacities in establishing enrichment and remedial sessions for disadvantaged gifted.

Numerous opportunities are provided for the trainee to observe and work with children in formal settings at the community centers in Tampa Model Cities Project and at other social agencies.

Saturday enrichment seminars for gifted children allow the teacher trainees opportunities to work with disadvantaged gifted students as well as with gifted students from upper and middle classes.

Teacher trainees receive valuable experience in the development of inservice and preservice materials. These describe how to identify disadvantaged gifted children through lists of behavioral characteristics or nonverbal measures and how to program after careful diagnosis enrichment and remedial materials for the disadvantaged gifted.

As Sisk points out, it is necessary to get direct and continuing contact with the target population that the teacher is going to be working with in order to provide an effective teacher preparation program.

Counseling Specialist

The teacher, however, is at a strong disadvantage in such a program unless he has the help of a diagnostic specialist, often a school psychologist or counselor. Although the teacher can observe that a child is manifestly unhappy in class, it is often much more difficult to determine the precise reason for the unhappiness. Even the child himself may not be aware of why he is so distraught and unhappy. If one asked Joe what was eating him, he might reply with a snarl that nothing was wrong with him at all and to leave him alone.

The school psychologist or counselor with special training in the problems of children, and techniques to discover these problems, can be of decided assistance. As indicated in Table 11–4, what is needed is a person skilled in diagnostic techniques who can sit down with the teacher and other team members and plan a reasonable program on the basis of what had been discovered.

Such a specialist should do more than diagnose or consult with the teacher, however; he should also know how to provide remedial help. Since Sam's problems are based on a realistic social situation, his need for personal counseling is less than Joe's, whose problems are partially based on a personal misinterpretation of his world.

The remedial counseling would depend upon the information that the counselor could obtain from the teacher, and the diagnostic specialist, in turn, would feed back information to the teacher regarding the performance of the youngster in this aspect of the remedial program. This diagnostic and remedial specialist should be assigned directly to the program for gifted children, and the state of Pennsatucky should partially reimburse school systems that employ such personnel.

To some critics of education, it seems that the hiring of each person who is not directly teaching in the classroom with the youngster is somehow evidence of educational luxuries or frills. In this age of complex social organizations, it is curious that many persons think of the ideal school as a group of teachers, each in his own self-contained classroom, with one principal on hand to mete out necessary discipline. The future school program promises to be an even more complex organization, with many different specialists applying their unique skills to the education of the next generation.

Sanborn, Pulvino, and Wunderlin (1971) reviewed a variety of research studies on the counseling of talented students and provided this summary of guidance services, which probably also indicates the nature of training that should take place (pp. 38–39).

1. *Direct contact with parents.* A student contact is never scheduled without also scheduling a parent conference, and subject matter for the parent conference is based, on the most part, on the most recent student contact. Guidance experiences of the students can be improved when parents interested in resources are systematically put to use.
2. *Counselor's understanding of education program.* The counselor often encounters situations which require some change in the student's environment and activities, if guidance and education needs are fully

met.   Counselors assuming appropriate responsibility for soliciting teacher action should be able to evaluate their programs, partially in terms of classroom policies and practices they help establish.

3. *Student participation.* Follow through actions on counselor suggestions for special provisions was increased dramatically when students were informed of counselors' communication with teachers and urged to take initial steps to get started with teachers on follow through activities.

4. *Professional teamwork.* Most of the studies point up the importance of the team approach to guidance work.   The teachers, parents, administrators and the students themselves are members of the team and equal in terms of responsibility for active follow through of guidance and counseling activities.

In short, the counselor's major responsibilities are to touch all aspects of the student's life that can help bring those forces to work in a positive fashion.   One of the issues that many counselors have so far failed to come to grips with in guiding the gifted is to what extent the counselor's own values are influencing his decisions.   Gifted students, such as Cranshaw or Zelda, or even Sam or Joe, have many options available in which they can do reasonably well.   Therefore, the counselor needs to provide those options clearly and openly to the student without necessarily imposing his or her own preference or choice.

Recently a gifted minority-group student from a southern rural area, now having attained status in medical school, was asked what he would recommend to other talented youngsters from similar economically disadvantaged backgrounds.   He commented that one rule he followed was to listen carefully to what the counselor said and then do exactly the opposite!   He said that if he had paid attention to his counselors, he would not have gone to a northern university but would have settled for a small technical or musical school and still be back in his old hometown teaching in a segregated school.   This remark, of course, is not meant to reflect on all counselors, but it is not rare either, and suggests that counselors still have a difficult time counseling highly talented youngsters.

PERSONNEL ALTERNATIVES BEYOND THE SCHOOL

One of the instructional principles that has been generally accepted is that a gifted student will learn concepts that are no more complex than the teacher has been able to master himself.   If the teacher does not understand advanced principles of economics, it is not likely that the teacher can help Zelda, Cranshaw, or Sam in these dimensions.

Cranshaw's current elementary teacher is not particularly strong in mathematics or mathematical theory. It is unlikely that deep understanding of mathematics will come through Cranshaw's contacts with that teacher. Sam's teacher in his school has himself come out of a limited educational background and is unable to present an intellectual scope that would challenge Sam. These limitations of course apply to all children in a self-contained classroom, but it is the gifted who constantly bump up against the ceiling of the teacher's own capabilities.

What is to be done about this? What are the strategies by which we can bring a wide variety of intellectual strength into contact with the gifted student? One of the strategies noted in the previous chapters on creativity and problem solving is to teach gifted children enough search or research techniques so that they become more independent of the particular current teacher and are able to search out ideas and procedures on their own. Although this is a useful technique, it has its limitations, in the sense that gifted students still need guidance in the general territory that they wish to explore or search. That is, they rarely know where to find historical sources or knowledge on the new physics without some adult guidance and instruction.

We are fond of saying that education is wider than the four walls of the school, but we are often not very adventuresome in acting on that idea. If the school staff does not have the necessary knowledge or talent, additional efforts need to be made to bring student and knowledge together.

Gifted students throughout history have found a means of coming into contact with other great minds through books, and access to a rich library is one of the fundamental criteria for a good program for gifted students. If a good library is not immediately handy, transportation of books or pupils seems called for.

A second device is to depend upon programmed-learning sequences that can utilize machine-operated or computer-assisted instruction devices to bring the student into contact with systematic bodies of knowledge that can be mastered without necessary interaction with the current teachers and instructors (see Chapter 8).

Third, the administrative aspects of the program can be so arranged that outstanding intellects are brought into the school program in a *mentor* arrangement where an older distinguished artist, scientist, or businessman will take one or a small number of students under his wing to explain more about his given field and his own operation. The mentor adds more talent to the program than would possibly be available under the usual school restrictions. A variation on such a theme would be to send youngsters out to various businesses, universities, or other work experiences, which would allow them access to a stronger intellectual input than they could get from the usual school staff.

When we think about additional personnel, it is only natural to consider noted artists and scientists, but it is possible to get help from another direction as well. Karnes, Teska, and Hodgins (1970) report on the training of paraprofessionals to help implement a program for young preschool gifted children. In this program, persons from the neighborhood without specific education training were brought in to work with the special teachers.

These paraprofessionals were given a strong orientation and training program in which they learned techniques of student observation and methods of helping children develop alternative behavior patterns so that the child learns to cope with aggression, fear, achievement, and so on. The paraprofessionals are expected to take responsibility for teaching, under supervision, carefully structured lessons, take data on children, and perform many assistant teacher functions. Under this system the trained teacher becomes an executive teacher who plans lessons, gives individual assistance, and does parent counseling.

STAFFING RURAL SCHOOLS

Even if the legislature of Pennsatucky decided to adopt the comprehensive program discussed here, it is likely that some of the local communities would still not participate. This is because the financial structure that supports the school systems is strained to the breaking point, and no additional staff will be added unless 100 percent reimbursement is guaranteed, something to which the state of Pennsatucky would not agree. How can children be aided in those districts, mostly rural, where this situation exists?

In addition to the culturally different children whom we discuss in other sections of this book, the most neglected children are those from rural areas where none of the staffs or programs discussed are available or could be available under existing circumstances. The programmed-learning sequences noted above would be one type of possible solution to the rural problem.

Another useful device that has been considered is the establishment of *technical assistance teams* (Gallagher, 1974, p. 7) that operate out of a regional center and provide specialized services to local school districts. Such a team, serving a major geographic region in a rural state, could provide the following services:

1. Give advice to local school systems on methods of screening talented children for special programs.
2. Do individual case studies and aid local schools in individualizing programs for specific gifted students.

3. Provide access to specialized books and reference materials to be provided on loan to gifted students.
4. Provide consultation to local teachers and counselors on issues related to the gifted.
5. Provide inservice training or workshops for teachers and educational staff on new methods and techniques to work with the gifted.

Such technical assistance teams could provide the needed link with the rest of the educational world that is so often missing in the isolated rural world.

SUMMARY

In the earlier chapters in this book we placed a strong emphasis on the need to develop special curricular content and on the use of different kinds of teacher styles in educating gifted children. Such demands obviously require specific changes in the procedures for preparing the educational personnel we expect to educate such students.

The shortcomings of existing teachers appear to be well known and accepted by both the general public and the teachers themselves. There are two major strategies that can be adopted to deal with these shortcomings and both are clearly in use. In the first instance, we can attempt to provide additional training for teachers working with the gifted, and second, we can attempt to get better-trained persons from a variety of backgrounds into contact with the gifted student, in and outside the traditional school program.

Special training is recommended for three levels of personnel: the teacher, the program consultant or supervisor, and the educational leader. In the teacher's case, there is a need for more emphasis on specific content skills (i.e., history or physics) and also on pedagogical techniques that can strengthen such approaches as "independent study." Teachers can improve their own teaching techniques by analyzing their classroom performance through review of videotapes or of notes taken by observers in the class, if the latter use a systematic observational system, as noted in the chapter.

The program consultant is an important addition to any training program for the gifted since he or she possesses knowledge of sources, special tests, and teaching techniques, and can provide continuing technical assistance to the teaching staff. A continuous inservice training program for all teachers can be organized by program consultants so that the latest in techniques and materials are available to on-line teachers.

Special leadership training can alert educational leaders, such as superintendents, state department personnel, and administrators, as to the special program needs and opportunities for the gifted. Such leaders are in the position to influence local and state policies so as to bring more resources to programs for the gifted and to communicate effectively with the general public on this issue if they themselves have been well briefed on the educational issues.

For those gifted youngsters who come from culturally different families or who are not responding well to the regular program, some additions should be made to training programs. Educational personnel, teachers and administrators, need to know the nature of any cultural differences involved in addition to understanding the dynamics of underachievement. They need to focus on techniques and methods that encourage motivation and that stress areas of special student strength, such as visual perception, while avoiding areas of relative weakness, such as verbal or linguistic facility—until the student becomes strongly motivated to carry out school-oriented tasks.

In addition, the use of mentors, paraprofessionals, and technical assistance personnel is encouraged in special circumstances and underlines the need to fit the special education program to the needs of the gifted children in a particular setting.

UNRESOLVED ISSUES

1. A much clearer description should be made of the nature of the special experiences and skills needed by teachers of gifted students. These should include the minimum content knowledge that should be available for (1) a curriculum specialist, or (2) a teacher of a self-contained program for the gifted. Such a description would also include the special pedagogical skills they should possess beyond those of the regular teacher.

2. Special inservice training programs in personality dynamics and emotional development need to be designed to aid teachers who must deal with chronic underachievers. Few traditional teacher training programs now provide such experience.

3. How can we convince university training programs to take a more vigorous role in graduate training programs for the gifted? Since the number of students would always be somewhat low, such a program will not be economically self-supporting and needs positive support by the university or an outside subsidy (such as from a State Department of Education) to flourish.

READINGS OF SPECIAL INTEREST

Bruner, J. *Toward a theory of instruction.* Cambridge, Mass.: Harvard University Press, 1966.

One of the most influential persons in education in the past two decades presents his ideas on a theory of instruction, based on current knowledge of the developing intelligence of young children and on current ideas as to how to stimulate it.

MARTINSON, R., & WIENER, J.   *The improvement of teaching procedures with gifted elementary and secondary school students.*   (Final Report)   Gardena, Calif.: California State College, 1968.

A report on the selection of forty-five teachers to use inservice self-study techniques to improve the qualitative level of classroom activities for the gifted.   These teachers conducted case studies, evolved classroom principles for higher thought processes, and made videotapes of classroom interaction. The significant improvement that resulted in classroom performance as a result of the self-study program suggested that this is a means by which teachers can be upgraded in skills.

SIMON, A., & BOYER, E. (Eds.).   *Mirrors for behavior: An anthology of classroom observation instruments.*   Philadelphia: Research for Better Schools, Inc., 1967.

A fifteen-volume compendium of over eighty classroom observation instruments that allow the cataloging of cognitive or affective behaviors on the part of the student and teacher.   The teacher wishing to find something to help analyze his own performance or the researcher interested in measuring tools for the classroom is almost sure to find something to his taste in this set.

STOVALL, B., & TONGUE, C.   *The itinerant resource teacher: A manual for programs with gifted children.*   Raleigh, N.C.: State Department of Public Instruction, 1970.

This manual discusses the potential role to be played by the itinerant resource teacher whose major responsibility is as a resource to the elementary or junior high teacher as well as to the children.   Sample schedules and implementation strategies are presented to show how such a professional can work in the public school setting.

SECTION V

Special Problem Areas

This section concerns the tragic waste of human potential: the concerto never written, the scientific discovery never made, the political solution never found. This tragedy has been widely celebrated in song and literature; as in the delicate phraseology of Thomas Gray's "Elegy Written in a Country Churchyard":

> Full many a gem of purest ray serene
> The dark unfathomed caves of ocean bear;
> Full many a flower is born to blush unseen,
> And waste its sweetness on the desert air.

And in the more modern, hammer-like cadence of Langston Hughes:

> What happens to a dream deferred;
> Does it dry up
>   like a raisin in the sun?
> Or fester like a sore—
> And then run?
>
> Does it stink like rotten meat?
> Or crust and sugar over—
>   like a syrupy sweet?
> Maybe it just sags
>   like a heavy load.
> Or does it explode? [1]

[1] Copyright 1951 by Langston Hughes. Reprinted from *The panther and the lash: Poems of our times*, by Langston Hughes, by permission of Alfred A. Knopf, Inc.

Unfortunately, more poets contemplate this issue than do educators; more writers worry about it than do budget allocators. So the problem continues to plague our educational programs and our talent-starved society.

The evidence presented in earlier chapters refutes the general belief that the early display of talent on the part of gifted students amounts to little in the long run. Generally speaking, the accomplishments of gifted children, even without special educational programming, have been impressive. We really don't know what they could do given a strong educational program. However, there are a number of exceptions to that general rule, as illustrated by the case studies of Joe and Sam; the two chapters in this section attempt to deal with some of these exceptions.

The failure of young people to make reasonable use of manifest talent is probably one of the most frustrating experiences for conscientious educators. Gifted underachievers who, year after year, fail to perform in any way close to their real talents raise disturbing images of "what might have been." Chapter 12, "Gifted Underachievers," takes a close look at the special characteristics of this group of children and explores whether there is a particular personality syndrome predisposing certain gifted children in this direction, or alternatively whether the schools, by consistent mishandling and by their failure to stimulate giftedness, may be at fault.

Chapter 13, "Culturally Different Gifted," focuses on special groups of talented children from family settings, and often neighborhoods, where the values and standards of behavior are quite different from those prevailing in the general community. Such talented children face a number of quite different problems in their cultural setting and in the educational system, and these are detailed in this chapter. Not the least of these problems is that their talents may never be discovered in the first place, as they may be hidden in the different cultural patterns. Once discovered, the problem arises as to how the school program should be adapted to meet their needs. How much should the child adapt to the majority culture, and how much should the system adapt to them? This is the basic issue. As elsewhere in the book, all three of the educational dimensions, content, skills, and learning environment, are explored for possible educational modifications.

12

Gifted Underachievers

We have found that many gifted children are doing efficient work in school and are performing well beyond the youngster of average intellectual abilities. Nevertheless, a small proportion of these gifted youngsters are doing quite poorly; these are referred to as *underachievers*. The term "underachiever" is a relatively new one in educational circles and suggests, among other things, that we can accurately tell how much achievement can be expected of a gifted child, since the term "underachiever" implies that the youngster has fallen short of that mark.

Some people question the existence of underachievers and think that the term represents some kind of statistical gimmick. Others report that a youngster, any youngster, is achieving just what he should be achieving because if we knew all of the factors influencing Joe, we would say that he is doing just what he should. Some of these objections are just playing with words. What is really being said is that we *can* make a reasonable prediction of academic performance from measures of cognitive ability. With certain youngsters those predictions are not fulfilled—these are the underachievers. There is the further assumption that if we could change certain unfavorable circumstances, achievement would improve.

If such identification is just a statistical trick, we would not expect to find these groups of children to be substantially different in any other characteristics from other groups of children. Nor would we expect that one group of such children, identified in one part of the country, would have the same characteristics as a group chosen similarly in other parts of the country. But in both instances, we would be wrong. Such groups, chosen because their achievement is far below what we would predict on the basis of high-IQ test results, do show consistent differences from group to group, and these differences fit an explainable pattern, as we shall see.

CHARACTERISTICS OF UNDERACHIEVERS

Children who are chronic underachievers, who seem to perform below their intellectual aptitude year after year, provide a most frustrating problem for the teacher. Every now and then a youngster such as Joe will show a flash of interest and ability which excites the teacher temporarily—only to plunge him into despair as Joe retreats into a more immature and passively hostile attitude. Such youngsters often give teachers a vague feeling of frustration and failure. They hint that somehow they will flower intellectually if the teachers only know the right buttons to push.

Joe's past academic record is peppered with teachers' comments to the effect that they suspect that this boy is bright, but he never seems to produce. His reaction to pressure, and to stern disciplinary measures, has been wholly unsatisfactory. What is Joe's problem? What is the basis for his seeming reluctance to use his ability? Is it the poor school program that is unstimulating? Is it the unfortunate values and attitudes of his peer group? Does the answer rest in his family relationships? Is it a part of Joe's own personality makeup? Naturally, these questions have to be answered on an individual basis. However, very interesting patterns have evolved from research and investigation on chronically underachieving youngsters such as Joe.

Family Relationships

FATHER. A number of investigators have suspected that the negative attitudes of the underachieving student, particularly the underachieving boy, are closely related to family attitudes and values. Accordingly, they have tried to compare underachieving gifted children with other groups of high-aptitude youngsters who have been performing up to expectations. Although the research on the family in the past three decades has concentrated mainly upon the importance of the mother and her relationships with the child, the father has lately come into his own as a factor of potential influence.

One instance of this influence can be seen in a study by Pierce and Bowman (1960), who found that high-achieving high school students felt that their fathers were a more important influence in their lives than did the low achievers. When asked who was the most important influence in their lives, the underachieving boys would often name a male figure outside the family, such as an uncle, a minister, or a teacher—in contrast to the high achievers, who would more often name their fathers.

A case-study method of investigating personality characteristics related to underachievement indicated that such youngsters had inadequate relationships with their fathers and were unable to express their negative feelings effectively (Kimball, 1953).

Another study (Karnes, McCoy, Zehrbach, Studley, & Wright, 1961) compared gifted overachievers with underachievers. A total of 223 children in grades two through five in a midwestern city were found to have IQ's of 120 and above. The top 16 percent and the bottom 16 percent of achievers, in relationship to their ability, were then chosen for this comparison. In terms of family relationships, the attitude and relationship to the father seemed to play a significant role. In this instance, the fathers of the underachieving children showed more hostility and rejection than did the fathers of the overachievers. Similar feelings, however, were not shown by the mothers.

One of the popular myths is that the child who is underachieving is doing so because he is bored and is really not being given a chance to show his unique and creative style. This comparison indicated quite clearly that, on measures of fluency, flexibility, and originality, the underachieving children were significantly poorer than the overachievers. They also obtained significantly lower ratings in peer relationships. In total, the underachieving child seems to be undercreating and to be having trouble in his social relationships. Just which of these many unfavorable factors is the causal "chicken" and which is the resulting "egg" is a problem that has yet to be solved.

Overall, there is the definite implication that, when the father is more punitive in his relationship with his children, particularly his sons, there is an increased possibility that the son will show disturbances in the academic area.

MOTHER. What about the mother? The mothers of underachievers seem to differ significantly from the mothers in families in which the youngster is performing effectively. One study indicated that the mothers of high-achieving boys were lower in authoritarianism than were the mothers of low-achieving boys. The combination of a father and mother, both high in rigid authoritarianism and low in acceptance of their youngster, could create a pattern of poor academic performance in the boy. However, the effect of mothers upon girls seems to be just the opposite. That is, the girls who are poor achievers seem to have mothers of low authoritarianism, whereas high-achieving girls seem to have mothers of high dominance (Pierce and Bowman, 1960).

In another study, the mothers of high-achieving children tended to be higher in dominance, whereas mothers with a laissez-faire attitude were more likely to have an underachiever. The authors concluded, "Parental intervention is necessary for the development of proper ego controls within the child so that he can adjust to the reality demands of the school room" (Drews and Teahan, 1957).

In Joe's case, he could have profited considerably by having a stronger and more dominant mother who might have partially offset his more rigid and authoritarian father, who seemed to be in complete mastery and control of this family. Strodtbeck (1958), in his study of family and cultural relationships, found that whenever the power structure in the family was relatively equal between mother and father, the chances were greater for high achievement in the children than if the power balance was strongly in favor of the father.

McGillivray (1964) split a group of 235 eighth graders who scored over 130 on an IQ test into two equal groups on the basis of achievement tests. In comparing the high achievers with the low achievers, he found what most teachers understand quite well. The crucial difference between the home of the achiever and the nonachiever lies in the psychological, rather than the physical, environment of the home. The parents of the high achievers spent more time with their children and showed a greater interest in education.

In summary, it is clear that most of the studies have discovered disturbances in the family relationship of underachievers. The next question to be asked is how these disturbances reveal themselves in the person's attitudes toward himself, his school, and his future goals.

Self-Attitudes

Let us for the moment entertain the notion that what has happened in the lives of many underachieving youngsters is a failure to identify with the parent of the same sex and, thus, a failure to introject, or take into oneself, the values and attitudes of that parent. However, if they cannot accept those standards and values, what then?

In the case of gifted children, as well as that of other children, who fail to make proper identification with adults because the model (i.e., the father or mother) is unacceptable to them for various reasons, they must find other models of behavior. Where are they to go for their values? It seems they often turn to their peer group and band together with other dissatisfied youngsters of similar background.

Gough (1955) suggests that the chronic underachiever has an *asocial personality* and rejects school as part of a total pattern of rejecting the values of society. Gough found that chronic underachievers scored higher on a scale measuring delinquent antisocial attitudes than did effective achievers. So we start with the personal values of the underachiever being described as antisocial, if not asocial.

Pierce (1959) found that underachievers showed a more negative attitude to *school, work,* and *imagination* than did good achievers. In a study in Portland, Oregon (1959), the underachievers were found to be rejecting school and teachers and, instead, valuing "fun" or a "good personality" more highly. These youngsters do not have trouble finding friends and, thus, will not appear as isolates in sociometric analyses. However, sometimes teachers might wish that they *were* isolates, since their choice of friends often seems to result in a social clique that has as its basis excitement seeking, a negative attitude toward school, and a decided trend toward violation of adult codes and standards.

Walsh (1956), using play techniques to investigate the self-concepts of elementary school underachieving boys, found that their expressed attitudes were closely allied to those discovered by other investigators. The low-achieving boys felt less accepted by their families, were more constricted in their actions, and generally more negativistic and defensive. The portrait of their world was that of an unfriendly and unsympathetic place, and this attitude apparently stemmed from their negative attitudes toward the "family." In short, the children, in reaction to the parents' unfriendly attitudes toward them, were hesitant to accept the values of the family or of the society.

Probably the most extensive study of underachievers has been carried out by Shaw (1961), who identified underachieving students in seventy-four schools in thirteen districts of one California county. The children were examined in grades four, seven, and ten. Children who obtained an IQ score of 115+ on the California Test of Mental Maturity were identified as academically talented. Those who had a grade-point average of 2.8 and below, or about a "C" and below, were called "underachievers"; those with a "B" average or above in grades were called achievers. A total of over 1,000 achievers and 628 underachievers were examined on various personality tests. The results indicated that the underachievers appeared different from the achievers in exhibiting a greater negative self-concept and a generally more negative outlook on life.

The achievers also differed from the underachievers on the expression of overt hostility. The achievers, although apparently experiencing feelings of hostility, suppressed them, whereas there was more overt expression of aggression and hostility among the underachievers. Although the achievers freely expressed negative self-attitudes in specific areas, they did not have an overall feeling of inadequacy, which seemed to be the lot of the underachievers.

Shaw raises the issue that underachievement may very well have different bases at various social class levels. It may well be that the general portrait of underachievement presented in this chapter merely fits the middle class. Underachievers from the lower social classes may have entirely different patterns of personality and motivation.

The fact that the chronic underachiever tends to be more constricted and less productive in all areas has been borne out by the Portland study

(1959), which shows that the underachievers have a narrow range of interests. These results would fit into the theory that those children who harbor feelings of hostility must expend considerable effort to control or disguise the hostility. They are not able to expend as much, therefore, on creative or productive school behavior.

The low-aspiration level of many underachievers is shown in some comments recorded in interviews in a study by Goldberg (1959):

> *"I just passed my subjects and that's all I care about."*
> *"I just want to be an average kid, nothing special. Why should I be the smartest kid in the world?"*
> *". . . I just want to be one of the crowd."*

Joe was asked, along with his classmates, to write a composition using a picture for a stimulus. The picture showed a boy staring out a window. There was no obvious setting or emotional reaction, so the theme and feelings in the story had to come from within the students themselves. Joe's story went like this:

> This boy is thinking about how lucky some people are. He is thinking about Pete who lives down the street from him. Pete has a nice family, a father that goes fishing with him instead of yelling at him all the time; his teachers like him so he gets good grades and he has money to buy his own Go Kart (miniature gas-powered racer). This boy wishes he could trade places with Pete.

Contained in this story are some of the themes often found in reactions of the underachiever. Somehow his troubles are the fault of someone else, or of fate. His feeling of not being understood in his family is not an uncommon theme; and note how the boy resolves the story. He does not ". . . take arms against a sea of troubles, and by opposing end them," but, instead, waits for luck or fate to turn his way—ignoring the possibility that he could, through actions of his own, improve his situation.

The belief in luck and fate, or rather bad luck, is often adopted when the individual no longer believes in himself. Building the confidence of a boy who wishes to avoid the very experiences that would bring self-confidence is a task that may well need greater professional experience and insight than is available in the classroom teacher.

The use of an ambiguous stimulus (such as the boy sitting at the window) to trigger expressive behavior can be one important tool for the teacher interested in the attitudes and feelings of his students. Naturally, it is the theme or themes that recur over and over again that will be important to the child, and to his advisers. No one story or production by itself will tell the teacher much.

It also seems well established that these attitudes and values that differentiate the achiever from the underachiever have been present from an early age. The Terman and Oden comparison (1947) between the personality traits of gifted achievers and nonachievers indicated the long-range nature of these traits. Terman and his associates identified the 150 men who seemed to have produced the poorest level of achievement in their longitudinal study of gifted individuals, and compared them with 150 markedly successful men. He also had a portion of each of these groups rated on personality characteristics by themselves, their wives, and their parents. Both the self-ratings of the individuals and the ratings of their wives and parents agreed on four major characteristics which differentiated these underachieving individuals from effective achievers. These characteristics were (1) lack of self-confidence, (2) the inability to persevere, (3) a lack of integration to goals, and (4) the presence of inferiority feelings.

A look at the school records of these individuals found that teachers' ratings showed the *same* differences between these youngsters, even at the preadolescent level. The personality patterns that set these two groups apart as adults were apparently manifested early in the school program. The clear implication of these findings is that, unless some major attempt is made to counteract these trends at an early age, these underachievers will turn out as relatively nonproductive members of our society, to the detriment of both society and themselves.

Another indication of the consistency of underachievement is given in a study by Shaw and McCuen (1960). They found 144 students in grades eleven and twelve who were in the upper quarter of their class in intellectual ability. Those whose grade-point average was above the average for the class were termed "achievers," while those who were below average in grades were termed "underachievers." The authors then reviewed the academic record of each of these students from grades one through eleven to see how they had done in their previous education.

Figure 12–1 gives a comparison of achievers' and underachievers' grade-point averages. It is easy to observe that, with the boys, underachievement has been chronic since their start in school. The difference between boy achievers and underachievers became significant from the third grade on.

A different situation is apparent with girl underachievers, as noted in Figure 12–1. In this instance, a difference between the achievers and underachievers was not found in the expected direction until grades nine and ten. It was hypothesized that girls do not display their self-directed tendencies, to the extent that boys do, until they approach adolescence.

This type of study does not give us information regarding students who had underachieved in elementary school and are now performing effectively in high school. There is enough evidence here, however, and in other studies, that underachievement is no temporary accident, brought

347

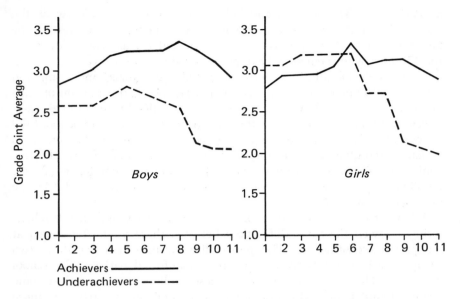

Achievers ————
Underachievers — — —

FIGURE 12–1. *Comparison of Achievement Patterns of Boy and Girl Achievers and Underachievers from Grades One Through Eleven. (From M. C. Shaw & J. T. McCuen. The onset of academic underachievement in bright children.* Journal of Educational Psychology, 1960, **51,** p. 105.)

on, possibly, by one poor teacher during one year. It is, with boys, a continuing problem stemming from basic personality and social problems, which needs treatment and care as early in the school program as is feasible. Further study is needed to understand the dynamics of the underachievement of girls.

There is a strong similarity in the findings of recent research on underachievers to those from a generation ago. Bachtold (1969) compared the personality characteristics of achieving and underachieving bright fifth-grade students by use of a children's personality questionnaire. Generally, underachieving girls seemed to lack self-confidence and were more excitable and less self-controlled than the high-achieving girls; high-ability and high-achieving males also tended to show a greater degree of emotional stability, seriousness, and sensitivity than underachieving males.

Again it is interesting to note that these personality characteristics seem fairly well established by the preadolescent elementary school level and that the program for remediation for these youngsters has to include the personality as well as the academic problems revealed by the youngsters.

O'Shea (1970) compared bright junior high school boys who were low achievers with those who were high achievers. The low achievers had significantly poorer family relationships and were less aggressive, less persistent, and less conforming. This portrait, so similar to the Terman underachievers, leaves little doubt that there are clear personality characteristics common to underachievers.

Table 12–1 gives a summary of the kinds of typical statements that a gifted underachiever might make in the process of protecting his bruised self-image. Each teacher with some experience can probably make a similar table out of his or her own experience. It is true, of course, that the gifted underachiever needs understanding—so do we all—but more is required of the skilled educator than just to understand. He must translate such understanding into a program that can improve the performance and confidence of the underachiever.

Classroom Behavior

What do underachieving boys and girls do in the classroom? Do they show any consistent patterns of behavior that would give a clue to their problems? Most of the available information of the underachiever concentrates on their personality characteristics, but an interesting study by Perkins (1965) examines the actual classroom behavior of thirty-six underachievers chosen from a sample of twenty-seven fifth-grade classrooms in suburban communities in Maryland. The determination of underachievement was made on the basis of a large discrepancy between IQ scores and achievement test scores.

These thirty-six underachievers, together with thirty-six children who served as control subjects, were observed by two-member observation teams in consecutive observations totaling almost eighty hours over a five-month period. The results tell us something about the continuing classroom problems of the underachievers. The most predominant feature of their behavior was the characteristic of *withdrawal*. The underachievers were observed more often than the achievers to be working in another academic area and engaged in nonacademic work. Arithmetic lessons showed a particularly high level of withdrawal.

Although there were no differences between the achievers and nonachievers in the amount of time spent listening and watching, reading or writing, or being highly active, the achievers did spend significantly more time in social, work-oriented interaction with peers.

In short, the underachiever has adopted classroom behavior that is nonadaptive for effective learning. His desire to escape from unpleasant experiences keeps him from effective confrontation with his environment. If Joe and his teacher both appear to be frustrated, it is because they both know that the pattern of behavior that Joe has adopted is bound to fail in the long run, but neither Joe nor his teacher knows what to do about it.

TABLE 12–1. *Protecting the Bruised Self-Image of the Chronic Under-achiever.*

WHAT HE SAYS	WHAT HE MAY MEAN
School is terrible. Teachers are against me and they aren't any good anyhow.	If the system is bad, no real blame can come to me if I don't succeed in it.
I think I would like to be a jet pilot or a movie star or a politician.	I want to do thrilling and glamorous things but cannot stand a position with a long period of training preceding it or where sustained hard work is needed (rarely choosing surgeon, electronics engineer, or president).
I really am not gifted and those tests are crazy anyhow.	The label "gifted" puts the pressure on me to succeed. One way to take the pressure off is to lose the lable.
Some people are lucky and some aren't. I wish I could hit it lucky for once. I dream about breaking the bank at Las Vegas.	If life is a game of chance, I am less personally responsible for my ultimate success or failure.
My old man is a grouch. He is from nowhere.	My father and I don't understand each other and cannot communicate. I can't model myself after him.
I like to get into a hopped up jalopy and go-go-go. Man, that really is living. Give me a bennie and watch me fly.	The excitement of speed and risk makes me feel competent. This is something I can do without sustained effort and it distracts me from my unpleasant self-image.
Future? What future? The "bomb" will take care of our future. If not, things will work out somehow.	To think of the future requires planning and effort. These are too painful since I have failed too often before. I prefer to ignore it and trust to luck, etc., to make things come out all right.
The only time I feel at home is with my buddies—when we go out searching for kicks, I feel like a person.	The only time my self-image is bolstered is when I am with other fellows who feel as I do and who help me explain away my problems.

Perhaps the greatest frustration that Joe presents to those adults who observe him is not only what he does at the present to frustrate those who wish to help him, but also the fact that he creates an unfavorable environment for his own future learning. The underachievers have a penchant for finding others in their peer groups who complement and feed the patterns of behavior antagonistic to learning and academic effort.

Morrow and Wilson (1961) compared the peer relations of forty-nine high school boys of superior mental ability (group IQ over 120) who had a low grade-point average with those who had a superior grade-point average. The underachievers described themselves as more impulsive, adventurous, and restless. They described their friends as uninterested in school achievement, negative toward authority, seeking excitement, and showing general dissatisfaction with life. The friends of the under-achiever thus seem to make up one more piece of the picture of the non-productive environment in which the underachiever operates, and which he actually seeks out.

The Bright Dropout

One of the popular stereotypes of the high school dropout has been that this is a student of lower-than-average intelligence with a long history of academic failure, belonging to a societal subgroup that does not value education. It is likely that the average dropout does fit this pattern, but we are concerned not with averages but with individuals, and the range of variation of ability in any group of dropouts is substantial.

Sam and Joe can be considered as first-rate candidates for potential dropout at the secondary school level despite their high ability, whereas Cranshaw and Zelda cannot. At least, this seems plausible on the basis of what we know now. French and Carden (1968) reported on the characteristics of 125 male and 81 female dropouts of high ability (IQ 110+). They concluded that the male dropouts were more uninhibited than male nondropouts and fought the strong pressures of the school for them to conform.

In addition, they were vocationally confused, although they were more "trade" than "college" oriented. Students with high ability almost automatically get placed in the academic college-bound program, whether they like these types of courses or not. The unmarried female dropouts followed a similar pattern. The authors suggest that more sensible vocational guidance, which allows talented youth to explore more avenues of work, and a systematic program for improving social skills could bring about a lesser incidence of dropouts.

On the other hand, the personality profile of the dropouts did not suggest that they rejected learning but indicated instead that the conforming nature of the school setting may have created a stumbling block for them. They were, as a group, mentally healthy individuals, and this pattern held true for both boys and girls. The talented male dropouts expressed concern that the schools were not preparing the students for the real world and disliked intensely the forces they perceived within the school toward conformity.   These students stressed the importance of being able to be an individual.   The talented girl dropouts showed similar attitudes, feeling that the school did not meet their needs with regard to vocational or professional goals.   Although these girls were not close to their teachers, they did not complain about unfair treatment or favoritism.

There is always the problem of whether the individual should adjust to the situation or the situation should adjust to the individual.   In this case, it seems as though the school setting was the problem rather than these mentally healthy, above-average-ability individuals.   In most situations we can expect that a combination of personal adjustment problems and limited programs in the schools cause the difficulties.

Summary

What do we know about Joe if he is typical of the groups that have been studied under this label of underachievement?   First, he is an insecure boy with negative feelings toward himself.   Let us not be fooled by manifestations of bravado or studied laziness or defiance; Joe is trying to tell us something in a language that most of us have difficulty translating.   He has trapped himself in the unrewarding posture of trying to protect a self-image at the expense of future attainment.   A great deal of his behavior can be characterized as defending the *self* at all costs.

In some ways, Joe resembles a boxer who has taken a fearful beating in his ten rounds of life.   Now he weaves and dodges and backs away. Others seeing this behavior may shout to him, as fans shout to the boxer, "That is no way to behave . . . how do you expect to win by running away . . . get in there and fight!" What neither the boxing fans nor Joe's teachers have considered is that Joe isn't trying to win (i.e., get A's or B's) any more.   Like the beaten boxer, he is merely trying to survive without too much damage to his shaky self-concept.   So he will deny his high ability, blame others for his shortcomings, state that the world's rewards are handed out by luck or chance or favoritism—anything to avoid another painful blow to his bruised self.   It is important that we recognize what Joe is trying to say so that we react to the real problems and not to Joe's defensive reactions and escape patterns.

EDUCATIONAL PROGRAMMING FOR UNDERACHIEVERS

One of the drawbacks to more effective planning for gifted underachievers has been the consistent tendency to underestimate the scope of the problem. As long as it is viewed as only a type of stubbornness, or a fit of laziness, or antagonism to a particular teacher on the part of the student, major efforts will not be undertaken to deal with the problem. As we have seen in the first part of this chapter, it is far from that. Instead, it is a total way of life, and attempts to change the pattern have to take due recognition of this important fact.

One way to look at the underachiever is that he is in the middle of a circle of barbed wire. It makes up his total environment, and all the elements of his environment have contributed to the building of this wire circle—his family, his friends, his school, and, most important, himself. Any movements that he attempts to make to get out of the barbed wire are going to be painful to him. Sometimes it is more comfortable to sit quietly and passively in the middle of his trap and bemoan his own fate than to risk getting scratched trying to get out.

What needs to be done then? Attempts can be made to clear away the barbed wire in a particular area and allow Joe a path out. Such a path can be taken through family counseling by placing him in a special school environment, or by trying to involve him with peers who are better models than his own group. One might give Joe, himself, some counseling to help him define his own life goals and aspirations more effectively. It would probably be best to make more than one of these efforts at the same time.

As an example of the daily problems caused by Joe, we can make a visit to the Washington Elementary School. A clear, crisp October day has given a certain buoyancy and enthusiasm to student and teacher alike. One would not think of this as a setting for the beginning of a sustained battle and conflict, but it is. The conflict is between Mr. Jenkins, teacher, and Joe, our underachieving gifted child. The battle lines are drawn when Mr. Jenkins calls Joe up to his desk.

Mr. Jenkins: I see that you were five minutes tardy today, Joe.

Joe: Yeh, there were a lot of boys makin' a big fuss in the hall so I came the long way around.

The first round is clearly Joe's. He implies that not only should he not be censured for being tardy but actually deserves a good deal of credit for having the moral strength to avoid the disorderly group in the hall. This is not the major reason for the conference, as both know, however, and Mr. Jenkins wisely moves on to the main topic.

Mr. Jenkins: Joe, I am a little disappointed in the story you turned in. In the first place it was a day late, and, in the second place, it is quite sloppy and poorly organized for a final draft.

Joe: Yeh, I know. It was late because there was one reference I wanted to get, and the library was closed when I went to get it so Mom said I'd better wait an extra day and get it before I turned the paper in. And I didn't think that you would worry so much about the form, the way which the paper looked. Mrs. Johnson last year said that what was important was to have good ideas first and then worry about how it looks afterwards. I was just trying to get the ideas down, was that wrong?

The deftness with which Joe sidesteps the teacher's complaints shows his experience in such matters. Again, his tardiness in turning in the paper turns out to be a *virtue*. He wanted to get the most important material into the paper, and quoting his mother and last year's teacher is a fine way to keep the present teacher off balance. Does Mr. Jenkins really want to get into an argument with Joe's absentee mother? For all he knows, Mrs. Johnson *may* have said this or something very much like it, and maybe Joe should be given the benefit of the doubt this time. One must not think, either, that Joe is necessarily callously misquoting or distorting Mrs. Johnson's views. He, like most human beings, has a tendency to remember those things which fit into his own attitudes and ideas and discard the rest. He probably does this without thinking very much about it, and with no intent to falsify.

Mr. Jenkins: Well, Joe, you did have some good ideas in the paper, but I looked at your records and I think I have a right to expect more from you than what you have done for me on the first paper.

Joe: Well, that's what I get from all my teachers. Ever since I took that IQ test, teachers have been telling me, "I expect a good deal from you." I don't see that this is fair at all. Why should I be expected to do any more than any other kid in class? Those tests are a lot of hooey anyway.

And so it goes. Joe has introduced Mr. Jenkins into the fascinating and baffling world of the passive-resistant underachiever, and, unless he is extremely skillful or extremely perceptive or both, this little scene, with minor variations, is likely to be replayed many times during the school year. The tragedy of such scenes is that each participant tends to go away reinforced in his own nonproductive beliefs. Joe will continue to maintain that his teachers are unfair and that they have too high expectations of him. As long as he holds to this position, he will not be motivated to change his habits. The teacher is impressed by the fact that here is a difficult student, one who is going to require a good deal of watching. This is the information he had received previously in that remarkable communication center known as the teacher's lounge.

Two major strategies have been used to intervene effectively in the nonproductive life pattern of the talented underachiever—counseling and changes in educational environment and programming. These two approaches represent very different assumptions regarding the relative plasticity of the underachiever. The counseling approach focuses on the poor emotional adjustment of the student and his inadequate self-concept. By helping the student to explore his view of himself and his world, counseling should (the argument goes) enable him to reorganize his self-concept and his perceptions into more constructive channels and, this, in turn, will result in better school performance.

The alternative educational approach maintains the theory that the basic problem of the student is his inability to adapt to the educational situation. His recognition of his failures intensify whatever feelings he has toward education and intensifies his unfavorable response. Therefore, a change in that environment that would allow the student to become more effective might change his behavior patterns directly, and those effective behavior patterns will enhance his self-concept and improve his emotional adjustment.

An oversimplified summary of these two approaches would be that counseling attempts to improve school performance through raising the student's self-concept, whereas the education approach attempts to enhance his self-concept through better school performance. In actual practice, few programs are restricted to one approach; most programs are mixtures of the two strategies.

Counseling

One natural plan stemming from our knowledge about Joe's personality problems is to attempt to modify the child's behavior through counseling. What kind and how? Should individual or group counseling be used? Should the teacher hold conferences with the student, or should trained counselors be employed? Do these students need an inspirational talk? Baymur and Patterson (1960) tried to evaluate three methods of helping underachieving high school students. One group of underachievers consisted of children who were individually counseled; a second group received group counseling; and a third group was given a one-session motivational talk. The underachievers were told, in the one-session talk, that they had high ability and that they should try to work up to their expectations. The fourth group was a control group that received no counseling at all. As has been found in other research, changing the attitudes of such youngsters is not an easy task; the results of the counseling were not clearly positive. There did seem to be some tendency for the counseled students to have a higher grade-point average than the noncounseled students, but there were only limited changes in their self-concept stemming from the short-term counseling.

One of the most interesting results of this research was that the inspirational talk, or "get-in-there-and-fight-fellows" approach, seemed to be a complete failure. These students even fell below the control group in performance on the measures of effectiveness. Baymur and Patterson point out that *this* is the type of approach most commonly used by parents and teachers when they attempt to raise the output of the underachiever. They comment, "It is suggested that it may be better to leave underachievers alone, rather than pointing out their failure to achieve adequately and exhorting them to do something about it." This author would add, "without telling them *how* to go about it."

The use of group counseling has been particularly recommended for gifted adolescents, on the grounds that they appreciate the opportunity to exchange ideas with peers. They seem to perceive themselves as struggling for independence against adults, and they much prefer peers' assistance in solving their problems to that of another adult. Another positive gain from this is that many of them seem genuinely reassured to find that other persons of their own age are having problems similar to their own.

One attempt at group counseling has been made by Broedel, Ohlsen, Proff, and Southard (1960), who worked with four groups of underachieving ninth graders. The sessions were planned upon the premise that, if a youngster discovers that other peers accept him, he will be better able to accept other persons, in turn, and eventually can better accept himself. After he begins to accept himself, then, and only then, can he accept the fact that he is gifted and make plans for the full use of his potentialities. These investigators also warn that underachievement, particularly at this age level, is not a surface phenomenon easily modified. It takes skillful counseling and a good deal of time to achieve even the modest results obtained in this experiment. Some improvement in self-concept and achievement was attained in individual cases.

The life patterns of the underachiever have been forming for fourteen, fifteen, or sixteen years, so they cannot be radically changed merely by a few good words, a pat on the back, or a stern growl. They appear to require an extensive period of self-discovery, of creating a proper atmosphere for the individual to look at himself in a nonthreatening situation, and of accepting both his positive and negative feelings about himself and others.

Joe, for instance, bitterly resented his father's attempts to get him to work harder. The thought that he would directly combat the wishes of his stern father was too frightening for him to contemplate, so he hid his resistance behind all sorts of rationalizations: "People are picking on me," "Teachers are unfair," and so on.

The sad part of this story is that Joe *must* find out the truth for himself. Even if someone else, say a neighbor or teacher, told Joe why he was doing this, he would probably laugh it off. *The great talent of the counselor lies in helping the student find out for himself what the counselor already knows.* This goal requires the highest level of professional competence and patience in order to obtain the desired results.

In a problem area where few traditional methods seem perfected, it is important that experimentation be tried on a wide number of different remedial practices in order to see which one might be most useful. Shaw (1960) initiated a family counseling technique for underachievers and their parents. The basis for this program was the hypothesis that the basic problem of the underachiever is a breakdown of communication between himself and his parents, causing him to feel unworthy and unaccepted. His reactions to these feelings would be resentment and hostility, which tend to create the personality and attitudinal framework that result in the underachievement.

In the family counseling technique, the parents and the children are seen together by a counselor. For one half of the period, the child listens to the parents' side of the problem; then, for the other half of the session, the parents listen to the child expressing his difficulties. In order to express feelings in the presence of his parents, the first two of the four sessions were arranged so that the student was with other students' parents and not his own. Shaw used twelve groups of twelve parents each, eight of the groups coming from a tenth-grade population and four groups coming from a seventh-grade population. They underwent four therapeutic sessions of an hour and a half each, with both a mother and a father present during the sessions.

The evaluation was quite informal in nature, but the program seemed to be successful enough to warrant continuation for another year. Both the parents and youths realized the value of having parents and youths in the same group. Shaw found that students were able to talk freely in front of adults and, with practice, could do so with their own parents. There seemed to be another advantage to this procedure, in that the students generally felt it was an honor to be considered an equal with adults in discussing problems. When one considers the low self-evaluation of the underachiever, one can see how this respect paid to them by the counselors can be an important part of remedial practice.

One final general finding needs to be repeated for both teachers and parents: "Lecturing at either parents or students fails to help, but setting a climate where both can learn from listening to each other makes the likelihood of learning greater" (Shaw, 1960, p. 276).

In contrast to the negative findings of other counseling approaches, Shouksmith and Taylor (1964) obtained strikingly positive results in a combined program for preadolescent underachievers and their parents, with eight of the twelve members of the counseled groups improving to the point where they could no longer be identified as underachievers in less than a year's time. How can one account for this seemingly contradictory set of findings?

For one thing it is easy to fall into the trap of assuming that a common label means common behavior. Is everything called "counseling" really the same type of behavior? Is counseling by a practitioner of thirty-years experience the same as that by an advanced graduate student? Is counseling done by a psychoanalytically oriented counselor the same as counseling by a vocationally oriented counselor? We need to look much more closely at just exactly what is going on between student and counselor to be able to judge the significance of the results of the various studies.

Classroom Modifications

It would be a mistake to believe that the warm and intimate relationship that may convince Joe to modify his approach to school, can be achieved *only* by counseling. Attempts have also been made to bring the remedial concept into the classroom.

One educational strategy has been to place a large number of underachievers together in one special class and then plan an educational program for them. Goldberg (1960) has reported on a program of research directed through the Talented Youth Project at Teachers College. In one experiment, 35 students were identified who had obtained IQ scores above 125, and who had relatively low grade-point averages. These students were given a homeroom teacher who was also their social studies teacher. The teacher was warm, accepting, and flexible in his demands on the students; they seemed to respond by obtaining slightly better grades than did their control sample colleagues in the regular program. During the following year, however, this same group was placed with a social studies teacher, who, while highly skillful in her own area, had rather rigid and high standards that she expected all students to meet. This group of students rebelled against this type of teaching, and, at the end of the year, were no further ahead, and in some cases less far ahead, than were the control subjects.

Another group of students who were in the top 10 percent of their class in ability and who had failed first-year algebra was placed in a special geometry class with a master teacher. These students did seem to respond to the instructor and to show improvement in geometry, but this was often at the expense of some of their other subjects.

On the basis of this indifferent success, it was concluded that the greatest need for the underachiever was to identify with a teacher and to have ample opportunity for help with both personal and academic problems. Another group of underachievers was identified and placed in a program that allowed time for individual conferences, help with work-study skills, and group discussions of common problems. Sad to relate, this particular treatment did not show sizable positive results either.

358

Since it is clearly possible to identify underachieving children (particularly boys) at a reasonably young age, more and more schools are turning toward attempts to deal with this problem in the early grades, where treatment could be given earlier, and with less investment of professional time. An attempt to evaluate different remedial methods has been carried out in Evanston, Illinois, by Miller (1962), in which three groups of underachieving second-grade children (about 35 each) were identified. One group of children was assigned to a counselor who held group-counseling sessions. A second group received individual tutoring from the reading specialist, while a third group served as a control sample receiving no special treatment. Over one semester, no significant changes were shown in any of the groups on reading scores, again substantiating how difficult it is to modify and change the pattern of adjustment of such youngsters. The plan is for this research to be continued over a longer period of time, in the hope that changes will begin to manifest themselves after the treatment or tutoring has been allowed to develop further.

Another interesting variation in the attempt of schools to deal with underachievers has been tried by Karnes, McCoy, Zehrbach, Wollersheim, and Clarizio (1961). They identified gifted underachieving children at the elementary school level in Champaign, Illinois. These children were divided into two groups; members of one group were placed in classes of gifted children that had been homogeneously grouped. No more than 20 percent of any class of gifted children would be composed of underachievers. The second group was placed in the ordinary educational setting, a standard heterogeneous grouping. Both groups were observed over a two-year period of time. At the end of that period, the gifted children in the homogeneously grouped classes showed significant improvement both in intellectual fluency *and* in their perceived parent attitudes. These results have considerable educational significance if they can be repeated in other communities, since one important goal is to modify the underachiever's attitudes. This study indicates that it *is* possible to modify attitudes, not by attacking them directly through counseling, but rather through modification of the educational environment of the child! The authors believed that the underachievers in the homogeneous class were introduced to many more stimulating ideas and concepts than were the gifted children in the heterogeneous class. In this community, the teachers in both programs had the advantage of the assistance of a full-time consultant on gifted children, a factor that might have been partly responsible for the results.

The changes perceived in attitudes toward parents is another illustration of how difficult it is to make a clear interpretation of educational research. There is always the possibility that the parents, fully aware of the research project, actually may have changed their attitudes toward their children in a positive direction, partly as a result of the project. If

359

this was the case, the positive attitude perceived in the students may represent a real change in parent behavior rather than a mere change in the perceptions of the youngster.

If these results could be duplicated elsewhere, it would suggest that manipulating the educational environment itself might be a more useful approach than counseling underachievers. At any rate, counseling still has to prove itself as an effective technique for dealing with under-achievers.

Program Evaluation: A Comment

It is only natural to look at the research efforts in this area with disbelief at the relative ineffectiveness of the various approaches to this problem. Some educators seem to think that research tends to speak with forked tongue, particularly when it fails to come up with answers that support practitioners' experience. In this area, it is more fair to say that most research speaks to one very specific situation, and that any one study is likely to be an inconclusive basis upon which to build educational practice.

There is one more caution that cannot be repeated too often to both counselor and teacher—and that is to warn against the *feelie* type of program evaluation that is all too common in schools. The reaction of the practitioner to negative or indifferent results obtained by researchers on their programs is often, "I don't care what your tests show, I just *feel* that some good is being done by the program." Now it may be that the tests aren't adequate. Such areas as motivation or personality changes are hard to measure.

But there is another possibility that must also be considered. Psychiatry has taught us that human beings possess an almost unlimited ability for self-deception, for believing what they wish to believe in the face of almost any kind of evidence. When the researcher comes up with no positive results on my program, and I feel that he is wrong, could it be that I am the one who can't see the reality?

How Much Pressure?

How hard should a gifted student work? This is a question asked by students, by their parents, and by their teachers. The question is phrased in a culture in which those who work with their hands are spending less and less time on the job, whereas those who work with their brains are spending more and more time at their work.

Unfortunately, some schools have adjusted to the demand for excellence, and to the knowledge explosion, by piling on lengthy homework assignments, instead of changing the complexity or meaningfulness of the assignments for the talented. This has led to the phenomenon of the conscientious secondary student spending four to six hours on homework assignments handed out by his various teachers. It is just as unwise, however, to ask for too little pressure to achieve, as it is to demand too much. As Gardner (1961, p. 148) has put it, "The best-kept secret in America today is that people would rather work hard for something they believe in than enjoy a pampered idleness."

Berkowitz (1964, p. 43), in summing up the field of achievement motivation, stresses the importance of providing difficult tasks that are *within the power of the individual to accomplish.*

> Remember that the person with strong achievement desires generally prefers to work on moderately difficult tasks. He tends to seek out the "optimal challenge," presumably because it is only through succeeding on a challenging, moderately risky task which tests his skill and ability that he can obtain the satisfaction of a job well done.

Helping the Underachiever in the Classroom

The entire force of the evidence available is that positive movement for the underachiever is a difficult matter at best. He would be better-off by far to be in a special program designed for his own needs. Nevertheless, it is unlikely that the majority of Joes around the country will be involved in such a special program. Instead, it is likely that their unusual and self-defeating behavior will confront one puzzled teacher after another. What can the ordinary teacher, or even one who has received some special training, do with Joe? Several general ideas could be kept in mind by the teacher.

1. *Causation probably lies outside the classroom.* When things go wrong in the classroom, the conscientious teacher often searches for reasons within himself for the disaster. It is appropriate that teachers do consider themselves first, particularly if such consideration leads to a change in teacher strategy. In Joe's case, however, the teacher would do well to consider his past history and the history of children like him. It is likely that Joe is pursuing a pattern of behavior constructed long before he had contact with his present teacher. Understanding that pattern—rather than futile soul-searching, or asking oneself, "What did I do that went wrong?"—would seem to be the more profitable approach.

2. *Remediation is a difficult road.* The dance of the underachiever can be symbolically described as three steps forward, two steps back, and one step sideways—pause for effect. There is a fantasy shared by almost all teachers that they (the pure in heart) can come onto the scene and through love, warmth, affection, or superior knowledge touch a child who has remained

impervious to the best efforts of other teachers, and thus magically cast away his affliction. We can call this the "Merlin the Magician" method. For the underachiever, a better image is that of teaching the cerebral-palsied or postpolio child to walk. There are no instant successes and the road is hard and slow but greatly rewarding, if one can be accepting of small successes and many setbacks.

3. *The underachiever's fear of failure.* Almost everything that he does, or does not do, seems colored by this fear. This is why he cannot sustain interest on a lengthy or complex problem. The experience of failure overwhelms him before he gets to the end and he retreats, thus confirming his own feelings of failure (see Table 12–1). The strategy to combat this fear is to give short and intrinsically interesting assignments so that his frustrations will not overwhelm him and cause him to retreat. Term papers or long reports are almost always overwhelming to the underachiever. Short assignments, where the material is immediately available stand the best chance for success. These can be gradually lengthened as Joe tends to tolerate his frustrations more. He must be weaned away gradually from the comforts of ignorance and anonymity!

4. *The fear of success.* Most teachers are familiar with the fear of failure and what that causes children to do, but not many are aware of the fear of success. An example of this in Joe's case was the time that Mr. Jenkins noticed Joe working on a short composition. The teacher had already commented favorably upon it, but Joe seemed to be more agitated about his work as it approached completion. Finally, he took an eraser and with great strength rubbed the eraser across the composition tearing the paper and ruining it. The impending success seemed to be too much for Joe and his "old shoe" comforts of mediocrity.

Mr. Jenkins, knowing Joe well, did not fall into the trap of scolding Joe for his carelessness but instead praised Joe for the quality of work that had been in the composition and helped him to mend it the best he could. He then wrote a note on the bottom of the composition. "Good work, Joe, this is a great improvement. I am encouraged, and I know that you are, too." Joe didn't say anything about it but seemed to sit up straighter and work a little longer the next day. But Mr. Jenkins knows that the end is not yet in sight, nor will it be for a long time, because these long-ingrained unfavorable habits are sure to emerge again when Joe becomes anxious, threatened, or just bored with the way things are.

SUMMARY

There is probably nothing more infuriating to an educator than to see a child with great talent fritter it away through a lack of action or apparent lack of care. The educator sees so many children with limited talent struggle hard to get what the talented child could do so easily if he would but make some small effort that he tends to have little sympathy for the underachievers.

The basic question is: "Do the underachievers' problems lie within themselves or within a school system that is not flexible enough to deal with their unusual talents?" Surely, the answer lies in a combination of these circumstances. It would be foolish to focus all our blame on uninteresting schools.

Certainly, the underachievers are clearly different from gifted achievers in their personal characteristics. They generally seem to be unsure and lacking in purpose and confidence in themselves. They often have a history of family conflict, particularly father–son conflict. Underachieving children have started their lackluster career of mediocre performance very early in the elementary grades and can be identified at that level, and they appear to want to protect their bruised egos from further hurt. Teachers and parents have expressed disappointment with their past performances. So they will do anything to delay or divert further negative evaluations of self. They will miss assignments, blame poor grades on others—they will do almost anything but the work necessary to get the grades and recognition needed to raise that self-image.

Many educators and educational programs fail to deal effectively with the gifted underachiever because they fail to realize the depth and intensity of the problem and therefore underestimate the resources needed to correct it. By the time the gifted underachiever has reached the middle elementary grades, his underachievement is a genuine life-style, and major educational readjustments or counseling over an extended period of time are often needed to change it.

A child who is chronically afraid of anything, whether it is big dogs or thunderstorms or *his own perceived failure,* needs much patience and tolerance of slow progress in order to overcome the fear. The typical underachievers are basically fearful children who have lost faith in themselves and their talents and abilities. The veneer of bravado, casual disdain for school, or a daily quarrelsome attitude, is most often a coverup. Once this basic lesson is learned, the teacher and educator are a giant step forward in seeking ways to aid the child to the fuller use of his or her talents.

Investments in intensive counseling and specially designed educational programs give hope of recovering some of the talent lost to these problems at both the elementary and secondary levels.

UNRESOLVED ISSUES

1. Can we design preventive programs for very young children who are predisposed to the patterns of underachievement as listed in this chapter? By beginning at an early age we can make a major effort to keep the known psychological defenses from hardening into patterns that, in adolescence, become very difficult to modify.

2. Can we devise parent-training programs so that the circular and self-defeating interactions of underachieving children and their parents can be broken and so that more effective parental rewards and stimulation can build the missing self-confidence in the underachieving student?

3. We have still found no truly satisfactory remedial education process for these gifted underachievers once they have reached the upper elementary grades. We need to seek out more imaginative and more effective remedial programs for such youngsters from whatever disciplines have something to offer—from psychoanalysis to behavior modification.

READINGS OF SPECIAL INTEREST

BACHTOLD, L. *Counseling: Instructional programs for intellectually gifted students.* Sacramento, Calif.: California State Department of Education, 1966. (ED 011 124)
A wide variety of techniques and methods are presented to deal with the intellectually gifted child. Some of these approaches have potential usefulness for the gifted underachiever.

CHAPMAN, M., & HILL, R. (Eds.) *Achievement motivation.* Philadelphia: Research for Better Schools, Inc., 1971.
A remarkably complete summary of the literature on achievement motivation. This source book covers such issues as influences that produce high achievement motivation and strategies for inducing high achievement motivation.

RAPH, J. B., GOLDBERG, M. L., & PASSOW, A. H. *Bright underachievers.* New York: Teachers College Press, Columbia University, 1966.
A detailed description of specific programs designed to improve the educational program for gifted underachievers at the secondary level. Important for its revelation that such problems are not easily remediated. An excellent review of the literature to 1965 is also included.

TERMAN, L. M., & ODEN, M. *Genetic studies of genius. Vol. 4. The gifted child grows up.* Stanford, Calif.: Stanford University Press, 1947.
Contains an excellent section discussing the special problems and characteristics of the gifted underachiever grown up, in the major longitudinal study of 1500 gifted students in California.

13

The Culturally Different
Gifted

For several decades the description of the Terman group of gifted children whose progress was followed into adulthood (reported in Chapter 2) has been taken as the composite portrait of gifted children. The super all-American characteristics of this group have served a useful purpose in dispelling the image of the gifted child as a bespectacled, puny bookworm.

On the other hand, it has become increasingly apparent that the Terman description is also incomplete. As Jacobs (1970) and others have pointed out, Terman obtained his sample initially through teacher nominations, which we know would stress the compliant, well-mannered child and would run the risk of overlooking the child from a culturally different environment. Even if a child from a Chicano or black family were nominated, he or she might not pass the 135 to 140 Binet IQ score necessary for membership, even though in native ability—environment aside—he or she might be equal.

In the past decade, increasing concern has been felt for identifying and planning for the talented child from cultural backgrounds far removed from the American middle-class stereotype. This search, this talent hunt, represents a recognition, in part, that the human resources of America are not unlimited, any more than are our physical resources. Further, we have more than enough problems to solve to provide all our intellectual youth full-time employment for some time to come.

SAM'S REFRAIN

It is rare that educators have a full appreciation of the diverse pressures that can be placed on talented youngsters who persist in deviating from acceptable neighborhood cultural norms. Sam had one such experience that was burned vividly into his memory and influenced his school behavior from then on.

During one class Sam became enthusiastic about an assignment, and the teacher was able to see past the rough exterior and grasp the diamond-like quality of Sam's intellect. For an electric moment their minds touched, and the teacher and Sam had an exhilarating conversation, almost forgetting the rest of the class in their mutual enthusiasm.

That evening as Sam trudged home from school, he turned a corner and was suddenly confronted by five of his male classmates, obviously waiting for him. He was sure that he could handle any one of them physically but equally sure that he was helpless before the group. Cold chills ran up his spine as the largest of the group approached him.

"Hey, Sam, how come you're suckin' up to the teach? We don't like guys actin' too smart, do we?"

A rumble of assent came from the assembled group and several further highly distinctive suggestions were made as to what might happen to someone who kept at such unacceptable behavior. Sam held his ground, but the next day he was very distant to the teacher and resisted all attempts to reinstitute that special relationship. He had made his choice. If he kept his distance from the teacher, and continued to excel athletically, his intellectual interests would be accepted, though not without some scorn. It is this type of compromise, in one form or another, that is forced upon talented students coming from a cultural background that is essentially hostile to the institution of the school or the pursuit of the intellect.

A different problem would face Sam's sister. She might not be threatened in so openly a physical way as Sam, but her aspirations to seek a writing career beyond the home and family, if expressed openly, might result in just as thorough an ostracizing as Sam's, in a subculture where women are supposed to produce babies, not books. So what do these youngsters do? With their peer group, they "cool it." They hide their interests and aspirations when with their friends, and they are very cautious in the classroom.

Educators need to do more than decry the values that cause these talented youngsters to disguise their talents. They need to find less public opportunities for such youngsters to show their talents. There is hardly any more public arena than the open classroom discussion. Everything said there is open to full group hearing and monitoring. The wise teacher, understanding these factors, probably would have waited until she had Sam aside for some reason for their discussion, so that he wouldn't have been socially endangered by his own intellect.

We do not often consider that an open show of intellect can be a socially dangerous step for a youngster; but it can.   It should not lie beyond the ingenuity of educators to create settings where such expression carries adult enthusiasm and praise, while not running the risk of peer censure.

CHARACTERISTICS OF THE CULTURALLY DIFFERENT GIFTED

Any attempt to specify general characteristics of such a broad group that would include American Indians, Puerto Ricans, recent immigrants from Europe, and so on has to be made with extraordinary caution.   We will try to be specific in discussing particular groups.

One of the major efforts to try to answer the question about the characteristics of talented children was conducted by Frierson (1965), who studied four groups of children: two gifted samples, one of upper socioeconomic status and the other of lower socioeconomic status; and two average samples of the same characteristics.   A wide variety of personality tests, interest tests, and home information data was collected; comparisons were then made to see whether the differences among the four samples were due more to ability or more to difference in socioeconomic status.   The primary difference between the two gifted groups from different socioeconomic backgrounds was found to be in the dimension of interests and attitudes.   There were no major differences between the groups on physical characteristics and few differences obtained on the personality tests.   The upper-status gifted spent a great deal more time and had a great deal more interest in *reading* in recreational hours, whereas the lower-status gifted seemed more interested in *action* and competitive team sports.

A second major question was: Were there differences between the lower-status gifted and the lower-status average student in the same way that differences have been found between the middle-class gifted and average students from comparable backgrounds? Some of the results suggested that the lower-status gifted were more likely to play musical instruments, to aspire to higher-status occupations, read the news sections of the newspaper, and so forth.

A similar study by Karnes, Zehrbach, Studley, and Wright (1965) found gifted children from lower-class homes to have more tension in the family and to be performing substantially lower than their predicted achievement levels.   Gallagher and Janzen (1965) found substantial interracial friendship choices in elementary classes for gifted children in a midwestern town, suggesting a less ingrained tendency to respond to stereotypes in gifted programs.

In short, distinct differences were found between the gifted and average groups regardless of the socioeconomic background that they came from. However, the interest and attitude differences of the lower-status gifted do point to some possible modifications and changes that might be made in the educational program for these students.

In an earlier chapter we discussed the finding that there are real differences among various ethnic groups as to the percentage of their subgroup that falls into the gifted category. But why? Some kind of genetic factor can, of course, be proposed, but the genetic pluralism of European societies and the polygenic nature of intelligence make it more plausible to seek possible cultural influences that might explain such differences in ethnic results.

One of the most provocative studies of cultural values has been performed by Strodtbeck (1958). He compared family and cultural values of forty-three Italian families and seventy-nine Jewish families in an eastern city. The Jewish families doubled the number of their members in the professional and upper-middle classes in one generation, whereas the Italian families did not increase their incidence in these classes from one generation to another. Strodtbeck found Jewish families placing greater stress upon certain values and philosophies of life, such as the following:

1. A belief that the world is orderly and amenable to rational mastery.
2. A willingness to leave home to make one's way in life.
3. A preference for individual rather than collective credit for work done.
4. The belief that man can improve himself through education and that one should not readily submit to fate.
5. A greater equality in the power structure between the mother and father in the family.

In the Italian families, Strodtbeck found a greater tendency to believe in the dominance of the father, in the preeminence of the family over the achievement and life goals of the youngster, and a greater tendency to believe in luck and chance as opposed to hard work. Strodtbeck concludes that cultures which support values like those found in Jewish families will produce more achievers than will cultures which support values antagonistic to them. This is a very provocative first step and deserves much research attention in the future.

IQ Constancy?

When differences are found in IQ scores, the interpretation of meaning depends upon our knowledge of how vulnerable the IQ score is to environmental influences. We return to the question, "Does an IQ score represent intellectual capacity?"

Serious doubts have already been expressed about the range of the typical IQ test. We can now consider additional questions concerning the long-range predictive ability of these measures. It is important to realize that long-range predictions depend on our belief that IQ scores could not be substantially changed by experience. This had led to the conclusion that, once a child scores over 130 IQ, he will always score over 130 IQ, and once a child scores below 130 IQ, he will always score below that level, allowing for minor fluctuations due to a variety of technical factors.

Much evidence on IQ consistency has been obtained, not on gifted children but on slow learners. The concern expressed for the slow learners has been that cultural deprivation might lower the already limited capacity of children from this background; but one may well ask: If it lowers the intellectual potential of slow learners, would it not also lower the intellectual potential of even the brightest of this particular group?

Efforts to develop "culture-free" IQ tests have been based upon the notion that the usual IQ test has items common to a middle-class culture and, thus, are unfair to lower-class children such as Sam. The principal function of IQ tests is, of course, to predict scholastic achievement. Since the schools *are* culturally biased (because they reflect the dominant cultural values of our society), any good predictive aptitude test will be culturally biased also. There is unfairness, all right, but it is the unfairness of unequal cultural backgrounds for American youth, or perhaps of a single standard for excellence. (This question is treated in detail below, in the section "Talent Misplaced or Talent Erased.")

In a ten-year longitudinal study, Sontag, Baker, and Nelson (1958) gave IQ tests periodically to children of above-average ability from infancy until they were 10 years of age. Among other things, they found that some children seemed to increase their IQ scores systematically as they grew older, while other children consistently seemed to decrease their IQ scores. When these two groups of children were closely examined to see what characteristics differentiated them, one of the major factors was found to be motivation. Those children who systematically gained in IQ seemed to be more highly motivated and more active than were the children whose scores decreased.

The Coleman Report

If we have established the pliability of the IQ score, we are now in a position to look at some information from a most famous and controversial study—the Coleman report (1966). Coleman and his associates sampled student performance across the country by region and by race. The tests used were shorter versions of the usual measures of intellectual ability.

Figure 13–1 shows some of the results of this extensive study. Each

371

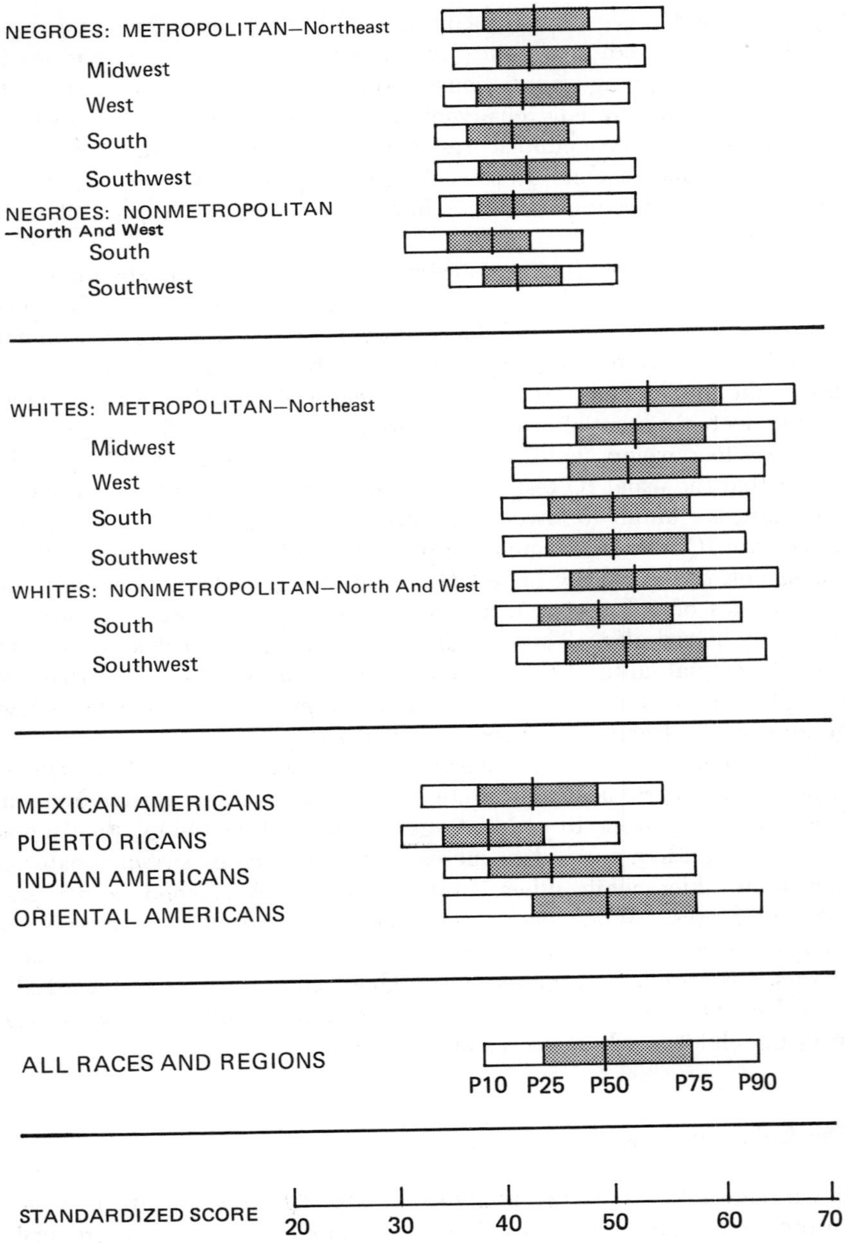

FIGURE 13–1. *Verbal Ability Test, Grade 6. (From J. S. Coleman, Campbell, E., Hobson, C., McPartland, J., Mood, A., Weinfeld, F., & York, R. Equality of educational opportunity. Washington, D.C.: U.S. Office of Education, 1966, p. 228.)*

distribution by race and region is represented on the graph in comparison to the overall norm for sixth-grade performance. The shaded areas of the bar represent the range in that population group from the top quarter to the bottom quarter. The full bar represents performance from the top 90 percent to the bottom 10 percent. Viewed in this perspective, there are obvious major differences among racial groups and among regions of the country.

Even with these differences, the overlap is substantial, with a part of the black population excelling the average of the white population and segments of southern students outstripping many of their colleagues in other parts of the country.

Of the other minority groups, it is interesting to note that the Oriental Americans perform close to the average of the white subgroups. The most common interpretation given to this finding appears to be the greater value placed on learning and a greater family solidarity in that subgroup than in the others.

Although these results are comparable to other findings, such as state-wide testing surveys, they have been brought under sharp attack by some representatives of minority groups, justifiably protesting a simple-minded interpretation of group inferiority in mental ability measured by a biased set of tests based on the white subculture.

If one remembers the influence of environment on IQ performance, an easy explanation is that generations of suppression and lack of stimulation can add up to the differences shown here. The only way to truly ascertain whether there is a "true" difference is to provide several generations of equal opportunity and then compare.

But that is not what concerns us here. If we accept the role played by environment in affecting the IQ, it is probable that the top level of any of these distributions, given equal opportunity, would likely be quite close to the top levels of the other distributions. A special emphasis on talent from culturally different populations requires a different type of identification, rather than the standard IQ score (see the discussion of Bruch (1970) later in the chapter).

Talent Misplaced or Talent Erased?

One of the more confusing and fruitless searches available in the field of educational measurement has been the search for a culture-free intelligence test that would avoid the cultural biases of the usual IQ test. It should be recognized that the assumption made by culture-free tests is that intelligence may be mislaid but not destroyed. Most of these efforts have centered on trying to find tests on which bright students from culturally different circumstances, or from lower social classes, would do as well as their more advantaged colleagues. One can have compassion for this psychological sleight-of-hand attempt to bring fairness to an unfair world.

The hard facts are that unfavorable environment and circumstances do not provide for the linguistic development necessary for success in a complex culture whose very nature is built around verbal and linguistic systems. Such talent suppressed is not easily regained. The embarrassing question not easily handled by those interested in culture-free tests is: Even if it were possible to construct such an instrument, what would we do with it once we had it? Surely such a test will not predict educational success when that success depends on the very verbal development that has been carefully excised from the test.

There are few doubts now about the ability of culturally different talented youth to perform, given proper preparation and motivation. Roberts and Nichols (1966) reported on the National Achievement Scholarship Programs for Negroes, in which the nation's secondary schools were invited to nominate outstanding black students for participation in the first annual competition.

The objective of the program was to call attention to the most able black youth and to help financially as many to attend college as funds would permit. In terms of family finances and intact families, these identified students were significantly better than the general nonwhite population. Sixty-two percent of the nominees were girls, which raises some questions about the predilections of the nominators or perhaps reflects the more difficult time of the black male in academic environments at that time.

A follow-up by Burgdorf (1969) of these more than 4000 students revealed that they were performing acceptably or better in college after their freshman year. Only 1 percent of the males and 3 percent of the females failed to complete their freshman year. The vast majority had made a good academic record. These results testified to the abilities of these students and of the tests used to select them in the first place.

It is the height of cultural insularity to assume that your own group has all the virtues, while the "others" have varying degrees of faults. It is more than just possible that differences found between groups lie, sometimes, in favor of the minority group. Torrance (1969, p. 73) states the basic issue this way:

> Should we seek to identify and cultivate those kinds of talents that the dominant society values, or look for talents of the type that are highly valued in the particular subcultures? Are there important kinds of talents commonly existent among disadvantaged subcultures?

Though much progress has been made in bringing cultural relevance into school readers in recent years, the following portrait of a beginning reader is still illustrative of the problem (Handlin, 1951, p. 246).

"This is Jack. This is Jack's house. This is Jack's daddy. Jack goes shopping. Jack goes to school. On the way he meets a cow. On the way he meets a sheep. Jack comes home. Jack falls asleep."

And surely enough, across the top from page to page the brightly colored pictures show it all. Blue-eyed and blonde, Jack himself stares out over the nice white collar and the neatly buttoned jacket. Across the green lawn, from the porch of the pretty yellow house, a miraculously slim mother waves. By the side of the road that dips through the fields of corn, the animals wait, each in turn to extend their greeting. There it all is, real as life.

Except that it is all a lie. There is no Jack, no house, no brightly smiling "Mummy." In the whole room there is not a boy with such a name, with such an appearance. One can walk streets without end and there will be never a glimpse of the yellow clapboards, of the close-cropped grass. Who sleeps like Jack alone in the prim room by the window to be wakened by singing birds? Good morning, Mr. Robin. The whole book is false because nothing in it touches on the experience of its readers and no element in their experience creeps into its pages.

When we speak of the disadvantaged, we are usually referring to students who are weak in verbal and semantic skills. But Torrance reminds us of other talents that often appear in much greater incidence in such groups (p. 75):

1. High nonverbal fluency and originality.
2. High creative productivity in small groups.
3. Adept in visual art activities.
4. Highly creative in movement, dance, and other physical activities.
5. Highly motivated by games, music, sport, humor, and concrete objects.
6. Language rich in imagery.

Smith (1965) also found children from "disadvantaged" backgrounds to do well in "creativity," which generally translates into more fluency and flexibility in responses to divergent thinking questions.

A recent conference was held to discuss the barriers standing in the way of talented children coming from culturally different environments, together with some possible solutions to overcome the barriers (Gallagher and Kinney, 1974). The conferees, most of whom came from culturally different backgrounds, felt the major barrier to be the middle-class bias that leads to school programs that are unrelated to the life of the child from culturally different backgrounds. This single middle-class oriented program also uses such tools as the IQ test as criteria for membership in special programs and curriculum materials that are highly inappropriate.

Several direct quotations from the conference will give something of the flavor of frustration and despair that is felt on this topic by those seeking larger opportunities for youths from minority or culturally different groups.

On testing. The tests themselves [IQ tests] are built on the assumption that this is the student's best performance. There is no such thing as their [culturally different gifted] giving a "best" performance because there is no motivation, there is no real concern.

On eligibility. My academic background in the use of IQ tests and my personal experiences with the many sociological factors affecting the lives of the prospective black students of this class made me defensive about the arbitrary IQ 130 cutoff point. I hated the idea of having to lower the standard for this class because it simply put a notch in the best of those who collect supportive data which point to deficiencies in an already maligned group of people.

On the classroom. Too often we have rewarded the rigid mind and docile spirit. . . . The sharp intelligent question has been rejected and the easy answer too often accepted. . . . Many of the strong and agile have left our ordered classrooms for the more challenging and seemingly less defeated atmosphere of the streets.

On language. Because the children go to the Bureau of Indian Affairs boarding schools, they are removed from their parents into a boarding school situation so that they cannot go home in the evenings to speak Navajo. . . . Also we have officials telling us that there are no talented Indians to be trained as teachers and they don't recruit our people.

The suggestions of the conference participants on helping the culturally different gifted are summarized (Gallagher and Kinney, p. 26). Several main themes emerge in the solutions. One of the most important is the cry for more respect for the concept of cultural pluralism in the educational program. The American culture has been enriched by the contributions of many different ethnic and racial groups. A school program that presents only the portrait of a Northern European culture inappropriately narrows the view of our society and discourages children from different backgrounds from making a full contribution.

A second major theme is that the schools should make a much fuller use of the resources of the total community. Persons without formal educational background but with outstanding talents and the ability to inspire gifted children from their own cultural background should be brought into the school program. Such a program would be a "school without walls." The boundaries of the school should be the boundaries of the community.

A third major theme involves the recruitment and training of persons who can apply their knowledge of cultural pluralism for the development of special educational techniques for the gifted. This means major changes in teacher-selection and teacher-training programs. The call for institutional reform was voiced together with some pessimism and hostility about the possibility that such reform will occur. Experience has taught many of the conference participants that schools and universities are highly resistant to change. Consistent citizen pressure seems required to force entrenched organizations such as public schools and universities to make major modifications in existing practices.

Finally, there was recognition that unless we reach key decision makers at the local, state, and federal levels, we will not be able to unlock needed resources to bring most of these suggested solutions into being. It is in the expenditure of scarce resources of money and people, not in the honeyed words of political leaders, that a culture establishes and molds its own character. Future generations will justifiably hold us responsible for how our money is spent now. It is the hope of this working conference group that the clearer delineation of needs and some specific program suggestions can lead to more favorable action for the "talent preservation" of this special group of children.

EDUCATIONAL PROGRAMMING FOR THE CULTURALLY DIFFERENT GIFTED

One of the things that we need to learn is that the educational planning designed for a diverse citizenry should reflect that diversity. It is a hard lesson to learn, and there doesn't seem to be much transfer of training. We should not pretend that because the mean IQ of disadvantaged groups is 85, that *one* program geared to that 85 IQ child fulfills our education responsibilities—any more than if we planned one curriculum for the 100 IQ child and called it American education.

The youngster who has talent and is two standard deviations above the mean of *his* subgroup requires special educational opportunities just as much as, and probably more than, the National Merit Scholarship students. Such an education should start early and take into account both the special conditions of his environment and his giftedness.

Not many educators have spoken on this problem. Riessman (1965) has thought seriously on the different learning styles one can identify with culturally different gifted. These special characteristics and their educational implications are presented in Table 13–1. Such a list is the portrait of a visual, rather than an auditory, learner. The auditory learner can use a linguistic system to hold some ideas and concepts in mind while actively working on related ones. Auditory learning is the mark of the theoretician, the fully arrived intellectual, who does not have to refer back to concrete events to pursue important lines of thought.

Although the curriculum for the talented deprived youngster needs to be formulated in the visual and limited temporal style to deal with the youngster as he is, the goal should be to progressively lead the child who has intellectual talents into an auditory mode, where he can live in the ocean of ideas without having to constantly snorkel his way back to

TABLE 13–1. *Program Adjustments for the Culturally Different Gifted.*

SPECIAL CHARACTERISTICS	EDUCATIONAL CHANGE IMPLICATIONS
Physical and visual rather than aural	Presentation of material should be concrete and a minimum amount of time devoted to teacher lecture or extended discussions; i.e., students should do experiments or go on field trips prior to discussions of general concepts. Role playing an effective device.
Content centered rather than form centered	The emphasis on inquiry training and creativity should be replaced, at least initially, by what is to be learned. The learning of a process or method of attack in problem solving is a more abstract concept and these students often not ready to consider that.
Externally oriented rather than introspective	Children from limited verbal environments tend not to be introverted or introspective and will not respond well to requests for self-examination of their own feelings or thoughts. Require the stimulation of concrete, external sources.
Problem centered rather than abstract centered	Should be presented with specific situations which only gradually lead to inductive thinking. The use of academic games and role playing bring forth the concrete and motoric response.
Slow, careful and patient rather than quick, clever and flexible	There is a temptation to skip steps and leap forward with gifted students. This should be resisted and a methodical orderly progression from one step to the next needed.
Need for structure and control	The elements of progressive education such as permissiveness, introspection, flexibility and lack of stress on discipline and authority ill-suited to this group. There is a need for firmness and structure, particularly in the beginning program stages.

Source: Adapted from F. Riessman. The slow gifted child. In J. Gallagher (Ed.), *Teaching gifted students.* Boston: Allyn and Bacon, 1965, p. 284.

the surface of reality. The ocean of ideas that he swims in should be a familiar ocean and the problems built around his experiences, at least at the elementary level. If he must learn about neighbors, let it be neighbors in surrounding New York or rural North Carolina and not Eskimos or Ecuadorians.

The ideas suggested by Riessman lead to certain kinds of programs. Given that the culturally different gifted like to deal directly with experience rather than with words, that they are externally oriented rather than introverted, and that a strongly structured program is desired, one of our major efforts should be to extend the program beyond the traditional school walls and to involve the surrounding community. The need for an appropriate model of behavior that the talented youngster can identify with and follow is given a sound theoretical base in the work of Bandura (1970). It is the best insurance that constructive patterns of behavior will be the outcome of an enlightened educational program.

Can we develop a program, for example, that will allow the gifted to leave the school for a period of time and spend that time in a business, in a laboratory, in a doctor's office, in a community service program, in those places where they can learn the essence of our culture? In these situations they are learning about the productive dimensions of this culture and not the destructive culture or ecology that many of them may be immersed in.

Taba and Elkins (1966), in discussing differential strategies for culturally disadvantaged students, suggested that the educational program must take into account the differences of their family and social environment (p. 16).

> Yet, for culturally deprived children, school must first both supplement and counteract their social learning if they are to have an equal opportunity to learn. School must also fill the gaps left by inadequate social learning at home and bridge the conflict between the culture of the home and that of the school.

There is a similar emphasis in this program to Riessman's emphasis on slow and orderly progression, without stressing introspective analysis.

Identification of the Culturally Different Gifted

Earlier in this chapter we suggested that a different set of identifying criteria needs to be considered for these groups. Bruch (1970) reanalyzed the data of Kennedy, Van de Riet, and White (1961), seeking to identify the cognitive strengths of a black sample from the southeastern region of the United States. On this basis, Bruch proposes the following criteria (pp. 47–48):

1. The primary identification criterion should be that a child exhibit outstanding powers in one or more abilities valued by his culture; the degree to which he manifests these abilities should be related both to national and to local cultural norms.
2. The secondary criterion would be that applicable to the usual identification tests: he should measure on national norms on both ability and achievement approximately at "bright average" levels or better.
3. A special consideration should be given to those children with demonstrated creativity.
4. Children who show social leadership potentials should also be given

special considerations as having a quality strengthening their identification as gifted.

As in other instances, the specific identification criteria for any program depends, in part, on the nature of the program itself. Identification in the absence of a program is a useless, and somewhat dishonest, activity, for it implies that some special program is about to follow.

Special Programs for Culturally Different Gifted

There are relatively few programs described that focus on the culturally different student of high academic potential from whatever cultural background. Obviously, any program must fit the goals and special needs of the group in question. In most instances the emphasis has been on students from these subcultures who are in serious academic difficulty and in which major remedial attempts are being made. This would seem to be an incomplete strategy. Special efforts must also be made to stimulate those disadvantaged students who have strong leadership potential and high intellectual talent that would, in turn, enable them to stimulate and develop the potential of their total cultural subgroups.

One distinctive program, reported in the literature by Tisdall (1968), was a residential high school for intellectually gifted but culturally disadvantaged children in the state of Kentucky. This program for ninth and tenth graders was a coeducational, nongraded, racially integrated, academic-year school located in a rural area of Shelby County, Kentucky. The objectives of the program were to provide a high school program preparing students for admission to colleges and universities, to provide remedial instruction for talented students who were not living up to their intellectual potential, and incidentally to provide us with more information about such students.

Of the 400 students attending, the average Wechsler IQ was 121. Considering the sociocultural background of the students, it is reasonable to believe that their aptitude was considerably higher. Upon entering the program, many of these students were quite unmotivated and indifferent toward learning. They did not know how to study or organize their work, were oriented toward short-range goals, and had a significant disregard for the fine arts. They liked structured activities and, as Riessman suggests, preferred concrete to abstract learning experiences.

Although the program content was not unusual for high school, including the standard science, social studies, English, language, and so on, the emphasis was on individual and small-group instruction, with no class having more than twelve pupils. The general estimate of the faculty was that although only 10 percent of the students who entered the school in September were achievers, at the end of the first year about half the student body could be so considered, with students winning prizes in national mathematics and writing contests, several accepted in the Upward Bound programs, and so forth.

An unhappy postscript, however, is that the program itself was disbanded after a couple of years, not, apparently, because of the failure of the program itself, but rather because of the social and racial problems that were generated by its interracial character in a southern state at that stage in history

A very similar program was carried out by Wessman (1972). He reports on a group of eighty-two low-income, disadvantaged boys with ability or academic promise who began a summer transition program at Dartmouth College in 1965. These students, following that transitional program, entered thirty-nine preparatory schools that fall, and the results obtained are mainly on the basis of a systematic two-year follow-up. The boys were 70 percent black and the rest a scattering of other culturally different youngsters, with 10 percent of the population white. The fathers' occupations were generally manual labor or low-status, white-collar jobs, and the mothers were predominantly housewives or engaged in unskilled labor.

The focus of the ABC summer program was to concentrate on strengthening these students' abilities in English, reading, and mathematics, and although the program was demanding, there were small classes and an unusual degree of individual help.

Significant changes were reported in terms of increased self-confidence and social ease, greater awareness, more direction and higher goals, and increased tolerance and flexibility. On the other hand, one fourth of the boys reported feeling more tense, anxious, and driven, apparently the price to be paid for stimulating higher expectations and goals.

Wessman concludes (p. 370):

> The findings have made it clear that educational miracles did not occur. According to the two-year reports, only about 30% of the boys actually fit the program's ideal of motivated academic risks, who had improved their scholastic performance through better teaching and their own hard work. . . . The remaining 46% had done mediocre and/or poor work, and in some cases had even declined scholastically.

There were some limited gains attained on the general achievement test, so that the major impact of the program seemed to lie in the dimension of personality attitudes, rather than academic performance *per se*.

The ABC students seemed to adjust reasonably well to their new situation, with less than a third having serious problems, and only a few obviously in deep conflict. Undoubtedly, as Wessman points out, a large measure of that kind of success can be attributed both to careful additional screening of prospects and also to the supportive treatment they received during the program itself. What we have seen is an increasing emphasis on using the summer program to strengthen and elaborate on the existing program for talented youth.

Stallings (1972) provided a series of suggestions for programs for culturally different gifted that went beyond the dimensions of the school setting itself and included suggestions related to the total environment surrounding the child or student. His program suggestions, which seem most appropriate for older students, were divided into four phases:

1. *Assist the child in planning his occupational goal.* Stallings strongly suggested that the child should be allowed to develop his own realistic and attainable goals rather than having such goals thrust upon him by another adult.
2. *Locate individuals in the community who can help in developing student's occupational model.* "A common conflict for the urban child is to realize the benefits of planning a career (which in many cases takes years) when a community hustler obtains instant success in a matter of weeks" (p. 4).
3. *Teachers should effectively start early communications with parents of gifted children.* The parents and teacher should work together to develop the child's motivation and the teacher should share with the parents materials to enhance learning in the home and should share knowledge with parents about vocational and scholastic opportunities.
4. *A clear standard of excellence is needed as a model for all areas of study.* Students should be informed by teachers of their talents by providing students with the opportunity to explore their talents and potential. The child needs to know a well-written paper when he sees one, and he needs to be rewarded for attaining his goal.

One of the temptations for teachers working with the culturally different gifted is to not require the same level of excellence from these students as from those of more traditional middle-class homes. They reason that with students with such a different background, teachers should be satisfied with a somewhat lesser performance. Although every effort should be made to relate the material to the background of the student (a critique of Wright's *Black Boy* or Stone's *King Strut* might be more appropriate content than Thomas Hardy's *Return of the Native*), the requirements of sharp and analytic thinking should not be relaxed.

It does no favor to the culturally different gifted to shade requirements in misdirected sympathy. Sooner or later, in college or before, they will be judged on the same yardstick as other students, and there is good reason to believe that, given a relevant and demanding educational experience, they can hold their own with other students of similar abilities.

One of the devices that can be used for special stimulation are summer programs that, unfettered by regular school and curriculum requirements, can be used experimentally to develop new materials and program activities. Torrance and Torrance (1972) reported on a summer workshop for creative problem solving for disadvantaged students at the elementary school level.

The workshop itself was run in a city park with the usual minimal recreational and crafts facilities, but with a fine ecological environment that could be used to encourage active problem solving and observational activities. Each day began with a large group activity, usually a creative dramatics and problem-solving session, a film made by participants, a dance contest, and the like. This was followed by moderate-sized groups in creative music or dance, or photography and crafts programs.

After a break the session shifted to small-group activities including painting, dramatics, and biology, and then the participants worked in four-person groups under adult supervision on brainstorming and creative problem-solving training and practice. Students were taught how to respond effectively to such questions as

> *"Produce as many ideas as you can about what might happen if water animals could live on land and land animals could live in the sea."*
> *"Produce as many ideas as you can for unusual uses for junked autos."*

Informal evaluation of this program was enthusiastic on the part of students and staff. Students seemed to be able to respond to the specific training and produce many more ideas in problem solving.

One of the standard inhibitors of action for the gifted, and particularly for the culturally different gifted, is the statement that "there is no money." It would be foolish to deny that this does not represent a major barrier, but just as unwise to think that lack of immediate support forecloses any useful program activity. One large community reorganized some of its program to provide the open and flexible program they wished for the culturally different gifted with little or no additional resources; instead they rejuggled the resources already available and instituted careful in-service training to prepare staff for their different roles. The results were program components as follows (Gallagher & Kinney, 1974, p. 120).

1. *Differential staffing and team teaching.* Teachers' aides and tutors supplemented the staff to create a more favorable ratio of students to adults, providing more personalized instruction. Teachers planned related lessons together whenever possible. As a result, students were better equipped to recognize and understand topics, solve problems requiring several skills, and learn subjects from several areas.

2. *Flexible scheduling.* This was dictated primarily by the activities

within a classroom rather than a specific time-block, and students within this flexible scheduling module were not programmed by the regular school class bells.

3. *Independent study and activity time.*   Students were allocated so much time each week to utilize and carry out independent study and work on their own projects individually or in groups.   This proved to be one of the most successful modules in which students felt they could achieve constructively and still get positive reinforcement from adults. Staff members felt the scheduling of still more independent study time would help students develop greater self-direction and initiative.

4. *Multi-media approach to learning.*   A utilization of multi-media devices and materials was an integral part of the learning program itself. It helped the students use various senses such as hearing, viewing, reading, feeling in the learning process and in the reinforcement of learning.

5. *Multi-modal approach.*   In this approach, class time could be scheduled for independent study or cluster activity in small, regular or large groups.

6. *Utilization of community resources.*   Students visited various businesses and industries, museums, and cultural organizations.   Speakers from these units were also pulled in to work with and be part of the major community resource component.

7. *Ungraded classes.*   Seventh, 8th and 9th grade students of high ability worked together in clusters, which changed as activities were restructured.   Combined with tutorials, the clusters provided a rich opportunity for interaction with adults and for peer group relationships.

8. *On-going evaluations.*   Records were maintained for each individual student so that all staff members knew what each student had accomplished.   Evaluations were discussed with the parents and students in the continuation of the on-going assessment.

We have not been overburdened with new educational ideas, concepts, or models in this area.   Hillson and Myers (1963) reported on the Demonstration Guidance Project in New York that later became the Higher Horizons Project, one of the first of the educational efforts to improve the educational status of talented youth from disadvantaged circumstances.   The results of these efforts have been reported as positive, particularly as it concerns improved motivation, reduction of failure, and helping students to continue within the educational stream.   Such projects have not multiplied, however.

Other, similar projects have been developed, such as Project Upward Bound, which uses the summer to help students correct academic deficiencies and provide them with inspiration to continue their studies. Massive attention of almost any sort can increase student motivation. The advantages of such programs can be maximized by providing a sound educational program that fits the needs of the disadvantaged. More sound experimentation with different models is clearly called for.

THE SCHOOL OR THE CULTURE

For some time now public education has served as a marvelously available scapegoat for the problems of a changing society. It is always visible, virtually powerless to strike back, and has enough faults to render plausible whatever the attack. If the child is not motivated to learn, it is the school's fault. If he drops out of school, it is the school's fault. But is it really?

The talented child from the culturally different family, such as Sam, can see farther than others into his own future, and that foresight can cause discouragement as well as enthusiasm. What he may well see in front of him is limited opportunity and a biased society that will not reward him in full measure for his efforts.

Coles (1971), in discussing children of crisis, paints a vivid picture of the discouragement that the migrant or sharecropper child and his family face. One mother is quoted discussing her son, "I want my boy to go plumb through school, but if he does, then what will he do?" What will he do, indeed? It is often the lack of a good answer to that question, rather than the dingy schools or lack of equipment, that can cause the perceptive and talented student to say to himself, "Is all this worth it?"

We can summarize what we have presented as follows:

1. Culturally different talented children do have different attitudes and cognitive characteristics which make them a distinctive educational problem. There are few current examples of exemplary programs in this special area.
2. We need to focus on clear examples and models of how to provide a better education for these children before we, as educators, can expect major support for such programs.
3. We should be open to programs that get outside the walls of the school and involve adults not ordinarily a part of the educational establishment.

SUMMARY

Until a decade or so ago, the portrait of the gifted child was that of a middle-class child from a well-established family well in tune with the majority cultural values of the community. The discovery of many children with substantial talent from other cultural subgroups of the society has come quite recently and creates special educational problems requiring special adjustment in content, style, and environment.

Intelligence does not survive unscratched from social pressures either from inside or outside the cultural subgroup. The verbal abilities so important to standard IQ measures generally are depressed in subcultures where the first language or dialect is different.

A greater interest in the discovery of talent from culturally different subgroups has led to a broadening of standard identification techniques. The emphasis now is on charting outstanding abilities that are specially valued by the subculture. These might be imaginative performance in games or art or dance or music. When these measures supplement the IQ score, where some appropriate adjustments can be made for cultural suppression, many talented youngsters can be found in any subgroup.

The special programming recommended for such groups would place special emphasis on starting from the cultural values of the subgroup. The program might focus more on visual and less on auditory types of input. If it is not the cultural style to be introspective, then the focus of lessons would be on the description of the outer world before attempts are made to bring the child to awareness of the rich inner world that he possesses.

It has been recommended that special attempts be made to use community resources and bring into the school program successful citizens, such as scientists, physicians, businessmen, and artists, who can add to the limited experience of the gifted students. A number of secondary programs for talented youth from cultural subgroups have been shown to be useful and successful.

In the end, the motivation needed to stick out the long and painful educational road is often determined by the children's perceptions of their opportunities in the future. If eight more years of schooling do not seem to get members of the subgroups demonstrably up the social or economic ladder, then their desire for higher education must be limited, no matter how they are counseled. We can enhance that positive motivation for achievement by making sure that America remains in fact, as well as in theory, the land of opportunity for all.

UNRESOLVED ISSUES

1. Can we find the blend of agreed-upon values of the dominant culture and the minority cultures so that a common standing place can be found for those interested in the development of all talented children, without making special education for the gifted elitist on the one hand or anarchistic on the other?

2. What is the nature of training experiences for teachers who come from the dominant culture but must develop a degree of respect and understanding for the special life situations of the culturally different gifted? It is clear that teaching prospective teachers "facts" is not, in itself, useful but it requires some experiences, as well.

3. What are the particular methods by which gifted youngsters can be early identified and placed in a program that allows them to keep pride in their heritage, in their language and patterns of the past, while at the same time allowing them to master the essential knowledge and skills of the dominant culture?

READINGS OF SPECIAL INTEREST

Coles, R. *Children of crisis.* Vol. 2. *Migrants, sharecroppers, mountaineers.* Boston: Little, Brown, 1971.

A detailed personal chronicle of the life settings of children growing up in a variety of difficult environments told by a psychiatrist who lived with the families in migrant camps and rural mountain areas. Rich insight into the emergence of values and interests of young children—the culturally different children.

Gallagher, J. J., & Kinney, L. (Eds.). *Talent delayed—talent denied: A Conference Report.* Reston, Va.: Foundation for Exceptional Children, 1974.

A report of a conference on the special problems and needs of gifted children from cultures different from the standard middle class. Emphasis is placed on the need for a pluralistic educational program to match the American pluralistic society.

Stallings, C. *Gifted disadvantaged children.* National Leadership Training Institute, Teacher Education/Early Childhood, Technical Paper. Storrs, Conn.: University of Connecticut, 1972.

A description of the types of program adjustments and teacher procedures that can be used for gifted students from urban settings. Stresses the use of the community as the learning environment and the need to salvage talent from urban ghettoes that may drop out.

Taba, H., & Elkins, D. *Teaching strategies for the culturally disadvantaged.* Chicago: Rand McNally, 1966.

The generation of particular strategies for a specific target group of children. Stresses the practical level using concrete experience that can later build inductively to larger conceptual understandings. Less emphasis on verbal or abstract ideas unsupported or illustrated by direct experience.

References

ABRAMOWITZ, J., & HALLIBURTON, W. *Searching for values: Pathways to the world of English.* New York: Globe, 1973.

ADLER, M. A study of the effects of ethnic origin on giftedness. *Gifted Child Quarterly,* 1963, **7,** 98–101.

AIKEN, L., JR. Attitudes towards mathematics. *Review of Educational Research,* 1970, **40,** 551–596.

ALTUS, W. Birth order and its sequelae. *Science,* 1966, **151,** 44–49.

ARNOLD, J. Useful creative techniques. In S. Parnes & H. Harding (Eds.), *A source book for creative thinking.* New York: Scribner's, 1962.

ASTIN, H. Sex differences on mathematical and scientific precocity. Paper presented at the meeting of the AAAS, Washington, D.C., 1972.

ATKIN, J. Research styles in science education. *Journal of Research in Science Teaching,* 1967–1968, **5,** 338–345.

ATKIN, J., & WYATT, S. *Astronomy: Charting the universe.* Urbana, Ill.: Elementary School Science Project, University of Illinois, 1962.

Baboons. Cambridge, Mass.: Education Development Center, 1968.

BACHTOLD, L. *Counseling: Instructional programs for intellectually gifted students.* Sacramento, Calif.: California State Department of Education, 1966. (ED 011 124)

BACHTOLD, L. Personality differences among high ability underachievers. *Journal of Educational Research,* 1969, **63,** 16–18.

BACHTOLD, L., & WERNER, E. Personality profiles of gifted women: Psychologists. *American Psychologist,* 1970, **25,** 234–243.

BANDURA, A. *Principles of behavior modification.* New York: Holt, 1969.

BARBE, W. Characteristics of gifted children. *Educational Administration and Supervision,* 1955, **41,** 207–217.

BARRON, F. *Creative person and creative process.* New York: Holt, 1969.

BAYLEY, N. Development of mental abilities. In P. Mussen (Ed.), *Carmichael's manual of child psychology.* Chicago: Rand McNally, 1970.

BAYLEY, N., & ODEN, M. The maintenance of intellectual ability in gifted adults. *Journal of Gerontology,* 1955, **10,** 91–107.

BAYLEY, N., & SCHAEFER, E. Relationships between socioeconomic variables and the behavior of mothers toward young children. *Journal of Genetic Psychology*, 1960, **96**, 61–77.

BAYMUR, F., & PATTERSON, C. H. Three methods of assisting underachieving high school students. *Journal of Counseling Psychology*, 1960, **7**, 83–90.

BEALS, A. *Culture in process.* New York: Holt, 1967.

BEBERMAN, M. The University of Illinois school mathematics program. *School Review*, 1957, **65**, 457–465.

BEGLE, E., & WILSON, J. Evaluation of mathematics programs. In *Mathematics education.* 69th Yearbook NSSE. Chicago: University of Chicago Press, 1970.

BERENSON, D. Methods of scientific thinking. *Grade Teacher*, 1966, **81**, 70–74.

BERKOWITZ, L. *The development of motives and values in the child.* New York: Basic Books, 1964.

BERNE, E. *Games people play.* New York: Grove Press, 1964.

Biological Science Curriculum Study. *Biological science: An inquiry into life.* New York: Harcourt, 1963.

Biological Science Curriculum Study. *Biological science: Molecules to man.* Boston: Houghton Mifflin, 1963.

Biological Science Curriculum Study. *High school biology.* Chicago: Rand McNally, 1963.

BISHOP, W. Successful teachers of the gifted. *Exceptional Children*, 1968, **34**, 317–325.

BORG, W. *An evaluation of ability grouping.* United States Office of Education Cooperative Research Project No. 577. Logan, Utah: Utah State University, 1964.

BOTTS, T. A changing mathematics program. In *Mathematics education.* 69th Yearbook NSSE. Chicago: University of Chicago Press, 1970.

BRAGA, J. Early admission: Opinion vs. evidence. *Elementary School Journal*, 1972, **72**, 35–46.

BRUCH, C. A proposed rationale for the identification and development of the gifted disadvantaged. *Gifted Child Newsletter*, 1970, **12**, 40–49.

BRUNER, J. *The process of education.* Cambridge, Mass.: Harvard University Press, 1960.

BRUNER, J. *Toward a theory of instruction.* Cambridge, Mass.: Belknap Press, 1966.

BRUNER, J. *Man: A course of study.* Cambridge, Mass.: Educational Development Center, 1970.

BURGDORF, K. *Outstanding Negro high school students: A one-year follow-up.* Evanston, Ill.: National Merit Scholarship Corporation, 1969.

Cambridge Conference on School Mathematics. *Goals for the correlation of elementary science and mathematics: The report on the correlation of science and mathematics in the schools.* Boston: Houghton Mifflin, 1969.

COLEMAN, J. S., CAMPBELL, E. Q., HOBSON, C. J., McPARTLAND, J., MOOD, A. M., WEINFELD, F. D., & YORK, R. L. *Equality of educational opportunity.* Washington, D.C.: U.S. Office of Education, 1966.

COLES, R. *Children of crisis.* Vol. 2. *Migrants, sharecroppers, mountaineers.* Boston: Little, Brown, 1971.

CONANT, J. B. *The American high school today.* New York: McGraw-Hill, 1959.

COVINGTON, M., CRUTCHFIELD, R., & DAVIES, L. *The productive thinking program.* Berkeley, Calif.: Brazelton Printing Co., 1966.

COX, C. *Genetic studies of genius.* Vol. 2. *The early mental traits of three hundred geniuses.* Stanford, Calif.: Stanford University Press, 1926.

CROWDER, T., & GALLAGHER, J. J. The adjustment of gifted children in the regular classroom: Case studies. *Exceptional Children,* 1957, **23,** 353–363, 396–398.

CRUTCHFIELD, R., & COVINGTON, M. Programmed instruction and creativity. *Programmed Instruction,* 1965, **4,** 1–2, 8–10.

DELLAS, M., & GAIER, E. L. Identification of creativity: The individual. *Psychological Bulletin,* 1970, **73,** 55–73.

DESSERT, D., & FRANDSEN, H. Research on teaching secondary school mathematics. In R. Travers (Ed.), *Second handbook of research on teaching.* Chicago: Rand McNally, 1973.

DEWING, K. Family influences on creativity: A review and discussion. *Journal of Special Education,* 1970, **4,** 399–404.

DODDER, C., & DODDER, B. *Decision making.* Boston: Beacon Press, 1968.

DREWS, E., & TEAHAN, J. Parental attitudes and academic achievement. *Journal of Clinical Psychology,* 1957, **13,** 328–332.

DUBOIS, R. *Pasteur and modern science.* New York: Anchor Books, Doubleday, 1960.

Education of the gifted and talented. Subcommittee on Labor & Public Welfare, U.S. Senate, March 1972.

Education of mentally gifted minors. Sacramento, Calif.: California State Department of Education, 1971.

ENDRES, M., LAMB, P., & LAZARUS, A. Selected objectives in the English language arts. *Elementary English,* 1969, **46,** 418–430.

ENNEVER, L., & HARLEN, W. *With objectives in mind.* Bristol, England: School Council Publications, School of Education, University of Bristol, 1971.

FEATHERSTONE, J. Experience in learning. *New Republic,* 1968, **159** (24).

FELDHUSEN, J., TREFFINGER, D., & ELIAS, R. The right of programmed instruction for the gifted. *National Society for Programmed Instruction Journal,* 1969, **8,** 6–11.

FINK, D. *Computers and the human mind.* New York: Anchor Books, Doubleday, 1966.

FLANAGAN, J. *Project Talent 1957–70: Selected findings and data.* Pittsburgh: University of Pittsburgh, 1970.

FLANAGAN, J. C., DAILEY, J. T., SHAYCOFT, M. F., GORHAM, W. A., ORR, D. B., & GOLDBERG, I. *Design for a study of American youth.* Boston: Houghton Mifflin Co., 1962.

FLANDERS, N. Interaction analysis in the classroom. In A. Simon & E. G.

Boyer (Eds.), *Mirrors for behavior.* Vol. 2. Philadelphia: Research for Better Schools, Inc., 1957.

FRENCH, J. L., & CARDEN, B. W. Characteristics of high mental ability dropouts. *Vocational Guidance Quarterly,* 1968, 162–168.

FRIERSON, E. C. Upper and lower status gifted children: A study of differences. *Exceptional Children,* 1965, **32,** 83–90.

GAIR, M. Rorschach characteristics of a group of very superior seven year old children. *Rorschach Research Exchange,* 1944, **8,** 31–37.

GALLAGHER, J. J. Social status of children related to intelligence, propinquity, and social perception. *Elementary School Journal,* 1958, **58,** 225–231.

GALLAGHER, J. J. Expressive thought by gifted children in the classroom. *Elementary English,* 1965, **42,** 559–568. (a)

GALLAGHER, J. J. The influence of a special school on cognitive style and attitudes of gifted students. Springfield, Ill.: Illinois Department for Program Planning for the Gifted, Office of the Superintendent of Public Instruction, 1965. (b)

GALLAGHER, J. J. (Ed.) *Teaching gifted students: A book of readings.* Boston: Allyn and Bacon, 1965. (c)

GALLAGHER, J. J. *Ethics and moral judgment in children: A pilot investigation.* Boston: Unitarian Universalist Association, 1966. (a)

GALLAGHER, J. J. *Leadership training for the gifted.* In Gallagher, J. J., Godman, V., Retzer, K., Schevers, M., Shaffer, F., Simmons, W., & Weiser, M. (Eds.), *Educational programs and planning for gifted students.* Urbana, Ill.: Institute for Research on Exceptional Children, University of Illinois, 1966. (b)

GALLAGHER, J. J. *Research summary on gifted child education.* Springfield, Ill.: Office of Superintendent of Public Instruction, 1966. (c)

GALLAGHER, J. J. Teacher variation in concept presentation in Biological Science Curriculum Study curriculum program. Biological Science Curriculum Study *Newsletter,* 1967, No. 30, 8–19.

GALLAGHER, J. J. Three studies of the classroom. In J. J. Gallagher, G. Nuthall, & B. Rosenshine, *Classroom observation.* AERA Monograph Series No. 6. Chicago: Rand McNally, 1970. Pp. 74–108.

GALLAGHER, J. Technical assistance—a new device for quality educational services for the gifted. *TAG Newsletter,* 1974, **16,** 5–8.

GALLAGHER, J. J., ASCHNER, M., & JENNE, W. *Productive thinking of gifted children in classroom interaction.* Council for Exceptional Children Research Monograph Series B5. Arlington, Va.: Council for Exceptional Children, 1967.

GALLAGHER, J. J., et al. *Analysis of hearings held by Regional Commissioners of Education on education of the gifted. Education of the gifted and talented.* Report to the Congress of the United States by the U.S. Commissioner of Education and background papers submitted to the U.S. Office of Education. Washington, D.C.: GPO, 1972.

GALLAGHER, J. J., & CROWDER, T. The adjustment of gifted children in the regular classroom. *Exceptional Children,* 1957, **23,** 306–312, 317–319.

GALLAGHER, J. J., GREENMAN, M., KARNES, M., & KING, A. Individual classroom adjustments for gifted children in elementary schools. *Exceptional Children*, 1960, **26**, 409–422, 432.

GALLAGHER, J. J., & KINNEY, L. (Eds.) *Talent delayed—talent denied: A conference report.* Reston, Va.: Foundation for Exceptional Children, 1974.

GALLAGHER, J. J., SHAFFER, F., PHILLIPS, S., ADDY, S., RAINER, M., & NELSON, T. *A system of topic classification.* Urbana: University of Illinois Institute for Research on Exceptional Children, 1966.

GETZELS, J. W., & DILLON, J. The nature of giftedness and the education of the gifted. In R. Travers (Ed.), *Second handbook of research on teaching.* Chicago: Rand McNally, 1973. Pp. 689–731.

GETZELS, J. W., & JACKSON, P. W. *Creativity and intelligence.* New York: Wiley, 1962.

GHISELIN, B. (Ed.) *The creative process.* New York: New American Library, 1952.

GLASS, B. The Japanese science education centers. *Science*, 1966, **154**, 221–228.

GOERTZEL, V., & GOERTZEL, M. *Cradles of eminence.* Boston: Little, Brown, 1962.

GOLDBERG, M. A three year program at DeWitt Clinton High School to help bright underachievers. *High Points*, 1959, **41**, 5–35.

GOLDBERG, M. *Research on the talented.* New York: Bureau of Publications, Teachers College, Columbia University, 1965.

GOLDBERG, M., PASSOW, A., JUSTMAN, J., & HAGE, G. *The effects of ability grouping.* New York: Bureau of Publications, Teachers College, Columbia University, 1965.

GOODLAD, J. I. *School curriculum reform in the United States.* New York: Fund for the Advancement of Education, 1964.

GOWAN, J. *Development of the creative individual.* San Diego, Calif.: Robert Knapp Publishers, 1972.

GOWAN, J., & GROTH, N. The development of vocational choice in gifted children. In J. Gowan (Ed.), *The guidance and measurement of intelligence development and creativity.* Northridge, Calif.: San Fernando Valley State College, 1972.

GRACE, H. A., & BOOTH, N. L. Is the gifted child a social isolate? *Peabody Journal of Education*, 1958, **35**, 195–196.

GRUPE, A. Adjustment and acceptance of mentally superior children in regular and special fifth grade classes in a public school system. Unpublished doctoral dissertation, University of Illinois, 1961.

GUILFORD, J. P. Creativity. *American Psychologist*, 1950, **5**, 444–454.

GUILFORD, J. P. Creativity: Yesterday, today, tomorrow. *Journal of Creative Behavior*, 1967. **1**, 3–14. (a)

GUILFORD, J. P. *The nature of human intelligence.* New York: McGraw-Hill, 1967. (b)

HANDLIN, O. *The uprooted.* New York: Grosset and Dunlap, 1951.

HARVEY, O. J. Some situational and cognitive determinants of dissonance resolution. *Journal of Personality and Social Psychology*, 1965, **1**(4), 349–355.

HATCH, M. Elementary number theory (mimeographed report). Palo Alto, Calif.: School Mathematics Study Group, 1965.

HAWKINS, D. Messing about in science. *Science and Children.* Washington, D.C.: National Science Teachers Association, 1965.

HERSEY, J. *The child buyer.* New York: Knopf, 1960.

HILDRETH, G. Characteristics of young gifted children. *Journal of Genetic Psychology,* 1938, **53,** 287–311.

HILLSON, H. T., & MYERS, F. The demonstration guidance project, 1957–1962. Albany: New York Board of Education, 1963.

HISKEY, M. Twelve years of early admission in Nebraska. In M. Reynolds (Ed.), *Early school admission for mentally advanced children.* Reston, Va.: Council for Exceptional Children, 1962.

HOLLINGWORTH, L. *Children above 180 IQ.* New York: World Book, 1942.

HOUSE, E., KERINS, T., & STEELE, J. *Illinois Gifted Program Evaluation.* Urbana, Ill.: Center for Instructional Research and Curriculum Evaluation, University of Illinois, 1972.

HOUSE, E., KERINS, T., & STEELE, J. *The demonstration center: An appraisal of the Illinois experience.* Urbana, Ill.: Center for Instructional Research and Curriculum Evaluation, University of Illinois, 1969.

HUGHES, L. *The dream keeper.* New York: Knopf, 1937.

Introduction to the elementary science study. Cambridge, Mass.: Educational Development Corporation, 1966.

JACKSON, D. M., & ROGGE, W. M. *Inservice education—an integral part of the Illinois plan for program development for gifted children.* Urbana: University of Illinois, 1965.

JOHNSON, G. *A history for Peter.* New York: Morrow, 1960.

JOHNSON, G. O., & KIRK, S. A. Are mentally handicapped children segregated in the regular grades? *Exceptional Children,* 1950, **17,** 65–68.

JOHNSON, G. W. *Communism: An American's view.* New York: Morrow, 1964.

JONES, R. *Fantasy and feeling in education.* New York: New York University Press, 1968.

KAGAN, J. Impulsive and reflective children: The significance of conceptual tempo. In J. Krumboltz (Ed.), *Learning and the educational process.* Chicago: Rand McNally, 1965. Pp. 133–161.

KARNES, M., McCOY, G. M., ZEHRBACH, R. R., WOLLERSHEIM, J., & CLARIZIO, H. F. The efficacy of two organizational plans for underachieving intellectually gifted children. *Exceptional Children,* 1963, **29,** 438–446.

KARNES, M. B., TESKA, J. A., & HODGINS, A. S. The successful implementation of a highly specific preschool instructional program by paraprofessional teachers. *Journal of Special Education,* 1970, 4, 69–80.

KARNES, M., ZEHRBACH, R. R., STUDLEY, W. M., & WRIGHT, W. R. *Culturally disadvantaged children of higher potential: Intellectual functioning and educational implications.* Champaign, Ill.: Champaign Community Unit 4 Schools, 1965.

KARPLUS, R. What's new in curriculum—physical sciences. *Nations Schools,* 1969, **84,** 35–36.

KEATING, D., & STANLEY, J. Extreme measures for the exceptionally gifted in mathematics and science. *Educational Researcher*, 1972, **1**, 3–7.

KELLEY, J. Number systems of arithmetic. In *Mathematics education*, 69th Yearbook NSSE. Chicago: University of Chicago Press, 1970.

KENNEDY, W., VAN DE RIET, V., & WHITE, J. *Standardization of the 1960 revision of the Stanford–Binet Intelligence Scale on Negro elementary school children in the southeast U.S.* Tallahassee: Human Development Clinic, Florida State University, 1961.

KIRK, S. A. *Educating exceptional children* (2nd ed.). Boston: Houghton Mifflin, 1972.

KLINE, M. *Why Johnny can't add: The failure of the new math.* New York: St. Martin's, 1973.

KLOPFER, L. Evaluation of learning in science. In B. Bloom, J. Hastings, & G. Madaus (Eds.), *Handbook on formative and summative evaluation of student learning.* New York: McGraw-Hill, 1971. Pp. 559–642.

KOESTLER, A. *The act of creation.* New York: Macmillan, 1964.

KOHLBERG, L, & TURIEL, E. Moral development and moral education. In G. Lesser (Ed.), *Psychology and educational practice.* Glenview, Ill.: Scott, Foresman, 1971, 410–465.

KOUGH, J. Administrative provisions for the gifted, in B. Shertzer (Ed.), *Working with superior students.* Chicago: Science Research Associates, 1960.

LAKE, T. P. Their classroom is the world. *Teaching Exceptional Children,* 1973, **6**(1), 6–15.

LIGHTFOOT, G. *Personality characteristics of bright and dull children.* Contributions to Education No. 969. New York: Teachers College, Columbia University, 1951.

LOMBROSO, C. *The man of genius.* London: Walter Scott. 1893.

LONNON, G. Noninterference—independent study. In W. Rogge & E. Stormer (Eds.), *Inservice training for teachers of the gifted.* Champaign, Ill.: Stipes Publ. Co., 1966.

LUCITO, L. J. Independence-conformity behavior as a function of intellect: Bright and dull children. *Exceptional Children,* 1964, **31**, 5–13.

LYON, H. *Learning to feel, feeling to learn.* Columbus, Ohio: Merrill, 1971.

MACKINNON, D. The nature and nurture of creative talent. *American Psychologist,* 1962. **17**, 484–495.

MACKWORTH, N. H. Originality. *American Psychologist,* 1965, **20**, 51–66.

MARLAND, S. *Education of the gifted and talented.* Report to the Subcommittee on Education, Committee on Labor and Public Welfare, U.S. Senate, Washington, D.C., 1972.

MARSH, P., & GORTNER, R. *Federal aid to science education.* Syracuse, N.Y.: Syracuse University Press, 1963.

MARTINSON, R. *Educational programs for gifted pupils.* Sacramento, Calif.: California State Department of Education, 1961. (Final report of the California Pilot Project)

MARTINSON, R. An analysis of problems and priorities: Advocate survey and statistics sources. *Education of the gifted and talented.* Report to the

Congress of the United States by the U.S. Commissioner of Education and background papers submitted to the U.S. Office of Education. Washington, D.C.: GPO, 1972.

MARTINSON, R., HERMANSON, D., & BANKS, G. An independent study-seminar program for the gifted. *Exceptional Children*, 1972, **5**, 421–425.

MARTINSON, R., & SEAGOE, M. *The abilities of young children.* Washington, D.C.: Council for Exceptional Children, 1967.

MASLOW, A. *Motivation and personality* (2nd ed.). New York: Harper & Row, 1970.

MAYOR, J. *The University of Maryland Mathematics Project.* Progress Report No. 11. College Park, Md.: University of Maryland, College of Education, 1966.

McGILLIVRAY, R. H. Differences in home background between high-achieving and low-achieving gifted children: A study of one hundred grade eight pupils in the City of Toronto Public Schools. *Ontario Journal of Educational Research*, 1964, **6**, 99–106.

MEEKER, M. *The structure of intellect: Its interpretation and uses.* Columbus, Ohio: Merrill, 1969.

MENSH, I. Rorschach study of the gifted child. *Exceptional Children*, 1950, **17**, 8–14.

MILLER, R. V. Social status and socioempathetic differences among mentally superior, mentally typical and mentally retarded children. *Exceptional Children*, 1956, **23**, 114–119.

MITCHELL, JONI, "Both sides, now." New York: Siquomb Publ. Corp. (Division of Warner Bros.), 1967.

MORRIS, G. A stimulating seminar for rural youth. *Journal of the National Association of Women Deans and Counselors*, 1957, **21**, 31–34.

MORRISON, P. The curricular triangle and its style. Educational Services, Inc. *Quarterly Report.* Cambridge, Mass.: Educational Services, 1964 (Summer–Fall ed.)

MORROW, W. R., & WILSON, R. C. Family relations of bright high achieving and underachieving high school boys. *Child Development*, 1961, **32**, 501–510.

NEWELL, A., SHAW, J. C., & SIMON, H. H. The processes of creative thinking. In H. Gruber, G. Terrell, & M. Wertheimer (Eds.), *Contemporary approaches to creative thinking.* New York: Atherton, 1962.

NICHOLS, R. C. The National Merit Twin Study. In S. G. Vandenberg (Ed.), *Methods and goals in human behavior genetics.* New York: Academic Press, 1965.

NICHOLS, R. C. The origin and development of talent. *National Merit Scholarship Corporation Research Reports*, 1966, **2**(10), 20 pp.

ODEN, M. *The fulfillment of promise: Forty-year follow-up of the Terman Gifted Group.* Stanford, Calif.: Stanford University, Department of Psychology, Genetic Psychology Monographs, Vol. 77, 1968, 3–93.

O'SHEA, A. Low achievement syndrome among bright junior high school boys. *Journal of Educational Research*, 1970, **63**, 257–262.

PAGE, D. A. Probability. In *24th Year Book.* Washington, D.C.: The National Council of Teachers of Mathematics, 1959. Pp. 229–271.

PAGE, D. A. Maneuvers on lattices. In W. Martin & D. Pinck (Eds.), *Curriculum improvement and innovation.* Cambridge, Mass.: Robert Bentley, 1966.

PARNES, S. J. *Programming creative behavior.* Buffalo, N.Y.: State University of New York, 1966.

PARNES, S. J., & NOLLER, R. B. Applied creativity: The Creative Studies Project II. Results of the two year program. *Journal of Creative Behavior,* 1972, **6**(3), 164–186.

PERKINS, H. V. Classroom behavior and underachievement. *American Educational Research Journal,* 1965, **2**, 1–12.

PIAGET, J. Piaget's theory. In P. Mussen (Ed.), *Carmichael's manual of child psychology.* Chicago: Rand McNally, 1970.

PIERCE, J. V. Personality and achievement among able high school boys. *Journal of Individual Psychology,* 1961, **17**, 101–102.

PIERCE, J. W., & BOWMAN, P. Motivation patterns of superior high school students. *Cooperative Research Monograph No. 2,* 1960, 33–66.

PLOWMAN, P., & RICE, J. *California Project Talent. Final report.* Sacramento, Calif.: California State Department of Education, 1967.

POSTELTHWAIT, S., NOVAK, J., & MURRAY, H. *The audio-tutorial approach to learning: Through independent study and integrated experiences.* Minneapolis: Burgess, 1969.

POSTMAN, N., & WEINGARTNER, C. *Teaching as a subversive activity.* New York: Delacorte Press, 1969.

POTTER, S. *The theory and practice of gamesmanship.* New York: Holt, 1948.

POTTER, S. *Oneupmanship.* New York: Holt, 1962.

PRESSEY, S. L. Concerning the nature and nurture of genius. *Science,* 1955, **68**, 123–129.

PROVUS, M. Ability grouping in arithmetic. *Elementary School Journal,* 1960, **60**, 391–398.

RABI, I. I. *Science, the center of culture.* New York: World, 1970.

RAMASESHAN, P. H. The social and emotional adjustment of the gifted. Unpublished doctoral dissertation, University of Nebraska, 1957.

RAPH, J. B., GOLDBERG, M. L., & PASSOW, A. H. *Bright underachievers.* New York: Teachers College Press, Columbia University, 1966.

RATHS, L., HARMEN, M., & SIMON, S. *Values and teaching: Working with values in the classroom.* Columbus, Ohio: Merrill, 1966.

REESE, H., & PARNES, S. Programming creative behavior. *Child Development.* 1970, **41**, 413–423.

RENZULLI, J. S. Identifying key features in programs for the gifted. *Exceptional Children,* 1968, 35, 217–221.

RENZULLI, J. *New directions in creativity.* New York: Harper & Row, 1973.

REYNOLDS, M., BIRCH, J., & TUSETH, A. Review of research on early admission. In M. Reynolds (Ed.), *Early school admission for mentally advanced children.* Reston, Va.: Council for Exceptional Children, 1962.

RICE, J. California Project Talent: A unique educational development. Paper presented at the California Project Talent Western Regional Conference, San Francisco, Calif., November 1966.

RICE, J. *The gifted: Developing total talent.* Springfield, Ill.: Charles C Thomas, 1970.

RICE, J., & BANKS, G. Opinions of gifted students regarding secondary school programs. *Exceptional Children,* 1967, **34**, 269–273.

RIEDSEL, C., & BURNS, P. Research on the teaching of elementary school mathematics. In R. Travers (Ed.), *Second handbook of research on teaching.* Chicago: Rand McNally, 1973. Pp. 1149–1176.

RIESSMAN, F. The slow gifted child. In J. Gallagher (Ed.), *Teaching gifted students: A book of readings.* Boston: Allyn and Bacon, 1965.

ROBECK, M. Special classes for intellectually gifted students. In P. Plowman & J. Rice (Eds.), *California Project Talent.* Sacramento, Calif.: California State Department of Education, 1967.

ROE, A. *The making of a scientist.* New York: Dodd, Mead, 1952.

ROGGE, W., & STORMER, G. *Inservice training for teachers of the gifted.* Champaign, Ill.: Stipes Publ. Co., 1966.

ROSSMILLER, R., HALE, J., & FROHREICH, L. *Educational programs for exceptional children: Resource configurations and costs.* Washington, D.C.: National Education Finance Project, 1970.

ROTHNEY, J., & SANBORN, M. P. *Promising practices in the education of superior students: A demonstration program.* Madison, Wis.: University of Wisconsin, 1968.

RUTHERFORD, F., HOLTON, G., & WATSON, F. *The project physics course.* New York: Holt, 1970.

RYDER, V. A docent program in science for gifted elementary pupils. *Exceptional Children,* 1972, **38**, 629–631.

SANBORN, M., & NIEMIEC, C. Identifying values of superior high school students. *The School Counselor,* 1971, **18**, 237–245.

SANBORN, M., PULVINO, C., & WUNDERLIN, R. *Research reports: Superior students in Wisconsin high schools.* Madison, Wis.: University of Wisconsin, 1971.

SANFORD, N. Personality development during the college years. *Journal of Social Issues,* 1956, **12**(4), 3–70.

SATO, I. Institute on the gifted and the talented: A multipurposed project. *TAG Gifted Children Newsletter,* 1973, 1–16.

SCHAEFER, C. A psychological study of ten exceptionally creative adolescent girls. *Exceptional Children,* 1970, **36**, 431–441.

School Mathematics Study Group. *Junior high school mathematics units.* Vol. 3. *Applications.* New Haven, Conn.: Yale University Press, 1959.

SCHWAB, J. J. Structure of the disciplines: Meanings and significances. In G. W. Ford & L. Pugno (Eds.), *The structure of knowledge and the curriculum.* Chicago: Rand McNally, 1964.

SCHWARTZ, P. A compendium of methods for the teaching of science to gifted children. *Science Education,* 1968, **52**, 130–134.

SCOTT, L. *Trends in elementary school mathematics.* Chicago: Rand McNally, 1966.

SCRIVEN, M. *Applied logic: An introduction to scientific reasoning.* Palo Alto, Calif.: Behavioral Research Laboratories, 1965.

SEARS, R. R., MACCOBY, E., & LEVIN, H. *Patterns of child rearing*. New York: Harper and Row, 1957.

SELYE, H. *The stress of life*. New York: McGraw-Hill, 1956.

SENESH, L. The organic curriculum: A new experience in economic education. In J. Gallagher (Ed.), *Teaching gifted students: A book of readings*. Boston: Allyn and Bacon, 1965.

SHAFTEL, F., & SHAFTEL, G. *Role playing for social values*. Englewood Cliffs, N.J.: Prentice-Hall, 1967.

SHAW, M. C. *The interrelationship of selected personality factors in high ability underachieving school children, Project 58–M–1*. Sacremento Calif.: California State Department of Public Health, 1961.

SHAW, M. C., & McCUEN, J. T. The onset of academic underachievement in bright children. *Journal of Educational Psychology*, 1960, **51**, 103–108.

SHOUKSMITH, G., & TAYLOR, J. W. The effect of counseling on the achievement of high-ability pupils. *British Journal of Educational Psychology*, 1964, **34**, 51–57.

SHULMAN, L. Psychology and mathematics education. In *Mathematics education*, 69th Yearbook NSSE. Chicago: University of Chicago Press, 1970.

SHULMAN, L., & TAMIR, F. Research on teaching in the natural sciences. In R. Travers (Ed.), *Second handbook of research in teaching*. Chicago: Rand McNally, 1973.

SILBERMAN, C. *Crisis in the classroom*. New York: Random House, 1970.

SIMON, A., & BOYER, E. (Eds.). *Mirrors for behavior*. Philadelphia: Center for the Study of Teaching, Temple University, 1967.

SISK, D. Teacher must understand the complexities of urban culture. *The Gifted Pupil* (Newsletter of Programs for Mentally Gifted Minors, California State Department of Education), 1970, **5**, 11–12.

SISTER JOSEPHINA. Teachers' reaction to gifted children. *Gifted Child Quarterly*, 1961, **5**, 42–44.

SKLARSKY, S., & BAXTER, M. R. Science study with a community accent. *Elementary School Journal*, 1961, **61**, 301–307.

SMITH, H. A. *The teaching of a concept*. Washington, D.C.: National Science Teachers Association, 1966.

SMITH, R. M. *The relationship of creativity to social class*, United States Office of Education Cooperative Research Project No. 2250. Pittsburgh: University of Pittsburgh, 1965.

SNOW, C. P. *The two cultures and the scientific revolution*. New York: Cambridge University Press, 1960.

STALLINGS, C. *Gifted disadvantaged children*. National Leadership Institute, Teacher Education/Early Childhood, Technical Paper. Storrs, Conn.: University of Connecticut, 1972.

STEELE, J., HOUSE, E., LAPAN, S., & KERINS, T. *Instructional climate in Illinois gifted classes*. Urbana, Ill.: University of Illinois Center for Instructional Research and Curriculum Evaluation, 1970.

STRODTBECK, F. Family interaction values and achievement. In D. McClelland (Ed.), *Talent and society*. Princeton, N.J.: Van Nostrand Reinhold, 1958.

SUCHMAN, R. Inquiry and education. In J. Gallagher (Ed.), *Teaching gifted students: A book of readings*. Boston: Allyn and Bacon, 1965.

SUPPES, P. *Sets and numbers: Teacher's manual for Book 1*. Stanford, Calif.: Stanford University, 1960.

SUPPES, P., & SEARLE, B. The computer teaches arithmetic. *School Review*, 1971, **78**, 213–225.

TABA, H., & ELKINS, D. *Teaching strategies for the culturally disadvantaged*. Chicago: Rand McNally, 1966.

TABA, H., & HILLS, J. L. *Teacher handbook for Contra Costa social studies, Grades 1–6*. San Francisco: San Francisco State College, 1965.

TANNENBAUM, A. *Adolescent attitudes toward academic brilliance*. New York: Bureau of Publications, Teachers College, Columbia University, 1962.

TENENBERG, M., & DETHLEFSEN, E. *Students and teachers: Strategies for discussion, and what is anthropology*. Washington, D.C.: American Anthropological Association, 1972.

TERMAN, L. The discovery and encouragement of exceptional talent. *American Psychologist*, 1954, **9**, 221–230.

TERMAN, L., & ODEN, M. *Genetic studies of genius*. Vol. 4. *The gifted child grows up*. Stanford, Calif.: Stanford University Press, 1947.

TERMAN, L. W., & ODEN, M. The Stanford studies of the gifted. In P. Witty (Ed.), *The gifted child*. Boston: Heath, 1951.

TERMAN, L., & ODEN, M. *Genetic studies of genius*. Vol. 5. *The gifted group at mid life*. Stanford, Calif.: Stanford University Press, 1959.

TISDALL, W. A high school for disadvantaged students of high academic potential. *The High School Journal*, 1968, **52**, 51–61.

TOFFLER, A. *Future shock*. New York: Bantam, 1971.

TORRANCE, E. P. Explorations in creative thinking in the early school years. IV: Highly intelligent and highly creative children in a laboratory school. *Research Memorandum BER 59–7*. Minneapolis: University of Minnesota, Bureau of Educational Research, College of Education, 1959.

TORRANCE, E. P. *Rewarding creative behavior*. Englewood Cliffs, N.J.: Prentice-Hall, 1965.

TORRANCE, E. P. *Creativity*. Belmont, Calif.: Dimensions Publ. Co., 1969.

TORRANCE, E. Are the Torrance tests of creative thinking biased against or in favor of "disadvantaged" groups? *Gifted Child Quarterly*, 1971, **15**, 75–80.

TORRANCE, E. Creative young women in today's world. *Exceptional Children*, 1972, **39**, 597–603.

TORRANCE, E. Broadening concepts of giftedness in the 70's. In S. Kirk & F. Lord (Eds.), *Exceptional children: Educational resources and perspectives*. Boston: Houghton Mifflin, 1974.

TORRANCE, E., & TORRANCE, P. Combining creative problem-solving with creative expressive activities in the education of disadvantaged young people. *Journal of Creative Behavior*, 1972, **6**, 1–10.

TOYNBEE, A. Is America neglecting her creative talents? In C. Taylor (Ed.), *Creativity across education*. Ogden, Utah: University of Utah Press, 1968.

TREFFINGER, D., & RIPPLE, R. Programmed instruction in creative problem solving. *Educational Leadership*, 1971, 667–675.

TURIEL, E. Stage transition in moral development. In R. Travers (Ed.), *The second handbook of research on teaching*. Chicago: Rand McNally, 1973.

WALBERG, H. Physics, feminity and creativity. *Developmental Psychology*, 1969, 1, 47–54.

WALLACH, M. Creativity. In *Carmichael's Manual of Child Psychology*. Vol. 1. New York: Wiley, 1970.

WALLACH, M., & KOGAN, N. *Modes of thinking in young children*. New York: Holt, 1965.

WALLACH, M., & WING, C. *The talented student. A validation of the creativity-intelligence distinction*. New York: Holt, 1969.

WALLAS, G. *The art of thought*. New York: Harcourt, 1926.

WALSH, A. *Self concepts of bright boys with learning difficulties*. New York: Teachers College, Columbia University, 1956.

WESSMAN, A. E. Scholastic and psychological effects of a compensatory education program for disadvantaged high school students: Project ABC. *American Educational Research Journal*, 1972, 9, 361–372.

WHITING, J. W. M. Resource mediation and learning by identification. In I. Iscoe & H. W. Stevenson (Eds.), *Personality development in children*. Austin, Tex.: University of Texas Press, 1960.

WIENER, J. Attitudes of psychologists and psychometrists toward gifted children and programs for the gifted. *Exceptional Children*, 1968, 34, 354.

WIENER, J. L., & O'SHEA, H. Attitudes of university faculty, administrators, teachers, supervisors and university students toward the gifted. *Exceptional Children*, 1963, 30, 162–165.

WILDER, R. Historical background of innovations in mathematics curricula. In *Mathematics education*, 69th Yearbook NSSE. Chicago: University of Chicago Press, 1970.

WILLIAMS, F. *Classroom ideas for encouraging thinking and feeling*. Buffalo, N.Y.: Dissemination of Knowledge, Publishers, 1970.

WOLFF, P. From subject to citizen. In W. Martin & D. Pinck (Eds.), *Curriculum improvement and innovation*. Cambridge, Mass.: Bentley, 1966.

WOOTON, W. (Ed.). School Mathematics Study Group: *The making of a curriculum*. New Haven, Conn.: Yale University Press, 1965.

WRIGHT, R. *Black boy*. New York: Harper & Row, 1945.

YAMAMOTO, K. Creativity–A blind man's report on the elephant. *Journal of Counseling Psychology*, 1965, 12, 428–434.

YEOMANS, E. Education for initiative and responsibility (Pamphlet). Boston: National Association of Independent Schools, 1967.

ZACCHARIAS, J. R. Learning by teaching. In W. T. Martin & D.C. Pinck (Eds.), *Curriculum improvement and innovation*. Cambridge, Mass.: Robert Bentley, 1966.

APPENDIX A

Gifted and Talented Children
and Youth: A Selected Guide
to Resources for Information,
Materials, and Assistance[1]

NATIONAL RESOURCES FOR THE GIFTED AND TALENTED

Office of the Gifted and Talented

> Office of the Gifted and Talented
> U.S. Office of Education
> Washington, D.C.   20202
> 202/962–4038

The Office of the Gifted and Talented was established in response to the findings of the 1971 Report to the Congress, *Education of the Gifted and Talented.* The office coordinates federal leadership in education of the gifted and talented.

Each of the ten regional offices of education has personnel with assigned responsibilities in the area of education of the gifted and talented.

Region I: Connecticut, Maine, Massachusetts, New Hampshire, Rhode Island, Vermont
Harvey Liebergott
U.S. Office of Education, Region I
John F. Kennedy Federal Building
Government Center

Boston, Massachusetts   02203
617/223–5453

Region II: New Jersey, New York, Puerto Rico, Virgin Islands
Robert H. Seitzer
Commissioner

[1] Compiled and edited by The National Clearinghouse for the Gifted and Talented.

U.S. Office of Education, Region II
Federal Building
26 Federal Plaza
New York, New York   10007
212/264–4370
Roger W. Ming
Supervisor
Education for the Gifted
State Education Department
Room 314A, Main Building
Albany, New York   12224
518/474–4973

Region III: Delaware, District of Columbia, Maryland, Pennsylvania, Virginia, West Virginia
Joseph Hendrick
U.S. Office of Education, Region III
401 North Broad Street
Philadelphia, Pennsylvania   19108
215/597–1011

Region IV: Alabama, Florida, Georgia, Kentucky, Mississippi, North Carolina, South Carolina, Tennessee
Ellen Lyles
Program Officer
Vocational Technical Education
U.S. Office of Education, Region IV
50 Seventh Street, N.E., Room 550
Atlanta, Georgia   20223
404/526–5311

Region V: Illinois, Indiana, Michigan, Minnesota, Ohio, Wisconsin
Richard H. Naber
U.S. Office of Education, Region V
HEW–OE 32nd Floor
300 South Wacker Drive
Chicago, Illinois   60606
312/353–1743

Region VI: Arkansas, Louisiana, New Mexico, Oklahoma, Texas
James R. Frazier
U.S. Office of Education, Region VI
1114 Commerce Street

Dallas, Texas   75202
214/749–2634

Region VII: Iowa, Kansas, Missouri, Nebraska
Harold Blackburn
Assistant Regional Commissioner
U.S. Office of Education, Region VII
Federal Office Building
601 East 12th Street
Kansas City, Missouri   64106
816/374–2528

Region VIII: Colorado, Montana, North Dakota, South Dakota, Utah, Wyoming
John Runkel
Director, School Systems
U.S. Office of Education, Region VIII
Federal Office Building, Room 9017
1961 Stout Street
Denver, Colorado   80202
303/837–3676

Region IX: American Samoa, Arizona, California, Guam, Hawaii, Nevada, Trust Territory of the Pacific Islands
Mary Ann Clark Faris
Information Officer
U.S. Office of Education, Region IX
Federal Office Building
50 Fulton Street
San Francisco, California   94102
415/556–3441

Region X: Alaska, Idaho, Oregon, Washington
Robert A. Radford
Director, Urban and Community Education Programs
U.S. Office of Education, Region X
Mail Stop 628
1321 Second Avenue
Seattle, Washington   98101
206/442–0450

National/State Leadership Training Institute on the Gifted and Talented

National/State Leadership Training Institute
on the Gifted and Talented
316 West Second Street, Suite 708
Los Angeles, California 90012
213/489–7470

This federally funded program aims to provide leadership training and technical assistance to the education of gifted and talented, primarily through state education agencies.

National Clearinghouse for the Gifted and Talented

National Clearinghouse for the Gifted and Talented
The Council for Exceptional Children
1920 Association Drive
Reston, Virginia 22091
703/620–3660

The clearinghouse acquires, synthesizes, and disseminates information relevant to the education of the gifted and talented.

Alliance for Arts Education

Alliance for Arts Education
John F. Kennedy Center for the Performing Arts
2700 F Street, N.W.
Washington, D.C. 20007
202/254–3250

A project sponsored jointly by the Office of Education and the John F. Kennedy Center for the Performing Arts to coordinate national and regional efforts to develop programs for the talented in the field of the fine arts.

NATIONAL ORGANIZATIONS FOR THE GIFTED AND TALENTED

The Association for the Gifted (TAG)

The Association for the Gifted
The Council for Exceptional Children
1920 Association Drive
Reston, Virginia 22091
703/620–3660

A Division of the Council for Exceptional Children since 1958, the Association for the Gifted (TAG) plays a major part in helping both professionals and parents deal more effectively with the gifted and talented. TAG conducts annual national and regional conferences and provides current information to members and affiliate organizations.

National Association for Gifted Children

National Association for Gifted Children
Route 5, Box 630 A
Hot Springs, Arkansas 71901
501/767–2669

A professional organization with membership open to parents, NAGC conducts inservice training and consultation services for schools. The organization also holds an annual conference and publishes *The Gifted Child Quarterly*.

The Gifted Child Research Institute

The Gifted Child Research Institute
300 West 55th Street
New York, New York   10019
212/541–7059

The American Association for the Gifted

The American Association for the Gifted
15 Gramercy Park
New York, New York   10003
212/473–4266

This organization consists of a small group of professional personnel who meet annually to discuss the various problems facing the education of the gifted. They have assisted in publication of texts and articles on the gifted.

The Council of State Directors of Programs for the Gifted

Joyce Runyon, President
The Council of State Directors of Programs for the Gifted
Florida State Department of Education
319 Knott Building
Tallahassee, Florida   32304
904/599–5807

Additional information on other supportive national organizations with specific interests in the gifted and talented, such as MENSA, National Science Foundation, National Endowment for the Humanities, and National Endowment for the Arts, may be obtained by writing to the National Clearinghouse for the Gifted and Talented.

STATE RESOURCES FOR THE GIFTED AND TALENTED

State programs vary considerably in their ability to provide service to the gifted and talented. The states included in the list below were chosen for their ability to provide multiple services.

Northern California

Consultant for Mentally Gifted
California State Department of
   Education
721 Capitol Mall
Sacramento, California   95814
916/445–4036

Southern California

Consultant for Mentally Gifted
California State Department of
   Education
214 West First Street, Room 803–A
Los Angeles, California   90012
213/620–4224

Connecticut

Consultant for Gifted and Talented
Connecticut State Department of
   Education
P. O. Box 2219
Hartford, Connecticut   06115
203/566–2492

Florida

Consultant for the Gifted
Florida State Department of
   Education

319 Knott Building
Tallahassee, Florida   32304
904/599–5807

Georgia

Consultant for the Gifted
Georgia State Department of
   Education
State Office Building
Atlanta, Georgia   30334
404/656–2414

Illinois

Director
Programs for the Gifted
Illinois State Office of Public
   Instruction
316 South Second Street
Springfield, Illinois   62706
217/525–7830

Minnesota

Consultant
Gifted and Talented Division
Minnesota State Department of
   Education
500 Cedar Avenue
St. Paul, Minnesota   55101
612/296–4072

Nebraska

Consultant for Gifted and Talented
Nebraska State Department of
  Education
233 South Tenth Street
Lincoln, Nebraska 68508
402/471–2477

New York

Consultant
Special Education—Gifted
State Department of Education
Albany, New York 12224
518/474–4973

North Carolina

Gifted Child Section
North Carolina State Department of
  Public Instruction
Raleigh, North Carolina 27602
919/829–3931

Pennsylvania

Programs for Gifted and Talented
Pennsylvania Department of
  Education
P. O. Box 911
Harrisburg, Pennsylvania 17126
717/787–4714

Rhode Island

Education for the Gifted
Special Education, Department of
  Education
Roger Williams Building
Providence, Rhode Island 02908
401/277–3037

Virginia

Special Education
State Department of Education
Richmond, Virginia 23216
703/770–2674

STATE ORGANIZATIONS FOR THE GIFTED AND TALENTED

A selection of state organizations for the gifted and talented is listed below. Additional information on local county and school organizations may be obtained by writing to the National Clearinghouse for the Gifted and Talented.

California Association for the Gifted
Ruthe Lundy, President
School of Education
California State University at Long
  Beach
Long Beach, California 90801
213/373–2739

California Parents for the Gifted
Beverly King
5521 Reseda Boulevard, Suite 10
Tarzana, California 91356
213/345–1356

Connecticut Association for the Gifted
Rudolph Polh, President
Southern Connecticut State College
New Haven, Connecticut 06515
203/397–2101

Florida Association for the Gifted
Dorothy A. Sisk
University of Southern Florida
Special Education
Tampa, Florida 33620
813/974–2100

Georgia Association for Gifted
  Education
Marjorie Hatten, President
P. O. Box 557
Alamo, Georgia   30411

Massachusetts Commission on the
  Academically Talented
Joseph Plouffe, Chairman
Brockton Public Schools
Brockton, Massachusetts   02402
617/588–7800

Michigan Association for the
  Academically Talented, Inc.
517 Chamberlain Street
Flushing, Michigan   48433
313/659–5126

Minnesota Council for the Gifted
Barbara Ross
4567 Gaywood Drive
Minnetonka, Minnesota   55331
612/935–8055

Nebraska Association for the Gifted
John Dudley, President
Lincoln Public Schools
Administration Building
Lincoln, Nebraska   68508
402/475–1081, Extension 273

The Gifted Child Society, Inc.
Gina Ginsberg, Executive Secretary

59 Glen Gray Road
Oakland, New Jersey   07436
201/337–7058

Ohio Association for the Gifted
Betty J. McMillan, President
2320 McKinley Avenue
Lakewood, Ohio   44107
216/226–0610

Pennsylvania Association for the
  Study and Education of the
  Mentally Gifted
Eugene Hammer, President
Wilkes College
Wilkes-Barre, Pennsylvania   18703
717/824–4651, Extension 279

Texas Association for the Education
  of the Gifted
E. Beatrice Hall, Executive Director
P. O. Box 547
Austin, Texas   78767
512/472–4963

State Advisory Committee for the
  Gifted and Talented
Richard Mould
Superintendent of Public Instruction
Division of Curriculum Instruction
Old Capitol Building
Olympia, Washington   98504
206/753–3222

APPENDIX B

Potential Resource Organizations[1]

Arts and Humanities

Alliance for Arts Education
John F. Kennedy Center for the
    Performing Arts
2700 F Street, N.W.
Washington, D.C. 20007
202/254-3250

National Endowment for the Arts
806 15th Street, N.W.

Washington, D.C. 20005
202/382-6085

National Endowment for the
    Humanities
806 15th Street, N.W.
Washington, D.C. 20005
202/382-7465

Counseling

American Psychological Association
Division of School Psychology
1200 17th Street, N.W.
Washington, D.C. 20036
202/833-7600

American School Counselor
    Association
    (Division of American Personnel
    and Guidance Association)
1607 New Hampshire Avenue, N.W.
Washington, D.C. 20009
202/483-4633

Early Childhood

American Association of Elementary/
    Kindergarten/Nursery Educators
    (Affiliate of NEA)
1201 16th Street, N.W.
Washington, D.C. 20036
202/833-4000

Office of Child Development/Project
    Headstart
P.O. Box 1182
Washington, D.C. 20013
202/755-7782

[1] Compiled and edited by The National Clearinghouse for the Gifted and Talented.

APPENDIX B

General

American Association of University
  Women
2401 Virginia Avenue, N.W.
Washington, D.C.   20037
202/338–4300

Boys Clubs of America
771 First Avenue
New York, New York   10017
212/684–4400

Boy Scouts of America
U.S. Highway 1
North Brunswick, New Jersey   08903
201/349–6000

The Council of Churches
1239 Vermont Avenue, N.W.
Washington, D.C.   20005
202/638–1077

The Council for Exceptional Children
1920 Association Drive
Reston, Virginia 22091
703/620–3660

Girls Clubs of America
101 Park Avenue
New York, New York   10003
212/832–7756

Girl Scouts of America
830 Third Avenue
New York, New York   10003
212/751–6000

National Council of the YMCA's of
  the USA
291 Broadway
New York, New York   10007
212/349–0700

National Federation of Settlements
  and Neighborhood Centers
232 Madison Avenue
New York, New York   10016
212/679–6110

National Parent Teachers Association
700 North Rush Street
Chicago, Illinois   60611
312/787–0977

Neighborhood Youth Corps
Bureau of Work Programs
United States Department of Labor
Washington, D.C.   20036
212/961–2803

Young Women's Christian Association
600 Lexington Avenue
New York, New York   10222
212/752–4700

Gifted

Commission on Presidential Scholars
400 Maryland Avenue, S.W.
Room 1158
Washington, D.C.   20202
202/963–3116

ERIC Clearinghouse on the
  Handicapped and Gifted
The Council for Exceptional Children
1411 South Jefferson Davis Highway,
  Suite 900
Arlington, Virginia   22202
703/521–8820

Explorers' Club
46 East 70th Street
New York, New York   10021
212/628–8383

MENSA and Teen MENSA
50 East 42nd Street
New York, New York   10017
212/687–0037

National Association for Gifted
  Children
Route 5, Box 630A

Hot Springs, Arkansas 71901
501/767–2669

National Honor Society
1904 Association Drive
Reston, Virginia   20091
703/860–0200

National Merit Scholarship
    Corporation
99 Grove Street
Evanston, Illinois   60201
312/869–5100

National/State Leadership Training
    Institute on the Gifted and
    Talented

316 West Second Street, Suite 708
Los Angeles, California   90012
213/489–7470

Office of the Gifted and Talented
U.S. Office of Education
Washington, D.C.   20202
202/962–4038

The Association for the Gifted (TAG)
The Council for Exceptional Children
1920 Association Drive
Reston, Virginia 22091
703/620–3660

Organizations Focusing on Specific Minority Groups

A Better Chance, Inc.
1028 Connecticut Avenue, N.W.,
    Suite 616
Washington, D.C.   20036
202/833–2274

American Friends Service Committee
160 North 15th Street
Philadelphia, Pennsylvania   19102
215/563–9372

ASPIRA
296 6th Avenue
New York, New York   10003
212/244–1110

Division of Student Services
Indian Education Resource Center
Box 1788
Albuquerque, New Mexico   87103
505/766–3351

Follow Through Program
U.S. Office of Education
R.O.B. 3, Room 3642
7th and D Streets, S.W.
Washington, D.C.   20202
202/963–7731

National Association for the
    Advancement of Colored People

1790 Broadway
New York, New York   10019
212/245–2100

National Committee on the Education
    of Migrant Children (National
    Labor Committee)
145 East 32nd Street
New York, New York   10016
212/683–4545

National Education Task Force de la
    Raza
Graduate School of Education
University of California
405 Hillgard Avenue
Los Angeles, California   90024
213/825–2488

National Scholarship Service and
    Fund for Negro Students
6 East 82nd Street
New York, New York   10028
212/757–8100

Office of Education of the Bureau of
    Indian Affairs
Department of the Interior
1951 Constitution Avenue, N.W.
Washington, D.C.   20245
202/343–7387

413

Office of Spanish Speaking American Affairs
400 Maryland Avenue, S.W., Room 1152
Washington, D.C.   20202
202/962–8566

Program Development Branch
U.S. Office of Education (Contact agency for Talent Search—Upward Bound)
R.O.B. 3, Room 4642
Washington, D.C.   20202
202/962–4588

Rural Education Association
NEA Midatlantic Region
7617 Little River Turnpike, Suite 400
Annandale, Virginia   22002
703/941–6686

United Scholarship Service
P.O. Box 18285
Capitol Hill Station
Denver, Colorado   80218
303/222–3841

Urban League
55 East 52nd Street
New York, New York   10022
212/751–0300

Museums

American Association of Museums
2233 Wisconsin Avenue, N.W.
Washington, D.C.   20007
202/338–5300

Association of Art Museum Directors for the U.S. and Canada
c/o National Gallery of Canada

Ottawa 4, Ontario
Canada
613/992–4636

Association of Science Museums
Illinois State Museum
Springfield, Illinois   62704
217/525–7386

Science

American Association for the Advancement of Science
1515 Massachusetts Avenue, N.W.
Washington, D.C.   20005
202/467–4400

National Science Foundation
1800 G Street, N.W.

Washington, D.C.   20006
202/655–4000

Science Service
1719 N Street, N.W.
Washington, D.C.   20036
202/785–2255

Supervisors and Administrators

American Association of School Administrators
1801 North Moore Street
Arlington, Virginia   22209
703/528–0700

Council of Chief State School Officers
1201 16th Street, N.W.
Washington, D.C.   20036
202/833–4000

Music Educators National Conference
(Affiliate of NEA)
1201 16th Street, N.W.
Washington, D.C.   20036
202/833–4000

National Art Education Association—
Division of Supervisors (Affiliate
of NEA)
1201 16th Street, N.W.
Washington, D.C.   20036
202/833–4000

National Association of Elementary
School Principals
1801 North Moore Street
Arlington, Virginia   22209
703/528–5627

National Association of Secondary
School Principals
1904 Association Drive
Reston, Virginia   22091
703/860–0200

National Association of State Directors
of Special Education
Exceptional Child Division
State Department of Education
Tallahassee, Florida   32304
904/488–3205

National Council of State Supervisors
of Music (Affiliate of NEA)
1201 16th Street, N.W.
Washington, D.C.   20036
202/833–4000

National Council of Teachers of
English Supervisors Conference
508 6th Street
Champaign, Illinois   61820
217/353–0523

National School Boards Association
1233 Central Street
Evanston, Illinois   60201
312/869–7730

Index

A

ABC summer program, 381–382
Ability (*see also* IQ):
 racial and ethnic differences in,
  52–53
Ability grouping:
 impact of, 291–292
 in language arts, 178
 objections to, 271
 by subject, 282–283
Academic achievement (*see*
  Achievement)
Acceleration, 285–290
 by Advanced Placement Program,
  286
 Conant's recommendations
  concerning, 284
 curriculum, and student, 141–144
  early, 143–144
 by early admittance, 286, 288–290
 effects of, 287–288
 by grade-skipping, 286, 288–289
 objections to, 289
 operational feasibility of, 289–290
Achievement (*see also*
  Underachievement):
 of gifted in Terman research,
  35–36
 of highly creative, 56
 of highly gifted, 37–38
Achievement tests, shortcomings of,
  37–38
Adler, M., 53
Administration:
 adaptations in:
  in elementary school, 276–280
  in secondary school, 280–290
 changes in, for gifted, 269–306
  objectives in, 271
  unresolved issues concerning,
   305–306
  for gifted, 267–335
Administrators, educational,
  responsibility of, 256
Advanced Placement Program, 286
Aiken, L., Jr., 115
Altus, W., 47
Anthropology Curriculum Study
  Project (ACSP), 160–161
Antiintellectualism, 121
Antiscience, 121
Arithmetic (*see also* Mathematics):
 and high IQ, 37–38
 laws of, 108–109
Arnold, J., 185–186
Artists and scientists, 125–126
Aschner, M., 15, 48
Astin, H., 49
Athletics and social status, 40
Atkin, J., 139–140, 142–143
Attitude:
 of public toward gifted program,
  271
 of public toward grouping, 271
 toward scientists, 121

B

Bachtold, L., 51, 183–185, 348
Baker, C., 371
Bandura, A., 197, 379
Banks, G., 176, 318
Barbe, W., 294–295
Bardeen, John, 143
Barron, F., 61, 233–234, 246, 261
Baxter, M. R., 279
Bayley, N., 35, 49
Baymur, F., 355–356
Beals, A., 159
Beberman, M., 75

V

Value sheet, 195–196
Values:
 clarification of, stimuli and
  devices for, 195–196
 of creative, 57–63
 development of, 187–199
  additional teaching techniques
   in, 195–198
  drawbacks to teaching, 191–192,
   199
 of gifted, 57–63
 of Jews, 370
 of teacher, and creativity, 255–258
Van de Riet, V., 379
Very high ability children, 43–46
 incidence of, 44
 social problems of, 43–44
Von Braun, Werner, 45, 46

W

Walberg, H., 48
Wallach, M., 60–61, 245
Wallas, G., 249–250
Walsh, A., 345
Watson, F., 122
Wechsler Adult Intelligence Scale
 (WAIS), 12
Wechsler Intelligence Scale for
 Children (WISC), 12
Werner, E., 51
Wessman, A. E., 381–382
White, J., 379
Whitney, J. W. M., 197–198
Wiener, J., 314, 315
Wiener, Norbert, 45–46, 143
Wilder, R., 96–97
Williams, F., 256–258, 263
Wilson, J., 106, 115

Wilson, R. C., 351
Withdrawal of underachievers, 349
Wollersheim, J., 359
Women:
 creative, 248–249, 263
 professional, characteristics of, 51
Word games in language arts,
  187–190
Workshops, summer:
 for culturally different gifted,
  382–383
 for educational personnel, 323
Wright, H. F., 343
Wright, W. R., 369
Wunderlin, R., 330–331
Wyatt, S., 142–143

Y

Yeomans, E., 278

Z

Zacharias, Jerrold, 141
Zehrbach, R. R., 343, 359, 369
Zelda (case study):
 ability profile of, 21–22
 and acceleration, 287, 289
 characteristics of, 20–21
 cognitive memory of, 251–252
 empathy of, 187
 family background of, 21
 as gifted girl, 47–48
 and independent study, 205, 317
 lack of creativity of, 54–55, 244,
  245
 and language arts, 175
 and mathematics, 100, 102
 social difficulties of, 20, 21, 23, 40
 and social studies, 149, 150